THE SOUND OF
THE ONE HAND

THE SOUND OF
THE ONE HAND

281 ZEN KOANS
WITH ANSWERS

TRANSLATED, WITH A COMMENTARY BY

YOEL HOFFMANN

FOREWORD BY ZEN MASTER HIRANO SŌJŌ

INTRODUCTION BY BEN-AMI SCHARFSTEIN

Basic Books, Inc., Publishers

NEW YORK

TO MY PARENTS

FRÄNZE AND AVRAHAM HOFFMANN

TO MY WIFE

VARDA

CONTENTS

PART FOUR

THE SOUND OF
THE ONE HAND

FOREWORD

When the Japanese edition of this book, *Gendai Sōjizen Hyōron* ("A Critique of Present-day Pseudo-Zen"), was first published in 1916, it caused a great sensation. The reason for this lay in the fact that the koans and their answers had been secretly transmitted from master to pupil in the Rinzai sect since the origination of the koan-teaching system in Japan by Zen Master Hakuin (1685–1768). This publication of the "secrets" of Zen seems to have embarrassed many masters at that time. Furthermore, I have heard that the recent appearance of photocopies of this 1916 edition has caused alarm among Zen masters of today. Yet . . . if anyone finds himself troubled, he has only himself to blame—the book itself is not to blame. As for myself, I feel there is no reason whatsoever to be alarmed in any way.

The attempt to prevent such publications is not new in the history of Zen. For example, the widely known Zen classic, *Hekiganroku* ("The Green Grotto Record"), consists of one hundred koans selected by Zen Master Setchō (A.D. 980–1052), including his comments, and to which the comments of Zen Master Engo (1063–1135) were later added. Master Dai-e, Engo's disciple (1085–1163), was of the firm conviction that such a book should not be made public, and he burned it. In time, however, this book became a Zen classic; not only was it harmless to the koan teaching, on the contrary, it did much to aid the understanding of Zen.

More than fifty years have passed since the Japanese publication of *Gendai Sōjizen Hyōron*, which can now be said to deserve the status of a classic of Zen. Therefore those who would wish to prevent the contents of this book from being made public are misguided. Of course, in judging such matters, what is most important is the attitude of those reading the book. What is revealed in this publication is the approach of Zen masters of approximately two centuries ago to the Zen koans. It should by no means be assumed that those reading the book today will come to an "understanding" in a flash. However, I am convinced that this book, like the *Hekiganroku*, *Rinzairoku*, and other Zen classics, will have the effect of contributing to the attainment of a correct conception of Zen.

ZEN MASTER HIRANO SŌJŌ

INTRODUCTION
ZEN: THE TACTICS
OF EMPTINESS

You have opened the pages of an odd, tension-filled book. If you already know Zen well enough, or if you are simply impatient, skip this introduction and go on immediately to the text. It is the text that should be read, for reasons that I shall try to make clear.

Now, at the beginning, I ask you to remember that the world you are entering is odd to almost everyone, even to those who have lived in it for a long time. It multiplies paradoxes; and yet its oddness, like the paradoxical oddness of a dream, verges on the familiar. Odd and familiar as a dream, Zen is meant, however, to occupy the daylight, by means of an irrational reversal of the quality of our lives. For Zen says that we are self-deceived, split, and unhappy. Its disciples are trained to arrive at least at equanimity. This aim is, no doubt, subject to practical limitations. Maybe it, too, is a dream of sorts; but, if you are open-minded, you may prefer to consider it tentatively before deciding whether or not to shrug it off. Even if Zen is not what it takes itself to be, it is an unusually interesting human and cultural phenomenon.

Zen History

Let me begin with a word of Zen history. Indian Buddhism, spread abroad by missionaries, seems to have entered China during the first century A.D. Foreign by nature to the Chinese, it assumed the disguise of a native Chinese philosophy and religion, that of Taoism. This disguise was possible because, like Taoism, it cultivated a ritual and a technique of breathing, which was related to a technique of meditation, and because it was concerned with survival beyond the ordinary span of life. Missionaries continued to bring scriptures to China, but centuries passed before translations of these scriptures became genuinely intelligible, and before the Chinese were able to see Buddhism for what it was, a detailed proposal to teach mankind how to escape from life's inescapable sufferings by escaping from life itself.

When this message and its practical consequences became clear, traditionally minded Chinese protested. To them, the monks, who lived on charity, were no more than parasites. To them, the monks' celibacy and shift of allegiance from family and emperor to religious master and monastery were endangering the survival of society. Furthermore, they said, the monks, though supposedly indifferent to worldly things, were accumulating monastic wealth and power. It was also a particularly galling and un-Chinese insult that the monks were ready to be cremated at death and so to destroy their bodies, which the traditional Chinese regarded as gifts that their ancestors had put into their safekeeping.

On the whole, however, Buddhism prospered and became increasingly Chinese and increasingly assimilated into Chinese culture. I shall not attempt to say anything of the contribution of Buddhism to Chinese culture, much of which still lay in the future, or of its involvement in the politics of the imperial court, where its fortunes rose and fell. But in the middle of the ninth century, in an atmosphere of hostility to everything foreign, a great attack was leveled on Buddhism. Its monasteries were destroyed, its wealth confiscated, its icons melted down, its leaders scattered, and its monks and nuns forced to return to lay life.

The Buddhism that survived was predominantly of two kinds, Pure Land and Ch'an. Looked at in a somewhat unkind light, Pure Land Buddhism may be said to have succeeded because it demanded little and promised much, for which reason the common people turned to it enthusiastically. Pure Land Buddhism fostered the belief that the Buddha of Mercy would actively help to rescue everyone, regardless of who he was or what he had done. Its panacea, by which, it taught, anyone could attain salvation, was simple: repeat and repeat the name of a Buddha or the title of a Buddhist scripture. Ch'an Buddhism, which I shall from now on call Zen Buddhism, in deference to the Japanese origin and content of the present book, was also an adaptation to Chinese life, though of a very different kind. No one knows just why Zen survived the decline of the other forms of Buddhism, but a number of plausible reasons can be given. One reason may well have been geographical. Zen was strong in provincial centers that were remote from imperial influence and perhaps resistant to it. Zen was intuitive and down-to-earth, and therefore acceptable to the Chinese, who fostered these qualities. Zen was also optimistic, because it believed that nirvana, the state to which every Buddhist aspired, could be reached in a single lifetime, and not only as the result of a prolonged series of merit-accumulating lives. Finally, in spite of an express scriptural prohibition which forbade Buddhist monks to farm the land, because a farmer necessarily destroys plants and other living things, the Zen novitiates worked as farmers. Zen accepted the motto, "One day no work, one day no food." Zen diligence thus answered the accusation of parasitism and, in any case, helped to maintain the Zen community.

Zen might even be described as a kind of monastic humanism. Robust, earthy, and energetic, it reacted against the tendency of each of the competing sects to favor one particular scripture, and, in general, it opposed heavy reliance upon sacred texts. According to Zen tradition, men of lesser understanding might need the aid of words and scriptures, but Buddhism, in the highest sense, was wordless. The tradition said that when Buddha had turned a flower in his fingers, only his disciple, Kashyapa, had understood what was meant. Kashyapa, understanding, had smiled, so Buddha chose to transmit his enlightenment to him, wordlessly and directly. As a sign of the transmission, Buddha handed him his robe and begging bowl and initiated the formal act of transmission that has been preserved in Zen in various ways.

The tradition says that Zen Buddhism was brought from India to China by the monk, Bodhidharma. In the course of time, Zen Buddhism prospered, but it split into sects, each organized around some dominant master, with his own personality, conceptions, and methods. Many of these masters are named in the present text; but the one who most concerns us is Lin-chi, called Rinzai in Japanese. He was the originator of the sect whose attitude informs this collection of koans. I shall say of him now only that he was a magnetic, enigmatic, inventive man, perhaps, as he has been described, a sort of less reasoning Socrates.

Between Rinzai and Hakuin, the Zen master I should like to mention next, there lies a whole complex history. Zen was effectively transferred from China to Japan in the twelfth and thirteenth centuries. It encountered hostility in Japan, and, like the other Buddhist sects, it engaged in politics. Like the other sects, it, too, contributed much to both the aristocratic and popular culture of Japan.

Hakuin, a distant but attractive and energetic inheritor of Rinzai Zen, was born in 1686 and died in 1769. It was he and his pupils who devised the training method embodied in this book, and it was the tradition stemming from him that established, not only the kind and sequence of koans to be used in training, but also the "rightness" of the answers that are given here. Hakuin's personal experience had taught him that the Zen riddles, as the koans may be called, were the essential source of enlightenment. The rival sect, the Soto school of Zen, thought that extensive reliance upon koans might be an attempt to force enlightenment, and it therefore preferred enlightenment to come "silently," by itself. But Hakuin wanted active, unremitting questioning by means of koans. Again and again he insisted that "dead sitting and silent illumination" were destructive. To him, the ideal was the commingling of meditation with the activity of life, until the two became indistinguishable, whether in the life of the monk or of the layman. If, he said, "dead sitting and silent illumination" prevailed, so would its ideal of passivity, and then everyone would abandon his work, and the country would collapse. "Then the people, in their anger and resentment, would be sure to say that Zen was an evil and ill-omened thing."

Although a Buddhist who has achieved enlightenment ought not to hate anything or anyone, I suspect that Hakuin hated those whom he accused of destroying Buddhism. He particularly opposed the union of Pure Land with Zen. The tendency to unite them was old and quite in keeping with the Chinese desire to mitigate human friction by means of compromise. When the Chinese Zen master, Hui-hai, had been asked whether Confucianism, Taoism, and Buddhism were one doctrine or three, his answer had been that when employed by men of great understanding, they were the same. This tendency to harmonize became particularly strong in China during the sixteenth and seventeenth centuries. The famous Zen monk, Chun-hung (1535–1615), who is said to have revived Buddhism by synthesizing Pure Land and Zen, was deeply opposed to sectarianism. "Whoever clings to Ch'an and denigrates Pure Land," he said, "is denigrating his own Original Mind. He is denigrating the Buddha. He is denigrating his own Ch'an doctrine. He is simply not thinking."

This view carried the day in China, where Pure Land and Zen were freely joined. The tendency to harmonize was imported, like everything else Chinese, into Japanese Zen, but it was overcome there in time by the force of Hakuin's objection. The method adopted by Pure Land, of simply repeating a Buddha's name, was lazy, shallow, and ineffective, he said. It could not provoke the crisis of doubt that was necessary, he was sure, to provoke enlightenment. He therefore said that Chu-hung had "displayed an incredibly shallow understanding of Zen." It does seem as if Japanese Zen remained more determinedly pure and sectarian than its Chinese counterpart.

Zen Discipline

It may already be clear from what I have said that Zen has had a strong element of individualism and even rebelliousness. This should not obscure the fact that Zen monks have lived under severe discipline. Their very skepticism of scriptures made their dependence upon their masters more complete. Dogen, the relatively conservative monk who established Soto Zen, retained his respect for scriptures, but insisted that "if a learned priest says that a toad or a worm is the Buddha, then one must abandon ordinary knowledge and believe that a toad or a worm is the Buddha." When asked why meditation was carried on only in the sitting position, he answered that monks had always meditated sitting down and that the matter should not be questioned any further.

This conservative outlook, which may not have been shared by his own Chinese masters, led him to expect absolute conformity to the rules of Zen, which were and which remain minute and strict. Hakuin also demanded strict obedience to the rules. These regulate the monk's sleeping, arising, washing, eating, evacuating, conversing, and, of course, praying and meditating. The differences that distinguish Soto from Rinzai Zen lend themselves easily to satire. Jonathan Swift could have made much of the little fact that monks in Soto Zen monasteries must sleep on their right sides, while those in Rinzai Zen monasteries must sleep on their backs.

An investigator, Holmes Welch, has gathered testimony from Chinese Zen monks on monastic life during the first half of the twentieth century. Much of their testimony is on the Chin

Shan monastery, which was situated on the Yangtze River, between Nanking and Shanghai. Its meditation hall was regarded as the foremost in all China. To make clear the nature and minuteness of the discipline at such a monastery, let me cite Welch's descriptions of the ceremonies on awakening, of the rather ceremonious evacuation that follows breakfast, and of the manner of meditation.

First, the ceremonies on awakening:

> The monks get up to the sound of four strokes on a small portable board. They have slept only five hours and the sun will not rise for two hours more. It is dark and cold. They have put on their full-sleeved gowns and over this their robes. The clang of the large bell has led into the booming of the large drum and by the time the drum has ceased, they are ready to march in procession to the great shrine hall. . . .
>
> In the great shrine hall all the monks of the monastery except the kitchen staff have gathered to recite morning devotions. Here too everyone has his place. . . . The center of the hall is occupied by hundreds of monks, standing row on row. In general, the higher their rank, the closer they stand to the Buddha image. . . . No one may leave without the permission of the proctor and he is a fierce disciplinarian.

We leave this scene even before the morning liturgy has begun and shift to something more profane, by non-Zen standards, that of the rules of the evacuation that follows breakfast:

> The manner of excretion is exactly prescribed. . . . Defecation is full of taboos. The code of rules of the Kao-min Ssu [i.e., Kao-min monastery] prescribes that the lid must be lifted silently and then the monk must "snap the fingers of his right hand three times toward the opening of the pit. This is to avoid having the excrement dirty the heads of the hungry ghosts, thus incurring their revengeful wrath. It is terribly important." Certain kinds of hungry ghosts are apparently attracted by the smell of faeces. After snapping his fingers and seating himself, the monk must sit up straight and keep his legs covered with the corners of his underclothes. "He must not look this way or that, talk with people nearby, lean against the partition, or scratch his private parts"—and he must be quick about it, because others are waiting. When he is finished, the code of rules prescribes that he go to the

water basin, dip in the middle two fingers of his right hand, wipe them on his left palm, and then run his hands quickly over the towel.

And now to the critical business of meditation:

> Almost everyone sits in the order of rank. . . . In a well-run hall the monk should be able to forget his body and let it be guided like an automaton by the bell and board. He sits on the narrow bench, his eyes fixed on a point no further than the third and no nearer than the second row of tiles on the floor. He tries to keep his spine perfectly straight and to control his respiration. Talking is forbidden. The silence must be absolute. If a monk in the east makes a sound, the precentor goes over and beats him then and there with his incense board—and beats him hard. . . .
>
> Those who are new at meditation usually sit cross-legged with only one foot up. Even then it may be so painful that they cannot sleep at night. Some lose courage and flee the monastery. According to one informant, "The pain is cumulative. It hurts until the sweat pours from your body. Some people cheat by uncrossing both legs under cover of their gowns, but eventually the precentor will catch them at it and give them a beating. The loss of face is one reason why so many run away." How many? "About 30 percent in the first week or two of each semester."
>
> Old hands, of course, are untroubled by leg cramps and sit with both feet up. A few even learn to sleep in this posture and do not retire to the sleeping platform at night. But no one is allowed to sleep or even to doze during meditation. If they do, they are awakened by a meditation patrol, who stands facing the altar, holding an incense board horizontally before him in two hands. . . . At eight o'clock the hand-chime is struck. This signifies the end of the "morning meditation period."

And so on and, on.

Zen Meditation and Enlightenment

The word "meditation" has already been used here many times, and it has become necessary, I think, to say a preliminary word on its nature and effects. In Rinzai Zen, with which we are here concerned, to meditate on a koan is to engage in an active process, like that we engage in when we try to solve a mathematical problem. As in mathematics, the solution is supposed to come suddenly. But Zen's belief in the suddenness of enlightenment has not been accepted by many of the other Buddhists. This difference in belief requires us to return for a moment to the history of Buddhism.

In seventh- and eighth-century China there was a long and finally bitter controversy between those of the Zen Buddhists who believed in gradual and those who believed in sudden enlightenment. The debate had begun in India. Indian Buddhists had usually assumed that the understanding of the truth was progressive. The training system that expressed this assumption was long and complicated, and there were, therefore, Buddhists who tried to simplify it. The most radical simplification was aimed at the instantaneous understanding of the truth. The mere exclamation, "Oh suffering!," it was said, could lead to instantaneous enlightenment. The justification for this belief was based not only upon appropriate scriptural passages but also on the idea that once we see illusion for what it is, the truth can be grasped all at once.

During the first few centuries of Buddhism, the two theses, that of slow, successive and that of unique, "in one time" enlightenment confronted one another. There was a venomous debate in eighth-century Tibet, in which the "sudden" method, represented by a Chinese master, was defeated by the "gradual" method, represented by the Indian master, Kamalashila.

The variant of this debate conducted in China itself also led to bitterness. The exponents of gradualism, known as the Northern school, were charged with attempting to steal Bodhidharma's robe, with mutilating the stele that recorded the transmission of enlightenment, and with cutting the head of the Sixth Patriarch from his mummified body. On the other side, the leader of the "sudden" or Southern school was charged with sedition.

Neither the Northern nor the Southern schools remained in existence very long, but in Zen Buddhism it was the sudden method that was victorious. It was accepted, as an old Buddhist master had put it, that "the fruit drops when it is ripe," or, in the kind of landscape metaphor that the Chinese understood, "When the mountain has been climbed the landscape of the goal appears all at once."

It seems that in China conciliation eventually settled this issue too. Holmes Welch, whom I have previously cited on the life of Zen monks in China, reports that none of the monks he questioned saw any contradiction between sudden and gradual enlightenment. "As they put it, the sudden enlightenment of the Sixth Patriarch [the founder of the "sudden" school] must have been the result of long training and self-cultivation in earlier lives." In other words, the few who reach sudden enlightenment must have been prepared by long, gradual efforts, extending over many lives.

Welch asked the Chinese monks why they were willing to put up with the austerities of the meditation hall, "leg cramps, mosquitoes, the exhaustion of meditation weeks, the confinement within the monastery, and, most of all, the inherent boredom of trying to think about the same thing for nine to fifteen hours a day." Most of his informants denied having been bored. The enigmatic question that had been posed was effective, they said. "A monk pursued it and concentrated all his energy upon it. He also learned to control his mind—to watch the stream of consciousness and, as soon as bad thoughts arose (greed, anger or stupidity), to dissolve them in the silent recitation of Buddha's name. Thus busied with learning, how could he get bored? Furthermore, his character was improved. Bad habits were weeded out. Through meditation even the most active person became peaceful and indifferent to the abuse of others."

But when Welch asked the abbot of Chin Shan about the possibility of boredom he got what he took to be a franker answer. "If you did not have the mental equipment to cope with the work," he said, "then the meditation hall was worse than prison. So every year there were monks who fled. On the other hand, if your mind was really on your work, then there was nothing boring about it. Those who were doing well with meditation could hardly wait to get started each day."

The question on whether or not any enlightenment was achieved was usually not answered. Welch says, "I have been largely unsuccessful in getting an answer to this question. For one thing, it has not pleased the venerable monks with whom I have raised it. To them it seems inappropriate and in bad taste. Other people's spiritual accomplishments were their personal affair and, baldly put, none of my business. If I wanted to find out about spiritual accomplishments, I had better have some of my own. This was not because such things were esoteric or mysterious, but because they were private, like a man's intimate relation with his wife."

Yet reward there must have been. Otherwise, asks Welch, why would so many of the monks have enrolled for a second and third year? He draws on the testimony of John Blofield, who sat relatively long in a Chinese meditation hall, and who reported that some of the monks found meditation an ordeal, while others profited greatly. Blofield recalled one of those who profited as saying:

> I don't know how many of us younger monks here really understand the Preceptor [instructor]. I find his lectures far from clear. Still, I have discovered for myself that if I just sit perfectly still, so still that I am conscious of the blood drumming in my ears and open my mind to—no, not to anything—just open my mind; though nothing happens the first time or the second, one day I begin to feel some response. My heart seems to be talking to me, revealing secrets of which I have never so much as dreamed. Afterwards I am left in a state of marvelous happiness. A Light shines within me and about me and they are One. . . . Then, sooner or later, from habit I do something which brings me against the current of the stream; the Light fades and I am as before, but for a while I am as lonely as when I first separated from my mother.

Zen literature itself has many reports of the experience of enlightenment; but while some of those queried by Welch brought up the experiences of the famous monks, others refused to be drawn into such evaluations. An old rector, that is, a high-ranking monk, told him that he had often seen cases of enlightenment. He could tell them, he said, from the way people answered questions during tutorials. However, "the abbot of Chin Shan took the opposite position. When I asked him whether he could detect enlightenment in the monks who came to him for tutorials, he replied: 'No, for I have not gotten paranormal powers. . . . Only with paranormal powers—telepathic powers—could I have known whether a disciple was enlightened or not.'"

Zen Words

For whatever it is worth, my own attitude toward words is favorable. I think that the intellectual and other difficulties we run into are inherent in the situation or in ourselves, and not particularly in words as such. But there is an old, deeply rooted suspicion, most obvious in certain poets and in mystically inclined philosophers, that words are essentially inaccurate and unable to convey whatever matters to us most. This suspicion is expressed early in India in the Upanishads, in China in Lao-tzu and Chuang-tzu, and in Greece in Plato. Closer to Zen Buddhism, the Lankavatara Sutra says that true learning requires familiarity with meaning and not with words.

In Zen itself, as in other religions, scriptures were (and are) often recited without understanding. Reacting to this situation, a Zen master forbade people to recite sutras, that is scriptures, and explained, "Such people are like parrots mimicking human speech without understanding its meaning. . . . To comprehend meaning we should go beyond unsteady words; we should leap beyond writings. . . . That is why those seeking enlightenment forget all about wording after having arrived at the meaning." Then, alluding to some apt words in Chuang-tzu, the master said, "Awakening to reality, they throw away the doctrine just as a fisherman, having caught his fish, pays no more attention to his nets."

It appears to have been only a short step from an attack on the uncomprehending use of words and on the distance created between words and "meaning" to an attack on words as such, and therefore to a rejection of scriptures because they were composed of words. I doubt that this rejection was ever consistent and unequivocal, but some Zen masters, speaking with their customary earthy directness, heaped scorn on Zen scriptures, masters, and images. One of them warmed himself with a statue of Buddha he had set afire. Another said, starkly, that the Buddha was a barbarian turd and sainthood an empty name. Rinzai, using the same stark terminology, said, "Do not take the Buddha for the Ultimate. As I look at him, he is still like the hole in the privy." And Hakuin, echoing Rinzai, said, "All the scriptures are only paper good for wiping off shit." In an excess of enthusiasm, which, if taken seriously, would have ended his career, he said as well, "Studying Zen under a teacher is an empty delusion."

This attack on words may seem to you arbitrary or theatrical, by which I mean, consciously designed to shock. It may not have been difficult to enlist the latent resentment of monks against the scriptures they had so often parroted; but we, I assume, are not party to their resentment. What are we to think of the attack? I have already said that I like words and have no general fault to find with them. But they can be used without a sense of their nature and limitations. Philosophers, for example, may press them to artificial extremes, and almost anyone may sometimes be tempted to confuse a word or set of words with something it is not. There is, then, a basic truth in the Zen attack on words, at least in their more philosophical and abstractly coercive uses, and I should like to put this truth to you in my own way.

I am writing these words, on the inadequacy of words, in the circle of light cast by my lamp. This is a moment in my life much like many others, and yet, though I find it hard to say exactly how, it is unique. As I write, I repeat the words softly to myself. In spite of their generality, there is something absolutely individual in myself and in them as I am using them now.

The quality of absolute individuality is one that philosophers have considered and even invented names for. It is the inseparable "thisness," the *haecceitas*, of every object, according to the medieval European philosopher, Duns Scotus. The Indian philosophers known as the Vaisheshika call it *vishesha*. Buddhist philosophers express that which is unique, with no tinge of otherness, with the concept of *sva-lakshana*. But although suitable names have been invented for absolute individuality, no one, not even a philosopher, can live in a world all made up of unique particulars. If everything would be completely different from everything else, it would be impossible to learn from experience. Strictly speaking, such a world, consisting of nothing but unique particulars, cannot even be thought, because thinking, whatever else it may be, is also a generalizing and a relating. Is it a sophism, or is it the lack of a theory of levels of language that tempts us to say that absolute individuals have their individuality in common, as is demonstrated by the use for all of them of the same name, whether *haecceitas*, *vishesha*, or *sva-lakshana*. Does not every argument in their favor have to generalize about them and therefore imply that they are not merely individual particulars?

I think I know where the trouble lies, though I have no ambition to analyze it exactly. Concepts, that is, abstractions, are useful because they are isolating. We use proper names to name natural beings that are more or less complete in themselves; but we use abstractions to stand for characteristics that have no independent existence. The number system is a simple, persuasive example. We could hardly get along without numbers. Even animals need an ability equivalent to counting. We need and believe in numbers firmly enough to feel uncomfortable when someone suggests that their reality may be qualified. Yet, whatever in the end we care to think of numbers, it is true that nothing we perceive with our senses, not even the symbol for number, is simply "one" in itself, or "two." It is always one thing of some particular sort, or two things, and so on.

The difficulty arises when abstractions come to be regarded as if they were things or parts of things, or when it is supposed that reality is made up of "abstractions," or that reality must conform exactly to abstractions, be cut, so to speak, to exactly their pattern. Sometimes I think that the tendency, so evident in the history of thought, to see reality in this light, is only the philosopher's obsession with neatness, as if he could not bear to live in a world he had not swept clean, straightened up, and protected with anti-macassars wherever an oily head or sweaty arm might lean. We know well enough that even the most useful abstractions cannot fit experience perfectly or exhaustively. The strict "either-or" of the logician is not always more adequate to experience than the paradoxical-sounding union of opposites of the mystic, or the mystic's refusal to commit himself to any clear final statement. I do not think that this is true because of any radical defect in the principle of contradiction, but because of the inadequate ways in which we choose or are impelled to use it. We often use it crudely in a world that remains beyond even our subtlest analysis.

What I am saying suggests the unease felt by many philosophers at the uncomprehending use of abstractions. Wittgenstein was particularly uneasy at the use of abstractions of the philosophical kind. Speaking in his name, his disciple Renford Bambrough insists that the normal "yes-no" or "either-or" standard of reasoning may not work well in philosophy. That is, it may happen that a certain statement or proposition, p, and its contradictory, *not-p*, may both be misleading. We may then try to say what we need without either making the crucial-seeming statement or contradicting it. "Wittgenstein preaches this method and he often practices it. When he 'assembles reminders for a particular purpose,' when he abjures explanations and allows what used to be called 'aseptic' description to take its place, he is doing his best to escape from the standard philosophical forms of words precisely because he has noticed that they are incurably misleading, that to deny what is expressed by one of them is as misleading as to assert what is expressed by it."

Chuang-tzu makes much the same point, though more radically. He knows, as we do, that analytic thought must, by its very nature, apply definite names, concepts, and values to our experience. All these are necessarily subjective, because they are derived from particular and limited points of view, and all are necessarily too definite, because they are inadequate to the fluidity, to the ebb and flow of nature. All these are therefore necessarily distorting. They lead us, he says, to become entangled in contradictions. We should learn to relax our conceptual definiteness and our incessant distinguishing between one thing and another. Things merge no less than they separate. Consider, for example, fixity and change, or, in words with a more human connotation, living and dying. Everything that exists is changing and so vanishing, and so to live is in a sense to die; and dying is a process that, as such, takes place, that is, exists, and so to die is in a sense to persist or live. Opposites are in a sense the same, "the admissible is simultaneously the inadmissible," and every definite thing, every "it," as the translator puts Chuang-tzu's word, is also the same as that which is other than itself. "What is 'it,'" says Chuang-tzu, "is also 'other,' what is 'other' is also 'it.' . . . Are there really It and Other? Or really no It and Other?"

The question can have no answer. "Therefore," says Chuang-tzu, "the glitter of glib debate is despised by the sage. The contrived 'that's it' he does not use, but finds things in their places as usual. It is this that I call 'throwing things open to the light.'"

Chuang-tzu does his best to stretch the medium of words to what he thinks it can or cannot quite express. He appears to agree that unambiguously unique or particular things are impossible, and that words, which signify that things are unambiguously definite, are always problematic. He uses words and recognizes their use; he sees their imperfections; he asks about them but gives no dogmatic answer. He takes the middle, indefinite path. He says, "Words are not just wind. Words have something to say. But if what they have to say is not fixed, then do they really say something? Or do they say nothing? People suppose that words are different from the peeps of baby birds, but is there any difference or isn't there?"

Can such a view be put without Chuang-tzu's impish paradoxicality? Perhaps. Perhaps it is put more clearly by the Indian philosophers of the Jain sect, when they insist that all ordinary descriptions of reality, because they must be made from a limited standpoint, should be prefixed, "in a sense" or "somehow." It is a mistake, they say, to describe the whole of reality by means of a single predicate, such as "unchanging" or "changing." Reality is neither the Vedantist's permanence nor the Buddhist's impermanence, but change *in* permanence and permanence *in* change. To drive this argument home, they tell the now famous parable of the blind men trying to describe an elephant. One of the blind men said that an elephant was ear-shaped, another that it was trunk-shaped, a third that it was tail-shaped, and so on. But reality has ears, a trunk, a tail, and very much else, and it is not just one of them and maybe not even exactly all of them either separately or together.

The Taoists and the Jains are both saying that abstractions, like mass-produced clothing, cannot fit all natures perfectly, and certainly not nature as such, in the absolute. Like many Indian philosophers and like the neo-Platonists, they try to get below the surface of things and find inexpressible reality there. Inexpressible it must be if it is unique, either in the sense of a unique whole or that of a whole made of unique parts. It must then be inexpressible because uniqueness evades the generality of abstract words. Both radical monists and radical pluralists ought to be silent. But silence, like speech, has its shortcomings. As a Zen master said, "Both speech and silence transgress."

The disciple of Wittgenstein that I have quoted ascribes to his teacher an approximation of this last Zen moral. He says, plausibly enough, that Wittgenstein maintains that there is something *impossible* about words in their philosophical use:

A characteristically philosophical form of words is always capable both of expressing something true and of expressing something false, and when such a form of words is used the speaker may mean by it only what is true or only what is false or *both* what is true *and* what is false in what the expression is naturally capable of expressing. Correspondingly, someone who denies an assertion made with such an expression may intend to deny the false content of the assertion, or the true content, or both. (This paragraph is itself a most misleading philosophical remark.)

Chuang-tzu, who takes a similar position, says:

> Treat as 'it' even what is not, treat as 'so' even what is not. . . . Therefore behind dividing there is something undivided, behind disputation there is something not argued out. 'What?' you ask. The sage keeps it in his breast.

I know that these words on the inadequacy of words are unclear. Let me try, then, to explain, because I have no ambition to rival Zen or other riddles with any of my own making.

If what I am saying makes no sense to you, I am not really speaking, certainly not to you. But suppose the contrary. Here we are, you and I. We are invisible to one another. We are at different times. We do not know one another at all. Each of us comes from a different place and is going somewhere else, every day and all his life, and has different thoughts and fantasies filling his mind. And yet, as I am writing and you are reading these words, they enter the consciousness of each of us, and as long as they remain at the center of my consciousness and yours, you and I are thinking the same thoughts. In this sense we are internally one.

I will be more radical. I am not simply writing to you, and you are not simply reading me. I am you and you are I because we are simultaneously having the same thoughts—simultaneously, not at the same clock time, but at the intended simultaneity of writer and reader. I could go further still and say that at the moment that we share the same thoughts I am not speaking to you, because, if I am the same as you, I cannot speak to you—speaking to someone else implies that he is different from me. It is of course true that we speak to ourselves, and true that, when we do so, we divide ourselves into two; but in this condition the words sinking into the consciousness of the listener, who is also the speaker, unite the two.

Because I am talking about difference and oneness, let me suggest an impossible experiment in counting. If we could now take off our hands, feet, and bodies, how many consciousnesses would there be left? If, all containing the same thoughts, they would all be the same, why not say "one"? Or if "one" seems too definite and arithmetical a number for a situation so hard to count, why not say, with the Taoists and Zen Buddhists, "neither one nor many"? Listen to Chuang-tzu again as he states such a paradox (in a necessarily interpretive translation):

The universe and I exist together, and all things and I are one. Since all things are one, what room is there for speech? But since I have already said that all things are one, how can speech not exist?

Difference and sameness, manyness and unity, illusion and reality. Do these really constitute a problem or are they, paired or single, merely the nature of the world, which we should accept as it obviously is, without surprise? Read the Zen paradoxes in this book and the reactions to them, and see if an answer insinuates itself into your mind. The English philosopher John Wisdom said, Wittgenstein-like, "I have said that philosophers' questions and theories are really verbal. But if you like we will not say this or we will also say the contradictory." It may be helpful to set koans and Wisdoms in some framework if we recall the opinion of a strange, mystical genius, the mathematician Luitzen Brouwer. "The language of introspective wisdom," he wrote, "appears disorderly, illogical, because it can never proceed by systems of entities which have been imprinted on life, but can only accompany their rupture and in this way perhaps aid the unfolding of the wisdom that causes the rupture."

Zen Koans

Koan, or, in Chinese, *kung-an*, means "public case." I am not sure whether the relevant connotation of the word is "record of a public discussion" or "precedent for public use." Koans appear to have developed out of Zen conversations and out of stories describing the masters' intuitive wisdom. The old Zen masters were resourceful educators, and they must have vied with one another in the invention of verbal and physical techniques to arouse their students to the elusive truth. It was inevitable that the words of the revered old masters, the "old cases," should be collected, systematized to a degree, and provided when necessary with answers, clarifications, and atmospherically fitting verses. Zen tradition came to see the koans as exemplifications of the transcendent principle, received silently from the Buddha himself, and, as such, beyond logic, beyond transmission in writing, and beyond measure by reason. To use one of the grander expressions of Zen rhetoric, the koan is "a divine mirror that reflects the original face of both the sacred and the secular."

It has been said, with what degree of truth I do not know, that the early Zen masters of China put things more simply, less enigmatically, and that some of them were even prepared to accept philosophically logical answers. On the whole, however, the koans were designed to break down ordinary rationality. Rationality or intellectuality was regarded as a defense against the truth. Intellectually plausible answers were therefore taken to be "dead words," and only non-rational, apparently irrelevant ones to be "living words." The disciple, given a koan to see through, was encouraged to put his whole strength into the singleminded search for its solution, to be "like a thirsty rat seeking for water, like a child thinking of its mother." The disciple was to carry the problem with him everywhere, until suddenly, if he were successful, the solution came, or, as the Zen phrase went, "the ball of doubt was shattered." This vivid expression had been lifted out of an old Zen poem, whose author had written:

> Everywhere I went I met with words,
> But I couldn't understand them.
> The ball of doubt within my heart
> Was as big as a wicker basket.

However, as the poem recounts, the doubt was shattered by an opportune blow delivered by the Zen master:

> The Master, from his mat of felt,
> Rose up like a dragon,
> And, baring his right arm,
> Struck my chest a single blow.
> My ball of doubt, fright-shattered,
> Fell to the ground with a crash!

Hakuin himself always emphasized that the koan could lead to enlightenment only through such enormous effort that the Great Doubt, as he called it, would be aroused. The shattering of the Great Doubt was enlightenment and the welling up of a flood of exaltation. The koan that gives this book its title was devised by him as the most effective possible way of evoking the Great Doubt and leading to the first stage of enlightenment. "If you take up one koan," he said, "and investigate it unceasingly, your mind will die and your will will be destroyed. It is as though a vast, empty abyss lay before you, with no place to set your hands and feet. You face death and your bosom feels as though it were fire. Then suddenly you are one with the koan, and body and mind are cast off. . . . This is known as seeking into one's nature. You must push forward relentlessly and with the help of this complete concentration you will penetrate without fail to the basic source of your own nature."

As the poem on the shattering of the ball of doubt intimates, and as this whole book shows, the Zen master used what might be called, somewhat pretentiously, psychophysical methods. Rinzai, with a dialectical verve that belies his anti–intellectualism, carried on the practice of therapeutic hitting that he had learned from his teacher. He administered his blows selectively. "Many students," he said, "are not free from the entanglement of objective things. I treat them right on the spot. If their trouble is due to grasping hands, I strike them there. If their trouble comes from their mouths, it is there I strike. So far I have not found anyone who can be set free by himself. That is because all have been entangled in the useless mechanics of their old masters. As for me, I do not have a single method to give to everyone, but what I can do is relieve the troubles and set them free."

Rinzai was famous, not only for his hitting, but also for his effective shouting of *Katsu!*, which, like the precisely timed interpretation of a psychoanalyst, was meant to catalyze insight. *Katsu!*, like blows, was used discriminatingly by Rinzai, who has therefore been said to have constituted a semantic system of the cry. It is only one of a group of now conventionalized cries used to respond to koans. The Zen cries, and, sometimes, Zen blows, may be used in a kind of dialectical duel, in which each contestant tries to transfix his partner on the sword of enlightenment.

Other techniques were resorted to, as ingenuity or experience suggested. These techniques included the giving of an irrelevant response, the repetition of the question as the answer to the same question, and the use of a disconcerting negation or series of negations. Nose twisting, we learn, was also available to the enterprising master.

Like any educational technique, that of koan Zen has sometimes, in its own terms, succeeded and sometimes failed. At its extreme, Zen technique suggests a strain of masochism or sadism. The first is suggested by the story of Bodhidharma's would–be disciple, who proved his sincerity and earned his discipleship by cutting off his arm. The second, sadism, is more than hinted at by the famous koan, which can be read in the following pages, in which the master, Nansen, makes his point by cutting a cat into halves, a deed that would have horrified the many generations of Buddhists who believed in the utmost mercy for every living thing.

It should perhaps be said here that, although Hakuin was a benign and public-spirited man, there was something military and even militant in his attitudes, as his language often betrays. He told a disciple to *raise* his mental lance, *destroy* the enemy to enlightenment, *march against* the black demon of sleep, and *attack* the concepts of active and passive and right and wrong. It should perhaps also be said that Zen Buddhism was prominent in the education of the Japanese warriors. It taught them a single-minded, at once alert and relaxed use of weapons. As this swordsman's ideology and training was put in the fifteenth century, "The essence of swordsmanship consists in giving yourself up altogether to the business of striking down the opponent." Zen also trained warriors to lose their fear of death. Hakuin commended his koan training for the production of courageous soldiers. Zen Buddhism was evidently a double-edged sword, good for the conquest of both enlightenment and territory.

Something more must be said of the possibly unfavorable effects of koan training. Zen monasteries, like all such places of refuge from the world, have always had their share of the outcast, the unfortunate, and the unstable. It is natural that psychotic breakdowns occur among them. But the method itself of koan meditation is said to be capable of inducing depressions and hallucinations, that is, a specific "Zen sickness." Hakuin recalls predecessors attacked by it and gives a moving description of his own suffering and his recovery, made with the help of an old monk.

The victims or apparent victims of Zen training also appear in the account of the lives of twentieth-century Zen monks in China:

> One hears of monks who found it impossible to make any mental breakthrough either because they were "stupid" or because they could not stop thinking about their parents, wife, children, and the other things they had left behind. At first they would be unable to keep their minds on anything. Then they would begin to have hallucinations and "talk nonsense." At this point they were usually locked in a room and a Chinese doctor called to examine them. Some re-

covered; some died. According to one informant, fatalities were most common during meditation weeks and the bodies were not buried immediately. It was felt that their death must be retribution for sins committed in former lives, so they were wrapped in quilts and left to be disposed of when the meditation weeks were over.

Zen Dada

The fantastic humor of Zen Buddhism is derived not from India but from China, specifically from Taoism, and, more specifically, from that wild and subtle philosopher (or group of philosophers) called Chuang-tzu. He enjoyed dissolving clever debates into long, clever metaphors and humorous fantasies. When Hui-tzu told him that his words were big and useless, just like Hui's own big, gnarled tree, no good for lumber or anything else, Chuang-tzu answered:

> Now you have this big tree and you're distressed because it's useless. Why don't you plant it in Not-Even-Anything Village, or the field of Broad-and-Boundless, relax and do nothing by its side, or lie down for a free and easy sleep under it? Axes will not shorten its life, nothing can ever harm it. If there's no use for it, how can it come to grief or pain?

Such philosophical Taoism resisted duties and artificiality and fostered a not unmystical "naturalness." Its adherents believed in floating along with nature in general and their own natures in particular. Infected with this naturalness, there were Chinese poets and painters who indulged and even paraded their idiosyncrasies. They came to regard themselves as the men of "wind and stream," who lived each one in accord with himself. They tried, like the yet non-existent Zen Buddhists, to respond to things but not to be ensnared by them. The more intellectual among them conducted terse and maybe precious "pure conversations."

It is amusing to see how Taoistic behavior was converted, sometimes with minimal change, into Zen behavior. Take for example the story of a Taoist, Huan Yi, famous for his skill with the flute. Another Taoist worthy heard that he was traveling nearby and sent a messenger to ask him to come and play for him.

So Huan Yi "descended from his chariot, sat on a chair, and played the flute three times. After that, he ascended his chariot and went away. The two men did not exchange even a single word."

In its Zen transmutation this becomes the story of the Zen master, Kakua, an early pioneer of Zen in Japan. When he returned from China, the emperor asked him to tell him everything he had learned of this new sect. Kakua produced a flute, blew a note on it, bowed politely, and walked out.

We are also told of a Chinese Zen master who answered questions by rolling the wooden balls he played with, and another who did his meditation perched, like a bird, in a tree. More ominously, we hear that the Zen monasteries of China "ended by turning into madhouses." We hear, too, that in the sixteenth century, a period of social disorganization in China, there were Zen-inspired Confucians with "a truly remarkable ability to bring a person to sudden enlightenment by means of clever dialogue." They formed a "realization" school, whose members included a "mad" group. The "madmen" despised rules and attacked the conventions that, they said, kept men imprisoned. One of them went so far as to proclaim freedom of speech and equality of the sexes. It is said that such Confucians and followers of Zen "gave birth to the heresy of mad and irresponsible actions" and deliberately flouted the moral code.

There is something in this anti-establishmentarianism, stubborn whimsicality, and creative disorder that recalls the spirit of Dadaism. I am referring to the less bitter, more benign and creative Dadaists, such as Schwitters and Arp. Let me make some comparisons to persuade you of what I have just said. You will discover in the present book that Master Mumon pondered for six years on the koan on Mu. Then he suddenly achieved enlightenment and composed the following poem:

Mu! Mu! Mu! Mu! Mu!
Mu! Mu! Mu! Mu! Mu!
Mu! Mu! Mu! Mu! Mu!
Mu! Mu! Mu! Mu! Mu!

It may be only my own stubbornness that leads me to insist, as I do, that, granted the cultural differences involved, this repeated Mu! is a Dadaist poem, reveling in its own literal meaninglessness and irony.

The same variant of the same koan may also be answered by

the recitation of the first twenty letters of the alphabet. The letters of the alphabet, in or out of their fixed order, are the substance of more than one Dadaist poem, for example, Schwitters' "Register [elementary]," beginning

$$Z$$
$$A \quad R \quad P$$
$$A \quad B \quad C$$

and ending, as the alphabet dictates,

$$Z$$
$$Z$$
$$Z$$

Further comparisons are easy. It is easy to recall the "Ursonata" of Schwitters, composed of meaningless sounds, his "Poem 25," made up completely of numbers, and his "Composed Picture Poem," which looks like a more complicated and mechanical version of the circles, signifying "emptiness," or the quasi-symbolic square-triangle-circle that Zen artists used to paint. The purely typographical poems and pictures, called, in our times, "concrete poetry" or "concrete art," also come to mind.

The comparison between Zen and Dada extends to the explicit ideas of Dadaists and Surrealists. Arp, for example, believed that we should not create by imposing artificial forms upon nature, but by submitting to chance, which "embraces all other laws and is as unfathomable to us as the depths from which all life arises." Only by submission to the law of chance, he said, can one attain perfect life, the perfection and order of which are the perfection and order of nature itself.

In the vein of Zen "suchness," the ninth-century Zen master Ch'an-sha Ching-ts'en (Chosha Keijin, in Japanese) once said to his monks:

> The entire universe is your eye; the entire universe is your own luminance; the entire universe is within your own luminance. In the entire universe there is no one who is not your own self.

Kurt Schwitters, somewhat likewise, and for somewhat similar reasons, though in the vein of European pantheism, wrote:

> I am the hand.
> The hand is the man.

The man is the hand.
The earth is the world.
We men are great.
Never do men overbear over.
I am the hand.
Never do hands overbear over.

Zen Hands

The technique of the Zen koan is, obviously, to tempt the learner into logic, into the giving, that is, of a rational response. He must be taught to resist the temptation. His response must reflect reality unqualified, unanalyzed, unrationalized. The Zen response is therefore often by act rather than by word. Consider three examples.

The first example is the following dialogue:

> MONK: Where is the reality in appearance?
> MASTER: Wherever there is appearance, there is reality.
> MONK: How does it manifest itself?
> The master lifted his saucer.

The second example, from the koan on the one finger, ends in typical Zen hyperbole:

> Whenever Master Gutei was asked a question, he would simply raise one finger.
> ANSWER: The pupil raises one finger.
> MASTER: What if I cut this finger off?
> ANSWER: Even if you cut it, it cannot be cut. From the top of the thirty-third heaven down to the deepest layer of earth, it is the one finger.

The third and last example is from the koan on the sound of the one hand:

> MASTER: In clapping both hands a sound is heard. What is the sound of the one hand?
> ANSWER: The pupil faces his master, takes a correct posture, and, without a word, thrusts one hand forward.

This demonstrative, wordless form of argument is not totally foreign to Western thought. When Boswell told Samuel Johnson that the philosopher, Berkeley, had argued that matter did not exist, Johnson made a famous response. In Boswell's words:

> After we came out of the church, we stood talking for
> some time together of Bishop Berkeley's ingenious sophistry
> to prove the non-existence of matter, and that everything
> in the universe is merely ideal. I observed that though we are
> satisfied his doctrine is not true, it is impossible to refute it.
> I shall never forget the alacrity with which Johnson answered,
> striking his foot with mighty force against a large stone, till
> he rebounded from it, "I refute it *thus!*"

Boswell adds, "To me it is inconceivable how Berkeley can be
answered by pure reasoning." But this is precisely why, by Zen
standards, Johnson is right. To answer Berkeley's reasoning with
reasoning would be a mistake, a trap, Zen would say. Johnson is
not engaged in the philosopher's usual epistemological analysis,
and, indeed, most philosophers regard his response as irrelevant.
After all, you can't really kick an argument. But by Zen and
Johnsonian standards, the kick, though technically irrelevant,
is relevant in fact. That is to say, Berkeley has not only an abstract
argument, but a goal. He wants to get rid of the belief in matter
and, by doing so, to cause a change in attitude toward the world.
Johnson commonsensically denies Berkeley's right to tamper with
his natural reaction to objects or, for that matter, with his religious
views. In Johnson's world, stones are not, as Berkeley would have
them, immaterial messages being spoken immaterially to an
immaterial Johnson by an immaterial God. Berkeley, or the stone
that represented him, had the kick coming to him, or to it.

But not only philosophically unsophisticated men have come
on this kind of demonstrative argument. It was used, not very
many years ago, by the English philosopher G. E. Moore. His
purpose was to refute Kant, who held that the only possible proof
for the existence of external things was the one that he, Kant,
had given. Moore's response was:

> I can now give a large number of different proofs, each of
> which is a perfectly rigorous proof. . . . I can prove now, for
> instance, that two human hands exist. How? By holding up
> my two hands, and saying, as I make a certain gesture with the
> right hand, "Here is one hand," and by adding, as I make a
> certain gesture with the left, "and here is another." And if,
> by doing this, I have proved *ipso facto* the existence of external

things, you will see that I can also do it now in numbers of other ways: there is no need to multiply examples.

But did I prove just now that two human hands were then in existence? I want to insist that I did; that the proof I gave was a perfectly rigorous one; and that it is perhaps impossible to give a better or more rigorous proof of anything whatever.

Contemporary philosophers may or may not be satisfied with Moore's proof. Zen Buddhists would surely approve it, though they might sadly note that the tradition of English philosophizing made it necessary for Moore to accompany the motion of his hands with explanatory words. Even the few he used would be too many for the pure Zen taste.

Zen and Other Riddles
and the Reasons for Riddling

If we look at the koans historically, it is not difficult to see how they were evolved and how they came into vogue as a training method. But I should like to try to understand, independently of the Zen tradition, what their usefulness might have been.

What are riddles and enigmas good for, apart from amusement? They have been created everywhere, I suppose, and seem to be a natural accompaniment of the pleasure humans take in exercising their intelligence. Black Africa, for example, abounds in them. Riddles have been used there as an instrument of traditional education and as a challenge to verbal contests. African riddles may have symbolic meanings known only to initiates. My rather offhand explanation of the interest in riddles in Africa and else-where is this: riddles pose difficulties that, when solved, give much of the satisfaction of having solved real, that is, really disturbing difficulties of which the riddles are the invented simulacra. When solved, they also give the feeling of an ability to solve mysteries and penetrate secret intentions. To solve a riddle is to gain or regain confidence in oneself.

If, however, we choose Africa for the comparison, we find that Zen koans resemble African riddles less than they do African dilemma tales, tales that end with difficult alternative conclusions. Some such tales are provided with a "correct" answer, but, in any case, they provoke lively discussion.

Let me give an example of an African dilemma tale, "The

Leftover Eye." It begins with the situation of four blind persons, a man, his wife, his mother, and his wife's mother, all living together on an impossibly poor farm. To improve their lot, they leave the farm. On the road, the man stumbles over something. This something turns out to be seven eyes. He immediately gives two eyes to his wife and two to himself. Of the remaining three eyes, he gives one to his mother and one to his wife's mother. He now has a single eye left in his hand. To whom should he give it, to his mother or his wife's mother. "If," says the tale, "he gives the eye to his mother he will forever be ashamed before his wife and her mother. If he gives it to his wife's mother, he will fear the angry and disappointed heart of his own mother. A mother, know you, is not something to be played with."

The dilemma is rubbed in a bit more, and then the narrator ends with the question, "If this thing would come to you, which would you choose?"

The African imagination shown in this tale resembles that of Zen in that both seize on imaginative dilemmas in order to force apparently impossible solutions.

Before I comment further on dilemmas, I should like to contrast a pair, one of them African, the other Zen.

According to the African dilemma tale, "a man's helpless mother was fed by his wife. One day she bit the wife's hand and would not let go. Not knowing what to do, the man asked the judge, and the judge asked the people. The young people said, 'Break the old lady's jaw.' The old people said, 'Cut off the young woman's hand.' The judge was unable to decide. What would you do?"

The Zen dilemma is one of the koans of this book. "Let us suppose," it begins, "that a man climbs up a tree." It continues, rather implausibly, "He grips the branches with his teeth, his hands do not hold onto the tree, and his feet do not touch the ground. A monk below asks him about the meaning of our founder's coming from the West [i.e., about the essential meaning of Buddhism]. If he does not answer, he will be avoiding the monk's question [and demonstrating cruelty, which is forbidden to a Buddhist]. But if he opens his mouth and utters a word, he will fall to death. Under such circumstances, what would the man do?"

Here, in this book, the sensible comment is made that it is plausible to assume that the man would, anyway, soon fall.

"Answering or not is not his problem. He needs not philosophy but someone kind and courageous enough to help him down."

How do the two dilemmas compare? They have at least their drastic alternatives and black humor in common, and they are equally difficult to answer persuasively. An African will normally weigh alternatives and choose the one that seems best to him, or he will think of a clever strategem to solve the dilemma. The Zen monk, in contrast, will try to cut through the difficulty, as if it were the proverbial Gordian knot. Both African and Japanese dilemmas provoke an attempt to apply traditional rules or modes of vision to perplexing particular cases. The dilemma is, then, an exercise in the maintenance of a traditional set of values, and, further, an exercise in self-revelation, for the individual who attempts to solve a dilemma must decide how he would interpret these values. The dilemma also shows all those who join in the attempt to solve it what they have in common.

To speak of the Zen koan alone, it does appear to have both an individual and a social usefulness. This becomes clear if the context of monastic life is recalled. Riddle-solving, under the personal direction of a teacher, provides an important degree of autonomy given within a highly regulated life; for every monk knows that the effort is engaged in for his own sake, at his own pace, and must, if it is to be successfully concluded, end in an internal victory achieved by himself.

If we remember, too, that many of the monks are orphans or others cast adrift or troubled by life, we see that the koan training, if sincerely practiced, represents their attempt to fulfil themselves by means of a viable integration of mind and body, or intellect and emotion. The monks have a vague but sufficiently orienting background of explicit philosophy, they find a truth for the simple-minded and another, higher one for the more demanding or insightful, and they learn that they must always preserve an intimate communion between thought and action. Briefly, koan training is a formal method of giving the monk his personal value and satisfaction, and it is, no less, the method of linking him tightly to master and monastery, the master guiding and the monastery disciplining him, and together making his personal accomplishment possible.

This said, it should also be remembered that Zen Buddhism was a training ground for poets, artists, and warriors. I cannot think of anything much better than koan meditation to drive home the lesson, so well learned in traditional China and Japan, that the aim of the poet, artist, or warrior is creative intuition, and that this is achieved by the attentive fusing of discipline, intelligence, and emotion.

This granted, the possible usefulness of koan meditation to the individual can be stated. As I have said, it unites the externally imposed discipline of the monastic community with his self-interest. His meditation is conducted under the rule of the master, who acts the role of a super-parent. The strain of meditation may trigger a psychosis, but, generally speaking, meditation makes use of the monk's inward sense of omnipotence and his mystical tendencies in order to stimulate him to feel an essential identity between himself, his community, and the universe. His meditation merges solitariness and sociability, limitation and infinity.

When I say this, I am reminded of a friend who could not remain at peace with himself unless he heard a concert of classical music every week. It seemed to me that the music first aroused his emotions, as, in its initial development, it ranged from soft to loud and low to high. His emotions were then carried along by the music and accentuated and made to clash, for classical music, before it ends, enters into a war with itself. Finally, music and emotion having become one, both came as one to a classic, harmonious resolution.

The very strain, it seems to me, of koan meditation is not unlike the self-imposed strain of a creative mathematician, writer, or artist. Such a person deliberately sets himself difficult problems, and deliberately renews them once they have been solved, in order, so to speak, to compose or harmonize or solve himself by his internalization of the difficulty that he is composing, harmonizing, or solving. He is using his effort, ostensibly directed at something external, so that, by ordering the external object, he can order himself internally. The result of such a self-conquest can be an access of pleasure, optimism, and self-confidence. It can bring on the ecstatic states of which Hakuin speaks with great emotion. These states can feel good, better, or superlative. The process, by which one rises from doubt or ambivalence to pleasure or more, suggests what psychotherapists have often said, that, to be healed, one must first bring to the surface difficulties that have been suppressed and, because suppressed, have brought on neurotic suffering. One must, they have said, summon up trouble in order to get rid of it. Zen meditation is at least a form of psychotherapy, and, as such, its most obvious aim is psychophysical wholeness.

Zen Ordinariness

Zen teaches vigilant carelessness and detached involvement. In a more high-sounding phrase, it teaches transcendental ordinariness. In a simpler, more sympathetic phrase, it teaches nothing but ordinariness itself.

Long before Zen came into existence, when, in India, mysticism had flourished and had been attacked by philosophical opponents and unmystical realities, there had been Buddhist philosophers who arrived at a subtle solution of the problem. What problem? The one that has been stated in these pages in various forms. One form is that of impermanence and permanence, which, when put in the light of human concerns, becomes the problem of death and survival, which, put in another form, is the problem of relative and absolute. The philosophers I am speaking of put this problem in terms of "emptiness," which is to say that they regarded everything as devoid of substance and, in the final analysis, as inconceivable. The philosophers of emptiness, having despaired of the philosophers' prolonged debate, regarded the debate as essentially insoluble—Kant, in Europe, said the same. It is true, these Buddhists said, that there is no immutable substance, nothing, at least nothing that can be put into words or logic, that underlies the eternal flux. Nothing either positive or negative can be said to characterize reality. Reality, they said, is not dual, for there is no essential difference between subject and object, impure and pure, or relative and absolute; but neither is reality single. It is neither individual nor non-individual, neither one nor many. It is, instead, "empty."

It should be obvious that this was the conclusion adopted by the Zen Buddhists; except that they had usually grown to dislike the too explicit philosophizing by which it had been maintained. They also adopted the "empty" Buddhist conclusion that there was and could be no difference between the ordinary world, the round of birth and death, as the Buddhists saw it, and the superlative goal of Buddhism, nirvana. In Buddhist terminology, they concluded that *samsara* is identical with nirvana. Common sense reality, therefore, cannot be denied, because it is identical with superlative reality. The moral is that we ought to learn to experience the "suchness" or "thisness" of the common sense world.

All, then, that we can do, and all that enlightenment can teach, is the paradox of the enlightened acceptance of the world as it is. Be empty, the Zen masters advised, or, in other words, be intuitively ordinary. When a monk said to a Zen master, "Your disciple is sick all over. Please cure me," the master answered, "I will not cure you." When the monk asked, "Why don't you cure me?," the master's answer was, "So that you neither live nor die." And when another monk asked another master where silence, that is, emptiness, would finally be expressed, the master's answer was, "Last night at midnight I lost three pennies by my bed." His meaning was, "Get your attention back where it belongs, on ordinary life."

Ordinariness is not difficult unless one makes it particularly elusive. When an early Chinese Zen master, thinking of the difficulties of achieving enlightenment, allowed the words "Difficult, difficult, difficult" to escape him, his wife, who, at the moment, was wiser than he, answered, "Easy, easy, easy, just like touching your feet to the ground when you get out of bed." Her response, however, seemed too explicit to another Zen master, who added the characteristic formula, "Neither difficult nor easy."

It was ordinariness that led Rinzai to say to his disciples, with a touch of exasperation, that they had come from everywhere to search for deliverance from the world; but if delivered from the world, where, he asked, could they go? The advice he gave was to be ordinary. "Just carry on an ordinary task," he said, "without attachments," meaning, without blind, enslaving desire. "Shit and piss, wear your clothes, eat your meals. When you're tired, lie down. The fool will laugh at you, but the wise man will understand."

But the most charming expression of ordinariness, to my mind, is the invitation to have a cup of tea. Look at the contrast between poetic transcendence and courteous ordinariness, which is the invitation to have a cup of tea, in the following koan and the insightful response to it:

> The disciple Hokoji visited Master Baso and asked, "Who is he that transcends existence?" Baso said, "When you have

swallowed the waters of the West River in one gulp, I shall answer you." In an instant Hokoji realized the answer and said the poem which goes: "People from all over come and meet together; each one seeks to learn the way of non-doing. This is the place where Buddhas are born. I, having been chosen for holding the heart of nothingness, can now go back."

Answer: "I'll have a cup of tea," the pupil says, taking a cup of tea.

To Zen, tea, like ordinariness, cures everything.

Zen Terminable and Interminable

In one of his later essays Freud asked whether a psychoanalysis could ever be terminated. He said that it was evident that analysis could never attain absolute psychic normality, or that, if something like such normality appeared to have been attained, it was probably because the person in question had been spared from too searching a fate. The analysts themselves, said Freud, could not quite reach the standards of normality that they set for their patients. At this point, he added endearingly, "It almost looks as if analysis were the third of those 'impossible' professions in which one can be quite sure of unsatisfying results. The other two, much older-established, are the bringing up of children and the government of nations." I wonder if the profession of Zen master should be added to Freud's list.

Freud went on to say that every analyst ought to reenter analysis at intervals because his task, like the patient's, is in fact interminable. But he continued, as common sense dictates, that in practice analyses do come to an end.

Compare Hakuin's view. Hakuin, when speaking of enlightenment, told of a famous Chinese master who had experienced eighteen "great awakenings" and an uncountable number of smaller ones. Hakuin himself experienced great awakenings at least six or seven times, each awakening superseding in insight those that had preceded. Hakuin believed, as a result, that once the student attained the initial awakening, he had to go on with the study of his koans, arranged to become progressively more difficult.

Perhaps Zen, like psychoanalysis, should be regarded as an

ideally interminable education. I doubt if any Zen master has said so explicitly because, if he has, he might seem to be reverting from belief in sudden enlightenment to belief in gradual enlightenment. Yet there must be something interminable in Zen meditation, for what master could accept his condition of ordinariness and yet claim never to lapse from enlightenment? Zen is, as it claims to be, the condition of ordinary men and is embodied in ordinary institutions. But ordinariness is an ambiguous state, and the goal may be lost sight of. Institutionalization, for instance, has dangers that can never be escaped for long, by Zen or anything.

I say this because, before I end, I want to pay tribute to the Zen master whose introduction opens this book. Without his help, the translation of these koans and answers would necessarily have been less authentic, and their traditional intent could only have been guessed at. Surely the tendency, so clear in this book, to institutionalize the questions and, above all, the answers works against the Zen demand that we should remain spontaneous and open. The fear that the publication of the secret answers might weaken the whole system of Zen education is a comment on the dilution that the Zen ideal has suffered. By its own best standards, it should be reformed. That is why the help given by Master Hirano Sōjō demonstrates that respect for the truth is everywhere the same.

BEN–AMI SCHARFSTEIN

TRANSLATOR'S NOTE

This book contains all the koans which the Zen novice has to answer during the long course of his training for qualification as a Zen master, together with their traditional answers. My decision to bring the translation of this book before the general public was not easily made, and I am well aware that there will be Zen masters and Zen disciples in Japan and elsewhere who may regard such a publication with discomfort. One can hardly expect the teachers and disciples of a religious sect to welcome the publication of the "secrets" of their sect.

Since the publication of this book in 1916 and its republication in 1917, there has been no new edition. In Kyoto, only a photocopy of it is sold in a shop that specializes in Buddhist literature. To the best of my knowledge, this book cannot be found in libraries, nor does it appear in bibliographies on Buddhism or Zen. I have been told by the shop owner in Kyoto that almost all the buyers of the book are Zen novices. A certain Japanese Zen master told me that he had tried to compose his own koans in order to prevent his novices from relying on the answers in the book. He admitted, however, that he found it extremely difficult and was, in the end, forced to rely on the traditional koan teaching as presented in this book.

Though the teaching of Zen was introduced into Japan as early as the seventh century, it was not until the beginning of the eighteenth century that the koans were first systematized into the traditional method of teaching presented here. It was the Japanese Zen Master Hakuin (1686–1769) who first selected the koans in this book from among those recorded in Chinese sources. (There are close to two thousand recorded koans altogether.) It was he who also determined the order of their presentation to novices and composed many of the traditional answers. Hakuin created many koans of his own, the most famous of them being the koan on "the sound of the one hand." This system was further developed by Hakuin's disciples, Inzan Ien (1751–1814) and Takujū Kosen (1760–1833), into the teaching method which has prevailed in Japan until the present day. In the course of time, Hakuin's teaching came to be interpreted by a number of different schools, each using the method to give different answers to some of the koans. But these differences are, for the most part, nonessential.

Most scholars of Zen believe that "the koans that Hakuin created are still transmitted only by word of mouth to the student in the master's room."[1] But it is in fact the custom in Zen monasteries that the novice compiles his own notes on the various koans and their answers, exactly as transmitted to him by his master. When the novice, after ten or more years of practice, is qualified as a Zen master, his master goes over the notes and corrects and approves them. The pupil then vows to keep the notes a secret and, when he himself becomes a master, to transmit them only to his own disciples. Taking into account the traditional loyalty of the Japanese to their teachers and masters, it is no wonder that scholars of Zen in Japan and the West were led to believe that there existed no written records of the koans and their answers. The present book must have created a scandalous sensation when first published nearly sixty years ago. Why so few Japanese scholars and, it seems, not even a single Western scholar knew about this publication remains a mystery.[2] Ruth F. Sasaki writes, "Neither Hakuin nor his disciples compiled any collection of koans, at least none that were ever published.[3] It seems that the silence of Japanese scholars and students concerning the existence of this publication was, in effect, a clever method of dealing with the scandal, much more effective than the destruction of the book.

The lack of sources for the answers to the koans has created a serious handicap for researchers on Zen. In Japan, very few Zen masters work on the translation of the koans into modern Japanese; but even those who do, being bound by their vow to reveal the answers only in "dokusan" (the private meeting between novice and master), are extremely reluctant to refer even to the "meaning" of koans, not to speak of their answers. Thus scholars who are

---

[1] I. Miura and R.F. Sasaki, *The Zen Koan* (Kyoto: First Zen Institute of America, 1965), p. 28.
[2] After these words were written, I found a reference to the book in P.B. Yampolsky, *The Zen Master Hakuin* (New York: Columbia University Press, 1971), p. 13n.
[3] Miura and Sasaki, *The Zen Koan*, p. 28.

forced to rely on no more than the Chinese version of the koan have to speculate on the meaning of phrases and expressions which could be clarified if they knew the "official" answer to the koan, or at least the way the koan was presented and commented upon by the Zen master in private meetings.

Zen research in the West suffers from the same handicap. Because none of the translators knew the answers to the koans, they had to rely upon their own intuitions as to their meanings or on the mood or usage of the particular koan in the context of Zen teaching. As a result, many of the translations, though linguistically possible, have often missed the essential point of a koan. I suspect that even D.T. Suzuki, who introduced Zen to the West a few decades ago, did not know the answers to the koans. His presentation of the doctrine of Zen, its history, and its affinity with other Buddhist schools of thought is scholarly and reliable. However, Zen masters generally agree that his comments on koans are impressionistic and in many cases excessively "Western." When Zen began to attract the attention of intellectuals outside Japan, many Westerners took to writing on Zen. Some of these writers, endowed with poetic sensitivity, have given insight into the meaning of some koans. However, comments such as theirs cannot generally convey the rooted attitudes of Zen tradition.

My decision, then, to translate and publish this book was above all motivated by my firm conviction that it would introduce to the Western world the clearest, most detailed, and most correct picture of Zen. In trying to make the translation as clear as possible to the Western reader, I have refrained whenever possible from using terms that would not be understood by a reader with a limited knowledge of Buddhism. Where Buddhist terms were unavoidable, I provided their explanation either in the text itself or in notes. The notes I have added to the koans deal mainly with the philosophical background and the psychological relations between the persons who appear in the koan in question. The notes to the answers are designed, above all, to explain the reasons for the pupil's specific response.

For those interested in further research into the koans, I have provided a list of the Chinese sources to the koans of Part Three. As for the discourse on the two koans of Part One, a great part of the koans of Part Two, and the answers to the koans of Part Three, there is, to the best of my knowledge, no source other than the Japanese edition of this book.

The Japanese Edition and Its Author

The translation presented here includes the main part of the Japanese edition. It includes, that is, the complete body of "Hakuin-Zen"—two hundred and eighty-one koans and their answers according to the traditional order of the koan teaching system. The Japanese edition also includes some one hundred additional koans which are used only rarely in Zen teaching; the Zen monastic law; and a doctrine concerning the five stages of enlightenment related in its structure to an ancient Chinese divination system. None of these is included in the present book.

The Japanese edition was entitled *Gendai Sōjizen Hyōron*. *Gendai* means "modern" or "present-day"; *sōji* means "resemblance" or "similarity"; and *hyōron* means "critique." The title as a whole may be translated "A Critique of Present-Day Pseudo-Zen." The author of the book wrote under a pseudonym to "protect" himself, as he says, and to avoid "unnecessary" quarrels. The pseudonym chosen by him was "Hauhōō." The character of "ha" means "break" or "destroy"; "u" means "existent"; "hō," "law" or "order"; and "ō," "king." The name as a whole may be translated as "The Arch-Destroyer of the Existent Order." It is not clear at what age the author published his book, but he could not possibly have been young, for the material he revealed on the various "schools" of Zen indicated that he had completed the whole course of training for the position of a Zen master at least once, and had repeated parts of the course under several masters before he published these "secret" notes. The author considered himself a "reformer" of Japanese Buddhism in general, and of the Rinzai Zen sect in particular. As his pseudonym suggests, his "reform" was meant to be primarily destructive.

The author considered contemporary Zen masters (those of the end of the Meiji and the beginning of the Taishō era) and most of their followers to be fakes, and he declared himself determined to reveal their "true face." He added that it was useless to look for enlightenment among the Zen masters for they were nothing but "envoys of the devil clad in a monk's robe." He declared that his real masters were the Chinese Zen masters of the past, such as Rinzai, Chūhō, Bassui, and Takusui. In this way, he was suggesting that he accepted the Chinese koans as "Zen teaching" but rejected both the Japanese koans and the answers to the Chinese koans composed by Hakuin and his disciples. In his attacks on masters and novices of his time, the author avoided revealing their real names. He justified this restraint by his desire to prevent sensationalism, but it is clear he wished to hide his own identity.

The author declared that his aim in revealing the secrets of Zen was to destroy the position of the "masters" of his time. From now on, he said, anyone who read this book would know no less that the Zen masters—that is, he would be able to speak and act "Zen." Therefore, *anyone* could become a Zen master. The author also presented his own viewpoint on questions of Buddhist doctrine: generally speaking, he believed that the essence of Buddhist teaching is "deliverance from the cycle of life and death" and "insight into one's true nature." He thought that the koan system of "Hakuin-Zen," as revealed in this book and as employed by Zen masters, did not satisfactorily describe the essence of Buddhism.

From the author's approach to religion, his style, and the mood of his writing, it is quite obvious that whatever the state of institutionalized Zen in his time may have been, he was by his nature not suited for the world of Zen. He must have been the uncompromising, puritanical kind of reformer. He apparently could not find much in common with his masters and fellow novices, and seemed to have moved from one master to another in search for a "real" master. Disappointed and bitter, he finally gave it all up and devoted himself to an all-out attack on what he calls "pseudo-Zen."

There is, however, much truth in the author's criticism that some of the koans and quite a few of the answers are stereotyped and artificial. Many of the answers also seem to be missing the point of the koan. It seems fair to assume that the worst part of the traditional system of "Hakuin-Zen" was not composed by Master Hakuin himself but by some of his less-gifted disciples. It can only be hoped that the Zen masters of our time have enough insight to distinguish between what is old and good, and what is simply old.

I am deeply grateful to Zen Master Hirano Sōjō, who unsparingly gave his time, went over the Japanese edition with me, and offered invaluable suggestions as to the meaning of the koans. This book could not have been completed without his generous help.

I acknowledge my indebtedness to Mr. Leung Hau Yeong, Mr. Iwamoto Mitsuyoshi, and Miss Carol Chinaka for their help in preparing the translation. Especially deep thanks are due to Carol for her devoted work.

Had I not been blessed throughout the years with the guidance of a true teacher and thinker, I could never have written this work. I owe more than can be expressed in words to Professor Ben-Ami Scharfstein.

YOEL HOFFMANN

PART ONE

THE KOAN ON THE SOUND OF THE ONE HAND AND THE KOAN ON MU

THE KOAN ON THE SOUND
OF THE ONE HAND
AND THE KOAN ON MU

I

The Way of the Inzan School

A. *The Koan on the Sound of the One Hand*

In clapping both hands a sound is heard; what is the sound of the one hand?

ANSWER
The pupil faces his master, takes a correct posture, and without a word, thrusts one hand forward.

DISCOURSE
1   MASTER
If you've heard the sound of the one hand, prove it.

ANSWER
Without a word, the pupil thrusts one hand forward.

2   MASTER
It's said that if one hears the sound of the one hand, one becomes a Buddha [i.e., becomes enlightened]. Well then, how will you do it?

ANSWER
Without a word, the pupil thrusts one hand forward.

(47)

3   MASTER

After you've become ashes, how will you hear it?

         ANSWER

Without a word, the pupil thrusts one hand forward.

4   MASTER

What if the one hand is cut by the Suimo Sword?

         ANSWER

"It can't be."
Or:
"If it can, let me see you do it." So saying, the pupil extends his hand forward.
Or:
Without a word, the pupil thrusts one hand forward.

5   MASTER

Why can't it cut the one hand?

         ANSWER

"Because the one hand pervades the universe."

6   MASTER

Then show me something that contains the universe.

         ANSWER

Without a word, the pupil thrusts one hand forward.

7   MASTER

The before-birth-one-hand, what is it like?

         ANSWER

Without a word, the pupil thrusts one hand forward.

8   MASTER

The Mt.-Fuji-summit-one-hand, what is it like?

         ANSWER

The pupil, shading his eyes with one hand, takes the pose of looking down from the summit of Mt. Fuji and says, "What a splendid view!" naming several places to be seen from Mt. Fuji—or others would name places visible from where they happen to be.

9   MASTER
Attach a quote to the-Mt.-Fuji-summit-one-hand.

ANSWER

(Quote)

> Floating clouds connected the sea and the
>   mountain,
> And white flat plains spread into the states of
>   Sei and Jo.

10   MASTER
Did you hear the sound of the one hand from the back or from the front?

ANSWER

Extending one hand, the pupil repeatedly says, "Whether it's from the front or from the back, you can hear it as you please." *Or:*
"From the back it's caw! caw! [the sound of a crow]. From the front it's chirp, chirp [the sound of a sparrow]."

11   MASTER
Now that you've heard the sound of the one hand, what are you going to do?

ANSWER

"I'll pull weeds, scrub the floor, and if you're tired, give you a massage."

12   MASTER
If it's that convenient a thing, let me hear it too!

ANSWER

Without a word, the pupil slaps his master's face.

13   MASTER
The one hand—how far will it reach?

The pupil places his hand on the floor and says, "This is how far it goes."

14 MASTER

The before-the-fifteenth-day-one-hand, the after-the-fifteenth-day-one-hand, the fifteenth-day-one-hand, what's it like?

ANSWER

The pupil extends his right hand and says, "This is the before-the-fifteenth-day-one-hand." Extending his left hand he says, "This is the after-the-fifteenth-day-one-hand." Bringing his hands together he says, "This is the fifteenth-day-one-hand."

15 MASTER

The sublime-sound-of-the-one-hand, what is it like?

ANSWER

The pupil immediately imitates the sound he happens to hear when sitting in front of his master. That is, if it happens to be raining outside, he imitates the sound of rain, "Pitter-patter"; if at that moment a bird happens to call, he says, "Caw! Caw!" imitating the bird's call.

16 MASTER

The soundless-voice-of-the-one-hand, what is it like?

ANSWER

Without a word, the pupil abruptly stands up, then sits down again, bowing in front of his master.

17 MASTER

The true-[mental]-sphere-of-the-one-hand, what's it like?

ANSWER

"I take it to be as fleeting as a dream or phantom, or as something like an illusory flower. That's how I think of it."

18 MASTER

The source-of-the-one-hand, what is it?

"On the plain there is not the slightest breeze that stirs the smallest grain of sand."
(Quote)

> All communication with places north of the
>> White Wolf River is disconnected,
> And south to the Red Phoenix City,
>> autumn nights have grown so long.

Or:
"It is from the place where there is not even one rabbit's hair that I have struck the sound of the one hand."
(Quote)

> The wind blows and clears the sky of all
>> floating clouds,
> And the moon rises above those green hills
>> like a piece of round white jade.

Or:

> Arriving at the river, the territories of the
>> state of Go seem to come to an end,
> Yet on the other bank, the mountains of the
>> state of Etsu look so far away.

B. *The Koan on Mu*

A monk asked Master Jōshū, "Does a dog have Buddha-nature?" Jōshū said, "Mu" [i.e., "no," "non-existence," or "no-thing"].

ANSWER

Sitting erect in front of his master, the pupil yells, "Mu——!" with all his might.

DISCOURSE

I   MASTER
Well then, bring forth the proof of this "mu."

ANSWER

Sitting erect in front of his master, the pupil yells, "Mu——!" with all his might.

2   MASTER
If so, in what way will you become a Buddha [i.e., be enlightened]?

ANSWER

Sitting erect in front of his master, the pupil yells, "Mu——!" with all his might.

3   MASTER

Well then, this "mu"—after you've become ashes, how do you see it?

ANSWER

Sitting erect in front of his master, the pupil yells, "Mu——!" with all his might.

4   MASTER

Jōshū, on another occasion, when asked whether a dog has Buddha-nature or not, responded in the affirmative [i.e., "yes" or "there is"]. What do you think of that?

ANSWER

"Even if Jōshū says there is Buddha-nature in a dog, I'll simply yell 'Mu——!' with all my might."

5   MASTER

If I say that a dog does not have Buddha-nature because of his karma [non-enlightened state], how about that?

ANSWER

The pupil yells, "Mu——!" with all his might.

6   MASTER

When Jōshū was asked why he responded in the affirmative, he answered, "Knowing yet trespassing." How about that?

ANSWER

Sitting erect in front of his master, the pupil yells, "Mu——!" with all his might.

7   MASTER

Master Mumon recited "mu" twenty times. You do it in one breath.

ANSWER

The host and I do not know one another.

(Quote)

> I sit here for a moment because of the trees
>> and spring.
> Please do not worry yourself wantonly about
>> buying wine.
> Money will be there in your pocket all right.

[The above Chinese quote is composed of twenty characters. It is in the sum of characters that the Master's question is answered. Therefore, any quote consisting of twenty characters or syllables, or even, as some monks respond, the plain recitation of the first twenty letters of the alphabet will do.]

8   MASTER
The essence of "mu"—what's it like?

                                     ANSWER
Without a word, the pupil places both hands on his chest and stands up.

9   MASTER
The working of "mu"—what's it like?

                                     ANSWER
The pupil stands up and, swinging his arms back and forth, walks five or six steps saying, "When it's necessary to go, go." Sitting down again he says, "When it's necessary to sit, sit."

10   MASTER
Explain the difference between the "mu" state and the ignorance [or karma] state.

                                     ANSWER
The pupil describes the course one takes four to eight miles to and from his place of meditation. For example, if he meditates in Ueno [a place in Tokyo] he may say, "From here [Ueno] I went out to Hirokoji Street, got on a streetcar which passed the stops of Sudachō, Kyōbashi, Nihonbashi, Shinbashi, and got off at Shinagawa. After completing my business, I again got on the streetcar at Shinagawa and returned the same way."

11   MASTER
Attach a quote to that.

ANSWER

(Quote)

> It has just gone away with the fragrant
> grasses,
> Yet returns again chasing after the falling
> flowers.

Or:

> I entered the East Gate living quarters in the
> morning,
> And went up to the Kayō Bridge in the
> evening.

12   MASTER

The source of "mu"—what's it like?

ANSWER

"From   there-is-not-the-slightest-breeze-that-stirs-the-smallest-grain-of-sand-vast-plain, the sky, the earth, mountains, rivers all come into view."

Or:

"There is no sky, no earth, nor mountains nor rivers, no trees, no plants. There is nothing—neither I nor any other. Even these, my words, are no-thing ['mu']."

II

The Way of the Takujū School

A. *The Koan on the Sound of the One Hand*

> There is no sound to the one hand—
> Come hear this soundless voice.

ANSWER

In some cases the response is identical to that of the Inzan School: the pupil faces his master, takes a correct posture, and without a word thrusts one hand forward.

However, with certain Zen masters, the pupil may also reply

using words similar to the following: "The sky is the one hand, the earth is the one hand; man, woman, you, me are the one hand; grass, trees, cows, horses are the one hand; everything, all things are the one hand."

DISCOURSE

1   MASTER
If you've heard the soundless voice of the one hand, prove it.

2   MASTER
If you've heard the sound of the one hand, can you be absolutely delivered from life and death, or can't you?

ANSWER
To questions (1) and (2) the pupil, without a word, thrusts one hand forward.

3   MASTER
What if the one hand is cut by the Suimo Sword?

ANSWER
"Try it—no matter how hard one tries, it couldn't be cut. The sword's no match for the one hand."

4   MASTER
The essence of the one hand—in what way does it exist?

ANSWER
"It pervades all—extending from the top of Mt. Shumi [a legendary mountain signifying the top of the universe] down to the bottom of the lowest layer of hell."

5   MASTER
What is the shape of the one hand?

ANSWER
The pupil places both hands on his chest and stands up.

6   MASTER
What if the one hand is burnt?

ANSWER

"Even if you burn it, it won't be burnt."

7   MASTER

What is the-Mt.-Fuji-summit-one-hand like?

ANSWER

(Identical with that of the Inzan School)

Shading his eyes with one hand, the pupil takes the pose of looking down from the summit of Mt. Fuji and says, "What a splendid view!," naming several places to be seen from Mt. Fuji—or others would name places visible from where they happen to be. (*Quote*)

> Arriving at the river, the territories of the
>   state of Go seem to come to an end,
> Yet on the other bank, many are the hills
>   in the state of Etsu.

8   MASTER

Now that you've heard the sound of the one hand, of what use is it?

ANSWER

"Get up in the morning, wash your face, read your prayer, take your bowl to the dining room, eat your rice porridge, perform your evening duties. . . . " In this way, the pupil enumerates the daily routine.

Or:

"Light the charcoal brazier, boil water in the kettle, rub the ink stick, light the incense."

9   MASTER

Grind the one hand into powder and swallow it.

ANSWER

"Red pepper is powder and is to be eaten; noodles made from powder one eats."

10   MASTER

Did you hear the one hand in Kyoto or did you hear it in Harima [a district in the Hyogo Prefecture]?

ANSWER

"In Kyoto, at Gion, Maruyama, Kinkakuji [places in Kyoto].
In Harima at Suma, Maiko, and Awashi [places in Harima]."

11   MASTER

The lifting of the one hand—say something about it.

                            ANSWER

"Any garbage for pickup? Beans, bean curd for sale!" So saying,
the pupil imitates the ways of traveling peddlers.

12   MASTER

Burn the one hand, gather the ashes into a fist and bring it here.

                            ANSWER

"You think one can do such a stupid thing?!" With that the
pupil slaps the face of his master.

13   MASTER

If you've heard the sound of the one hand, let me hear it too.

                            ANSWER

Again the pupil slaps the face of his master.

14   MASTER

The source-of-the-one-hand, what's it like?

                            ANSWER

"Don't be stupid—there's no such thing! Nyaaa!" [He makes a
face]. With that the pupil stands up as if to leave.

15   MASTER

Did you hear the one hand from the back or from the front?

                            ANSWER

"From the back as well as from the front. During the first fifteen
days of the month, I heard it from the front; the latter fifteen days,
from the back."
Or:
"On the road in front, a man, a cart go by; at the back road, the
sparrow calls chirp, chirp, the crow calls caw!"

16   MASTER

The-Zen-monk-one-hand, what's it like?

ANSWER

"To eat meat, to take a wife is absolutely forbidden."

17   MASTER

When every possible effort is made, every means exhausted, the absolute, decisive one hand—how is it?

ANSWER

Concentrating all his energy, his eyes sharp as though burning with anger, the pupil thrusts one hand forward.

18   MASTER

Encompassing the whole of the one-hand koan, recite a quotation.

ANSWER

(Quote)

> The white plain is desolate under the
>   autumn sky,
> But someone is coming east on horseback.
> Do you know who he is?

B. *The Koan on Mu*

A monk asked Master Jōshū, "Does a dog have Buddha-nature?" Jōshū said, "Mu" [i.e., "no," "non-existence," or "no-thing"].

ANSWER

Sitting erect in front of his master, the pupil yells, "Mu——!" with all his might.
This answer is identical with that of the Inzan School.

DISCOURSE

1   MASTER

When you don't say "mu," what do you say?

ANSWER

The pupil yells, "U——!" [opposite of "mu," meaning "is" or "existence"].

(58)

2   MASTER
Distinguish between "mu" and "u."

                           ANSWER
The pupil separately yells, "Mu——!" "U——!"

3   MASTER
How far away is "mu" from "u"?

                           ANSWER
From where he sits in the room, the pupil points to objects [for instance, the threshold or door] and says, "From here to the threshold is so-and-so-many feet; up to that door it's so-and-so-many feet."

4   MASTER
The whole of "mu," how far does it reach?

                           ANSWER
The pupil stands up and with one hand pointing towards the sky says, "It extends from the summit of Mt. Shumi" [the top of the universe]. Then, stamping his foot once, he points to the ground with the other hand continuing, "And down to the bottom of the lowest layer in hell."

5   MASTER
Hand "mu" over to me.

                           ANSWER
The pupil takes whatever object is on hand and hands it over to his master.

6   MASTER
Let me see you use "mu" with ease.

                           ANSWER
"Jakenpo," the pupil says, with his hands making the forms of scissors-stone-paper [a Japanese children's game].
Or:
"One, two, three, four . . ." bending his fingers, the pupil counts to ten.

7 MASTER

Cut "mu" into dice form and bring it to me.

ANSWER

"Please have some yakkodōfu" [bean curd cut in cubes and served with soy sauce], the pupil says and makes a gesture of offering it to his master.

8 MASTER

Put "mu" through a strainer and bring me the strained "mu."

ANSWER

The pupil says, "Please have some wheat flour" and makes a gesture of offering it to his master.

9 MASTER

Tell me how tall "mu" is.

ANSWER

The pupil gives his own height.

10 MASTER

What form of figure does "mu" take?

ANSWER

The pupil places both hands on his chest and stands up.

11 MASTER

What does "mu" look like from the back?

ANSWER

With both hands still on his chest, the pupil turns around and turns his back to his master.

12 MASTER

The measurements for "mu," about how many inches is it?

ANSWER

"The cuff length is such-and-such inches, the full length is such-and-such inches." Thus the pupil enumerates the measurements of the gown which he is wearing.

13   MASTER
Make the "mu" walk seven steps in a circle.

                                ANSWER
The pupil walks one circle around the room.

14   MASTER
The "mu" of this fan (which I am holding now)—first know it
well, then let me see you use it.

                                ANSWER
The pupil takes the fan which the master extended to him and
examining it carefully, appreciates it saying, "What a beautiful
fan this is! The frame is made of bamboo, the calligraphy in
front is so-and-so, the design in the back is so-and-so, etc." Then
without further ado he casually fans himself.

15   MASTER
Say the "mu" clearly enough that even a child can understand
and then put it into practice.

                                ANSWER
The pupil says, "Yoshi, yoshi," as if nursing a child.

16   MASTER
Now that you've seen "mu," what will you do?

                                ANSWER
"Get up in the morning, wash my face, clean up, eat . . . ." Thus
the pupil enumerates the daily routine.
Or:
In accordance with the tradition of other Zen masters, the following may also be said: "Being the master of the house, being
the servant; being a welder, a carpenter, a plasterer; being a fish
peddler, etc." Thus the pupil enumerates and imitates the various
occupations of people.

17   MASTER
If you've seen "mu," fill the "mu-mind" [or the "mindless-mind"]
in a bottomless bowl and bring it here.

The pupil spreads out his arms and recites, "A bottomless bowl"; next, using both hands as if forming some concrete object, he recites, "Mu-mind." On top of that, as if raising a huge bowl high into the air, he recites, "Fill it and bring it."

18   MASTER
In an unhampered and free manner, distinguish "mu" and use it.

ANSWER
The pupil imitates the behavior and actions of various occupations such as a carpenter, a plasterer, a fencing teacher.
Or:
The pupil says, "Use 'mu' in an unhampered and free manner" and answers, "Getting up, sitting down, lying, walking . . ." accompanying his words with gestures.

19   MASTER
In the selling of common, everyday articles, distinguish "u" ["is," "being"] from "mu" ["no," "no-thing"].

ANSWER
"One yard of this cloth costs so-and-so, half a yard will be so-and-so."
(Quote)
> The same tree bathed by the spring wind has
>   two different states:
> The southern branches facing warmth, the
>   northern ones facing cold.

Popular Saying
The sprawling clusters of calabash originate in one stem.

20   MASTER
Capture "mu" and show it forth.

ANSWER
The pupil takes hold of any object lying about him and extends it toward his master.

21   MASTER
(Quote)
Master Daie said, "Jōshū said 'mu' like this." (How about that?)

The pupil energetically yells "Mu——!"

22   MASTER
(Quote)
The ancients said, "What if the monk had never asked about Buddha-nature and Jōshū had never answered 'mu'?" (How about that?)
ANSWER
The pupil energetically yells "Mu——!"

23   MASTER
(Quote)
The song on "mu," written by Zen master Ryōfu, says:
> "Jōshū's dog has no Buddha-nature,
> Ten thousand green mountains are hidden in
>   an ancient mirror,
> The one-footed Persian goes into China,
> And the eight-armed Nata carries out
>   administrative orders."

How about this?
ANSWER
a. The pupil says loudly, "Jōshū's dog has no Buddha-nature" and then yells, "Mu——!"
b. While surveying his surroundings, the pupil recites, "Ten thousand green mountains are hidden in an ancient mirror." With that he drops his head and steadily stares at his chest.
c. The pupil imitates a weary traveler coming from far away, walking with a cane and sighing, "Ahh, it hurts, it hurts."
Or:
Limping, he walks around the room. "You bloody bastard! How dare you not obey my command!" With that the pupil hits his master's back.
Or:
First the pupil says, "Mu." Then, making a fist, he punches the base of his master's skull. In this case, the master says, "Explain!" and the pupil answers, "This is called the-hit-on-the-base-of-the-skull."

24   MASTER
The eight "mu's" of Master Chūhō. (What about that?)

"When eating a meal, 'mu'; when drinking tea, 'mu'; when sleeping, 'mu'; when getting up, 'mu' . . . ." The pupil continues enumerating eight actions, reciting "mu" after each one.

Or:

"When eating a meal, when drinking tea, when sleeping, when getting up, when walking, when sitting, when cold, when warm, when farting, when shitting, when a bird cries, when a dog barks—mu, mu, mu," and on and on the pupil continues until his master says, "That's enough!"

25   MASTER

The twenty "mu's" of Master Mumon—recite in a quote.

ANSWER

(Quote)

> My heart is like the autumn moon and the
>   blue lake clear and bright,
> Nothing affords a comparison, how can you
>   make me explain?

[This quote is composed of twenty characters. Any quote consisting of twenty characters or syllables may be recited.]

26   MASTER

In a way that even a child can understand, recite it (the twenty "mu's" of Master Mumon).

ANSWER

"A B, C, D, E, F, G, H, I, J, K, L, M, N, O, P, Q, R, S, T."

27   MASTER

What is the distinction between "u" and "mu"?

ANSWER

"Well, if you're 'u,' then I'm 'mu.'"

28   MASTER

What's the distance between "u" and "mu"?

ANSWER

"If the threshold is 'u,' then the pillar is 'mu'; if the ceiling is 'u,' then the floor is 'mu.'"

29   MASTER

It is said that in Zen we do not rely upon words for enlightenment, nor do we instruct the way through the written letter. Well, without the use of letters—ultimately, HOW IS IT?!

ANSWER

"The threshold lies flat."

30   MASTER

Well then, using letters, ultimately, HOW IS IT?!

ANSWER

"The pillar stands erect."

31   MASTER

Rush into this leather bag.

ANSWER

"Each and every god, Buddha, Dharma, Confucius, Mencius are all in this stomach." So saying, the pupil pats his belly.

32   MASTER

The source of "mu"—what's it like?

ANSWER

"Don't be stupid! There's no such thing! Why don't you go wash your face," he snickers. "Nyaa!" [Any gesture of ridicule.] With that the pupil stands up and leaves, slamming the door shut. (Quote)

> The cold nocturnal hours came to an end
>   while I was listening to the rain,
> I opened the door and found that fallen
>   leaves were plentiful.

Or:

> The bottom of the sea can finally be seen
>   when it dries,
> But a man's heart can never be known even
>   till he dies.

Or:

> Clouds stood still after the rain, and the day
>   had just begun to dawn.

The few peaks looked picturesque with their
green height and massiveness.

33   MASTER
The "mu" of karma [non-enlightened state of mind]—go and see
what it's like.

                     ANSWER
With a grave, heavy voice, the pupil recites, "Karma, karma . . . ."

34   MASTER
Let's see you say it [i.e., "karma"] in simpler words.

                     ANSWER
"How hateful; how charming, I don't want to lose it; I wish it
were mine. . . . "

35   MASTER
Separate non-enlightenment [karma] into two.

                     ANSWER
"U." "Mu."

36   MASTER
Master Jōshū (on another occasion, when asked whether a dog
has Buddha-nature or not) said, "U ['is,' 'being']." How about
that?
                     ANSWER
"U."

37   MASTER
Let me see you say "u" in simpler words.

                     ANSWER
"Thinking of that which is not a man, as man; of that which is not
a woman, as woman; of that which is not a mountain, river, or
flower, as mountain, river, flower—this is 'u.'"

38   MASTER
Now, there's the state of consciousness of one's deeds [or of one's
karma—such as realizing something is wrong yet still doing
it]. What do you think of that?

"Standing on the border of life and death with complete freedom; facing heaven and hell and all forms of life with a playful mind, stable, unshakable. This being so, should I become a cat or a dog, it wouldn't make the slightest difference—I couldn't care less."
Or:
[The pupil says something like] "Cold is white, snow is black."

39   MASTER
Taking the whole of [the koan on] "mu," say a quote.

ANSWER
(Quote)
> The clouds obscured the three thousand miles
>   of the Kenkaku mountain range,
> And water separated the twelve peaks
>   of the Kutō gorge.

40   MASTER
Show me proof that you have understood [the koan on] "mu."

ANSWER
The pupil yells, "Mu——!" with all his might.

41   MASTER
If you've understood "mu," can you be absolutely delivered from life and death?

ANSWER
The pupil yells, "Mu——!" with all his might.

42   MASTER
Burning "mu," it becomes ashes; bury it, it becomes earth—what do you think of that?

ANSWER
The pupil yells, "Mu——!" with all his might.

PART TWO

MISCELLANEOUS KOANS

MISCELLANEOUS KOANS

1   MASTER
The original face—the face before you were brought into this
world by your mother and father—what is it?

ANSWER
Placing both hands on his chest, the pupil stands up.

2   MASTER
(Quote)
It is questioned, "What is the body of truth [Dharma-body]?"
It is answered, "A metal ship floating on water." (What of it?)

ANSWER
Placing both hands on his chest, the pupil stands up.

3   MASTER
(Quote)
When someone asks you in a dream about the purpose of our
founder coming from the west, how will you answer? If you
can't answer this, then the truth of Buddhism will have no effect
on you.

ANSWER
The pupil snores, "Zzz . . . zzz," imitating one soundly asleep.
Or:
With certain masters, should the pupil respond as above, they
immediately demand, "You think this answers it?" If the pupil
answers, the master fails him. If, without a word, the pupil
continues the pretense of sleeping soundly, the master passes him.

MASTER
Give a popular [Japanese] saying for that.

ANSWER

(Quote)

> In this world, there is nothing more carefree
> than sleep,
> But the dumb folk of this floating world
> get up and work.

MASTER

Give a [Chinese] quote for that.

ANSWER

(Quote)

> I slept so soundly that I did not know the
> mountain rain had stopped.
> Waking up, I felt the whole house airy
> and cool.

4   MASTER

A man walks straight. How will you walk straight through the forty-nine curves of the narrow mountain road?

ANSWER

Twisting and turning, the pupil winds about the room as if walking a narrow mountain road.

5   MASTER

It is said, "To pick up a stone from the bottom of the deep Ise Sea without even wetting your sleeve." How do you understand this?

ANSWER

The pupil pretends to jump into the ocean and bring up a big stone.

6   MASTER

What is this stone called?

ANSWER

The pupil gives his own name.

7   MASTER

About how heavy is this stone?

ANSWER

The pupil gives his own weight.

8   MASTER

On the sea, a Chinese junk with its sails full is racing in the wind. Stop it!

ANSWER

Standing up, opening his arms wide, and freeing his kimono sleeves, the pupil imitates a sailboat racing on the sea.

9   MASTER

There's a rowboat—stop it.

ANSWER

Getting up and imitating the creaking of oars, the pupil pretends to row a boat.

10   MASTER

There's a quarrel going on across the river—stop it.

ANSWER

"What the hell is that bastard muttering about?! You bloody fool! I'll kick your sides in and slam this damn bottle into your guts!" So saying, the pupil grabs his master by the neck and with his face raging with anger, he pretends to fling his fist at his master.

11   MASTER

Stop the sound (or echo) of the bell.

ANSWER

"Gonggg——." The pupil imitates the lingering, resonant sound of the bell.

12   MASTER

What'll you do if four different sounds come at once?

ANSWER

"Boom, boom [sound of a drum]; strum, strum [sound of a

stringed instrument]; jingle, jingle [sound of a bell]; tweet, tweet [sound of a whistle]."
Or:
"Boom, strum, jingle, tweet," the pupil combines the sounds.

13   MASTER
Extinguish the light that lies a thousand miles away.

                            ANSWER
"The lamp is lit in the other room but with no one there, it's dangerous and a waste of fuel so I'll go and blow it out...
whoosh!" So saying, the pupil pretends to blow out a lamp.
Or:
With the tips of his fingers, the pupil makes the form of a rising flame. Then, saying "Whoosh," he blows it out.

14   MASTER
From the second drawer of the medicine case draw out Mt. Tate [the highest mountain in the Hokuriku district].

                            ANSWER
"Master, if your stomach hurts let me give you some mankintan [an old-fashioned restorative medicine]."

                            OR
                          MASTER
From the first drawer of the medicine case draw out Mt. Fuji; from the second drawer, Mt. Haku [in the Ishikawa prefecture]; from the third drawer, Mt. So-and-so.

                            ANSWER
"Let me give you some seishintan, seikaigan, hōtan [names of old-fashioned Oriental medicines]."

15   MASTER
Without using your hands, make me stand.

                            ANSWER
The pupil stands up and walks two or three steps.

OR

MASTER

Without using your hands, make this old monk [i.e., me] get up.

ANSWER

"Ahhh." With a heavy sigh, the pupil imitates an old man getting up.

16   MASTER

Walk Mt. Fuji in three steps.

ANSWER

The pupil stands up and takes three steps.

17   MASTER

Make the Tōji [a temple in Kyoto] Pagoda stand in a teapot.

ANSWER

The pupil stands erect.

18   MASTER

In the middle of a duck egg, grind the tea mill.

ANSWER

The pupil walks in a circle around the room.

19   MASTER

What's the age of Monju [a legendary Buddha representing wisdom]?

ANSWER

"This year it's so-and-so (giving his own age), the exact age of Amida [the Buddha of the Western Paradise sect]."

MASTER

How old is Amida Buddha?

ANSWER

"As old as I am."

20   MASTER

Say the Five Moral Principles and the Five Cardinal Virtues [of Confucianism] in one breath.

"It's a nice day today!"

21   MASTER
How high is the sky?

ANSWER
Pointing toward the ceiling, the pupil says, "From here it's seven feet."

22   MASTER
Let me see you enter this stick [referring to the flat rod used by Zen masters when hitting novices].

ANSWER
The pupil hides the stick in his bosom.

23   MASTER
Rush into this pillar!

ANSWER
The pupil rams his whole body against the pillar.
Popular Saying
Leave me but it's not the end; I'll stick a five-inch nail into a straw doll and curse you to hell.

24   MASTER
Let me see you take out the Tennoji [a temple in Ōsaka] Pagoda from a teapot.

ANSWER
"If Your Reverence is thirsty, let me offer you some tea."

25   MASTER
Why do birds shit on Buddha's head?

ANSWER
"What the hell! Some damned bird shit on my head!" Saying this, the pupil makes the pretense of shaking it off his head.

26   MASTER
(Quote)
The wooden cock crows, midnight.

                      ANSWER
"Cock-a-doodle-doo" [the pupil crows like a rooster].

27   MASTER
(Quote)
The straw dog barks, daybreak.

                      ANSWER
"Bow-wow" [the pupil barks like a dog].

28   MASTER
(Quote)
Drink up all the water of the Seikō River [a river in China] in one gulp.

                      ANSWER
The pupil pretends to swallow the five continents in one gulp.

29   MASTER
(Quote)
The peonies of the city of Rakuyō [a Chinese city] have just come to blossom.

                      ANSWER
"The peonies growing in the garden have indeed blossomed beautifully."

30   MASTER
(Quote)
I arrived at the Western Heaven [India] in the morning, and evening saw me returning to the Eastern Earth [China].

                      ANSWER
While repeating the above quote, the pupil walks around the room.

31   MASTER
(Quote)
Hit a piece of wood and you hear no sound. Knock the empty air
and there comes a noise.

                                ANSWER
While saying, "Hit a piece of wood and you hear no sound,"
the pupil hits the floor. Continuing, "Knock the empty air and
there comes a noise," he strikes the air.
Or:
In either case the pupil hits the floor.

32   MASTER
(Quote)
Hold the spade empty-handedly.

                                ANSWER
The pupil pretends to take a spade and dig the earth.

33   MASTER
(Quote)
Ride a buffalo while walking.

                                ANSWER
Rolling up his trousers, the pupil pretends to cross the river.
Or:
Getting on all fours, the pupil pretends to be a buffalo.
Or:
Jumping on his master's back the pupil says, "Giddy-up!"
slapping the master's rear end.

34   MASTER
(Quote)
A man walked past on a bridge.

                                ANSWER
Crossing his arms and saying, "Clack, clack" [sound of wooden
sandals], the pupil assumes the pose of walking across a stone
bridge.

35   MASTER
(Quote)
The bridge flows on while the water does not.

                            ANSWER
Placing both hands on the floor, the pupil bends his body into a bridge. Then, rolling over, he pretends to be a running river.
Or:
Taking his kimono sleeve and fluttering it in the air, he makes the form of waves.

36   MASTER
There's a story about the lady-in-waiting Kasuga who saved a spirit [from this world of suffering] by filling a teacup with water. Then, taking her hair ornaments, she laid them, one after another, on the rim of the cup. Now you, a Zen monk, how would you save it?

                            ANSWER
The pupil makes a terrifying face (imitating a revengeful spirit) saying, "I'll have my revenge! I'll have my revenge!"

                            OR
                          MASTER
                      (Simply saying)
Let me see you save a spirit.

                            ANSWER
Imitating a spirit pleading for salvation, the pupil brings together both hands begging, "Please! Save me!"

37   MASTER
Bind up space with a thick rope and bring it here.

                            ANSWER
The pupil takes any object within reach, pretends to tie it up, and hands it over.

38   MASTER
Make space into a vegetable salad and bring it here.

ANSWER

"This soup is made of turnip leaves. Please have some," the pupil says as he pretends to offer it to his master.

39   MASTER

Make space into powder and bring it here.

ANSWER

The pupil pretends to offer to his master buckwheat flour or any other type of food made from flour.

40   MASTER

Is Shōki the Devil-Queller a god [of Shinto] or a Buddha?

ANSWER

"Any dummy who asks such a question must be out of his mind!"

41   MASTER

In the Chinese character "dai" of the word Daijingu [Ise shrine] there is a dot. The striking of this dot [in brushwriting] is considered to be a secret mystery of Shinto. Well then, in the case of Buddhism, where [in what character] will you strike such a dot?

ANSWER

Standing up, the pupil points one finger to the sky, the other finger to the earth, and recites, "Between heaven and earth there is nothing nobler than I."

42   MASTER

In the painting of Buddha's entrance into nirvana, where is the inexpressible subtlety?

ANSWER

"If you, my master, were to pass away at this moment, alas! whom will I turn to as my teacher?" So saying, the pupil pretends to be dejected.

43   MASTER

The state of nirvana—what's it like?

ANSWER

Facing his head to the north and lying on his side, the pupil recreates the reclining state of Buddha entering nirvana [as depicted in the famous paintings].

MASTER

But the *real* state of nirvana—what's it like?

ANSWER

As above; however when the master places his hand over the pupil's mouth to see if he is breathing, the pupil must hold his breath for a while.

44   MASTER

In Tōfukuji [a temple in Kyoto], why is there a cat in the picture of Buddha entering nirvana?

ANSWER

"Why isn't there a mouse?"
Or:
"Why don't you have a wife?"

45   MASTER

From what direction does Amaterasu [the Sun Goddess of Shinto] proceed?

ANSWER

(Quote)

> There are no two suns in the universe,
> And there is only one man between heaven
>   and earth.

46   MASTER

When the world was created, in what way did Kunitokutachi [a Shinto god—the founder of Japan] appear?

ANSWER

Placing both hands on his chest, the pupil stands up.

47   MASTER

Next, give birth to a mountain [as Kunitokutachi did].

ANSWER

Palms facing, hands tense and slightly spread apart, the pupil stands up and says, "This is one mountain."

48   MASTER
Now give birth to a land.

ANSWER
Prostrating himself on the floor, the pupil says, "This is land so-and-so of great Japan," naming a part of Japan.

49   MASTER
Recently I made a statue of Buddha. Where do you think it should be placed?

ANSWER
"Please have a cushion." So saying, the pupil pretends to welcome a guest.

50   MASTER
It is said that when Master Kyō-ō left his mountain monastery, he received fire as a parting gift. How should it be taken?

ANSWER
"Please put it in here." So saying, the pupil opens wide his kimono sleeve [usually used to carry small objects].

51   MASTER
The tea ladle which passes through the heat and cold of hell has no mind and therefore suffers not. This "has no mind and therefore suffers not" needs to be restated. How would you do it?

ANSWER
"If there's no mind, gobo-gobo [imitating the gurgling sound of boiling water]."

52   MASTER
Where will you go after death?

ANSWER
"Excuse me for a minute, I have to go to the toilet."

53   MASTER
(Quote)
On top of Mt. Godai the clouds are steaming rice.

ANSWER

"In the kitchen, they are cooking the noon rice."

54   MASTER
(*Quote*)
In front of the old Buddhist temple, a dog urinates towards the sky.

ANSWER

"A dog has pissed on the telephone pole."

55   MASTER
(*Quote*)
To fry hammers on top of a ten-foot pole.

ANSWER

"They're cooking potatoes and turnips in the kitchen."

56   MASTER
(*Quote*)
Three monkeys tossed coins at night.

ANSWER

"On the road in front, the children are tossing coins and playing gambling games."

57   MASTER
(*Quote*)
The cow in the state of Kai eats the rice plants, but it is the stomach of the horse in the state of Eki that gets swollen.

ANSWER

"If only you eat, that's enough for me. It doesn't matter if I don't."

58   MASTER
(*Quote*)
Chōkō drank wine and Rikō got drunk.

ANSWER

"If only you eat, that's enough for me. It doesn't matter if I don't."

(Quote)

Last night the clay cows fought their way into the sea, and nothing has been heard about them till this hour of the night.

ANSWER

"Isn't that Seijuro over there? That sure looks like his umbrella."

60   MASTER

Master Suiō said to Master Tōrei, "Lately, wherever you go everybody is impudently saying, 'I've heard the sound of the one hand! I've heard the sound of the one hand!' But all these people, just what sound do they think they have heard?!" Now you monk, taking the place of Master Tōrei, how would you answer? Hurry up—say it! say it!

ANSWER

"Hmmph! Such troublesome things you talk about! Your mouth ought to be clamped shut with a horse bit." So saying, the pupil clamps his master's mouth with his hand.

61   MASTER

How many hairs do I have in my nose?

ANSWER

The pupil points his finger at the master's nose and counts, "One, two, three. . . . "

62   MASTER

The other day there were these two young monks cleaning up. One of them picked up a piece of broken tile, placed it on a rock, turned to the other, and said, "Say something!" The other monk remained silent. If it were you, what would you have said?

ANSWER

"What do you think you're saying?!" With that the pupil raises his foot and kicks his master's knee.

63   MASTER

The light's blown out—where did it go? The darkness is back in the room as before.

"The maid's washing clothes at the side of the well. The servant is pissing in the field."
Or:
The pupil may use one or several of the following answers [in response to the second half of the master's koan]:
"Let's dig up the burdock root from the back field."
"I'll ram my head into that pole."
"I slipped on a watermelon rind."
"To pull the cow out from the back shed."

64   MASTER
Put the Great Buddha of Nara [a huge statue] on your back and bring it here.

ANSWER
While saying, "Well, I'll pack it on my back; I'm packing it," the pupil pretends to pack his master on his back.

65   MASTER
The light of the night soil bucket [container of excreta], what is it? Say it quick! Say it!

ANSWER
"Ugh, it stinks! It stinks!" the pupil says, holding his nose.
(Quote)
The stupid and the wise send out light one after another.

66   MASTER
There is a golden chime attached to the lion's neck—who can grab it?

ANSWER
"Excuse me," the pupil says, removing the upper covering of his master's gown.

67   MASTER
All the Buddhas of past, present, and future—what do they now preach?

ANSWER
"Chirp, chirp [the sound of a sparrow]; caw, caw [the sound of a crow]; meow, meow [the cry of a cat]; bow-wow [the bark of a dog]."

68   MASTER

The main pillar of the house—what does it preach?

ANSWER

"The Zen master wakes up early in the morning and takes care of his pupils. In an ordinary house, the father, from early morning, raises his voice and looks after his family's affairs."

69   MASTER

Try entering this incense burner.

ANSWER

Discreetly, the pupil takes the incense with his fingers, thanks his master and pretends to burn it.

70   MASTER

From where were you born and to where will you return?

ANSWER

"I just came from the temple hall and I'll return there again."

71   MASTER

It is said that big waters and small waters all return to the eastern sea. The waters of the Sumida River [in Tokyo]—where will they flow back to?

ANSWER

The pupil opens the front of his kimono and pretends to urinate.

72   MASTER

Take a bone from the body of the living Dharma [Bodhidharma— the founder of Zen Buddhism].

ANSWER

The pupil pretends to take out ear wax from his ear and hands it over to his master.

73   MASTER

If you're a Zen monk, try and say it with your mouth closed.

ANSWER

"Whether it can be said or not—you try it first." So saying, the pupil covers his master's mouth.

74   MASTER

There is the famous stone bridge of Mt. Tendai [in China, noted as a center of Buddhism]. Where would you start working on it?

ANSWER

The pupil takes his master's hand, stands up, and while saying, "Heave ho! Heave ho!" [the cry of encouragement workers use to keep time as they pull in unison], he drags his master.
Popular Saying
Once you've played with a geisha at Seki [a place in Japan], your wife looks like an old badger from over the hills.

75   MASTER

In building the wooden gate of Asakusa Temple [in Tokyo], where does the ax first fall?

ANSWER

The pupil stands up saying, "Chop! Chop!" as he pretends to use an ax.

76   MASTER

In the room a monster lies spread out on the floor, sleeping. If you were told, "There are some important documents on the shelf in that room, just go and get them for me," what would you do?

ANSWER

"Please forgive me," the pupil says, opening the door. "I'm terribly sorry to disturb your sleep and very much obliged to you, but please excuse me awhile," as he goes over to the shelf and takes the documents. Returning to the door he says, "Thank you most kindly. Have a good sleep."
Or:
The pupil may simply say, "Excuse me" as he pretends to walk around the pillow.

77   MASTER

This fan—did it fall down from heaven or spring up from earth?

ANSWER

"I bought it at the shop of Haibara in Nihonbashi in Tokyo for twenty-five yen."

78   MASTER

How many hairs in the back of your head?

ANSWER

The pupil stands in back of his master and counts, "One hair, two hairs, three hairs. . . . "

79   MASTER

What is the color of wind?

ANSWER

Taking his kimono, the pupil describes it, saying, "The front is black cotton cloth, the inside is lined in the color of rust."

Popular Saying

The young girl in the spring field picking herbs; the wind from the valley blowing her kimono hem.

(Quote)

> The pink cheeks and green brows of the ladies
>   complemented the round clouds of the
>   State of So.
> With peach blossoms blooming, someone in
>   a pomegranate dress was riding on horse-
>   back.

Or:

> The birds seemed whiter because of the green
>   river,
> And the flowers looked as if they were ready
>   to burst into flame in the verdant hills.

80   MASTER

Where does rain come from?

ANSWER

Taking the sleeve of his robe and shaking it in the air, the pupil says, "Zaa——zaa——" [the sound of heavy rain], imitating the fall of rain.

Or:

Using his ten fingers, the pupil flutters them over his master's head in the form of falling rain.

(Quote)

> Clouds were patrolling along the waistline of
>   the hills,

> Thunder and a downpour are certain
> tomorrow.

Or:

> The southern mountain became cloudy,
> And the northern mountain got rain.

Or:

"Pitter-patter," the pupil imitates the sound of rain.

Or:

With certain masters, the pupil may answer: "From the meditation hall, I came to the bell of summons [used to announce the entrance of the pupil into the master's room]; from there I entered into the consultation room. Hereafter I'll pass the summons bell and return immediately to the meditation hall."

81   MASTER
(Quote)
You cannot do it this way, you cannot do it the other way. This or that are all impossible.

ANSWER

Extending both hands in one direction the pupil says, "Wonder what it's like over there." Extending both hands in the other direction, he says, "Wonder what it's like over here." Then placing both hands on his lap, "Whew!" he heaves a sigh, relaxing. In this way, the pupil takes the rhythmic stances [of a Japanese dance].

82   MASTER
Deliver [enlighten] this ink stick.

ANSWER

The pupil pretends to rub the ink stick on an ink stone.

83   MASTER
That flower in the garden in front—is it alive or dead?

ANSWER

Staring at the garden the pupil says, "It has indeed blossomed beautifully."

84   MASTER
In this whole wide world—how many raindrops fall?

Looking outdoors the pupil counts, "One drop, two drops, three drops. . . . "

85   MASTER
Well, the tree in the garden in front—how many leaves are there?

ANSWER
Looking outdoors the pupil counts, "One leaf, two leaves, three leaves. . . . "

86   MASTER
Well then, how many stars in heaven?

ANSWER
Looking upwards the pupil counts, "One, two, three stars, four. . . . "
Or:
"Aren't there five or six; or is it twelve or thirteen?" the pupil says nonchalantly.

87   MASTER
All living things are flesh and bones. Why is a turtle flesh and bones?

ANSWER
Drawing in his hands and feet, the pupil imitates a turtle stretching its neck, withdrawing its neck.

88   MASTER
Go in and out of this wine flask.

ANSWER
As if holding a wine flask, the pupil says, "Master, let me pour you a glass."

89   MASTER
Among the eight dragon gods, which is the one that makes the rain fall?

ANSWER
The pupil pretends to urinate in front of his master.

90   MASTER

Show me the tree that does not move in a strong wind.

ANSWER

The pupil stands up and waves his hands in the air. Saying, "Ooooo——" [the sound of wind blowing], he sways to and fro like a tree.

91   MASTER

Stamp [as Sumo wrestlers do] on bean curd.

ANSWER

The pupil stands up, and saying, "At the wrestling arena," stamps his foot.

92   MASTER

The woman coming from over there, is she the older sister or is she the younger sister?

ANSWER

The pupil imitates a woman walking.

93   MASTER

Try and pass through a smoking pipe.

ANSWER

Lying straight on his side and twisting only his neck into the form of a pipe bowl, the pupil takes the pose of a smoking pipe.

94   MASTER

The ashes of the cigarette smoked the day before yesterday— bring them here.

ANSWER

Making his body round, the pupil takes the pose of cigarette ashes.

95   MASTER

You're put behind a stone gate which is bolted from the outside. How are you going to get out?

"Hey! Somebody let me out of here!," the pupil says, making the pretense of shaking the gate.

96   MASTER
The essence of the wind and the working of the wind—what's it like?

ANSWER
Extending both hands in front and gently waving them, the pupil says, "Ooooo, ooooo," imitating a passing breeze. [This is for "essence".] Next, "Up to now it's been south wind; it seems as though it's changing into east wind." So saying, the pupil points out the direction of the wind. [This is for "working."]

97   MASTER
It is said that Master Ummon [864–949] was reborn into Master Daitō [1282–1337]. During the several hundred years in between, what in the world was he doing?

ANSWER
The pupil briefly enumerates his personal history from childhood to the present.

98   MASTER
Say this room in one phrase!

ANSWER
"Ultimately, ku" ["void"], the pupil solemnly declares.

99   MASTER
Bring forth Mt. Fuji tied up with a lamp wick.

ANSWER
"Even this tattered rag will do as a head cover . . . it's time to go." So saying, the pupil moves to leave, heading toward the door. *Or:*
"Can you do such a thing? If that's possible, let me see *you* do it."

100   MASTER
Through the left sleeve, survey the eight hundred and eight towns of Edo [Tokyo].

ANSWER

Peering into his sleeve, the pupil says, "I can see the string of the loincloth; under the armpit, lice are scurrying around."

101   MASTER

Without taking the cover from the lunch box, say what's inside.

ANSWER

The pupil pretends to take the cover from the lunch box and says, "Ah, rice cakes! Thank you very much!"

102   MASTER

Look at the back of your head.

ANSWER

Facing his master the pupil says, "Master, would you turn around and I'll look at it for you?"

103   MASTER
(Quote)
When he and I die, where shall we meet?

ANSWER

Imitating a chance meeting with an acquaintance on the street, the pupil says, "My, it's been such a long time! How are you?"

104   MASTER
(Quote)
Turn the heavenly switch, and spin the earthly axis.

ANSWER

The pupil turns a somersault in front of his master.

105   MASTER
(Quote)

> I sauntered along and the murmer of the
> brook was crushed beneath my feet.
> The traces of the birds I recognized in a
> panoramic view.

As against, "*I sauntered along and the murmur of the brook was crushed beneath my feet.*"

ANSWER

Rolling the hem of his kimono to his waist, the pupil pretends to cross a stream.

Or:

Folding his arms across his chest and saying, "Trickle, trickle [murmer of a brook]" the pupil pretends to slowly walk along a brook.

As against, "*The traces of the birds I recognized in a panoramic view.*"

ANSWER

The pupil imitates a flying sparrow that comes to pick up crumbs.

Or:

Emitting, "Coo, coo" [a bird call], the pupil imitates a bird in flight.

106   MASTER

(Quote)

"The realm-of-no-thought" [enlightenment] is for what kind of people?

ANSWER

"In the Zen world—the distinguished Dokuon, Keichū, Kaion, Gasan [Zen monks of the Meiji era] have passed away. How truly sorrowful this is. In the secular world—Ito, Inoue, Katsura, Nogi [statesmen of the Meiji era] have died. What a pity."

107   MASTER

In the universe there are greatly enlightened ones. How do they reveal themselves?

ANSWER

"See how the many are gathered for the sake of practice [in search of enlightenment]. There is some affinity to it."

(Quote)

> Fire goes where it is dry,
> And water flows to where it is damp.

108   MASTER

(Quote)

People who endeavor to know the truth do not really know it only because they, having once in their studies come across the miraculous power of Buddha, and heard about the origin of life and death countless eons ago, call the unenlightened self the true self. What is the ultimate truth really like?

ANSWER

"In looking for that, you achieve nothing."

109   MASTER
The great sky is a drum and Mt. Shumi its drumstick. Who can hit it?

ANSWER

"You can't hit a broken drum, can you?"

110   MASTER
The Emperor Shukusō asked his Zen teacher, Etchū, "My teacher, what sort of wisdom have you acquired?" Master Etchū replied, "Your Majesty, do you see the piece of white cloud in the sky?" The emperor said, "Yes, I see it." The master said, "Is it being pinned up by a nail or is it dangling in midair?"

ANSWER

Looking down saying, "Fuuu, fuuu——," the pupil imitates a floating cloud.

111   MASTER
(Quote—Monk Daiji and His Mind-Reading Power)
There came the monk Daiji from the west to the capital. He said he possessed the unusual power of mind reading. Emperor Daisō ordered that his teacher Etchū should test the monk. The moment the monk met the master, he bowed and stepped aside to the right. The master said, "Have you got the power of mind reading?" "To some extent," said the monk in reply. "Tell me where I am at this moment," the master said. "You, the teacher of a nation, how can you go to the West River to see the boat race?" "Tell me where I am at this moment," the master said again. "You, the teacher of a nation, how can you stay on the Tenshin Bridge and watch monkeys performing tricks?" "Tell me where I am at this moment," the master said a third time. After quite awhile the monk still could not find the master's whereabouts. The master

scolded, "You fox! Where is your mind-reading ability?" The monk gave no answer. The master then said to the emperor, "Your Majesty, please do not be taken in by foreigners!"
WHERE DID THE MASTER GO?

ANSWER

With a fierce expression, the pupil exclaims, "What a despicable wretch!"
[In reference to the above answer the book comments, "Namely, being found out twice by Daiji, his whole being is consumed with hate."]

112   MASTER
(Quote)
If Jōshū drew out the blade of his sword, its light dazzling like cold, biting frost, and you were just about to inquire further concerning its meaning, you would be broken into two halves.

ANSWER

Pretending to draw out a sword, poised to attack, the pupil waves it, saying, "Pika, pika, chika, chika [referring to the glitter and shine of the sword]."

113   MASTER
Monju [a legendary Buddha representing wisdom] rides a lion. Fugen [a legendary Buddha of meditation and practice] rides a giant elephant. I wonder, what does [the historical] Buddha ride?

ANSWER

"Let's lay out a cushion."
Or:
"On a worn cushion I'm sitting, immovable."

114   MASTER
Make the teapot walk [around the room, as done during the reading of sutras].

ANSWER

The pupil folds his arms across his chest and walks a circle around the room as done during the reading of sutras.

115   MASTER
(Quote)
How can you enter the realm of Buddha without leaving the realm of the devils?

ANSWER
"When in the living quarters, I converse with the guests. When returning to the meditation hall, I sit in meditation."

116   MASTER
(Quote)
How to answer the calls from different directions with one body.

ANSWER
"Becoming densu [the monk in charge of reading the sutras], becoming tenzō [the monk in charge of cooking], becoming fuzui [the monk in charge of household affairs]."

117   MASTER
When the light has appeared, where does the darkness go?

ANSWER
"When it becomes light, the lantern is put into the closet and the mattress is folded away onto the shelf."

118   MASTER
(Quote)
All Buddhas of past, present, and future do not know that there is. Yet the raccoons and the white oxen know that there is.

ANSWER
"The sparrow—chirp, chirp; the crow—caw, caw; the dog—bow-wow; the cat—meow."

119   MASTER
(Quote)
> The clouds lay on the summit in a can't-be-
> more-leisurely manner,
> While the water hurries down the stream
> with excessive fervor.

As against, "The clouds lay on the summit in a can't-be-more-leisurely manner."

ANSWER

Saying, "Beer, sake, wine, tobacco, matches, rice balls," the pupil pretends to move about in a flurry.

As against, "While the water hurries down the stream with excessive fervor."

ANSWER

Shouting, "Japan won! Russia lost!" [referring to the Russo—Japanese War], the pupil dances around the room.

120   MASTER
(Quote)
To girdle a hundred thousand kan [1 kan = 8.25 pounds] around one's waist, and fly down to the city of Yōshū riding a crane.

ANSWER

"I've come from such-and-such a place carrying all these bags and I'm so exhausted. Ahh, my back hurts! My back hurts!" So saying, the pupil pounds his own back.

121   MASTER
(Quote)
Master Shishi said, "[In a fight] is it best to aim at a man's head, or is it best to aim at his waist, or is aiming at his feet best? The moment you hesitate [like that] your life is done for."

ANSWER

The pupil takes a wrestling pose in front of his master.

122   MASTER
(Quote)
A gentleman who loves money will get it through the proper channels.

ANSWER

"Anything given, I'll take."

123   MASTER
(Quote)
Morning—face to face with people. Evening—mingling with folks in a friendly way.

"It's not just morning and evening; right now, aren't we sitting facing each other?"

124   MASTER
(Quote)
Passion is the highest wisdom.

                                       ANSWER

"How hateful . . . how lovely . . ." the pupil says solemnly.
Popular Saying
When I think of you the bright sun clouds up, the clear moon turns dark.

125   MASTER
(Quote)
The one who is good at shooting does not hit the center of the target.

                                       ANSWER
The pupil pretends to fix an arrow on the bow and upon shooting it [says] "Oh."

126   MASTER
(Quote)
When suddenly caught from behind by a powerful giant ghost and thrown into a dazzling pit of fire, is there a way of escape?

                                       ANSWER
The pupil pretends to have fallen into a fire. He screams, "Hot! Hot! Hot!" as he writhes in pain.

127   MASTER
(Quote)
Is the teaching of our founder and the teaching of the later masters the same or different? The ancients had said, "When cold, chickens go up the tree while ducks go to the water." Show the meaning of this in a quote.

                                       ANSWER
(Quote)
            A cow drinks water and it becomes milk,
            A snake drinks water and it becomes poison.

Or:

> Blow and you can extinguish a fire.
> Blow and you can make a fire.

Or:

> When you breathe out, the air is hot.
> When you breathe in, the air is cold.

128   MASTER
(Quote)
If a man wants to know throughly about all the Buddhas of the past, the present, and the future, he should understand that the realm of existence is but the creation of mind.
As against, "Past, present, and future."

ANSWER
"Yesterday, today, tomorrow."
Or:
"Just before, now, soon after."
As against, "All the Buddhas."

ANSWER
The pupil replies, "Mr. A, Mr. B, Master, me . . . " thus enumerating names of people nearby.
As against, "All existence is but the creation of mind."

ANSWER
"The bean curd man makes bean curd, the carpenter builds a house."

129   MASTER
(Quote)
The Kongōkyō [the Diamond Sutra] says, "This being is shared by all and there is no such thing as the high and low in it." Well then, how come Mt. Shu is high and Mt. An is low?

ANSWER
"Mt. Fuji is high, Mt. Kamakura is low."

130   MASTER
(Quote)
The same scripture says, "Even though it is not a world, it is called a world."

ANSWER

"To the west as far as Tansui City in Taiwan, to the east as far as the Kurile Islands in Saghalien" [the frontiers of old Japan].

131   MASTER
(*Quote*)

The same scripture says, "The miraculous eye [that sees the smallest particle] and absolute wisdom [that knows every existence] all originate in this scripture." But how about the scripture [itself]?

ANSWER

The pupil slaps his master's face once.

132   MASTER
(*Quote*)

The same scripture says, "If a man sees me [i.e., Buddha] in a physical object, or searches for me through sound, then this man has walked astray; he will not see the Truth."

ANSWER

With single-hearted concentration, the pupil in a loud voice recites a passage from the Hannyashin Sutra or from the Daihiju Sutra.
Or:
Reciting, "He-will-not-see-the-Truth," the pupil says, "I see into each and every."

133   MASTER
(*Quote*)

The same scripture says, "It is impossible to have a past mind, it is impossible to have a present mind, neither can you have a future mind." With which mind do you eat?

ANSWER

"Old woman, I'm hungry. How much are these rice cakes? I'll have three or four."
Or:
"Up till now, I've only looked at the sutra and meditated. Now I am being taught in the master's room. Afterward, I'll go back and pull weeds."

(Quote)

The same scripture says, "That [true] mind comes into being when the mind does not dwell on any thought."

ANSWER
(As father)

"You lazybones! Get out of here!"
(As mother)

"Who are you saying get out to? Isn't it our dear son?"

Popular Saying

Upon seeing dumplings, "How cute"; upon seeing flowers, "How cute."

Or:

"Meditation, consultation, pulling weeds, cleaning, heating the bath. . . . " The pupil enumerates the daily routine, adding, "Not even a minute of rest."

135 MASTER

(Quote)

The breeze blows over the dark pine trees. The closer you come, the better the rustling of the leaves sounds.

ANSWER

With his right hand on his ear the pupil says, "Shhuu, shhuu" [the sound of wind in the trees], as he pretends to be listening to the breeze in the pine trees.

MASTER

[Additional quote added here by Master Hakuin] Listening close, just what do you hear?

ANSWER

"Oh that. It's a secret, so come close." Saying this, the pupil pretends to whisper some confidential talk into his master's ear.

PART THREE

THE ONE HUNDRED FORTY-FOUR KOANS

THE ONE HUNDRED
FORTY-FOUR KOANS

1. *The Man up the Tree*

Zen Master Kyōgen said, "Let us suppose that a man climbs up a tree. He grips the branches with his teeth, his hands do not hold onto the tree, and his feet do not touch the ground. A monk below asks him about the meaning of our founder coming from the west. If he does not answer, he will be avoiding the monk's question. But if he opens his mouth and utters a word, he will fall to his death. Under such circumstances, what should the man do?" A certain monk by the name of Kotō said, "Once the man is up the tree, no question should be raised. The man should ask the monk if the latter has anything to say to him before he goes up the tree." On hearing this, Kyōgen laughed out loud.

Later, Master Setchō commented, "It is easy to say it up on the tree. To say it under the tree is difficult. So I shall climb the tree myself. Come, ask me a question!"
As against, "*On the tree.*"

ANSWER

The pupil stands up and takes the pose of hanging down from a tree.

With certain masters, there are pupils who may stick a finger in the mouth; utter, "Uh . . . uh"; and, shaking the body slightly, give the pretense of one trying to answer but unable to.
As against, "*Under the tree.*"

ANSWER

The pupil pretends to fall from a tree. Landing on his bottom, he says, "Ouch! That hurt!"

2. The Man in the Well

Master Shōkū was asked by a monk, "What is the meaning of our founder coming from the west?" The master said, "It is like getting a man out of a thousand-foot-deep well without using one single inch of rope. This answers your enquiry." The monk said, "The monk Ō of the district of Konan recently became famous and that too has become the subject of people's gossip." Upon this Shōkū summoned the young monk Jaku and said, "Drag out the corpse."

Master Kyōzan (who heard about this dialogue) asked Master Tangen, "How can you get the man in the well out?" Tangen said, "You stupid fool! Who is in the well?" Kyōzan said nothing. Again, he later asked Master Isan, "How can you get the man in the well out?" Isan called out, "Kyōzan!" Kyōzan answered the call and Isan said, "He is out of the well already!"

Kyōzan always used to tell the story described above to the people, saying, "I got the principle from Tangen and learned the use from Isan."

ANSWER

Pretending to have fallen into a well, the pupil struggles in anguish, gasping for air.

Or:

Pretending to have fallen into a well, the pupil struggles in anguish, gasping for air. Then, as if choking and coughing up water, he says, "Oh, it was cold! It was cold! I thought I was inside the well, but it was right here in the master's room, wasn't it? Oh! How rude of me! Please forgive me!"

Or:

Pretending to have fallen to the bottom of a well, the pupil grabs onto the walls. Looking up, he says in a low voice, "Please help me. Please help me," as if pleading for sympathy.

3. Why a Monk's Garment?

Master Ummon said, "The world is so wide, why at the chime of the bell do you choose to put on a monk's garment?"

ANSWER

As if hearing the summons bell, the pupil pretends to put on his gown and go out to join the monks walking around the hall.

> When the king summons, one has to go
>> at once without waiting for a vehicle.
> When one's father calls, one has to answer
>> "Yes" without hesitation.

Or:

> The red headgeared night watchman
>> announced the morning hour.
> The king's wardrobe keeper had just carried
>> in a robe with green cloud patterns.

Popular Saying

At the clapping of hands, bring in the tea. When the clapping sounds again, fetch the ashtray.

4. The World a Grain of Rice

Master Seppō said, "The whole world, when gathered with the fingers, is no bigger than a grain of rice. Throw it before us, it will be impossible to find. Strike the drum for summons—let us all come together and look for it."

ANSWER

The pupil, as if present in a high place, pretends to survey many peaks at a glance.

(Quote)

> The states of Go and So extend toward
>> the southeast.
> Heaven and earth, day and night, are all
>> floating on the water.

Or:

"To the west as far as Taiwan, to the east as far as the Kurile Islands in Saghalien." Thus the pupil demonstrates the phrase from the Kongōkyō [the Diamond Sutra] which says, "The world is non-world; upon this it is named world."

5. The Three Gates of Master Ōryū

Master Ōryū asked Master Ryūkei, "Everyone has got an origin, where is your origin?" Ryūkei answered, "I had eaten some gruel this morning and now I feel hungry again." "How is my hand when compared with the hand of Buddha?" Ōryū asked. "Playing biwa [a musical instrument] under the moon," Ryūkei answered. "How are my feet when compared with those of a mule?" he asked. Ryūkei answered, "A heron standing in the snow, not of the same color."

Ōryū always asked students these three questions, and none could reach the correct meaning. Monks the world over called them "the three gates." Even if someone returned to answer, the master never said yes or no. He just sat there erect and shut his eyes and none could guess what he meant. After a while, someone would ask the master again for the reason. Ōryū said, "For he who has passed the gate will wave his arms and go straight on without caring for the gatekeeper. If you ask the gatekeeper for permission, it shows that you have not yet passed the gate." *As against, "Where is your origin?"*

ANSWER

The pupil asks, "Where is the place that you are?" To this the master answers, "It's useless to ask for the place where I am."
Or:
The pupil says, "Yes, I was born in so-and-so prefecture, in so-and-so district, in so-and-so village," thus giving his own birthplace.
Or:
The pupil says, "Your reverence is where your reverence is, I am where I am."
(Quote)
Where do you live? I live in Ōtō [a district in China].
Or:

A bird cried of cold on a dry branch,
And wild monkeys whined amidst empty
mountains.

Or:

Once again I crossed the Sōken River for
no apparent reason,
And I wished Henshū were my native place.
As against, "How is my hand when compared with that of Buddha?"

ANSWER

Stretching his leg out, the pupil asks, "Why is a leg called a leg?"
(Quote)
To play biwa under the moon.
Or:
To change hands and hit the chest.

As against, *"How are my feet when compared with those of a mule?"*
ANSWER
Thrusting his hand in front, the pupil asks, "Why is a hand called a hand?"
(Quote)
To imprint the green moss with the sole of a clog.
Or:
To walk to and fro.

6.   *Where Do the Snowflakes Fall?*

The time came when the layman Hōkoji bade farewell to Master Yakusan. Yakusan sent ten of his pupils to accompany Hōkoji to the front gate. Hōkoji pointed to the clouds in the sky and said, "All these lovely snowflakes do not fall on any particular place." At that time a monk by the name of Zen said, "Where do they fall then?" Hōkoji slapped him. Zen said, "Hōkoji, you should not treat me that roughly!" Hōkoji said, "How can you call yourself a Zen monk when the god of justice didn't place you as one!" Zen retorted, "What about you, Hōkoji?" Hōkoji gave him another slap and said, "You see, but you are just like the blind. You speak, yet you are no different from the dumb."

Later, Master Setchō commented, "I would have just hit him with a snowball when he first raised such a question!"

The pupil gives the image of snow gently falling to the ground.
(Quote)
> The mountain dwellers are rich with a
>   thousand trees of silver,
> And the fishermen are elegant with their
>   straw raincoats covered with pearls.

MASTER
[Certain masters may ask] The "particular place" of "All these lovely snowflakes do not fall on any particular place"—what does it mean?
ANSWER
The pupil slaps his master's face.
MASTER
This "I would have just hit him with a snowball when he first raised such a question!"—what does it mean?

ANSWER

The pupil slaps his master's face.

MASTER

"To hit with a ball of snow, to hit with a ball of snow"—what of it?

ANSWER

The pupil slaps his master's face.

7. *Round Are the Lotus Leaves*

> Round are the lotus leaves, round like a mirror.
> Pointed are the water chestnuts, pointed like a
> drill.
> The wind blows and willow flowers roll like
> hairy balls.
> The rain beats and plum blossoms flutter like
> butterflies.

MASTER

"Round are the lotus leaves, round like a mirror"—from the standpoint of self-centeredness, what's it like?

ANSWER

Stroking his head, the pupil says, "It's round like this."

MASTER

How is it like from the other-centered point of view?

ANSWER

"Gonbē and Hachibē and Ohachi and also Osan [common Japanese names of the working class], covered from head to toe with mud, are working."
(*Quote*)

> Everything in the southern and northern
> villages is soaked in rain.
> The newly married woman is serving her
> mother-in-law food,
> While her father-in-law is feeding the son.

MASTER

"Pointed are the water chestnuts, pointed like a drill"—from the standpoint of self-centeredness, what's it like?

ANSWER

"Sharper than a drill," the pupil says, violently spreading out his crossed arms.

MASTER

How is it like from the other-centered point of view?

ANSWER

"The merchant poring over his abacus is fighting for every single penny."

MASTER

"The wind blows and willow flowers roll like hairy balls. The rain beats and plum blossoms flutter like butterflies"—how about this?

ANSWER

Mimicking the striking sound of the master's stick and the chime of bells, the pupil imitates the various happenings in the meditation hall.

OR

(According to another school)

As against, "Round are the lotus leaves, round like a mirror. Pointed are the water chestnuts, pointed like a drill."

ANSWER

"With an iron pot to boil water, with a lamp to light a flame, with a set of drawers to store goods away, with an incense burner to burn incense."

(Quote)

> The monkey retreats to the back of the green
> mountain, carrying its offspring.
> The bird flies down the blue cliff, holding
> flowers in its beak.

Or:

> Blow at the stove of burning charcoal
> below the pot and it will be
> extinguished.
> Roar, the forest of swords and the mountain
> of knives will crumble and fall.

"The wind blows and willow flowers roll like hairy balls. The rain beats and plum blossoms flutter like butterflies"—how about this?

ANSWER

"When the rain falls, the plum blossoms will scatter. When the wind blows, the willow flowers will scatter."
(Quote)
When cold, chickens go up the tree while ducks go to the water.
Or:

> Stand on top of a high peak without getting
> your head damp with dew.
> Walk at the bottom of a deep sea without
> getting your feet wet.

Or:

> To jump over the four big continents in one
> leap,
> And to bring down Mt. Shumi in one blow.

OR

(According to another school)
As against, "Round are the lotus leaves."

ANSWER

From his sitting position, the pupil folds his body and rolls around in a circle.
As against, "Water chestnuts."

ANSWER

The pupil pretends to float on the water as water chestnuts do.
As against, "Willow flowers" and "butterflies."

ANSWER

For both, the pupil uses his body to imitate their appearance.
As against the master's, "Distinguish the four phrases of the koan in accordance with the four classes" [warrior, farmer, artisan, merchant].

ANSWER

The pupil compares the lotus leaves with the appearance of a farmer wearing a rain hat; water chestnuts he compares with the strict ranking of warriors; the hairy balls he compares with merchandise; and the fluttering plum blossoms he compares with artisans.

(112)

8. The Sound of Rain

Master Kyōshō asked a monk, "What is the noise outside?" The monk said, "The sound of rain." Kyōshō said, "The people are in a topsy-turvy condition, they have blinded themselves in the pursuit of material pleasure." The monk said, "How about you, Your Reverend?" Kyōshō said, "I can almost understand myself perfectly." The monk said, "What does understanding oneself perfectly mean?" Kyōshō said, "To be enlightened is easy. To put it into words is difficult."

ANSWER

"Bisha, bisha." The pupil imitates the sound of rain.

9. The Three Questions of Master Tosō

Master Tosō set up three questions to examine students. He said:
1. "One clears the weeds of idiocy and is enlightened by Buddha's teaching so that one can see one's nature. Now where is human nature?"
2. "After you have learned of your true nature, then you can escape from the cycle of life and death. But when you're on the brink of death, how will you escape?"
3. "If you have left the cycle of life and death, you will know where to go. But when the four elements [that form a physical body] are separated, where will you go?"

As against, "Now where is human nature?"

ANSWER

The pupil looks around, giving the pretense of one searching. At this point, the master adds, "Everything is filled with it. It is not that it does not exist, only it cannot be seen by the eye."

(Quote)

> I only know that I am in the middle of this
>   mountain,
> But the clouds are so thick that I cannot
>   figure out where exactly I am.

Or:

> The lotus leaves trembled though it was
>   windless.
> Definitely there were fish moving about
>   underneath.

Or:

> When the forest is dense, the cries of the
> monkeys become loud.
> When the water is clear, the reflection of
> the wild geese becomes sharp.

Popular Saying

Every year it blooms—the mountain cherry blossoms of Yoshino [near Nara]. Come, let's split the tree apart. From where the flowers bloom?

Or:

> The voice is heard but the figure unseen,
> You, hiding in lush fields—the grasshopper.

As against, "On the brink of death."

ANSWER

The pupil gives the pretense of one in agony—grappling his arms in the air, kicking his legs, twisting, turning, writhing in pain.

(Quote)

> Poisoned arrows stuck in the breast.
> Like the falcon seizing the dove.

Or:

At the lion's roar, the fox's brain is shattered.

As against, "When the four elements are separated, where will you go?"

ANSWER

Lying on his back, the pupil takes the pose of a corpse.

MASTER

(Quote)

What happens when there are not enough places to go?

ANSWER

The pupil retains the above pose of a corpse.

(Quote)

A monumental stone lay broken across an ancient path.

Or:

The monumental stone dedicated to Shin-u [a legendary figure] at the summit of Peak Shunrō.

Or:

Nothing but a slab of stone is left standing eternally on Mt. Enzan.

Or:

[With certain masters, in response to "Where will you go?"]:

It has just gone away with the fragrant
    grasses,
Yet returns again chasing falling flowers.

10. *The Sentence of Being and the Sentence of Nothing*

Master Ran-an said, "The sentence of being ['u'] and the
sentence of nothing ['mu'] are just like a wisteria vine twining
around a tree." Master Sozan heard of this and said, "I have
something to say to that old man." So at the end of that summer,
he went to the province of Bin to see Ran-an. When Sozan came
to him, Ran-an was plastering a wall. Sozan asked, "'The sentence of being and the sentence of nothing are just like a wisteria
vine twining around a tree,' are those Your Reverend's words?"
Ran-an said, "Yes." Sozan said, "If suddenly the tree falls and the
wisteria vine withers, where will those sentences go?" Ran-an put
down his plaster tray and laughed aloud. Then he went back to his
living quarters. Sozan said, "But I have sold my sheets and come
here from a place three thousand miles away especially for this matter! Why won't Your Reverend speak to me?" Ran-an called his
servant, "Bring some money and give it to this small priest."
Then he turned to Sozan and said, "Someday a single-eyed man
will explain to you."
    Later, Sozan went to Master Meishō and told the above story.
Meishō said, "Ran-an is a straight man from head to toe, only he
has not encountered someone who knows him." Sozan said,
"If suddenly the tree falls and the wisteria vine withers, where will
those sentences go?" Meishō said, "This will make Ran-an
laugh anew." Right at that moment, enlightenment dawned on
Sozan and he said, "In fact, there was a knife in Ran-an's laughter."
    In a later period, Master Dai-e [when still a novice] joined
Master Engo. Engo gave him the post of a servant. Every day
Dai-e sent to Engo's room, accompanying the officials [who
came to visit Engo]. Engo would say nothing except that the
sentence of being and the sentence of nothing are just like a
wisteria vine twining around a tree. Whenever Dai-e opened his
mouth to say something, Engo would say, "No, not like this."
In this manner almost half a year passed. One day while Dai-e
was eating with the official Jōhyōshi, he held the chopsticks in
his hands and forgot about the rice. Engo looked at Dai-e, turned
to Jōhyōshi and said, "This fellow is practicing the zen of the

box tree [from which chopsticks are made]. . . . " And to Dai-e he said, "You have fallen into a pit and will have to stay there awhile." A moment later Dai-e turned to Engo and said, "I have heard that Your Reverend had asked Master Hōen [Engo's teacher] about the sentence of being and the sentence of nothing before. I wonder if you remember the answer." Engo only laughed. Dai-e said, "If I ask this question in front of gods and men, will there be no one who knows?!" Engo said, "Once I asked Hōen, 'What if the sentence of being and the sentence of nothing are like a wisteria vine twining around a tree?' Hōen answered, 'It is no use to make a sketch of it.' I asked again, 'What if suddenly the tree falls and the wisteria vine withers?' Hōen said, 'They come in succession.'" [Or, 'They go together.'] When Dai-e heard the story he called out, "I've got it!" Engo said, "I am afraid you don't thoroughly understand this koan." Dai-e said, "Will Your Reverend raise questions to test me?" So Engo asked him questions and Dai-e replied with no hesitation. Engo said, "So today you know I have not cheated you. . . . "

MASTER

Ran-an said, "The sentence of being and the sentence of nothing are like a wisteria vine twining around a tree." Using your own insight, how do you understand the sentence of being and the sentence of nothing?

ANSWER

"In the middle of the field, a sole pine tree."
(Quote)

> A lonely pine flourishes on top of the winter mountain.

Or:

> The single pine stood high on top of the mountain.

Or:

> The pine tree will still be green for a thousand years.

11. Subject, Object

When the head monks of the two [meditation] halls came to see Master Rinzai, they shouted ["Katsu!"] at each other at the same time. A monk asked Rinzai, "At the instant these two head monks shouted at each other, were there subject ['host'] and object ['guest']?" The master said, "The role of 'host' and 'guest' are clearly distinct." And he added, "If you people want to understand my sentence concerning 'host' and 'guest,' go to the hall where the two head monks are and ask them."

"The pillar stands and the threshold lies; the mountain is high, the river low."
(Quote)
A mountain is a mountain, a stream a stream.
Or:
The willow is green and the flowers are red.
Or:
Straight is the pine and crooked is the briar.

OR
(According to another school)
ANSWER
The master is seated on the high seat, listening to the pupil who has come in for discussion. The pupil kneels on the floor, bowing his head.
(Quote)

> There is a three-foot-long sword at the head
> of the bed,
> And in the vase there is a branch of plum
> blossoms.

OR
(According to another school)
ANSWER
Alternately pointing his finger at his master and himself, the pupil says, "Guest and host are in this way clearly distinguished."

12. The Unrankable Being

Master Rinzai said in his lecture, "In your physical bodies of flesh, there is an unrankable being who often goes in and out of the doors of your faces. For those who have not yet proven the truth, see it! See it!" At that moment a monk came out and asked, "What is it [the unrankable being]?" The master came down from his seat, grabbed the monk, and said, "Say it! Say it!" Just as the monk was about to speak, the master pushed him away and said, "What dry dung is the unrankable being!" Then he returned to his room.

ANSWER

The pupil places one hand on his forehead, shading his eyes. [Taking the pose of "See it! See it!"]
(Quote)

> It may be that she has got a well-developed
> body,
> That she looks elegant naturally without
> putting on pink powder.

Or:

> On the contrary, she disliked cosmetics
> for they smeared her face.
> With brows lightly drawn, she went up
> to the emperor.

Or:

> He leaned his back on cold rocks, his face
> shining like a full moon
> Of which everyone on earth could see but
> one side.

OR

(According to another school)

MASTER

"See it! See it!"—what's it mean?

ANSWER

The pupil pretends to fall down in surprise.

MASTER

[The master comes down from his seat, grabs the pupil and says] "Say it! Say it!"

ANSWER

"I earnestly ask your pardon."

MASTER

The difference between "unrankable" and "not-unrankable"— say it quick! Say it quick!

"I earnestly beg your forgiveness."

13. *A Flower in Bloom*

A monk asked Master Ummon, "What is the pure body of truth?" Ummon said, "A flower in bloom." The monk asked, "At such a time, what is it like?" Ummon said, "A lion of golden fur."

As against, "A flower in bloom."

ANSWER

The pupil places both hands on his chest, stands up and says, "This shit hole."

As against, "A lion of golden fur."

ANSWER

The pupil pretends to shit in front of his master.

(Quote)

A refreshing wind moving inside torn clothes.

Or:

> There is a dead deer in the wilderness.
> I wrap it with beautiful flowers.

Or:

A flower vase holding waste matter.

OR
(According to another school)

MASTER

"A flower in bloom"—what's it mean?

ANSWER

"Maggots in the shit hole, pus of leprosy, scab over a boil."

(Quote)

To add rubbish on top of a pile of garbage.

MASTER

"A lion of golden fur"—what's it mean?

ANSWER

The pupil imitates a lion's roar.

14. *Will IT Be Destroyed?*

A monk asked Master Daizui, "When the fire of destruction blazes, the whole universe will be destroyed. I wonder if *IT* will be destroyed too?" Daizui said, "Yes, destroyed." The monk said, "Then shall we go with it?" Daizui said, "Yes, go with it!"

MASTER
Daizui said "destroyed"—what's it mean?

ANSWER
Saying, "Bari, bari, bari, bari," the pupil flickers his hands, giving the image of a blazing fire spreading in all directions.

MASTER
Daizui said, "Yes, go with it!"—what's it mean?

ANSWER
Saying, "Dotsu, dotsu, dotsu," the pupil moves his hands, giving the image of a streaming fire.

15. *Where Will ONE Return To?*

A monk asked Master Jōshū, "All existences return to *ONE*, but where will *ONE* itself return to?" Jōshū said, "When I was in the district of Sei, I made a cotton dress. It weighed seven jin" [1 jin = 14 ounces].

MASTER
"All existences return to *ONE*"—what's it mean?

ANSWER
The pupil slaps his knee, "Ah!" [i.e., "I see!"].
Or:
With his finger, the pupil writes the number one on the floor.

MASTER
"Where will the *ONE* return to?"—what's it mean?

ANSWER
"The *ONE* returns to the many."

Or:

[With certain masters]: "The *ONE* returns to the two, to the three, to the four, five, six, seven, eight, nine, ten, hundred, thousand, ten thousand, million, billion."

(Quote)

> There are plums at the end of the branch.
> Seven is the number of the fruit.

Or:

> The seven palaces crumbled because of the
> revolt started by one single man.

Popular Saying

In Mt. Hakone there is the man riding in the sedan chair. There is the one who pulls the sedan chair. And there is the one who makes the straw sandals of the one pulling the sedan chair.

16. *There Is No Such Thing as Holy*

Emperor Butei of the Ryō dynasty asked Daruma [Bodhidharma—founder of Zen Buddhism], "What is the highest of holy truth?" Daruma said, "There is no such thing as holy." The emperor said, "Who is it that answers me?" Daruma said, "I do not know." The emperor said nothing further. Daruma thus crossed the River Yōsukō and went into the state of Gi. The emperor later asked the same question of the Zen disciple Shikō and Shikō replied, "Does Your Majesty know this person by now?" The emperor said, "No, I do not know him." Shikō said, "This person is the incarnation of the Buddha of Mercy [Kannon] and he spreads the teaching of Buddha." The emperor felt regret and sent a mission to invite Daruma back. But Shikō said, "Even if the whole nation goes to carry him, he will not come back; to say nothing of Your Majesty's sending a mission to get him."

MASTER

"There is no such thing as holy"—what's it mean?

ANSWER

Folding his arms across his chest, the pupil stands up.

Or:

"Gonbe, Hachi, and San [common names], covered with mud, are working."

(Quote)
> Everything in the southern and northern
> villages is soaked in rain.
> The newly married woman is serving her
> mother-in-law food,
> While her father-in-law is feeding the son.

MASTER
[Daruma's] "I do not know"—what's it mean?

ANSWER
"If Daruma says he doesn't know, how should I know?"

MASTER
Why don't you know?

ANSWER
"Buddha as well as Amida don't know."
(Quote)
(Referring to "I do not know"):
> The light of the sun and moon cannot
> reach it,
> Neither can heaven nor earth completely
> cover it.

Or:
> The noise of talking woodcutters can never
> be heard in a deep mountain valley,
> While hunters can be found passing under
> shadowy cliffs.

17. *Words*

Master Jōshū said, "To reach the way of Zen is not difficult. The only setback is that of choice. The moment you use words, it is a matter of either choice or understanding. I am not in the realm of understanding. But you, are you not still thinking highly of it?" Then a monk asked, "Since you are not in the realm of understanding, what is there that you say should not be thought highly of?" Jōshū answered, "I do not know it myself." The monk said, "You say you do not know, but why then did you

say you are not in the realm of understanding?" Jōshū said, "It is only because you asked that I answered. Now go away."
As against, "Reach the way."

ANSWER

The pupil folds his arms, stands up and says, "Reach the way."
As against, "Not difficult."

ANSWER

"The mountain is high, the river low, the pillar stands, the threshold lies."
As against, "The only setback is choice."

ANSWER

"What a pity! I want! How hateful! Lovable! Good! Bad!"

MASTER

[Some masters may pose.] In "reach the way" and "not difficult," is it true that whichever way you see it there is no choice?

ANSWER

"Everything is provided for in 'reach the way.'"
(Quote)

> I only love to read the new calendar
> published by the observatory,
> And am reluctant to glance over the dry
> prose sent by Kantaishi [a poet].

MASTER

"I am not in the realm of understanding"—what's it mean?

ANSWER

"I will never forget your favor to me for the rest of my life."

MASTER

"Words reach from edge to edge" [from a quote attached to this koan by Master Setchō]—how about it?

ANSWER

"Shut up!" the pupil says and slaps his master's face.
(Quote)
ONE has many varieties, but TWO has got none.

OR

ANSWER

"In one hand, five fingers. Five fingers make one hand."

18. *The Four Ways of Master Rinzai*

Master Rinzai said, "Sometimes you take away the man without taking the land; sometimes you take away the land without taking the man; sometimes you take away both the land and the man; and sometimes you take away neither the land nor the man."

MASTER

Using your hand as "land," your body as "man," demonstrate the four ways.

As against, "Take away the man without taking the land."

ANSWER

The pupil stretches out his hand and covers his master's face.
(Quote)

> When the music ended, no one was to be
>   seen;
> Only the peaks along the river looked so
>   green.

Or:

> The bright moon comes and is gone again by
>   itself,
> There are no more people leaning against the
>   jade railings.

As against, "Take away the land without taking the man."

ANSWER

Hiding a hand behind his back, the pupil edges his body forward a bit.
(Quote)

> There cannot be two suns in the universe,
> And there is only one man between heaven
>   and earth.

Or:

> King Kō shouted angrily till his voice broke,
> And the thousand soldiers were nullified.

As against, "Take away both the land and the man."

ANSWER

The pupil quickly runs and hides behind the door.
(Quote)

> The universe is still void of the sun and moon
>   of Shin Dynasty,
> And the Kan Dynasty emperor and his subjects
>   are nowhere to be seen in the land . . .

As against, "Take away neither the land nor the man."
The pupil folds his arms across his chest and stands up.
(Quote)

> When evening falls in picturesque spots on the
>   river,
> Fishermen wearing straw raincoats are on
>   their way homeward bound.

Or:

> Wild geese flew over the city wall against a
>   night sky sparingly dotted with faint
>   stars.
> A long drawn note of the flute arose and
>   someone was leaning on the balcony.

OR
(According to another school)
As against, "Take away the man without taking the land."
ANSWER
"Ceiling, door, floor, charcoal brazier, stick"; the pupil thus enumerates the things within the room. Namely, these are things which take away the subject.
(Quote)

> The moon of the frosty night had climbed
>   right above my head.
> It would follow its natural course and fall
>   under the stream in front.

As against, "Take away the land without taking the man."
ANSWER
"In the whole world there is only me; I alone am the ruler of the universe."
(Quote)
Between sky and earth, I alone fill the universe.
Or:

> The four seas are under the enlightened rule
>   of the emperor.
> Who dares to invade our boundaries from
>   south, west, or north?

As against, "Take away both the land and the man."
ANSWER
'On the Tōkaidō Highway there's not a single man; on old Mt.

Kiso there's not a single cat; in old Tokyo there's not a single man;
in Asakusa Park [in Tokyo] there's not a single man."
(*Quote*)

> The states of Shin and So failed for excessive
> wealth.
> Fun-iku the warrior failed for courage.

Or:

Break into the city of Saishūjō and kill off Gogensai the rebel.
As against, "Take away neither the land nor the man."

ANSWER

"Host [subject], guest [object], things—where they are as they
are."
(*Quote*)

The emperor has no greed, the people are all virtuous.

Or:

> There were five or six adults, six or seven
> children.
> We bathed in the river, sang to the dance
> music played when people prayed for
> rain,
> And then went home reciting poems.

Or:

> Young men from wealthy and noble families
> gathered under sweet-smelling trees.
> Delightful songs and dances were performed
> among falling petals.

19.   *The Three Sentences of Master Rinzai*

When Master Rinzai came up to the lecture hall a monk
asked him, "What is the first sentence?" Rinzai said, "When the
seal is removed, the red ink comes into view. Even though the
script has not been read yet, the role of host [subject] and guest
[object] is already decided."

The monk asked, "What is the second sentence?" Rinzai
said, "How can reckless questions be permitted for such a wonderful thought? And why should the working be inferior to the
ideal?" The monk asked, "What is the third sentence?" Rinzai
said, "Look at the puppet show on stage. The pulling is done by
people within."

The first sentence—what of it?

ANSWER
"A, B, C, D, E, F, G."

MASTER
The second sentence—what of it?

ANSWER
"H, I, J, K, L, M, N."

MASTER
The third sentence—what of it?

ANSWER
"O, P, Q, R, S, T, U."

OR
ANSWER
"Today's a nice day [for the first sentence]!"
"Won't you have some tea [for the second sentence]?"
"Well, goodbye [for the third sentence]!"

20. Before and After

A monk asked Master Chimon, "What is the lotus flower before it appears above water?" Chimon said, "It is a lotus flower." The monk said, "What is it after it has appeared above water?" Chimon said, "It is a lotus leaf."

MASTER
"Before it appears above water"—in place of Chimon, on your own, answer the question.

ANSWER
"An earthenware mortar."

MASTER
"After it has appeared above water"—what of it?

ANSWER
"A rice cake."

21. To Beat the Drum

Master Kasan quoted, "To study is 'mon' [the character meaning "hear"]. To cut off study is 'rin' [the character meaning "near"]. Above these two there is 'shin'" [the character meaning "true"].

A monk asked, "What is 'shin' like?" Kasan answered, "To be able to beat the drum." The same monk asked again, "The essence of 'shin,' what is it like?" Kasan answered, "To be able to beat the drum." The monk asked once more, "I won't ask about the-mind-as-it-is-being-Buddha, but the-no-mind-no-Buddha, how about that?" Kasan answered, "To be able to beat the drum." The monk asked again, "If a person who is earnestly and wholeheartedly seeking for the truth comes to you, how will you treat him?" Kasan answered, "To be able be beat the drum."

ANSWER

"Boom, boom, boom, boom" [the sound of a drum].
(Quote)
> Gall is bitter to the root,
> Melon is sweet clear through.

22. No Great Masters?

Master Ōbaku said, "You are all leftover eaters! If you walk around the world and search for truth in such a manner, what achievement can you expect? Do you know that there are no more Zen masters in China?" Then a monk stepped out and said, "Aren't there those who walk around earnestly instructing the masses? What of them?" Ōbaku said, "I did not say there is no Zen anymore, only that there are no great masters."

As against, "Do you know that there are no more Zen masters in China?"

ANSWER

"I alone am the ruler of the universe."
(Quote)
> King Kō shouted angrily till his voice broke,
> And the thousand soldiers were nullified.

As against, "I did not say there is no Zen anymore, only that there are no great masters!"

ANSWER

"You're right, you're right; I was wrong."

(Quote)

> A man of [the state of] So lit the fire,
> And everything turned into ashes.

OR

(According to another school)

As against, "All of you are leftover eaters!"

ANSWER

"This wretched leftover eater of a monk!"

As against, "What achievement can you expect?"

ANSWER

"If you dilly-dally you won't make headway, you know!"

As against, "Do you know that there are no more Zen masters in China?"

ANSWER

"In the great empire of China, with more than four hundred prefectures, there is not even one worthy to be called a man. This is really a lamentable state of affairs!"

(Quote)

> To surrender is to be left in the hands of
>   barbarians for the rest of my life.
> To fight, and I end up exposing my bones in
>   the desert waste.

As against, "I did not say there is no Zen anymore, only that there are no great masters!"

ANSWER

"What? If it weren't for your great compassion, master, where would I be today?"

23. *Where Did Nansen Go after His Death?*

Sanshō made monk Shū ask Master Chōsa the following question, "Where did Master Nansen go after his death?" Chōsa answered, "When Master Sekitō was a young priest he met Master Enō." Shū said, "I didn't ask anything about Sekitō's young priesthood. I asked, 'Where did Nansen go after his death?'" Chōsa said, "Go and ask Nansen!" Shū said, "Although Your Reverence possesses a thousand-foot-high pine tree that can stand severe cold, you have not got a small stalagmite." Chōsa was silent. Then Shū said, "I thank you for answering me." Chōsa remained silent. Shū went back and reported the above to Sanshō. Sanshō said, "If it is so, Chōsa must be somewhat greater than

Master Rinzai. But I shall go and see for myself tomorrow."
The next day he went and said, "I have the pleasure of hearing
about your answer concerning Nansen's whereabouts after death.
It can be fairly termed as unprecedented and will be unique in the
years to come. It really is something rarely heard of." Chōsa was
still silent.

*As against, "When Master Sekitō was a young priest he met Master
Enō."*

ANSWER

"Monk So-and-so went out to buy bean curd."

*As against, "I didn't ask anything about Sekitō's young priesthood.
I asked, 'Where did Nansen go after his death?'"*

ANSWER

"There's a guest coming today so I'll prepare dinner."

As against, "The master was still silent."

ANSWER

The pupil just remains silent.
Or:
"Shut up!"
(Quote)

> I am now on the northern bank of River I,
>   under a tree below the spring heaven,
> While you somewhere east of Yōsukō River
>   may be staring at the clouds of twilight at
>   this moment.

Or:

> Spring is fading away in the city of Buryō.
> Trees behind tall buildings are getting green
>   and shady.

Or:

> The color of autumn trees on the plain,
> And the sound of an evening bell from the
>   foot of the sandy hill.

Or:

> As years go by my strength is leaving me.
> When people come to see me I am reluctant
>   to get down from my seat.

Or:

> A stream flows down by a path in the cold
>   mountain air.
> Enshrouded in thick clouds, a big temple bell
>   sounded.

As against, "Go and ask Nansen!"

ANSWER

Looking all around, the pupil says, "I wonder where he's gone at this time?"

(Quote)

> The bundle of willow twigs scattered apart,
> Was blown with the wind on white jade
>   railings.

Or:

> When, alas, my luck failed me, I began to
>   meditate deep and long;
> I thought I saw my emperor in a dream, but
>   on awakening I was not too sure.

Or:

> On a night when cold frost falls,
> The moon as it is glides into the valley in
>   front.

Popular Saying

Isn't that Seijuro over there? That sure looks like his umbrella.

OR

(According to another school)

As against, "Where did Nansen go after his death?"

ANSWER

"Excuse me a while—I'm going to the front gate to buy some straw sandals."

MASTER

Forget about the sandals awhile—"Where did Nansen go after his death?"

ANSWER

"Excuse me—I'm going to buy some paper."

(Quote)

> At night I departed from Seikei and headed
>   for Sankyō,
> I thought about you, but couldn't find you,
>   so I went down to Yushū.

Popular Saying

Ichidōmaru, in search of his father, went up Mt. Kōya.

Or:

Wonder where the sparrow's nest is.

As against, "When Master Sekitō was a young priest he met Master Enō."

ANSWER

Pretending to humor a baby, the pupil says, "Buru, buru, buru," clicking his tongue.

As against, "Go and ask Nansen!"

ANSWER

"Be it a bean cake or flower—how cute, how cute!"

As against, "The master was still silent."

ANSWER

The pupil just remains silent.

Popular Saying

The Sea of Genkai [near Kyūshū], which even birds cannot fly over, how shall we cross it?

(Quote)

> The surface of the water like a mirror,
> The mountain like a painting no bird flies
>   across.

24.   One, Two, Three

As the monk in charge of building Master Sozan's monument had finished his task, he came and reported it to Sozan, who asked, "How much will you give the constructor?" The monk said, "Everything is up to Your Reverend to decide." The master said, "Which is the best thing to do—give the constructor three mon [a monetary unit], or give him two mon, or just give him one mon? If you cannot answer me, I shall build the monument myself." The monk was bewildered.

Master Rasan was at that time living in a temple on Mt. Daiyūrei. A monk who went to Mt. Daiyūrei reported the above story. Rasan said, "Has anyone answered yet?" The monk said, "No one has got the answer yet." Rasan said, "Go back and tell Sozan: 'If you give the constructor three mon, you will not have the monument built in your lifetime. If you give him two mon, you will both be extending one hand. If it is one mon, you will both lose your eyebrows and beard.'" The monk went back and told this to Sozan. Sozan, with due ceremony, turned in the direction of Mt. Daiyūrei, bowed, and said, "I thought there were no great masters anymore. I never dreamt that on Mt. Daiyūrei an old Buddha is now radiating light which shines all the way to this place. However, it is a December lotus flower." Rasan heard about that and said, "When I said that, the hair of the tortoise had long before grown several feet."

As against, "Which is the best thing to do—give the constructor three mon, or give him two mon, or just give him one mon?"

ANSWER

"Wow! Thank you for so much!"

As against, "An old Buddha is now radiating light which shines all the way to this place."

ANSWER

The pillar stands, the threshold lies."

(Quote)

> On the wide plain a light breeze blows.
> From the sky, scattered rains dimly, dimly.

As against [Rasan's], "If you give three mon, you will not have the monument built in your lifetime. If you give two mon, you will both be extending one hand. If you give one mon, you will both lose your eyebrows and beard."

ANSWER

"The first one is a pine tree at the pond. The second one is a pine tree in the garden. The third one is a drooping pine tree."

As against, "A December lotus flower."

ANSWER

"Well, it's easily done."

(Quote)

> The many mountains abide in the one
>   mountain,
> The many voices go to the sea and disappear.

OR

(According to another school)

MASTER

In place of the monk, you, say how many mon are to be given.

ANSWER

The pupil counts, "One mon, two mon, three mon."

(Quote)

One, two, three, four, five, six, seven; Daruma does not know how to count.

As against, "The radiant light shines all the way to this place."
ANSWER
The pupil recites, "The radiant light shines all the way to this place."

25. An Iron Cow

Master Fuketsu said, "Buddha-mind is just like an iron cow; if there is movement—there is no progress; if there is standstill—there is stagnation. Well, this 'no-movement-no-standstill,' should one be mindful of it? Should one be unmindful of it?"

At that time a monk by the name of Roha said, "I hold the working of the iron cow. Please, master, I wish you wouldn't be hindered by it." Fuketsu said, "I'm used to catching whales. I thought I had a whale of the great sea on my line, but all it was was a muddy, creepy, small frog." Roha, dumbfounded, was speechless. At that, Fuketsu yelled ["Katsu!"] at him and said, "Why can't you go on?!" Roha was bewildered. Fuketsu then hit Roha with a stick and said, "If you remember what was said, let me hear you say it!" Roha opened his mouth to speak when Fuketsu hit him again.

At that point, a monk named Bokushu said, "The law of Buddha and the law of the emperor are the same!" Fuketsu asked, "What do you mean by that?" Bokushu answered, "Not to cut when one should cut invites disorder." With that, Fuketsu got down from his seat and left.

As against, "Buddha-mind is like an iron cow."
ANSWER
"It's like a stone mill."

MASTER
Why is it so?

ANSWER
"It doesn't move a bit."
(Quote)
> Along the hedge chasing a butterfly,
> By the water's side toying with a frog.

Or:
> Carrying one's wine bottle to drink the
>   village-brewed wine;
> At home, wearing the kimono, be the
>   master of the house.

As against, "*If there is movement—there is no progress; if there is standstill—there is stagnation. This 'no-movement-no-standstill,' should one be mindful of it? Should one be unmindful of it?*"

MASTER

[He repeats the above quote and says], If I keep after you in this way, how will you answer?

ANSWER

The pupil slaps his master once.

26. *Similar to a Dream*

Official Rikkō and Master Nansen were conversing. Rikkō said, "The philosopher Jō once said, 'Heaven and earth are of the same root as myself; the universe and I are one.' It is really strange." Nansen pointed at a flower in the garden and said to Rikkō, "When people look at this flower, it is similar to a dream."

MASTER

It is said, "When people look at this flower it is similar to a dream." Now tell me—what's Rikkō's view? [i.e., How does Rikkō see the flower?]

ANSWER

"Like a mortar, like a rice cake."

MASTER

What is Nansen's view? [i.e., How does Nansen see the flower?]

ANSWER

"It has really blossomed beautifully."

MASTER

Distinguish the positions of Rikkō and Nansen.

ANSWER

"Rikkō's state is one of admitting the mysterious working [of Buddhism]. Nansen does not."

MASTER

Distinguish the positions of Rikkō and Nansen as to daily affairs.

"Rikkō, in ceremonial dress, is proper and formal. Nansen, in ordinary clothes, a pipe in his mouth, is just about to go out."

MASTER

(Quote)

To listen, to see, to learn, to know is not all. The mountains and rivers should not be seen through a mirror.

ANSWER

With his finger, the pupil points at things one by one, reciting, "To listen, to see, to learn, to know is not all." Then saying, "The mountains and rivers should not be seen through a mirror," he gives the appearance of taking all and everything into himself, folds his arms, and looks down.

MASTER

(Quote)

The moon is sinking from the frosty sky, and half of the night is almost gone. With whom can I cast a cold shadow upon the surface of the crystal pond?

ANSWER

"It's gotten late—well, since there's no one to talk to, guess I'll piss and go to bed."
(Quote)

> When Kōsen, king of Etsu, returned after
> defeating the state of Go,
> The righteous warriors went home all clad in
> silk,
> And maids were all over the spring palace
> like flowers,
> But now, nothing but wild birds can be seen
> flying about.

[In reference to the above quote, the book comments that the first three lines illustrate the bustling characteristic of Rikkō's view. The last line expresses the distinctionless, still position of Nansen.]
Or:

> The donkey stares at the well,
> The well stares at the donkey.

OR

(According to another school)

As against, "Heaven and earth are of the same root as myself."

ANSWER

The pupil recites, "Heaven and earth are of the same root as myself."

As against, "The universe and I are one."

ANSWER

"Be it the floor, be it the charcoal brazier, be it the sliding door, it's all one with myself."

As against, "It is similar to a dream."

ANSWER

Nodding his head, the pupil pretends to be asleep.

(Quote)

> He saw only the meandering of the stream,
> and the winding of the road
> Without realizing that he was in "peach
> paradise."

As against, "To listen, to see, to learn, to know is not all."

ANSWER

"Without a doubt I'm listening, seeing, learning, and knowing."

As against, "The mountains and rivers should not be seen through a mirror."

ANSWER

The pupil pretends to look at mountains, rivers. Then, dropping his eyes on his chest, he stops.

MASTER

(Quote)

The moon is sinking from the frosty sky and half of the night is almost gone. With whom can I cast a cold shadow upon the surface of the crystal pond?

ANSWER

"It's gotten late. Well, since there's no one to talk to, guess I'll go to bed."

27. *"Not Affected," "Not Deluded"*

Whenever Master Hyakujō held a meeting, there was always an old man in the crowd listening to him. When the crowd dispersed, the old man went with it. One day, however, the old man did not leave. So Hyakujō asked, "Who is it standing before me?" The old man answered, "I am not a human being. In ancient times I lived on this mountain. A student of the Way asked me if the enlightened were still affected by causality. I replied, saying that they were not affected. Because of that I was degraded to lead the life of a wild fox for five hundred lives. I now request you to answer one thing for me." Thus he asked if the enlightened were affected by causality. The master said, "They are not deluded by causality." The old man was enlightened upon hearing this. He bowed and said, "I am already liberated but my body as a fox is still at the back of this mountain. I am venturing to beg Your Reverence to treat me as you customarily do a dead monk."

The master then ordered the monk in charge of burial to beat the drum so as to announce to the people that there would be a service for a dead monk after the meal. The people started wondering and talking since everybody was safe and sound and there were no patients in the sick room. After the meal the master led the people to a big rock at the back of the mountain. From under the rock he dug out a dead wild fox with his stick and had it cremated.

When night fell, the master told the above story in his lecture. Master Ōbaku [Hyakujō's disciple] said, "The only mistake of the deceased was his answer which made him lead the life of a wild fox for five hundred lives. If he were right in every answer, what should he become?" Hyakujō said, "Come up and I'll tell you." So Ōbaku drew near and gave Hyakujō a slap. Hyakujō clapped his hands, laughed, and said, "I only thought that the barbarian's beard was red, I never realized it was a red-bearded barbarian."
As against, "Not affected by causality" and "not deluded by causality."

ANSWER

As against "not affected by causality," the pupil says, "Kon, kon" [the cry of a fox]. As against "not deluded by causality," he says, "Bow-wow" [the bark of a dog].

MASTER

In the vast mountain of Hyakujō's, why is there a dead fox?

ANSWER

"Within the boundaries of even this temple there is at least one dead skunk. All the more, in the vast mountain of Hyakujō, there's nothing strange about there being one dead fox."

As against, "*I only thought that the barbarian's beard was red, I never realized it was a red-bearded barbarian.*"

ANSWER

The pupil repeats, "I only thought that the barbarian's beard was red, I never thought it was a red-bearded barbarian."
(*Quote*)

> I thought that the yellow lily was sweet like
> honey,
> But in fact it is honey that is bitter like the
> yellow lily.

OR
(According to another school)

As against, "*Not affected by causality.*"

ANSWER

The pupil takes two to three steps forward, saying, "Kon, kon" [the cry of a fox].
As against, "*Not deluded by causality.*"

ANSWER

The pupil takes two to three steps backward, saying, "Bow-wow" [the bark of a dog].

OR
(According to another school)

As against, "*Not affected by causality.*"

ANSWER

The pupil, saying, "Kon, kon," acts out the falling into the state of a fox.
As against, "*Not deluded by causality.*"

ANSWER

The pupil, lying on his back, draws in his arms and legs, pretending to be a dead fox. Thus he shows the point of breaking loose from the fox's body.

28. *Where Thing Does Not Contradict Thing*

The four realms of existence of the Kegon sect are: (1) the realm of truth (idea); (2) the realm of things; (3) the realm where truth and things do not contradict each other; and (4) the realm where thing does not contradict thing.
As against, "*The realm of truth.*"

(139)

ANSWER

"The world throughout is clear. Not a speck of dust."
(Quote)
All this stretch of land is but a rod of iron.
Or:
In the wide world there is not an inch of land.
As against, "The realm of things."

ANSWER

"Each and all things are radiating a great light."
(Quote)

> The tidal water in the spring river joins the sea
> and is level with it.
> Over the sea, the bright moon is born
> with the tide.

As against, "The realm where truth and things do not contradict each other."

ANSWER

"The flower and moon relate as one, the mountain and river relate as one, night and day, man and woman, monk and layman relate as one."
(Quote)

> The mist of sunset sweeps the sky together
> with the lonely duck,
> And the autumn river is of the same color
> with the wide heaven.

As against, "The realm where thing does not contradict thing."

ANSWER

"The willow radiates a willowlike light; the flower radiates a flowerlike light; the mountain, a mountainlike light; the river, a riverlike light; man, a manlike light; and woman, a womanlike light."
(Quote)
Green is the grass and yellow the willow. Profuse are the blossoms of the peach and fragrant are those of the plum.

OR
(According to another school)
MASTER
Show me the four realms using your hand.

(140)

The pupil thrusts his hand forward saying:

1. "To see the hand as a hand is the realm of things."
2. "Not to see the hand as a hand is the realm of truth" [idea].
3. "To be at the point where the hand is not seen as a hand and yet still to see the hand as a hand is the realm of truth and things not contradicting each other."
4. "The one hand immediately becomes heaven, earth; it becomes mountain, river, grass, tree; it becomes each and every thing; each and all things come into the one hand." (This is the realm where thing does not contradict thing.)

(Quote)

> The one moon appears on all waters,
> All waters reflect the one moon.

29. *What Will You Call It?*

Master Isan said, "When I die, I will be transformed into a male buffalo at the house of the parishioner at the foot of the mountain. On the buffalo's lower left side will be written the five words, 'This is the monk Isan.' If you call it 'Isan,' it's a buffalo. If you call it 'buffalo,' it's Isan. Well then, what will you call it?" Here Kyōzan stepped out, bowed, and walked away.

"My name is so-and-so," the pupil says, giving his own name.
(Quote)
Whether you say Kōshi or Kyūchūji [names for Confucius] it's the same thing.

30. *Stick!*

Master Shuzan, taking a bamboo stick, said to the people, "If you call this a stick, you fall into the trap of words (or: You must eliminate that which prevents you from calling it a stick); but if you do not call it a stick, you oppose the fact. So what will you people call it?" At that time monk Sekken, who happened to be in the assembly, came forth. He snatched the stick, broke it in two, and threw the pieces down the stairs, saying, "What is this?" Shuzan said, "Blind!"

Master Dai-e added, "Say it quick! Say it quick!"

As against, "What will you call it?"
ANSWER
Clenching his hand into a fist, the pupil thrusts it forward saying, "Stick! Stick!"

MASTER
If you call a stick a stick, it is like a donkey forever tied to a pole.

ANSWER
The pupil says, "Then you may call it a night pot or a nightsoil dipper."

MASTER
What's the use of the stick?

ANSWER
"It may be a cane, chopsticks, a pestle, or a rice spoon."

MASTER
"If you call this a stick you fall into the trap of words (or: You must eliminate that which prevents you from calling it a stick)." Handle this.

ANSWER
The pupil, handling the stick, assumes the pose of putting it away in the corner of the shelf.

MASTER
(Quote)
If it cannot be called "emptiness" ["nothingness"], what should it be called?

ANSWER
The pupil turns a somersault in front of his master.

OR
(According to another school)
As against, "If you call this a stick, you fall into the trap of words."
ANSWER
"Stick."

MASTER
Ha! You trespass [i.e., you violate "nothingness"]!

(142)

"Hmm, it's a piece of wood," the pupil says, throwing it away.

[He says again] Ha! You trespass!

"Stick."

Without falling into the trap of words [without violating "nothingness"]—how will you deal with this?

"Falling into the trap . . . trespassing—what a bore. Break it to pieces, stick it under the bathtub and burn it up!"

Not involving yourself in trespassing, say the phrase.

The pupil quotes, "Originally empty, ultimately empty." (*Quote*)

> If it is the time of Tō and Gu [dynasties]
>   then we shall have ceremony and music;
> If it is the time of Ketsu and Chū [villain
>   kings] then we shall have only war

31.   *The Emperor and the Bowl*

[Enō's master decided that Enō would take his place as the next master, and as proof of the authority, he gave him his cloak and bowl. The other monks, displeased with this, chased after Enō. Near Mt. Daiyūrei they caught up with Enō and attempted to steal the bowl from him. However, when they tried to grab the bowl away, they could not lift it.]

One day Emperor Taisō of the Sō Dynasty held up a bowl, turned to his minister Ōzui and said, "Since the monks at Mt. Daiyūrei could not lift the bowl, how is it that I can?" Ōzui gave no reply.

ANSWER

"The holy virtue of the emperor is a vast and magnificent thing. All the surrounding nations are bathed in his glorious presence."

MASTER

(Quote)
The clouds are deep and thick; I'm not supposed to be able to go to the emperor's court; how is it that I am here?

ANSWER

"The holy virtue of the emperor is a vast and magnificent thing. Even the birds and beasts in the depths of the mountain are worshipping His Majesty."
(Quote)
> The four seas are completely under the enlightenment
> of the emperor.
> Who dares to invade our boundaries from the
> south, west and north?

32. *How Is Your Health?*

Master Baso was not feeling well. The head monk of the temple went to him and asked, "How is Your Reverence's health these days?" Baso said, "Nichimenbutsu, Getsumenbutsu [two legendary Buddhas]."

ANSWER

"Neither Shaka Buddha nor Amida Buddha know anything."

MASTER

(Quote)
When I die it is a good monk who bears not his bereavement for too long.

ANSWER

"A man's life is short lived. Very soon my life too is in danger."

OR
(According to another school)
ANSWER
The pupil turns to the right, saying, "Nichimenbutsu." Turning to the left he says, "Getsumenbutsu."

As against, "*When I die it is a good monk who bears not his bereavement for too long.*"

ANSWER

"Oh, what shall I do? If anything should happen to my master, hereafter under whom am I to study?"

OR

(With certain masters)

ANSWER

"Oh, the pain! The pain!"

33.   *The Gate!*

At the end of the summer session, Master Suigan said to the people, "I have been talking to you brothers for a summer; see if my eyebrows are still here." Hofuku said, "The thief is afraid." Chōkei said, "It grows!" Ummon said, "The gate!" [or: "Shut!"]. *As against, "Chōkei said, 'It grows!'"*

ANSWER

"It grew! It grew!"

MASTER

What kind of place is the place where it grows?

ANSWER

"From the mountain just beyond, to the place of the hedge, it is covered all over with green grass grown."
(Quote)
After it rains, the greenery of the green hills turns greener.
Or:

> Clouds stood still after the rain and the day
>   had just begun to dawn;
> The few peaks looked picturesque with their
>   green height and massiveness.

As against, "Hofuku said, 'The thief is afraid.'"

ANSWER

"The thief's heart is beating in fear."
As against, "Ummon said, 'The gate!'"

ANSWER

"GAAATE!" the pupil roars like a lion and hits the floor.
Or:
The pupil slaps the master once.

(Quote)

> The father is equipped with tricks that can
>   persuade his wayward son;
> The son has the fist that can beat his father.

Or:

An angry fist does not strike a smiling face.

OR

(According to another school)

MASTER

See if my eyebrows are here.

ANSWER

The pupil looks at his master's eyebrows.

MASTER

Suigan's feeling—what's it like?

ANSWER

"The feathers of the cormorant—not even one can be plucked,
not even one can be added."
As against, "Hofuku said, 'The thief is afraid.'"

ANSWER

"Somehow, the fellow who steals cannot relax."
As against, "Chōkei said, 'It grows!'"

ANSWER

"It certainly grows."
As against, "Ummon said, 'The gate!'"

ANSWER

"This 'gate'—in things good or bad, anything, everything, there
is nothing that is not the 'gate.' It hasn't got a single crack, this
not-even-an-ant-can-crawl-through GATE!"

(Quote)

To lose money and be accused of a crime.

Or:

An angry fist does not strike a smiling face.

Or:

> I stop the vehicle for love-to-sit-in-the-
>   twilight-forest-of-maple-trees.
> The leaves under the frost are redder than
>   flowers of February.

34. Unforgivable

That Daruma knows is forgivable. That Daruma understands is unforgivable.
As against, "That Daruma knows is forgivable."

ANSWER

"Yes, that's okay, that's okay."
As against, "That Daruma understands is unforgivable."

ANSWER

"No, no, that's bad."
(Quote)
His cleverness can be matched, but his foolishness is surpassing.
Or:
Make me a good courtier, don't make me a faithful courtier.

35. How Do You Say It?

Master Kinzan went together with Master Gantō and Master Seppō to see Master Tokusan. Kinzan said, "Master Tennō said it like this. Master Ryūtan said it like this too. [Tennō was the master of Ryūtan, and Ryūtan was the master of Tokusan.] I wonder how you say it?" Tokusan said, "Try and show me how Tennō and Ryūtan said it." This upset Kinzan and just as he was about to speak, Tokusan hit him.

On the way back Kinzan said, "I know he is right, but beating me was too much!" Gantō said, "If that is the way you are, do not ever say you have met Tokusan."

MASTER

"Master Tennō said it like this. Master Ryūtan said it like this too. I wonder how you say it? Now, you answer in place of Tokusan."

ANSWER

"I knew you'd ask that."

36. Discuss Buddhist Law

Master Nansen said, "Monju and Fugen [legendary Buddhas] discussed Buddhist law until late last night. I gave them each thirty strokes with my stick and sent them to Mt. Nitetchi [i.e., the farthest end of earth]." At that point Jōshū stepped out from the crowd and said, "How shall we have hit you?!" Nansen said, "What have I done wrong?" Jōshū bowed.

"Yesterday I awoke at midnight and started thinking about home and my family. I thought of this, I thought of that, then SHUNK! quit it and slept soundly till morning."
(*Quote*)

> To read out the verdict while carrying the
> stolen object in your arms.

Or:

> I cut out all the rights and wrongs of the
> human world,
> And shut the wooden door where white
> clouds lie thick and deep.

OR
(According to another school)
As against, "Discussed Buddhist law."
ANSWER
"Since last night my back and shoulders hurt—what a pain!"
As against, "Sent them to Mt. Nitetchi."
"This morning I sent for the masseur and after the treatment I'm completely well."

37. Simultaneous Doubt and Enlightenment

Master Nan-in said, "You know only 'simultaneous doubt and enlightenment' [i.e., when a chick is about to come out from an egg, it chirps. In response, the hen will peck at the egg so as to break the shell and free the chick. This process is compared to having doubt and receiving the solution right away] as a thing in itself, but you are not equipped to apply it." A monk came up with the question, "What is the application of 'simultaneous doubt and enlightenment?'" Nan-in said, "The truly great master does not hold onto the mold of 'simultaneous doubt and enlighten-ment.' One who does is deprived of its working." The monk said, "I still have some doubt." Nan-in said, "What is it that you doubt?" The monk said, "The so-called 'deprived of.'" At that, Nan-in struck him. The monk protested but Nan-in drove him away.

Later, this same monk went to the assembly of Master Ummon and reported the above story. A certain monk said, "So, Master Nan-in broke his stick." With that, the monk came to realization. He went back to see Nan-in, but Nan-in had just passed away. Instead he met Master Fuketsu. The moment he bowed, Fuketsu said, "Aren't you the monk who asked our deceased master about 'simultaneous doubt and enlightenment?'" The monk said, "Yes." Fuketsu said, "How did you understand it then?" The monk said, "At that time I was like one walking by the light of a lamp." Fuketsu said, "You have understood."

ANSWER

"I'm doing all that I can, so please don't worry about me."
Or:
"I've grown *THIS* big without the help of others," the pupil says standing up.
As against, "The application of 'stimultaneous doubt and enlighten-ment.'"

ANSWER

"When the bell rings—to the meditation hall.
When the gong strikes—to the dining room."

38. *Don't You Believe Me Now?*

One day, the official Chinsō along with other officials were climbing up a tall building when they saw several monks coming. One of the officials said, "Those coming are all Zen priests." Chinsō said, "They are not." The official said, "How do you know that they are not?" Chinsō said, "Wait till they come closer. I shall ask them." When the monks came to the front of the building, Chinsō called out suddenly, "Reverend!" [In Japanese, "joza"—a general term for Buddhist priests; not the specific term for a Zen priest.] The monks looked up. Chinsō said to the officials, "Don't you believe me now?"

ANSWER

"I am filled with awe realizing the height of your lordship's wisdom and virtue."

OR
(According to another school)

As against, "Don't you believe me now?"

"Don't you believe me now?"

Take the place of the officials and say something.

"Your judgment is truly admirable!"
(Quote)
> The cold weather is selfless;
> You should understand even before the
>   occasion arises.

Or:

> Without great intelligence, how can we get
>   this man?

Or:

> If you do not have the strength to lift up a
>   three-legged giant stove or to root up a
>   mountain,
> You will find it not easy to ride the black
>   horse that runs a thousand miles a day.

39.   I Never Said a Word . . .

Master Kassan said, "I have been living on this mountain for twenty years but I never said a word about our sect of religion." A monk then asked, "I have heard you say that you had been living on this mountain for twenty years yet you never said a word about our religious sect. Is it true?" Kassan said, "Yes it is." At that, the monk threw Kassan off his seat. Kassan dismissed the assembly and left. The next day he made the people dig a pit and then ordered his attendant, "Ask the monk who raised the question yesterday to come." When the monk arrived, Kassan said, "I talked of nothing but nonsense in the past twenty years, so I request you to beat me to death and bury me in the pit. If you do not kill me, you have to beat yourself to death and be buried in this pit." The monk gathered his things and sneaked away.

MASTER
Take the monk's place and say something.

(150)

The pupil makes a face. "Ha, ha! Good for you!"

40. *Where in the World Are They?*

It is said in our sect that Master Toku-un of Mt. Myōhō never came down from the mountain. Master Zenzai went to see him but was unable to meet him for seven days. However, one day they happened to meet each other on the peak of another mountain. Having met, Toku-un spoke to Zenzai about the truth that a single thought holds the wisdom of all the Buddhas of past, present, and future.

Master Engo commented on the above story, saying, "Since Toku-un never came down from Mt. Myōhō, how come they met each other on another mountain? If he did leave the mountain, then it is contrary to the belief in our sect that Toku-un never came down from Mt. Myōhō. When it comes to this—where in the world are Toku-un and Zenzai?"

ANSWER
"Master and I are facing each other like this."

41. *A Bottle Is a Bottle*

When Master Isan was still a pupil under Master Hyakujō, he was in charge of cooking. At that time, Hyakujō founded a temple on Mt. Daii and was about to choose the monk to become the chief priest of this temple. He asked the head monk to call those qualified enough to apply for this position. Then Hyakujō picked up a bottle and put it on the ground. He asked, "If you weren't allowed to call this a bottle, what would you call it?" The head monk replied, "You cannot call it a wooden log." Then Hyakujō asked Isan. Isan kicked the bottle over and walked away. Hyakujō laughed and said, "The head monk lost to Isan." Thus he appointed Isan to be the chief priest of the temple on Mt. Daii.
(Quote)

> Rain falling on tree leaves—jadelike beads of
>   water turning around,
> And the heron breaks through the misty
>   curtain hanging over the bamboo trees.

42. *A Silver Bowl Filled with Snow*

A monk asked Master Haryō, "What is the teaching of the Daiba Sect like?" Haryō said, "A silver bowl filled with snow."

ANSWER
"Such a thing—smash it to pieces!"

OR
(According to another school)
As against, "Daiba Sect."
ANSWER
"Don't blab around."
(Quote)
Open your mouth and your insides are seen.

43. *Every Coral Branch Supports the Moon*

A monk asked Master Haryō, "What is the sword that can cut a hair blown against its blade?" Haryō said, "Every coral branch is supporting the moon."

ANSWER
"Such a thing—I broke it and flung it into the western sea!"
(Quote)
> A broken mirror does not reflect images
> again,
> And it is difficult for fallen flowers to go up
> the branches.

OR
(According to another school)
As against, "The sword that can cut a hair blown against its blade."
ANSWER
"When standing, in standing; when sitting, in sitting; when listening, in listening; unhindered, unhampered, freely managing."
(Quote)
To howl at the moon and sleep in the clouds.
Or:
To sing to the flowers and recite poetry under the moon.

44. *An Open-eyed Man Falls into the Well*

A monk asked Master Haryō, "What is the way?" Haryō said, "An open-eyed man falling into the well."

ANSWER

"Whew! That was close! I almost fell in!" the pupil says as he imitates one narrowly escaping a fall.
(Quote)
The pit that entraps people is full every year.
Or:
The pitch-dark, deep pit is almost terror-inspiring.

45. *In Relation to One*

A monk asked Master Ummon, "What is the real religion that Buddha preached?" Ummon said, "It is in relation to one."

ANSWER

"In meeting a minister, preaching to a minister; in meeting a beggar, preaching to a beggar; meeting a man, preaching to a man; meeting a woman, preaching to a woman."
(Quote)
> In speaking to an inferior official one should
>   be pleasant and kind,
> In speaking to a superior official one should
>   be pleasant and upright.

Or:
Talk of various things by the side of a dung fire.

46. *In Opposition to One*

A monk asked Master Ummon, "What if it is neither a happening-right-before-your-eyes nor a thing-right-before-your-eyes?" Ummon said, "It is in opposition to one."

MASTER

"In opposition to one"—what's it mean? Attach a quote to this.

ANSWER

(Quote)

> There are two lines of tears on the coral
>   pillow.
> Half is for thinking of you, while the other
>   half is for hating you.

Or:

> I always recall places south of the Yōsukō
>   River in the month of March,
> With the hundred flowers sweetening the air
>   amid the chirping of the small birds.

MASTER

As against, "What if it is neither a happening-right-before-your-eyes nor a thing-right-before-your-eyes?"—how'd you answer it?

ANSWER

The pupil solemnly recites, "What if it is neither a happening-right-before-your-eyes nor a thing-right-before-your-eyes."
(Quote)

> Grab the thief's gun and kill him.

[In reference to the above, the book comments that this is a case of answering through snatching the question.]

47. *Are You Alive?*

A monk asked Master Kyōshō, "I am chirping, will my master peck for me?" [i.e., when a chick is about to come out from an egg, it chirps. In response, the hen will peck at the egg so as to break the shell and free the chick. In Zen, this process is compared to having doubt and receiving the solution right away.] Kyōshō said, "Are you alive?" The monk said, "If I were not alive, people would laugh at me." Kyōshō said, "That's quite a guy."

ANSWER

"Chirp, peck, chirp chirp, peck peck."

48. *The One-Piece Tower*

Emperor Shukusō asked his Zen master Etchū, "When you die, what am I to do?" Etchū said, "Build a one-piece tower for me." The emperor asked Etchū for the form of the tower. Etchū remained silent for awhile. Then he asked, "Do you understand?" The emperor said, "I do not understand." Etchū said, "Among my disciples there is the man called Tangen. He knows about it. You may ask him about it."

After Etchū died, the emperor called for Tangen and asked him about it. Tangen said, "It is south of the place called Shō and north of the place called Tan. [On this phrase Master Setchō later said: 'The one hand does not sound of itself.'] Within, it overflows with gold. [Setchō: "A cane in the shape of a mountain."] Under a shadeless tree rests a ferryboat. [Setchō: "The sea is quiet, the river is clear."] There is an emerald palace that holds no Buddhist priest of fame." [Setchō: "He brought it out right in front of your eyes."]

As against, "To ask the master for the form of the tower."

ANSWER

The pupil folds his arms across his chest and stands up.
As against, "Etchū remained silent."

ANSWER

(Quote)

> North of the River Isui, trees under the
> spring sun;
> East of the River Yōsukō, the clouds of
> twilight.

As against, "South of Shō, north of Tan."

ANSWER

"Here is the shelf, here is the door."
As against, "Within, it overflows with gold."

ANSWER

"In the living room, there is spread a fine carpet."
As against, "Under a shadeless tree rests a ferryboat."

ANSWER

"Thus I seat myself down." [So saying, the pupil sits down.]
As against, "There is an emerald palace that holds no Buddhist priest of fame."

ANSWER

"In the whole world there is not one who knows my mind."

49. *No Meaning*

Master Ryūge asked Master Suibi, "What is the meaning of our founder coming from the west?" [i.e., what is the meaning of Zen?] Suibi said, "Hand me the stick." Ryūge handed the stick

(155)

to Suibi who, upon receiving it, hit Ryūge with it. Ryūge said, "Hit me as you like, at any rate there is no meaning to our founder coming from the west."

Ryūge then asked Master Rinzai, "What is the meaning of our founder coming from the west?" Rinzai said, "Hand me the cushion." Ryūge handed the cushion to Rinzai who, upon receiving it, hit Ryūge with it. Ryūge said, "Hit me as you like, at any rate there is no meaning to our founder coming from the west."

MASTER

"There is no meaning to our founder coming from the west"— what's it mean?

ANSWER

"Starting with the koan on the one hand, I went through the various stages of the [koan] teaching; but what I've gained can't even be pinpointed with a single rabbit's hair."
(Quote)

> Last year we were so poor we had only land
> as big as a drill-point.
> This year our poverty is such that we haven't
> even got land as big as a drill-point.

50. *It Is Somewhat a Pity*

Master Hofuku and Master Chōkei were strolling in the mountains. Hofuku pointed his finger and said, "That is the peak of Mt. Myōhō." Chōkei said, "It is all right, but it is somewhat a pity."

Later Master Setchō commented, "What is it I want touring mountains with this man?" And he also said, "After one hundred years there will be few, but not none." Master Kyōshō commented, "If it were not for Chōkei, skeletons would scatter the wilderness."

As against, "That is the peak of Mt. Myōhō."

ANSWER

Shading his eyes with one hand, the pupil pretends to look afar and says, "What a beautiful view!"

As against, "It is all right, but it is somewhat a pity."

"To be taken in by beautiful scenery can't be helped—before it gets dark let's go. Let's go home!"
(Quote)

> Weeping, I held the sleeves of Riryō [a
>   famous general] in my hands.
> The thought of returning home made tears
>   wet the lapels of my clothes.

51.   *A Few Here, a Few There*

Monju [a legendary Buddha representing wisdom] asked Master Mujaku, "Where have you been recently?" Mujaku said, "I have been in the south." Monju said, "How is the teaching of Buddha faring in the south?" Mujaku said, "The teaching of Buddha is declining and monks hardly keep discipline." Monju said, "How many monks are there?" Mujaku said, "Sometimes three hundred, sometimes five hundred. It varies." He then asked Monju, "How are things getting on here?" Monju said, "The people and saints live together. Dragons and snakes mingle." Mujaku said, "How many monks are there?" Monju said, "Three three in front, three three in back" [i.e., a few here, a few there].

(Quote)
There are rubies in front and pearls in back.
Or:
With upright head and straight tail.
Popular Saying
The tail is long, the head is long—a long-tailed cock.
Or:
Hiding the head yet forgetting to hide the rear.
Or:
Clap the hands, slap the ass—horse market.

52.   *Where Is the Mind?*

Master Banzan left a saying, "There is no existence in the three realms of past, present, and future. Where is the mind?"

"The pillar stands, the threshold lies, the willow is green, the flower is red."
(Quote)

> Green is the grass and yellow the willow,
> Profuse are the blossoms of the peach and
> fragrant are those of the plum.

OR
(According to another school)
ANSWER
The pupil slaps his master's face once.

MASTER
"No existence"—what's it mean?

ANSWER
"I ask you to excuse me," the pupil says, bowing his head.

OR
(According to another school)
ANSWER
The pupil stands up, shades his eyes with one hand as he pretends to look afar, and says, "If you look over here you see Mt. So-and-so; if you look over there you see Mt. So-and-so."
(Quote)

> Arriving at the river, the territories of the
> state of Go seem to come to an end;
> Yet on the other bank, many are the hills in
> the state of Etsu.

Or:

> When evening falls in picturesque spots on
> the river,
> Fishermen wearing straw raincoats are on
> their way homeward bound.

53. *A Speck of Dust*

Master Fuketsu said, "Raise up a speck of dust and the nation will prosper; if a speck of dust is not raised, the nation will fall."

Later, Master Setchō said, "Is there no monk among you who will live and die like me?"

ANSWER

(Quote)

> Arriving at the river, the territories of the
>   state of Go seem to come to an end;
> Yet on the other bank, many are the hills in
>   the state of Etsu.

54. *Gya!*

One day a monk of the eastern hall and a monk of the western hall had a fight over a cat. Master Nansen saw this so he took the cat and held it up, saying, "If any of you can tell me the meaning of this, I shall not cut this cat." The monks said nothing in reply; Nansen cut the cat into two.

ANSWER

"Gya!" [the cry of a dying cat].

55. *Nyan*

Master Nansen told the previous story to Master Jōshū and asked him about it. Jōshū took off his sandals and put them on his head. Nansen said, "If you were there, you would have saved the cat."

ANSWER

"Nyan" [the cry of a come-alive cat].
(Quote)

> When one is angered with another,
>   the sword is drawn. [Nansen]
> To cure a malady, one takes medicine
>   from the chest. [Jōshū]

56. *Come and Eat Your Rice*

Whenever mealtime came, Master Kingyū would himself take the rice pot to the front of the hall, dance and laugh heartily, saying, "Ho, ye children of Buddha! Come and eat your rice!"

Later, Master Setchō commented, "Though Kingyū did that, he did not do it out of good nature."

A monk asked Master Chōkei, "When Kingyū said, 'Children

of Buddha, come eat your rice!' what did he mean?" Chōkei said, "It is very similar to reciting a song of praise for the meal."

"Children of Buddha, come eat your rice"—how'd you answer to that?

"I'm full," the pupil says, patting his belly.
As against, "Though Kingyū did that, he did not do it out of good nature."

"The rice pot's empty."
As against, "Chōkei said, 'It is very similar to reciting a song of praise for the meal.'"

The pupil recites a prayer usually said at mealtimes.

57. *Playing Ball on Rapid Water*

A monk asked Master Jōshū, "Has a newborn baby the six senses?" Jōshū said, "Playing ball on rapid water."
The monk then went to Master Tōsu and asked, "What does 'playing ball on rapid water' mean?" Tōsu said, "Thought after thought incessantly flows on."

The pupil draws in his arms and legs, lies on his back and says, "Ga, ga," imitating a baby.

58. *Playing with Mud*

A monk asked Master Yakusan, "On the plain where short grass grows, there are herds of deer. What should one do to shoot the deer among deer?" Yakusan said, "Watch out for my arrow!" The monk let himself fall. Yakusan said to his attendants, "Drag out this useless corpse!" The monk then went away. Yakusan said, "This fellow plays around with mud. He knows no limits."
Later, Master Setchō commented, "Though he [the monk] lives while he takes three steps, when he takes the fifth step, he has to die."

As against, *"Watch out for my arrow!"*
ANSWER
The pupil gives the pretense of one fixing an arrow and drawing the bow.
As against, *"Let himself fall."*
ANSWER
The pupil pretends to let himself fall.

MASTER
"Drag out this useless corpse!" Instead of the monk, you say something.
ANSWER
"The master has died."

59.   *The Sturdy Body of Truth*

A monk asked Master Tairyū, "The physical body will rot and decay, but what will happen to the sturdy body of truth?" Tairyū said, "The blossoms of the mountain flowers are like brocade and the brook is deep and looks so blue!"
As against, *"The blossoms of the mountain flowers are like brocade and the brook is deep and looks so blue!"*
ANSWER
The pupil, folding his arms across his chest, stands up, reciting, "Mountain flowers." Sitting down again, he recites, "The brook."

MASTER
[In reference to "mountain flowers" he quotes]—[If "mountain flowers" are the body of truth] when strong winds blow, what will happen?
ANSWER
The pupil, swaying his body, imitates falling flowers. Then, plop! he drops himself down.

MASTER
[In reference to "the brook" he quotes]—[If "the brook" is the body of truth] when the mountain slides, what will happen?

ANSWER
"Chin, don, shan" [chime of bells]. So saying, the pupil gives the air of a funeral.

Popular Saying
You think resentfully of the morning dew, yet in the end your body lying on the grass will pass away like dew.
Or:

> On a spring evening coming to the mountain
>   temple,
> Together with the evening bells the flowers
>   fall.

60. *Put Together*

Master Ummon said, "Put a famous master of old together with that pole outside the hall. How does that work?" He answered himself saying, "It gets cloudy south of the mountain, but it is north of the mountain that it rains."

ANSWER

"I've bought a bag of red pepper for two cents. I also bought turnips, fried bean curd, and potatoes for five or six cents." *(Quote)*

> Cream and cheese are mixed into one,
> Cake trays and head ornaments are melted
>   into one metal.

Or:

> A Taoist hat, Confucian shoes, and a Buddhist
>   cassock,
> Mix and harmonize them together and the
>   three schools become one.

61. *"Say Nothing" and Nothing Said*

Yuima [a legendary Buddhist layman] asked Monju [a legendary Buddha], "What is the only way to enlightenment?" Monju said, "Those who have the same idea as I do will say nothing, preach nothing, show nothing, learn nothing about any method. Avoid all questions and answers. This is the only way." Those around also gave their views. Then Monju turned to Yuima and said, "Now that we have each had our say, what is your view?" Yuima was silent.

Later, Master Setchō commented, "What did Yuima say?" Then he added, "I've got it."

"Yuima was silent"—what's the gut meaning of that?

The pupil slaps his master's face once.

The view of Monju—what's it like?

The pupil solemnly recites, "Say nothing, preach nothing, show nothing, learn nothing about any method. This is the only way."

62. *Which Is Your Self?*

Master Ummon said, "Medicines cure diseases. The whole earth is medicine, but which is your self?"

"TURRNIP of Oari" [a town near Nagoya], the pupil slowly recites.
[In reference to the above the book comments, "It is taking the other by surprise and sending him flying."]
(Quote)
The fusu [name of a plant] of Menshū [name of a place] and the ginger of Kanshū [name of a place].
Or:
When you come once again, it is for no other reason than the misty rain of Ro Mountain and the tide of River Sekkō.

63. *Blind, Deaf, Dumb*

Master Gensha said, "Our elders always tell us to meet nature and benefit the living. But if suddenly there came the sick of the following three kinds, how would you treat them? There is the blind, who even if you pick up a hammer and wave it before him, sees nothing. Then there is the deaf, who, no matter how you tell him of the wonder of Buddhism, hears nothing. There is also the dumb, who, no matter how you teach him to speak, simply cannot do it. How will you deal with them? If you cannot deal with them, the teaching of Buddha has no effect on you."

Later a monk asked Master Ummon about this. Ummon said, "Make a salute." The monk saluted and rose. Ummon struck with his stick. The monk stepped back. Ummon said, "You are not blind." Then he called him to come near. The monk drew near and Ummon said, "You are not deaf." Ummon then said, "Do you understand by now?" The monk answered, "I do not." Ummon said, "You are not dumb." At that the monk was enlightened.

As against, "There is the blind, who, even if you pick up a hammer and wave it before him, sees nothing."

ANSWER

"It's unseen by the eyes, but it's a beautiful flower, isn't it?"
As against, "There is the deaf, who, no matter how you try to make him hear, hears nothing."

ANSWER

"The ears can't hear a thing, but the clock is going tick-tock, tick-tock."
As against, "There is the dumb, who, no matter how you teach him to speak, simply cannot do it."

ANSWER

"I won't say it with my mouth."
(Quote)

> Only in buildings in the capital or in the big
> cities can the color of tiles be seen,
> And in the temple of the goddess of mercy
> nothing but the sound of bells can be
> heard.

Or:

> Raising the curtain, I saw the snow on top of
> Peak Kōrō,
> And leaning on my pillow, I heard the peal
> of the bell in Iai Temple.

Or:

> Morning saw the clouds floating along so
> freely,
> And evening heard the murmuring sounds of
> running streams.

64. Sound

One day Master Kyōgen was weeding the grass. A piece of

brick hit the bamboo. It made a sound. At that moment, Kyōgen was enlightened. He recited the following: "One stroke and all I know is forgotten. No further learning is needed. I gather myself and give up the old way, untrapped by the stealthy occasion. Not a trace to be found anywhere. Sight and sound make me forget about manners. Those who know the way will say this is an excellent occasion."

ANSWER

The pupil stands up and pretends to clean up, throwing away rubbish. At the same time he utters, "Clunk!," acting out the point of a stone hitting bamboo.

65. *What Do You Understand by This?*

Master Gettan said to a monk, "Make a hundred carts. Take off both ends of each cart and get rid of the axle. What do you understand by this?"

ANSWER

The pupil pretends to push a cart from behind up a slope saying, "Creak, creak, rattle, rumble," in imitation of the sounds a cart makes.

66. *Not Keeping Silent, Not Using Words*

Master Hōen said, "On the road you meet a man who understands the way. You cannot keep silent and you should not use words. Tell me how you do it."

ANSWER

"In order to get to so-and-so from here, you go out the front gate, pass so-and-so and head in the direction of so-and-so." In this way the pupil, using the temple as the starting point, enumerates the course one takes in going to a place three or four miles away.

67. *Taking a Bath*

It is said that when the Bodhisattva called Baddabara was taking a bath, in a flash he attained great enlightenment.

Master Setchō said, "How do you monks understand this?"

The pupil takes the pose of taking a bath. Very quietly he rubs his arms saying, "Suu, suu," expressing the delicate sensation of touch.

68.   *Without Cold, Without Heat*

A monk asked Master Tōzan, "How can one escape from winter cold and summer heat?" Tōzan said, "Why do you not go to a place where there is neither cold nor heat?" The monk said, "What is the place without cold, without heat?" Tōzan said, "When it is cold, the cold freezes you. When it is hot, the heat burns you."

ANSWER
"Hot. Cold," the pupil says with force in his voice.
[In reference to the meaning of the above answer the book comments, "If you wholly become cold and heat, there is neither cold nor heat."]

69.   *What Do You Have in Mind?*

Master Nansen along with Master Kisū and Master Mayoku went together to pay their respects to Master Etchū. When they were halfway there, Nansen drew a circle on the ground and said, "I shall go if you can tell me what this means." Kisū sat in the middle of the circle. Mayoku played the woman and bowed. Nansen said, "If it is like this, I am not going." Kisū said, "What do you have in mind?"

MASTER
He draws a circle in front of the pupil, saying, "Well, what now?"

ANSWER
The pupil, saying, "Oh, this is a nice present!" gives the pose of one accepting.

70.   *Don't Fancy*

Whenever Master Mugō was asked a question, he would simply say, "Don't fancy!"

ANSWER

The pupil folds his arms and gravely says, "Don't fancy."

71. *Buddha's Master*

Master Hōen said, "Even Buddha and Miroku [a legendary bodhisattva] are his slaves. Tell me who he is."

ANSWER

The pupil enumerates such names as "Gonbē, Hachibē, Ohichi, Osan" [common Japanese names of men and women].

72. *Swallow a River?!*

The disciple Hōkoji visited Master Baso and asked, "Who is he that transcends existence?" Baso said, "When you have swallowed the waters of the west river in one gulp, I shall answer you." In an instant Hōkoji realized the answer and said the following: "People from all over come and meet together; each seeks to learn the way of non-doing. This is the place where Buddhas are born. I, having been chosen for holding the heart of nothingness, can now go back."

ANSWER

"I'll have a cup of tea," the pupil says, taking a cup of tea.

73. *Thought of the Moment*

"The boundless world is not even a pinpoint's distance from me. The happenings of ten generations past and present are never absent from the thought of the moment."
As against, *"The boundless world is not even a pinpoint's distance from me."*

ANSWER

"With a mountain, become one with the mountain; with a river, become one with the river; master and I are one body."
(*Quote*)
Mt. Tendai is the pillow, the footsteps on Mt. Nangaku.
As against, *"The happenings of ten generations past and present are never absent from the thought of the moment."*

"How hateful; how charming; how desirable; how disappointing."
(Quote)

> Though my golden bracelet on my arm has
> grown an inch too loose,
> Yet when meeting people I still tell them I am
> not in love.

Or:

> Only the lines of tears can be seen wetting
> her face.
> Heaven alone knows on whom her heart's
> hate is centered.

Popular Saying
A woman's single thought can pass through even rock, and if it so
desires can cut a golden chain.
Or:
Be it rock, be it gold, it pierces right through—the-single-minded-
ceaseless-beat-the-bell.

74. *Where Is My Rhino?*

One day Master Enkan ordered his attendant, "Fetch me the
fan with a rhino on it." The attendant said, "The fan is broken."
Enkan said, "Since the fan is broken, then give me back my rhino."
The attendant could not answer.

[The following are comments of later masters]:
Master Tōsu said, "I would do anything to bring it out for you,
only I am afraid that its head and horn will not be perfect."
Later, Master Setchō commented to this, "I want imperfect head
and horn."

Master Sekisō said, "If I give it to Your Reverend, then it will
be no more." Setchō commented to this, "But the rhino is still
there."

Master Shifuku drew a circle and wrote the word "rhino" in
the center. Setchō commented to this, "Why didn't you bring
it out before?"

Master Hofuku said, "As Your Reverend is advanced in age,
I think it is better for you to ask somebody else to do it." Setchō
commented to this, "It is a pity that all efforts are in vain."
As against, "Give me back my rhino."

"Such a thing! I cracked it in half and threw it out on the rubbish pile."

As against, "*I want imperfect head and horn.*"

"I bought a piece of flower-patterned silk for sixty-five cents."

As against, "*Why didn't you bring it out before?*"

"It was here just a little while ago—now it's gone somewhere."
So saying, the pupil looks all around.

As against, "*All efforts are in vain.*"

The pupil, in a loud voice, weeps.
(Quote)

> Time is against me and my horse refuses to
> budge.
> What can I do now that my horse refuses to
> budge?
> Oh yu! Oh yu! What can I do?

75. Ōbaku's Stick

When Master Rinzai was still practicing under Master Ōbaku he performed his duties single-mindedly. The head monk praised him and said, "Though he is young, he is different from the rest." He asked Rinzai, "How long have you been here?" Rinzai said, "Three years." The head monk said, "Have you already met Master Ōbaku and asked him questions?" Rinzai said, "No, not yet. I do not know what to ask." The head monk suggested, "Why don't you go and ask Master Ōbaku what the gist of the teaching of Buddha is?" So Rinzai went and asked. However, before Rinzai could finish his question, Ōbaku hit him. Rinzai returned and the head monk asked him, "How was the inquiry?" Rinzai said, "Master Ōbaku hit me before I could finish my question. I don't understand why." The head monk said, "Just go and ask the master again." Rinzai went to ask Ōbaku and was beaten again. In this way he asked three times and was beaten three times. Rinzai went and said to the head monk, "I am fortunate in meeting you, who were kind enough to send me to inquire. I had asked Master Ōbaku three times but was beaten three times. I have only myself to blame for lacking the qualification to understand his deep meaning. I am leaving this day."

The head monk said, "If you leave you have to bid farewell to Master Ōbaku." Rinzai bowed and left. But before Rinzai got there, the head monk went to Ōbaku and said, "The man who asked you questions is young, but he has discipline. Please be available and see him. We should shape him into a big tree so that it can thereafter give shade to people all over the world." So when Rinzai came to bid farewell to Ōbaku, Ōbaku said, "You may not go anywhere else but to the place of Master Daigu. He will certainly explain things to you."

When Rinzai arrived at Daigu's place, Daigu asked, "Where do you come from?" Rinzai said, "I come from Master Ōbaku's place." Daigu said, "What did Ōbaku say?" Rinzai said, "I asked him three times about the gist of the teaching of Buddha and was beaten three times. I don't know if I have done anything wrong."

Daigu said, "Ōbaku was indeed kindhearted to you in sending you here." Upon hearing this Rinzai was enlightened. He then said, "Ōbaku's Buddhism is really nothing serious." Daigu caught hold of him and said, "You bed-wetting baby! Just now you asked if you were wrong and then you say Ōbaku's Buddhism is nothing serious. What is your reason? Say it quick! Say it quick!" Rinzai hit Daigu in the ribs thrice with his fist. Daigu pushed him away and said, "Your master is Ōbaku. It is none of my business."

Rinzai then left Daigu and returned to Ōbaku. When Ōbaku saw him he said, "What end can there be to this man's coming and going?" Rinzai bowed and said, "Just because your kindness urged me, I went and came back." Ōbaku said, "Where have you been?" Rinzai said, "Yesterday, in compliance with your order, I went to see Master Daigu." Ōbaku said, "What did Daigu say?" Rinzai then repeated the above story. Ōbaku said, "How can I get this man [Daigu] here so that I can give him a sound beating?" Rinzai said, "Why talk of waiting till he is here? You can have it now!" Having said that, he slapped Ōbaku. Ōbaku said, "This crazy man has come here to pluck the tiger's beard." Rinzai shouted at him. Ōbaku said to his attendants, "Take this crazy man to the hall."

Later Master Isan told this story to Master Kyōzan and asked, "At that time did Rinzai get the help of Daigu or the help of Ōbaku?" Kyōzan said, "He knows not only how to ride a tiger's head but also knows how to hold onto the tiger's tail."

"Have the taste of sixty strokes from Ōbaku's stick!"
(Quote)
> With a golden cup I come to you.
> Decline me not and fill it to the brim with
>   wine.

76. *The Three Sentences of Master Rinzai*

[Continuation of koan 19]

Master Rinzai also said, "Each sentence must hold three subtle gates; each gate must hold the three seals (or elements). To each of these there is its variation and its working. How do you understand this?" With that he stepped down from his seat.

ANSWER

"This one fan—at times it makes a paperweight, at times it holds things atop of it, at times it blows in the wind."

77. *On an Isolated Peak; At the Crossroads*

Master Rinzai said, "There is a man on top of an isolated peak not removed from the world. There is a man at the crossroads looking neither forward nor backward. Which one is in front? Which one is in back? Do not be like Yuima [who meditated in an isolated place], and do not be like Fudaishi [mixing with people in worldly affairs]. Take care of yourselves."
As against, "A man on top of an isolated peak not removed from the world."

ANSWER

"Even to Buddha or Amida I would not show my face."
As against, "A man at the crossroads looking neither forward nor backward."

ANSWER

"With an old man, old-man-like; with a child, childlike; with each as each is."

OR

(According to another school)

As against both, "A man on top of an isolated peak" and "a man at the crossroads."

ANSWER

"The old man goes to the mountain to gather firewood, the old woman to the river to wash clothes."

78. *Why Can't the Tail Go Through?*

Master Hōen said, "It is like a cow passing through a window frame. The head, the horns, the four legs have all gone through; why can't the tail go through?"

MASTER

This cow—when was it born?

ANSWER

"It was born before this world began."

MASTER

This cow—what's its form?

ANSWER

"The carpenter—tap, tap [with a hammer]; the plasterer—beto, beto [with a trowel]."
(*Quote*)
>Everything in the southern and northern
>>villages is soaked in rain,
>The newly married woman is serving her
>>mother-in-law food,
>While her father-in-law is feeding the son.

MASTER

Is it a female cow? A male cow?

ANSWER

"It's a huge-balls-hanging-down male cow."

MASTER

What's its color?

ANSWER

"The cloak is iron-blue, the kimono is gray, the underwear is white."

MASTER

How does it feed?

ANSWER

"For breakfast, wheat porridge; for lunch, the regular meal; for dinner, rice and vegetable porridge."

MASTER

Where is the cow?

ANSWER

(Quote)

> I sit by myself in the deep and quiet
> bamboo forest,
> Playing music and howling out loud.

MASTER

Where is its birthplace?

ANSWER

(Quote)
An octagonal millstone spinning in midair.

MASTER

Say the working of the cow.

ANSWER

"I waved up my horns and ran head-on into you."

MASTER

"Why can't the tail go through?"

ANSWER

The pupil holds the master by the nose, slaps his master's rear, saying, "Even if I say giddy-up, he doesn't budge an inch." *(Quote)*

> Where is the person with whom we came
> together to appreciate the moon?
> The scenery looks very much the same as
> that of last year.

OR
(According to another school)
As against, "A cow passing through a window frame."

ANSWER

The pupil gets on all fours and like a cow crawls around the room.

MASTER

What's the form of the cow?

ANSWER

Getting up, the pupil moves forward and backward, left and right.

MASTER

What's the height of the cow?

ANSWER

"So-and-so feet, so-and-so inches" [the pupil gives his own height].

MASTER

Is it a male cow? A female cow?

ANSWER

Sticking his nose in front of his master, the pupil says, "Moo——."

79. *What Is Jōshū?*

A monk asked Master Jōshū, "What is Jōshū?" Jōshū said, "The east gate, the west gate, the south gate, the north gate."

ANSWER

"Even Buddha or Amida will never see the face—what makes a fellow like you think you will?"

80. *A Shell Holding Moonlight*

A monk asked Master Chimon, "What is the essence of the supreme wisdom?" Chimon said, "A shell holding moonlight." The monk asked, "What is the working of the supreme wisdom?" Chimon said, "To bear the child of the rabbit [in the moon]." *As against, "The essence of the supreme wisdom."*

ANSWER

The pupil folds his arms.
As against, "The working of the supreme wisdom."

ANSWER
The pupil, his arms still folded, bends forward.

81. *It Is Your Hearts That Move*

Master Enō saw a banner fluttering in the wind. Two monks were arguing about it. One monk said, "It is the banner that moves." The other said, "It is the wind that moves." They argued back and forth without ever reaching the core of the matter. Enō said, "It is not the banner that moves. It is not the wind that moves. It is your hearts that move." The monks were stunned.

ANSWER
The pupil stands up, and using the sleeve of his cloak, flutters it like a banner in the wind.

82. *The Immovable Cloak*

[Enō's master decided that Enō would take his place as the next master, and as proof of the authority he gave him his cloak and bowl. The other monks, displeased with this, chased after Enō. Near Mt. Daiyūrei they caught up with Enō.]

The monk called Myō was among those chasing Enō. Enō, upon seeing Myō, threw his cloak and bowl on the rock and said, "This cloak represents faith; if it is in your power to lift it, I shall let you have it." Myō tried to lift it but it was as immovable as a mountain. Bewildered and scared, Myō said, "I came here to look for the Way. I did not come for the cloak. Master, I beg you to teach me."

ANSWER
The pupil solemnly recites, "It represents faith."

83. *What the Old Woman Meant*

A monk asked an old woman, "Which is the road to Mt. Tai?" The old woman said, "Go straight ahead." The monk had just taken a few steps when the old woman remarked, "This one, too, is no different from the others." Later, a monk reported this to Master Jōshū who said, "Let me ask this old woman for you." He went the next day and asked the old woman the same question.

The old woman answered as before. Jōshū then returned and told the people, "I have got for you what the old woman meant."

ANSWER

"The strong one beneath the porch."
(Quote)

> I only wish my emperor would notice me.
> To be seen, I would climb the tall building
>   several times, my eyebrows painted.

OR

(According to another school)

ANSWER

"Go straight ahead."
(Quote)

> The raising of a great god's hand is nothing
>   serious,
> But it is enough to split the thousand hills
>   of the mountain range of Ka.

OR

(According to another school)

ANSWER

Walking around in the room, the pupil acts out the monk's going and Jōshū's going.

OR

(With certain masters)

ANSWER

"A wrinkled-faced old woman!"

84. *The Tortoise Is a Turtle*

A monk asked Master Kōrinon, "What is the lamp in the room?" Kōrinon said, "Three men testify that the tortoise is a turtle."

ANSWER

The pupil rubs his head around, saying, "All catch hold of this fellow, saying, 'It's so-and-so, it's so-and-so.'"

OR

(According to another school)

ANSWER

The pupil rubs the straw mat, saying, "It feels like Bingo [a product of the Bingo District] and yet it doesn't feel like Bingo." *(Quote)*

> Please don't show that you dislike the stains
>   on the lapels;
> I, shedding tears, had sewn it in front of the
>   lamp.

85. *Cut!*

Master Gantō asked a monk, "Where do you come from?" The monk said, "From the western capital." Gantō said, "After Kōsō [a leader of a rebellion] was gone, can you still get a sword?" The monk said, "Yes, I can." Gantō then stretched out his neck and said, "Cut!" The monk said, "The master's head has fallen." Gantō laughed out loud.

The monk later went to Master Seppō. Seppō asked, "Where do you come from?" The monk said, "From Master Gantō." Seppō said, "What had Gantō said?" The monk told the above story. Seppō gave him thirty strokes and drove him away.

MASTER

"Gantō stretched out his neck and said, 'Cut!'" Take the place of the monk and say.

ANSWER

The pupil takes a leap back and, as if in dread, says, "Oh, that's danger! That's danger!"

MASTER

"Can you still get a sword?" Take the place of the monk and say.

ANSWER

The pupil, pointing his finger in front of him, says, "Just now it was there. It's gone somewhere."

OR
(According to another school)
As against, "Can you still get a sword?"
ANSWER
"Such a piece of junk! I threw it out."

86. *When the Sail Is Hoisted*

A monk asked Master Gantō, "How is it when the old sail is not yet hoisted?" Gantō said, "A small fish swallows a big fish." The monk said, "What becomes of it after the sail is hoisted?" Gantō said, "The donkey eats grass in the backyard."

Later Master Kidō asked Master Nanpo, "How is it when the old sail is not yet hoisted?" Nanpo said, "Mt. Shumi in the eyes of an insect." Kidō said, "What becomes of it after the sail is hoisted?" Nanpo said, "The yellow river flows northward."

As against, "How is it when the old sail is not yet hoisted?"

ANSWER

The pupil spreads both sleeves of his kimono and is silent.

As against, "What becomes of it after the sail is hoisted?"

ANSWER

"Today is the day of shaving the head, cleaning the temple in and out. When that's done, take a bath."

87. *Why Don't People In Know about Out?*

Master Kempō said, "The true self has three kinds of diseases and two kinds of light. You have to go through them before you are enlightened." Master Ummon stepped out and said, "Why don't people in the hermitage know anything about the outside of the hermitage?" Kempō laughed out loud. Ummon said, "I still have doubt." Kempō asked, "What are your thoughts?" Ummon said, "I need Your Reverend to tell me." Kempō said, "One has to be like that, observant and meticulous, before one is enlightened." Ummon said, "Yes, yes."

As against, "The true self has three kinds of diseases and two kinds of light. You have to go through them before you are enlightened."

ANSWER

The pupil gives a scornful laugh, saying, "Hm!"

(Quote)

> To grab a deer from the mouth of a fierce
> tiger,
> To take a rabbit from under the claws of a
> hungry eagle.

MASTER

Attach a quote that gives the gut meaning of Kempō.

(Quote)

> On the surface you see peach blossoms
>> among bamboo trees,
> But deep inside there are briars reaching for
>> the sky.

As against, "Why don't people in the hermitage know anything about the outside of the hermitage?"

ANSWER

The pupil opens the door slightly, saying, "What a nice garden! Over here, stepping stones; over there, a lantern; beyond is the toilet, isn't it? Before it stinks, let's close the door." With that, he slams the door shut.

(Quote)

Shun [a wise and virtuous king] had not the land to hold even a drill.

U [a wise and virtuous king] had no more than ten families to gather around him.

MASTER

This koan is on the "holy body" [of truth]. Attach to it a quote on the "holy body."

ANSWER

(Quote)

> We get our body, hair, and skin from our
>> parents;
> We dare not destroy them; that is the basic
>> requirement of filial piety.

OR
(According to another school)
MASTER

"Three kinds of diseases"—what's it mean?

ANSWER

"Greed, anger, stupidity."

MASTER

"Two kinds of light"—what's it mean?

ANSWER

"With the two lights of serene mind [samadhi] and wisdom, the three diseases of hatred, covetousness, and attachment are brought to salvation."

As against, "Why don't people in the hermitage know anything about the outside of the hermitage?"

ANSWER

The pupil opens the door and acts surprised at seeing the daybreak. (Quote)

> Without going beyond the garden gate,
> I can see all the rivers and mountains in their
> thousands.

Or:

> Together with the fall of night there comes
> the sound of wind and rain;
> Yet can you tell how many flowers have
> fallen from their trees?

OR

(According to another school)

ANSWER

As against, "the three kinds of diseases," the pupil enumerates three diseases [such as ulcers, lumbago]. As against, "the two kinds of light," he pulls at both eyes.

88. Where Is the Old Man Going?

Master Seppō was in charge of meals under Master Tokusan. One day the meal was late. Tokusan, carrying his bowl, came down to the dining hall. Seppō said, "The bell has not yet rung, neither has the drum been struck. Where is the old man going carrying his bowl?" Tokusan was silent, He bowed his head and returned to his room. Seppō told this to Master Gantō. Gantō said, "Tokusan does not know the last sentence" [the ultimate truth]. When Tokusan heard of this, he ordered his attendant to summon Gantō to his room. He said to Gantō, "You will not let me go at that, will you?" Gantō in a whisper revealed his intention. The next day when Tokusan came to the hall to give a lecture, he behaved in an unusual way. Gantō clapped his hands, laughed, and said, "I am glad that the old man knows the last sentence. From now on, people the world over will not know how to deal with him. However, he has only three years to live." After three years, Tokusan died.

As against, "Tokusan returned to his room."

ANSWER

The pupil stands up and gives the pretense of leaving.
(Quote)

> It has just gone away with the fragrant grasses,
> Yet returns again, chasing after the falling
> flowers.

MASTER

Gantō said, "Tokusan does not know the last sentence"—instead of Seppō, you answer Gantō.

ANSWER

"You talk big, but you yourself don't know, do you?"
Or:
"You stupid monk! You think there's such a thing as the last sentence?!"
(Quote)
A single hair pulling a weight of a thousand jun.
As against, "Gantō in a whisper revealed his intention."

ANSWER

"There's something there. There's something there."
(Quote)
The father shelters for the son and the son shelters for the father.
As against, "He has only three years to live."

ANSWER

"Can you foresee everything? That's pretty terrific what you know."

MASTER

What would happen if he didn't die?

ANSWER

"No matter what you say, life may end tonight."

MASTER

"The last sentence and the first sentence are not the same sentence"—how about that?

ANSWER

"You ever blab about last sentence, first sentence and I'll beat you to death!"

89. Yet I Should Not Be Rash

After Master Tokusan arrived at the place of Master Isan he, still in his traveling clothes, walked around the hall from east to west, west to east, looking around right in front of Isan and said, "Mu. Mu" ["Nothing. Nothing"]. Then he walked away. [Master Setchō commented, "He has got it!"] But when Tokusan reached the front door he said, "Yet I should not be rash." Thus with proper dignity and ceremony he went in again to meet Isan. Isan was sitting. Tokusan said, "Master!" Isan reached for his stick and Tokusan shouted ["Katsu!"]. With a sweep of his long sleeves, Tokusan went out. [Setchō commented, "He has got it!"] Tokusan, with his back to the lecture hall, put on his sandals and left. When night came Isan asked the head monk, "Where is the one who newly arrived?" The head monk said, "He has long before turned his back to the hall, put on his sandals, and walked out!" Isan said, "Later this fellow will go to the peak of Mt. Ko, build himself a hermitage of grass, and will set to scolding Buddha and our masters." [Setchō commented, "To add frost on top of snow."]

As against, "He has got it!" [Setchō's first comment].
ANSWER
The pupil, raising his voice says, "He has got it!"
(Quote)
Gall is bitter to the root.

As against, "He has got it!" [Setchō's second comment].
ANSWER
The pupil, raising his voice, says, "He has got it!"
(Quote)
Melon is sweet clear through.

As against, "To add frost on top of snow."
ANSWER
"It is the laughter of a monkey's bottom."
(Quote)
The prisoner tells everything honestly.

90. Every Day Is a Good Day

Master Ummon said, "About the fifteen days before [i.e., before enlightenment] I do not ask you. Now that fifteen days have passed, come, say something." Nobody answered. Ummon himself said, "Every day is a good day."

"The fifteen days before," one sentence—say it.

"The grocer." (Or: "How about some vegetables?")

"The fifteen days after," one sentence—say it.

"The bean curd man." (Or: "How about some bean curd?")

"The just fifteenth day," one sentence—say it.

"Yes, today is a fine day, isn't it?"
As against, "Every day is a good day."
"Yesterday Hachibē from near the front gate got hurt. This morning again, I heard that Ohachi is sick. Just now a cable from the country arrived saying that a relative has died."
(Quote)

When flowers bloom there is lots of rain and
wind.
In life there are enough partings.
Popular Saying
With no wife, no parents, no child, not even a house—with all this, wouldn't it be better to die?

91. *Without Caring, Go Straight*

The head of the hermitage, Master Renge, picked up his stick and said, "Why didn't the people before us like to stay here?" Nobody answered. Then he answered the question himself, saying, "Because they didn't rely upon the teaching of a superior master." Then he said, "But how is it finally?" Again he answered himself, saying, "To carry the stick on your shoulders and without caring for others, go straight into the thousand hills" [i.e., monastery].
As against, "Strike the ground with the stick once."

[The one stroke of the stick symbolizes the realization of the answer to which the people could not reach.]

"Goton!" [the sound of a stick striking the ground]. Here the master comments, "The whole universe is just the one 'goton!' It resounds from the highest sphere of heaven down through the bottom of the deepest layer."

As against, "Because they didn't rely upon the teaching of a superior master."

"By dropping your bottom steadfast into the evenness of the plane of enlightenment you cannot save the people."

As against, "To carry the stick on your shoulders and without caring for others, go straight into the thousand hills."

"To leap into the rabble of this world and lead the masses to salvation."

Or:

"To meet up with favorable circumstances without halting there; to meet up with adversity without halting there. Such a fellow is an all right Zen priest."

92. Seven

A monk asked Master Ummon, "What is the true self?" Ummon said, "It does not hold six things."

ANSWER

The pupil, moving his body a bit, recites in a stern voice, "One, two, three, four, five, six, seven."

MASTER

Say it in reference to the "other."

ANSWER

"The two next-door neighbors and the three across. The nandin tree is three feet high and the wall is five feet high."

93. I Have a Lot of Things to Do

Master Sanshō asked Master Seppō, "I wonder what the small fish that can pass through a small net eat." Seppō said, "I shall tell you if you bring me a net." Sanshō said, "Does any of the thousand and five hundred wise [of the past] understand what I have said?" Seppō said, "I have a lot of things to do."

"If you're hungry, have some wheat porridge; if you're thirsty, drink some tea."
As against, "I have a lot of things to do."
ANSWER
"You know today I'm busy so I've got no time to mess around with you."

94. *Rice in a Bowl, Water in a Bucket*

A monk asked Master Ummon, "What is all-the-wonders-hidden-in-a-small-dust-particle?" Ummon said, "Rice in a bowl, water in a bucket."

ANSWER
"The bean paste barrel is filled with bean paste to the top; in the pot, boiling potatoes are going 'gutsu, gutsu.'"

95. *I Have a Headache Today*

A monk asked Master Baso, "Without using the four sentences [concerning the division of existence], without resorting to the hundred negatives [to describe the nature of nirvana], tell me directly the meaning of Zen." Baso said, "I am tired today, I cannot tell you anything. Go and ask Master Chizō." The monk asked Chizō, who said, "Why don't you ask Baso?" The monk said, "But the master told me to ask you." Chizō said, "I have a headache today. I cannot tell you anything. Go and ask Master Ekai." The monk asked Ekai, who said, "But I do not understand this far." The monk told this to Baso. Baso said, "Chizō's head is white. Ekai's head is black."

MASTER
"Chizō's head is white. Ekai's head is black"—what's it mean?

ANSWER
"Should the parent be a shit dropper, then the offspring is a bed wetter."

(Quote)
The king behaves like a king, while his courtiers behave like courtiers.
Or:
The father shelters for the son, the son shelters for the father.

96. *"All Over"; "Throughout"*

Master Ungan asked Master Dōgo, "What are the many eyes and hands of Daihi Buddha [Kannon Buddha, representing compassion] for?" Dōgo said, "It is like people twisting their hands back to grope for their pillows in the middle of the night." Ungan said, "I've got it!" Dōgo said, "What do you understand?" Ungan said, "It means that the body is eyes and hands all over." Dōgo said, "You got only eighty percent right." Ungan said, "How would you say it then?" Dōgo said, "The body is eyes and hands throughout."

MASTER

"It is like people twisting their hands back to grope for their pillows in the middle of the night"—what's it mean?

ANSWER

The pupil rubs his hands together, saying, "Shall I pound your back for you; shall I rub your legs?"
As against, "All over the body and throughout the body."

ANSWER

"It's the same thing, but it may be called 'sensu' and it may be called 'ōgi'" [Japanese synonyms for "fan"].

97. *Why Is That Thing Not You?*

The scripture of Ryōgon says, "When I do not see, why cannot I see what I do not see? If you can see what you do not see, naturally that is not something which cannot be seen. If I cannot see what I do not see, that thing naturally is not an object." Why is that thing not you?
As against, "That thing is naturally not an object. Why is that thing not you?"

ANSWER

Looking left and right, the pupil says, "That thing is naturally not an object. Why is that thing not you?"
(Quote)

> There was dazzling light when Zōmō arrived,
> And there were sky-high waves wherever
> Rirō went.

98. *Go and Have Some Tea*

Master Chōkei said, "It is not good to say Buddha has two languages [one for the initiated, one for the laymen]. I will not say Buddha has no language, only that he does not have two languages." Master Hofuku said, "What is the language of Buddha?" Chōkei said, "How do the deaf hear?" Hofuku said, "[You missed!] Say it the other way." Chōkei asked, "What is the language of Buddha?" Hofuku said, "Go and have some tea."

ANSWER

"Only he does not have two languages."
Popular Saying
Looking from the top of a high mountain down to the bottom of the valley, the melon and eggplant are blossoming.
(Quote)

> There were five or six adults, six or seven
> children.
> We bathed in the river, sang to the dance music,
> played when people prayed for rain,
> And then went home reciting poems.

99. *Made a Fool Of*

The Kongōkyō [the Diamond Sutra] says, "When a person is made a fool of by others, the sins of his former lives are the cause. But at this point of falling into adversity, by being made a fool of, the sins of his former lives are erased."

ANSWER

The pupil curses, "Stinking fool of an asshole!"
Or:
"This stupid bald head of a monk—get out! get out!"

(Quote)
> When two persons are quarreling, meddle in.
> When two persons are spitting at each other,
> splash water over them.

100. *"Wrong!"*

When Master Tenpyō was a traveling monk, he visited Master Saiin. Tenpyō always used to say, "Never say you understand the teaching of Buddha. If you look for anyone who understands this, you will not find him." One day Saiin saw Tenpyō from afar and called out, "Tenpyō!" Tenpyō looked up and Saiin said, "Wrong!" Tenpyō moved two or three steps and again Saiin said, "Wrong!" When Tenpyō drew near Saiin said, "The two 'wrongs' just now, are they meant for you or for me?" Tenpyō said, "It is Tenpyō that is wrong." Saiin said, "Wrong!" Tenpyō was silent. Saiin said, "Stay here for the summer so that I may discuss with you the two 'wrongs.'" But Tenpyō left right away.

Later when Tenpyō became a permanent temple resident, he told the people, "When I was a traveling monk I was carried by the wind of destiny to the place of Master Saiin. He said 'wrong' twice and asked me to stay for the summer in order to discuss it with me. At that time I did not know exactly where I was wrong, but as soon as I set foot for the south, I knew I had made a mistake."

Later, Master Setchō commented on the above, "Tenpyō, thinking about what happened at Saiin's place, felt regret at being wrong. That is wrong."

MASTER
In what way is the mistake of Setchō similar to that of Tenpyō?

ANSWER
"Setchō's mistake is like dung, Tenpyō's mistake is like bean paste."

101. *Tread on the Head of Buddha*

Emperor Shukusō asked his teacher, Master Etchū, "What is Buddha?" Etchū said, "Tread on the head of Buddha." The emperor said, "I do not understand." Etchū said, "Do not think of yourself as pure, true self."

As against, "Tread on the head of Buddha."

ANSWER

"I am Buddha."
As against, "Do not think of yourself as pure, true self."

ANSWER

"Though the body is covered with all sorts of beautiful clothing, the bowls are filled with piss and shit. Though ruler of heaven and earth, it's the same as Gonbē or Hachibē" [common names of the lower class].

MASTER

Now you, as a monk, how do you say it?

ANSWER

"Gonbē, Hachibē, anyone holds the nature of Buddha."

102. *The Body Emits Autumn Wind*

A monk asked Master Ummon, "What happens when trees wither and leaves fall down?" Ummon said, "The body emits autumn wind."

MASTER

(Quote)
Don't you understand what it is to waste away languishing in love, yearning? This love song, where did it come from?

ANSWER

"The garden of the ancestors has become bleak and desolate. Hmm, how can we get it back to its former state?" the pupil says, heaving a deep sigh with an air of lamentation.

MASTER

What does it finally come to?

ANSWER

"Now [time], here [space] are interwoven."

103. *The Mind as It Is*

Master Daibai asked Master Baso, "What is Buddha?"
Baso answered, "The mind as it is, is Buddha."

The pupil, raising his eyes in a glare, says, "Hateful!"
Or:
"Hot! Cold!"
(Quote)
The angry Nata [a mythical figure] struck at the emperor's bell.
Or:

> When it is cold, the cold freezes you.
> When it is hot, the heat burns you.

Popular Saying
Even the thought of an ant can reach the sky.

104. *No Mind, No Buddha*

A monk asked Master Baso, "What is Buddha?" Baso said, "It is no mind, it is no Buddha."

ANSWER

"At the railroad crossing a frog is squashed by a train."

105. *One*

> One hair swallows the big sea.
> One seed holds Mt. Shumi.

ANSWER

"One cup of tea, one piece of rice cracker."

106. *Take Care!*

Master Kanzan said, "Take care! Take care! Past, present, or future, you may at any time fall to hell."

ANSWER

The pupil, clapping his hands in rhythm, says, "From here to Edo [Tokyo] it's three hundred miles. Such a trip, is it possible to take it naked?"
(Quote)

> In the morning, I go out of Fuyōki. At night,
>   I stop at Fuyōki.
> Two or three nights I have stopped at Fuyōki.
> I have never really left Fuyōki at all.

What's your present karma?

The pupil, taking the pose of a beggar, says, "If you have any leftover food, I'd be grateful if you'd give it to me."
Popular Saying
Last night, where did I sleep? Tonight, I'm here. Tomorrow, I'll sleep in the rice field with the footpath as my pillow.

OR
(According to another school)
ANSWER
"From the age of sixteen or seventeen, wearing a monk's cassock, handbox hanging from my neck, I left home and went to Oshū in the east, Kyūshū in the west, Shikoku, Saigoku, Chichibu, Bandō [districts in Japan]; not leaving out anywhere, I traveled all over Japan making the rounds of pilgrimage."
Popular Saying
Hey you, going here, going there, traveling monk! From here to Edo it's three hundred miles. Such a trip, is it possible to take it barefooted?

OR
(According to another school)
ANSWER
The pupil, clapping his hands in rhythm and walking around the room, from time to time recites, "Take care! Take care! Past, present, or future, you may at any time fall to hell."

107. *What Will You Do after Three or Four Shouts?*

Master Bokushū asked a monk, "Where have you been recently?" The monk shouted ["Katsu!"]. Bokushū said, "I am shouted at once by you." The monk shouted again. Bokushū said, "What will you do after three or four shouts?" The monk was speechless. Bokushū then hit him and said, "You empty-headed fool!"

ANSWER
At shouting, "Katsu!" the pupil hits the floor with his hand. [In reference to the above answer the book comments, "The answer shows the simultaneous working of the stick and the shout."]

108. Non-Attachment

What is real insight? Master Rinzai said, "No matter whether you are a commoner or a saint, or in the state of attachment or enlightenment; in whatever realm of existence, everywhere you can see the formation, the existence, the corruption, and the passing into nothingness of the world. Buddha came into this world to teach. He entered into nirvana but we cannot see his coming and going. It is impossible to investigate into his life and death. If you realize this, then you enter the realm of nothingness; you may roam every corner of its territories. There you see that every existence is no real existence at all. All is but nothingness. You come to realize that you who are now listening to the truth of non-attachment are the source of all Buddhas. Therefore a Buddha is actually born from non-attachment. If you can understand non-attachment, then all the Buddhas are nothing—such understanding is real insight."

ANSWER

"To pass through the forest of thorns without setting the foot down on one's own ground—that is my view."
(Quote)

> On a night when cold frost falls, the moon as
> it is glides into the valley in front.

MASTER

Finally, what is it like?

ANSWER

"On 'u' ['being'], on 'mu' ['nothing']—to halt not the foot."

109. Calamity! Calamity!

When Master Rinzai went up to the hall to give a lecture a monk asked him, "What if under the threat of a blade?" Rinzai said, "Calamity! Calamity!"

ANSWER

The pupil takes three to four steps; then abruptly he makes himself fall as one who dies, head cut off.

Or:

"Oh! Danger! Danger!" the pupil says, as if in fear.
(Quote)

> When waves are three stories high and fishes
>   change into dragons,
> The simpleton is still measuring the water of
>   the country pond with a bucket.

Or:

> Because a piece of white cloud lay across the
>   entrance to the valley,
> Many homeward-bound birds lost their way
>   to their nests.

110. *Use the Air as Paper*

Master Hōen said, "If one uses the air as paper, the sea as an inkstand, Mt. Shumi as a brush, can he write the words: 'The meaning of our founder coming from the west?' If any of you can, I shall give you the seat and bow to you in due ceremony."

ANSWER

"The wily old fox!" says the pupil.
(Quote)

> I let my hands go beyond the broad
>   firmament.
> People of the time are all unaware of it.

Or:

The pupil with his finger writes in the air in big letters: "The meaning of our founder coming from the west."

OR

(According to another school)

ANSWER

The pupil, in pretense, rubs the ink stick, spreads out paper, takes a brush, and on the floor writes a large numeral "one."

111. *What Is Your Feeling at This Moment?*

There was an old woman who looked after a hermit. For twenty years she always had a sixteen-year-old girl bring him rice and wait on him. One day she ordered the girl to hug the man and ask, "What is your feeling at this moment?" The hermit said,

"The old tree leaning against the cold cliff has no warmth in the winter months." The girl went back and reported this to the old woman. The woman said, "For twenty years of support I get only a good-for-nothing fellow." So she drove the man out and had the hermitage burnt down.

As against, "What is your feeling at this moment?"
ANSWER

"Good-for-nothing tramp! When the old woman says 'Jump!' she jumps. What a mess!" So saying, the pupil pushes the master away.

(Quote)

> When light and darkness overlap each other,
> Who can see me emerging beyond the sky?

Or:

"Ah! That's a beautiful kimono you're wearing today! Is it muslin? Is it printed silk? Who made it for you? Did your mother make it for you?"

As against, "Had the hermitage burnt down."

(Quote)

The crocodiles are dead, the people are appeased.

112. *Of a Different Color*

A monk asked Master Sōzan, "The snow covers a thousand hills, but why is only the one peak not white?" Sōzan said, "You should know the absurdity of absurdities." The monk asked, "What is the absurdity of absurdities?" Sōzan said, "Being of a different color from the rest of the hills."

ANSWER

The pupil, stroking his head around, says, "Ah, my hair too has lately been growing white."

(Quote)

Once I had great ambitions, but dilly-dally, I have reached the age of white hair.

OR
(According to another school)
ANSWER

The pupil, as if standing in the midst of falling snow, pretends to shake the snowflakes off his hair.

Finally, what's the gut meaning?

ANSWER

The pupil, pretending he can't stand the cold, brings his frozen hand to his mouth, blowing on it to warm it up.
(Quote)
>   Try to shake the snow off the branches,
>   You are sure to find flowers of the night.

Popular Saying
In the top of the pine tree, the-monkey-jumped-at-one-branch looks especially green.

113. *Beard*

Master Wakuan said, "Why doesn't Bodhidharma have a beard?"

ANSWER

The pupil reciting, "Why doesn't Bodhidharma have a beard?" pretends to stroke his beard.
(Quote)
Sōsō and Kanu [two generals] bear golden hair.
Or:
"I'm afraid that the razor blade is not sharp."

OR
(According to another school)
ANSWER

The pupil, stroking his chin, says, "At the last shaving day I had my beard shaved, but here it's already grown back."
Or:
[With certain masters] "It was getting on my nerves so I shaved it off." So saying, the pupil strokes his chin.
(Quote)
>   The wild fire cannot burn it out completely.
>   With the blowing of the spring wind they
>   come to life once more.

Or:
Weeds cannot be hoed up entirely.

114. *It Is Here*

A monk asked Master Kenpō, "I wonder, where is the road to Buddha [enlightenment]?" Kenpō took up his stick, drew a line in the air, and said, "It is here."

Later, the monk asked Master Ummon for his view. Ummon took up his fan and said, "This fan jumps up to the thirty-third heaven, hitting the nostril of Buddha. Give the carp of the eastern sea a stroke of the stick and rain will come down in torrents." *As against, "I wonder, where is the road to Buddha?"*

ANSWER

The pupil slaps his master once.

MASTER

"Buddha"—what's it mean?

ANSWER

Surveying his surroundings, the pupil says, "The realm of Buddha."

115. *Is There? Is There?*

Master Jōshū went to a hermitage and asked its master, "Is there? Is there?" The master raised his fist. Jōshū said, "This shallow water is no place to anchor my boat." He went away. He went to another hermitage and asked the master, "Is there? Is there?" This master also raised his fist. Jōshū said, "It can give, it can grab, it can kill, yet can make alive." He bowed.

As against, "It can give, it can grab, it can kill, yet can make alive."

ANSWER

The pupil recites, "It can give, it can grab, it can kill, yet can make alive," simultaneously raising up his fist.

(Quote)

> In places south of the Yellow River there is
> the small orange,
> In places north of the river there is the
> trifoliate orange.

Or:

> The plum blossoms in the cold clearly
> demonstrated the meaning of [the
> founder] coming from the west.

> One petal flies toward the west while
> > another flies toward the east.

Or:

> The same tree bathed by the spring wind has
> > two different states:
> The southern branches facing warmth,
> > the northern ones facing cold.

Popular Saying
When the place is changed, the thing changes—in Naniwa [Osaka] it is reed; in Ise it is rush.
Or:
Doing-this-doing-that-going-through-life-man—what an empty dream. Doesn't he know that it's the same as the reed of Naniwa?

116. *Where Do You Come From?*

In a small meeting Master Tokusan said, "I shall not answer any questions tonight. Anyone who asks will receive thirty blows of my stick." Then a monk stepped out and bowed. Tokusan beat him. The monk said, "I have not yet even asked, why do you beat me?" Tokusan said, "Where do you come from?" The monk said, "I am from Shinra [Korea]." Tokusan said, "It is high time to give you thirty strokes before you step into the boat." On hearing this the monk was enlightened.

Later, Master Hōgen commented, "The words of Tokusan are broken into two halves." And Master Enmei said, "Tokusan started well but ended badly."

In reference to the above comments of Hōgen and Enmei, Master Setchō said, "Though the two elders are good at cutting from the long in order to mend the short, giving up the heavy in order to take up the light, it is still impossible for them to know Tokusan. Why? It is because Tokusan is like one holding power over places outside the imperial city gate. He possesses the sword of quick decision. Do you people want to know the monk from Shinra? He is but a blind man who has knocked himself against the pillar outside the hall."

ANSWER
The pupil takes the master by the neck and gives thirty blows of the stick.

How would *you* take the thirty blows?

ANSWER

"I truly ask your forgiveness."

OR
(According to another school)
MASTER
(Quote)
"Whether you have anything to say or not—thirty blows"—
what's it mean?

ANSWER

While hitting the master on his back the pupil recites, "Whether
you have anything to say or not—thirty blows."

MASTER

Forget about Tokusan for awhile—the blows of my stick, how
would you take them?

ANSWER

Springing back, the pupil pretends to be in fear, and bringing
his hands together he pleads, "Forgive me! Forgive me!"

MASTER

Let's forget Tokusan for awhile—how does your stick work?

ANSWER

"What rubbish! I don't carry such trash around with me!"

117. *One Got It, One Missed It*

A monk came to consult Master Hōgen before mealtime.
Hōgen pointed to the curtain with his hand. At that, two monks
simultaneously went to pull the curtain up. Hōgen said, "One
got it. One missed it."
As against, "One got it."

ANSWER

The pupil takes hold of the stick and thrusts it in front of his
master.
As against, "One missed it."

ANSWER
The pupil drops the stick on the floor.

118.   Yes

Master Etchū called his attendant three times and three times the attendant answered back. Etchū said, "I thought I had done you wrong, but in fact it is you who had done me wrong."

ANSWER
"When called a thief of a monk, answer as a thief of a monk; when called a fool of a monk, answer as a fool of a monk; when the crow cries 'Caw!' answer 'Caw!'"

OR
(According to another school)
The master, taking the place of Master Hōgen, turns to the pupil, saying, "Attendant!" The pupil responds, "Yes!" This is repeated three times.
(Quote)
> Only the wild monkey knew the traveler's
> sorrow.
> On the waterway of Ekiyō I heard it wail a
> third time.

119.   Three Pounds of Flax

A monk asked Master Tōzan, "What is Buddha?" Tōzan said, "Three pounds of flax."

ANSWER
"One, two, three," the pupil acts as a fish peddler taking count.
(Quote)
It looks like flax, and it looks like millet too.

120.   Even Up Till Now

Bibashi Buddha [a legendary Buddha] has been practicing since very ancient times. In spite of this, he does not know the deep meaning, even up till now.

"On the slope the sun shines hot; at Suzuka [name of a place] it is cloudy; in Tsuchiyama [name of a place] it rains."

121. *One Finger*

Whenever Master Gutei was asked a question, he would simply raise one finger.

ANSWER

The pupil raises one finger.

MASTER

What if I cut this finger off?

ANSWER

"Even if you cut it, it cannot be cut. From the top of the thirty-third heaven down to the deepest layer of earth, it is the one finger."
(Quote)

> The one thing communicates with all natures,
> The one existence includes all existences,
> The one moon appears on all waters,
> All waters reflect the one moon.

Or:
A cut that cuts all cuts.
Or:
My way is run through by one single principle.
Or:
All this stretch of land is but a rod of iron.

122. *It Is Important that the World Be in Peace*

When Buddha was first born, he pointed with one hand to the sky, and with the other to the earth. He walked seven steps in a circle and, looking in the four directions, said, "I am the only one to be honored in and below heaven."

Master Ummon said, "If I were there I would have killed him with a stroke of my stick and would have given him to the dogs to eat. Because it is important that the world be in peace." On this, Master Rōyakaku commented, "Ummon says that one should offer one's body and soul to this world. This is called repaying the favor of Buddha."

ANSWER

The pupil stands up, and, pointing one finger toward the sky and the other toward the earth, says, "I am the only one to be honored." *As against, "It is important that the world be in peace."*

ANSWER

"Mister, mister, please bestow your favor on the blind," the pupil says, acting out a beggar.
(*Quote*)
Rain falling on tree leaves—jadelike beads of water turning round.

123. *Mother and Father*

Prince Nata [a mythological figure] tore up his flesh and returned it to his mother, broke up his bones and gave them back to his father. Then he revealed his original body, and, exercising great magical power, preached the truth for his parents.

ANSWER

"I have made the pilgrimage to Ise seven times, to Kumano three times, to Atago [all Shinto shrines] I go every month," the pupil says, singing and dancing around the room.
(*Quote*)
> Silk dresses and jeweled sashes were untied for
>   thee,
> En [district] songs and Jō [district] dances
>   were performed for thee.

OR
(With certain masters)
ANSWER

"Father, you must be tired. Mother, you must be tired. Shall I rub your shoulders for you?"

124. *The Eastern Mountain Walks on Water*

A monk asked Master Ummon, "Where is the place of origin of Buddha?" Ummon said, "The eastern mountain walks on water."

ANSWER

"In the monks' quarters the fuzui [the monk in charge of daily affairs] welcomes the guests and prepares the welcoming dinner, the tenzo [in charge of cooking] boils the rice, the densu [in charge of sutra reading] reads the evening chapter, the attendant cleans the place up. It is very busy."

OR
(According to another school)
ANSWER

The pupil folds his arms across his chest and, while wandering about the room, says, "Shush, shush," pretending to walk along a valley stream.

125. *Youngsters Like You Never Know of That*

Master Hōun said, "In the third year of Kinei, I held the post of the official in charge of papers and accounts in Hōshō Prefecture. In that year, there was a great landslide at Mt. Ka and villages within a span of eighty miles were completely buried. Youngsters like you never know of that."

ANSWER

"Well, well, we are indeed fortunate to have heard such a beneficial lesson. We shall remember it for the rest of our lives.

126. *The Guy Understands This Time*

When Master Kassan first lived in the temple of Keikō, a monk asked him, "What is the body of truth?" Kassan said, "The body of truth is formless." The monk asked again, "What is the eye of wisdom?" Kassan said, "The eye of wisdom is blemish-free." At that time Master Dōgo burst out laughing from his seat. Kassan then dispersed his followers and went to see Master Sensu. There he reached enlightenment. Later, he went back and gathered his followers once more. Dōgo then sent a monk to ask Kassan, "What is the body of truth?" Kassan said, "The body of truth is formless." The monk asked again, "What is the eye of wisdom?" Kassan said, "The eye of wisdom is blemish-free." The monk returned and reported the whole thing to Dōgo. Dōgo said, "The guy understands this time."
As against, "The body of truth is formless."

(202)

ANSWER

"The incense tray is formless, the mat is formless, the table is formless, the pillar is formless, the wall is formless, each and every thing is formless."
As against, *"The eye of wisdom is blemish-free."*

ANSWER

"A round thing is round, a square thing is square."
(Quote)
Curved is the squash and straight is the cucumber.

127. *How Can We Go Through Without Interfering?*

A monk asked Master Fuketsu, "We are in constant contact with existence and its workings whether we talk or keep silent. How can we go through without interfering with it?" Fuketsu said, "I always recall places south of the river in the month of March when the small birds sing amid the fragrance of a hundred flowers."

MASTER

"How can we go through without interfering?"—what's it mean?

ANSWER

The pupil looks around him.

MASTER

"I always recall places south of the river in the month of March when the small birds sing amid the fragrance of a hundred flowers"—what's it mean?

ANSWER

The pupil just recites the above.

128. *Peach Blossoms*

Master Reiun saw the peach blossoms and was enlightened. He recited a selection that goes: "I am a traveler who has been looking for a master for thirty years. Time and again leaves have fallen and new shoots sprouted. But ever since I saw the peach blossoms, I have never doubted again."
Later he told this to his master, Isan. Isan said, "Those who

are destined to join us will never fall back or be at a loss. Go on protecting and keeping your faith."

Master Gensha heard about this and said, "It is certainly very true, but I am sure that you [Reiun] are still not thoroughly clear." Master Ummon said, "Say nothing of thorough and not thorough again. Study thirty years more!" Afterward, Master Daisen was asked by a monk about the poem mentioned above. Daisen said, "The thief trembles within."

ANSWER

"If the seer is a flower, the seen is a flower too." [This can also be translated: "If you see a flower, it's a flower that is seen."]

129.   *I Have Nothing to Hide from You*

One day the poet Sankaku was conversing with Master Maidō. Maidō said, "There are a few sentences in the book [*The Analects of Confucius*] that you know of which go: [Confucius said] 'You fellows, do you think that I am hiding something from you? I have nothing to hide from you.' It is exactly the same with the affairs of Zen. Do you know this?" Sankoku said, "I do not know." Later, Maidō and Sankoku were walking in the mountain. Maidō asked, "Do you smell the fragrance of the flowers?" Sankoku said, "I do." Maidō said, "I have nothing to hide from you." At that moment Sankoku was enlightened.

Two months later, Sankoku again went to see Maidō. Maidō asked Sankoku, "When you and I die and are burned into two piles of ashes, when and where shall we meet?" At that Sankoku, bewildered, could do nothing. Later, at a certain place, Sankoku was taking an afternoon nap. The moment he opened his eyes he was greatly enlightened. He realized the working of Maidō. Thereafter his mind was perfectly free.

As against, "When you and I die and are burned into two piles of ashes, where and when shall we meet?"

ANSWER

"Oh, this must be the house where Rikiyo [a male figure in a Kabuki play] lives. I don't know why, but I feel a little shy."

130.   *Bamboo Shoots Sprout Sideways under a Rock*

A monk came to Master Nansen. Nansen said to him, "Now I am going up to the mountain. You stay here and cook the meal.

When you have finished, carry my share of the meal to the mountain." Saying this, he left. The monk cooked the meal, ate it all up, then he broke all the dishes, and he went to lie down on the bed. Nansen waited for the monk for a long time. As the monk did not show up he went back to the hermitage and saw the monk lying on the bed. Nansen lay down beside him. The monk got up and went away. After Nansen had come to live in a temple he said, "Before, when I was still living in a hermitage, there was a clever monk. But I have never seen him again up till now."

Later Master Kidō commented, "If Nansen did not recognize the monk, the monk could not have gotten up and left. However, bamboo shoots will sprout sideways under a rock, and flowers will grow down on an overhanging cliff." Kidō added, "Clad in short breeches, long gowns, and white linen headbands, people are noisily, hurriedly pushing their carts under the sun. Those one meets on the roads of Rakyō City are all merchants and businessmen."

Popular Saying
I've been waiting and waiting, but no word from him. I wonder what he's doing now.
(Quote)

> The white plain is desolate under the autumn
>   sky,
> But someone is coming east on horseback.
> Do you know who he is?

Or:

> There are thousands of miles along the river.
> How can I meet my wise and holy king?

131. *Not Enter Nirvana, Not Fall into Hell*

In the Mahahanya scripture preached by Monju [a legendary Buddha] it says, "Chaste practitioners will not enter nirvana, and monks who violate the rules will not fall into hell."

MASTER
"Chaste practitioners will not enter nirvana"—what's it mean?
As against, "The four classes of warrior, farmer, artisan, and merchant."
ANSWER
"The soldier with his rifle on his shoulder is drilling; the farmer

with hoe and plow is plowing the field; the carpenter with the plane is shaving a board; the merchant with the abacus is doing business."

MASTER

"Monks who violate the rules will not fall into hell"—what's it mean?

ANSWER

"The rooster from early morn crows the time, the dog all night long guards the gate, the cat catches mice."

MASTER

Why isn't there falling into hell?

ANSWER

"Already in hell, what's this talk about falling or not falling?"
(*Quote*)

> When spring is warm, the singing of
> nightingales seems so smooth;
> When the world is peaceful, people put on
> smiling faces.

Or:

> The white herons go down to the fields in a
> thousand dots of snow,
> The yellow birds fly up the tree to form a
> bunch of flowers.

Or:

[Master Hakuin's poem on this koan]

> The leisured ants fight to drag the dragonfly's
> wing while young swallows rest together
> on the willow twigs.
> The silkworm raiser carries a leaf-filled
> basket; her face reflects the blueness of
> the leaves.
> The village boy, to steal some bamboo shoots,
> crosses over the sparse fence.

Popular Saying

The ayu fish in the shallow waters of the river stays, the bird in the tree dwells, man in the midst of feeling lives.

OR
(According to another school)

MASTER

The "chaste practitioners"—where are they?

ANSWER

"Right here," the pupil says, pointing to himself.

MASTER

The "monks who violate the rules"—where are they?

ANSWER

"Right here," the pupil says, pointing to his master. Then he switches the order. Pointing at his master he says, "Chaste practitioners"; pointing to himself he says, "Monk who violates the rules."

MASTER

Now, this "chaste practitioner" and "monk who violates the rules"—distinguish them in the affairs of everyday life.

ANSWER

"The tongs are stuck in the charcoal brazier; the knife is on the cutting board."

132. *High Rank, Low Rank*

Once upon a time, Monju Buddha went to where the gods met. It so happened that the gods had all returned to their own places. There was only a woman sitting near the seat of Buddha in deep contemplation of quietude. Monju said, to Buddha, "Why is this woman allowed to sit near you when I am not?" Buddha told him, "You just wake this woman. Rouse her from her contemplation and ask her yourself." Monju walked around the woman thrice, snapped his fingers, and carried her to a high sphere of heaven. Yet despite all his efforts, he could not get her out of her contemplation. Buddha said, "Even if there were hundreds and thousands of Monjus, they still would not be able to get her out of her contemplation. You go to the lower sphere where Mōmyō [a Bodhisattva of low rank] is. He can rouse this woman from her contemplation." Then Mōmyō gushed out from the ground. He bowed to Buddha, who commanded him to stand in front of the woman. Mōmyō snapped his fingers once, and the woman woke from her contemplation and stood up.

MASTER

Why couldn't Monju rouse the woman?

ANSWER

"Monju is an extremely distinguished Buddha. He holds the source of wisdom. Therefore, 'rousing,' 'not rousing' is not the problem."

MASTER

Why could Mōmyō rouse the woman?

ANSWER

"Mōmyō is a Bodhisattva of low rank, functioning in the sphere of cause and effect. It is in this realm that he saw the reason for rousing the woman."

MASTER

The enlightenment of the Buddha and the enlightenment of Daruma [Bodhidharma—founder of Zen]—how are they distinct?

ANSWER

"By the enlightenment of the Buddha—'What a fine rosary!' By the enlightenment of Daruma—'This rosary is made from such-and-such tree, it is painted in gold leaf and attached with a tassel of silk. It's a fine thing!'"
(Quote)

> Wild geese flew over the city wall against a
> night sky sparingly dotted with faint
> stars.
> A long drawn note of the flute arose and
> someone was leaning on the balcony.

Or:

> Light boats are floating on the lonely waters.
> The purple flowers of the water plant are
> growing on the clear pool.

When night falls those who gather in the
overlooking pavilion are mostly
fishermen.

The following quote was composed as a comment to this koan:
"The Buddha together with Monju and Mōmyō entering into the
deep mountain bush." How about that?

ANSWER

"The view of making all equal is of no use."

133. *The Oak Tree in the Front Garden*

A monk asked Master Jōshū, "What is the meaning of our
founder coming from the west [i.e., the meaning of Zen]?"
Jōshū said, "The oak tree in the front garden." The monk said,
"Master, please do not show people the place your heart has
roamed to." Jōshū said, "I will not." The monk said, "What is
the meaning of our founder coming from the west?" Jōshū
said, "The oak tree in the front garden."

Afterward Master Hōgen asked Master Kakutesshi [Jōshū's
disciple], "I have heard that Jōshū said something about an oak
tree, didn't he?" Kakutesshi said, "My deceased master had never
said that. Do not slander him!" Hōgen said, "The real offspring
of a lion can roar like a lion."

ANSWER

The pupil folds his arms, stands up, and says, "Oak tree."
(*Quote*)
>The pine trees in the cold are of the same
>color,
>Yet the span of a thousand years has lapsed.

Or:
Pine trees will be green for a thousand years.
Or:
The withered trees flourish in the winter months.
Popular Saying
The good luck young pine—its branches flourish wide and far,
its leaves grow thick and green.
As against, "Do not slander the deceased master."

The pupil folds his arms, stands up, and says, "Oak tree."
(*Quote*)

> Bamboo shoots will sprout sideways under a rock,
> Flowers will grow down on an overhanging cliff.

Or:

> The whale swallowed up all the water in the sea.
> Thus coral branches were exposed.

MASTER

Give a quote expressing Kakutesshi.
(*Quote*)
A good son never uses his father's money.
Or:
A filial son knows that the father is kind.
Or:

> The trees in the garden, knowing not that all the people had gone,
> Still put forth the same flowers as in olden days.

MASTER

Give a quote for this koan as a whole.
(*Quote*)
The oak tree in the front garden.

MASTER

The root of the oak tree—how far does it go?

ANSWER

"Horizontally it stretches across the ten directions [of space]. Vertically it reaches the end of the three worlds [of time]."

MASTER

The leaf of the oak tree—what is its color?

ANSWER

"The peach tree is so fresh-looking, its leaves are so profuse."

(According to another school)

As against, "Oak tree."

ANSWER

The pupil stands up, makes an angry face, and, spreading his arms out wide in a slight angle upwards, he gives the form of an oak tree.

MASTER

This tree—when did it grow?

ANSWER

"It's about five or six years."

MASTER

If I ask you [about the meaning of our founder coming from the west]—how'd you answer it?

ANSWER

"I guess I'd say pine tree."

134. *That Is Still Not Enough*

Master Haku-un said to Master Hōen, "Once there came a few guests from Mt. Ro. Every one of them was enlightened. When they said something it was perfect. When asked about a koan, they understood it. They also attached the right quote to their answer. But that is still not enough."

ANSWER

"In every and anything, he is a well-rounded monk, isn't he?"

135. *Give, Grab*

Master Bashō said, "If you have a stick, I will give you a stick. If you do not have a stick, I will grab your stick."

ANSWER

"Master, here's tea for you, 'cause I'm taking a cake." So saying, the pupil pretends to take the cake box.

What's the gut meaning of Basho's "give and grab"?

ANSWER
"When giving, give even the maggots in the toilet; when grabbing, of course, not to mention the ashes under the stove, don't even leave a single hair of an ant behind."

136. The Three Sentences of Master Busshō

The three sentences of Master Busshō are:

1. If the way upward [to enlightenment] is shared with all [saints] alike, why then did [the man called] Chōtatsu fall to hell?

2. Daruma did not come to the east. And Master Niso [the second patriarch] did not go to India. Why did Master Gensha bruise his toe?

3. Where will those who have broken through the void rest themselves?

As against, "The way upward is shared by all [saints] alike."
ANSWER
"'The way upward?!' What're you doing, dilly-dallying, messing around—what's the good of it?"

As against, "Daruma did not come to the east."
ANSWER
"Take care!"

As against, "Those who have broken through the void."
ANSWER
"Now, right now, right here."

137. Which One Is Real?

[Once there was a woman named Seijo whose body and spirit were split apart. The one Seijo eloped and married her lover Ōchū, while the other Seijo remained in her parents' home ill and speechless in bed.]

Master Hōen asked a monk, "The body and spirit of Seijo are split apart. Which one is the real Seijo?"

ANSWER
"Which one is real?"

A single spark of the lightless flame [the world of bondage] will temper big men of the human race.

MASTER

The state of Seijo's existence—what's it like?

ANSWER

"Regrettable! Desirable! Hateful! Charming!"
(Quote)

> Though my golden bracelet on my arm has
>   grown one inch too long,
> Yet when meeting people I still tell them I am
>   not in love.

138. Only There Is a Word That Is Not Very Proper

Once during a general meeting, Master Eimei heard a log fall to the ground with a sound. He was enlightened. He said, "It is not other things that fell, it is not dust that rushes this way and that. Rivers, mountains, and the big earth all reveal the body of truth."

Master Kidō commented on this, "Eimei is just like a small Confucian scholar who went up to the big city which made him completely satisfied. Only there is a word [in what he said] that is not very proper."
As against, "There is a word that is not very proper."

ANSWER

The pupil points at his master's nose.

139. Functions Like Theft

Master Kanzan said, "The story of the oak tree functions like theft."

ANSWER

"When I think of you, the sunny day goes cloudy, the clear moonlit night turns pitch black."
(Quote)
Yojō [a robber] hid himself and swallowed charcoal.

Or:

> Only after it snows can the goodness of pines
> and oaks be known.
> And only a difficult experience can reveal the
> heart of man.

140. *The Four Shouts of Master Rinzai*

Master Rinzai asked a monk, "Sometimes a shout ["Katsu!"] is like a precious sword molded from the hardest of gold. Sometimes a shout is like a golden-haired lion crouching on the ground. Sometimes a shout is like a fishing rod with floating weeds [in the shadow of which fish gather]. Sometimes a shout does not function as a shout. What do you understand by this?" Just as the monk was about to speak, Rinzai shouted at him.
As against the first three shouts.

ANSWER

The pupil goes, "Katsu! Katsu! Katsu!"
As against, "The shout that does not function as a shout."

ANSWER

The pupil with all his might shouts, "KAATSU!" shaking heaven and earth.

[In reference to the above answer the book comments, "From the highest heaven down to the lowest layer of earth—the one 'katsu.'"]
(Quote)
From blue sky and bright sun, angrily the thunder rolls.

141. *First, Second, Third*

If you got the first sentence you will become the master of Buddha. If you got the second sentence you will become the master of men and gods. But if you got the third sentence you will not be able to redeem even yourself.

ANSWER

"Standing, she is a gladiolus; sitting, she is a peony; walking, she is a lily"

142. *Host and Guest*

One day Master Rinzai went to the town of Kafu. When the host Ōjōji asked Rinzai to take his seat, Master Mayoku stepped out and asked, "Kannon Buddha has a thousand hands and eyes; which is the eye proper?" Rinzai said, "Kannon has a thousand hands and eyes; which is the eye proper? Say it quick! Say it quick!" Mayoku dragged Rinzai down from his seat and seated himself. Rinzai drew near and said, "How are you doing?" Mayoku was about to say something in reply when Rinzai dragged him down from his seat and sat down again. Mayoku then went out and Rinzai stepped down from his seat.

ANSWER

"Sometimes you are the host [subject], sometimes you are the guest [object]. It is not set."
(Quote)

> The mist of sunset sweeps the sky together
> with the lonely duck,
> And the autumn river is of the same color
> with the wide heaven.

143. *The Dragon Bitten by a Snake*

Master Ungo was at [the place called] "the gate of dragons." One day a monk had his foot bitten by a snake. Master Butsugen asked Ungo, "If this is 'the gate of dragons,' why was the monk bitten by a snake?" Ungo said, "Of course, he is great as expected."

Later, Master Engo heard of this and commented, "Since there is such a monk in 'the gate of dragons,' the teaching of Master Hōen [Butsugen's teacher] will not yet die out."

ANSWER

The pupil, stretching one leg, says, "It hurts! It hurts!" pretending to have been bitten by a snake.

144. *Zen*

Master Kotoku said, "Say one sentence where intelligence does not tread."

ANSWER

"Good morning, Master."

PART FOUR
NOTES AND COMMENTARY

NOTES AND COMMENTARY

NOTES TO PART ONE

The Koan on the Sound of the One Hand and the Koan on Mu

The Way of the Inzan School

A: *The Koan on the Sound of the One Hand*   (pp. 47–51)

This koan was composed by the Japanese Zen Master Hakuin (1686–1769). It is either this koan or the koan on "mu" which the novice receives as his first koan upon entering the monastery. The pupil is usually expected to "contemplate" his first koan for a long time. It may take him up to three years to reach the answer. In the meantime, the master rejects all the answers that do not correspond to the answer of "thrusting one hand forward." However, the master may guide the pupil in various ways. For instance, if the pupil comes up with an answer such as, "It is half" (namely, half the sound of clapping both hands), the master may reject the answer, explaining that the pupil is taken in by "two" (i.e., dualistic thinking). The master may also hint at the answer in a more concrete way. He may say, for instance, "Think of handing over your ticket upon entering the train" (i.e., extending one hand forward). In this case however, there is the danger that the pupil, through guessing, reaches only the correct *form* of the answer without really realizing its "meaning."

It will not be of much use trying to "explain" the koan. The state of mind which it embodies is not fully understood if we take into consideration only its philosophical, or rather anti-philosophical (anti-rational) aspect. The formation of the koan and its answer are to be viewed in relation to *zazen* (Zen meditation).

In the "clapping of both hands" the phenomenon ("sound") is the outcome of the interaction between two (or more) factors. It is thus possible, through distinction and differentiation, to trace its "reason" in other phenomena. In rational thinking we are always concerned with the *relation* of one "thing" with the "other." When "the sound of the one hand" is "heard," not a thing has been excluded. Every thing *is* ("u") in as far as it cannot be denied. However, its raison d'être does not lie in any "other" thing, nor does it lie in some principle or truth beyond the thing itself. The essence of a thing is no-thing or nothing ("mu"). Thus the one who has heard "the sound of the one hand" has realized "mu" without denying "u."

ANSWER

The seemingly paradoxical requirement to hear the sound of the one hand is answered through an act of extreme simplicity. To reach this height of simplicity, the pupil's mind undergoes a process of ever-growing sophistication. Yet however sophisticated rational thinking may be, its basic function is still that of adding one to one. Through seeing each one in itself and all as one, the pupil abandons rational thinking as a mode of being. This does not of necessity imply that logical thinking can no longer be employed for pragmatic purposes.

The pattern of response in the answer may be expressed in the following way:

Question: "What is the sound of *two* hands?"
Answer: Clapping *both* hands.
Question: "What is the sound of the *one* hand?"
Answer: Extending *one* hand forward.

Or to give another example—no one in the usual state of mind would ever answer three successive calls in the same manner. Now imagine the following exchange:

Hey you.	Yes.	
Hey you.	Yes.	Same intonation,
Hey you.	Yes.	same pitch

In this manner of response, there is such an extreme immediacy between every call and its answer that it is impossible to describe the situation as a process developing according to normal "reason."

(It may start anywhere and it may end anywhere.) If we apply the above to the koan, we get the following pattern:

Question: "Two hands!"

Answer: Extending (or clapping) *two* hands.

Question: "One hand!"

Answer: Extending *one* hand.

DISCOURSE

1. ★The pupil is not taken in by "prove it." He evades explanations by simply implying "that's it."

2. The pupil is not taken in by "enlightenment–non-enlightenment." The answer implies "here, now."

3. The pupil is not taken in by "existence–non-existence." Through the immediacy of his response, the pupil implies "here, now." The "after death" notion exists only while one is alive.

4. Suimo sword—the sharpest of all swords. "Suimo" is composed of the characters meaning "blow" and "hair"; namely, the sword that is so sharp that it cuts a hair that is blown against it.

There is nothing to be cut. Cut (or divide) no-thing and you still have nothing ("mu"). The third answer, because of its immediacy, is the best.

5. Surprisingly enough, the pupil responds to the "why" with a "philosophical" answer. However, it should be assumed that the response (if genuine) is of a more immediate nature than in the usual process of philosophical reasoning. The answer implies "non-distinction."

6. No comment necessary.

7. Similar to note 3. The pupil is not taken in by "life–death." The notion of "before life" is artificial and can be entertained only while alive (i.e., here, now).

8. The "essence" of a situation is the situation itself and nothing beyond it. When asked, 'What is actually happening now?" there is no way of answering the "what is actually" phrase. All that can be said is to repeat the "happening now." Thus the pupil responds to "summit" in a natural way by describing the view from the summit.

9. There is no need to speculate too much about the "meaning" of quotes. The pupil simply responds to "summit" and quotes a Chinese poem on a landscape viewed from a summit.

10. This question is a trap. The master tests whether the pupil

★ The note numbers correspond to the numbers in the text.—Translator.

is taken in by distinction or not. The "sound of the one hand" is not to be located spatially. Nevertheless it is not unrelated to space. Both answers imply that whether from the back or from the front it is just the same. However, it seems that through the second answer the pupil also implies that he has seen through the master's trap.

11. The pupil answers according to his own situation. As for the reader, the answer would be, "I'll go on reading" (or anything else he intends to do).

12. The pupil answers the challenge of the trap-question by slapping his master. By slapping he also implies that the master should not underestimate his understanding of the koan.

13. Again, a simple trap-question. The "one hand" is not to be located in space, but the pupil naively responds to the question within the frame of common sense.

14. This trap-question is intended to test if the pupil is taken in by distinctions of time or phase (beginning, middle, end) as to the "sound of the one hand." The answer implies "there is not much difference," no more than the simple difference of before a certain fixed limit and after that limit. More concretely, in terms of "beginning, middle, end," the answer is a simple response showing "this end" (right hand), "that end" (left hand), and "middle" (both hands together).

"Before-the-fifteenth-day" and "after-the-fifteenth-day" is sometimes also used as a set phrase for "before enlightenment" and "after enlightenment." This question may also be interpreted in such a way which does not differ much from the above inter- pretation. In such a case however, the reader should not read into the bringing of the hands together on the "fifteenth day" (the time of enlightenment) as an overtly abstract philosophical meaning (such as "unity" or "non-distinction"). The question is of the same pattern as question 10. Thus, instead of the answer in the book (extending right hand, then left hand, then bringing hands together), the pupil may, as in question 10, answer through sound imitations of three animals, or through the enumeration of three examples of any other phenomena of the same category.

15. The trap lies in the notion of "sublime." The expectation of a supermundane experience is perhaps the greatest obstacle in the way of Zen enlightenment. Through his answer, the pupil implies that he is not taken in by the distinction of "sublime–mundane."

16.   The pupil's action is an imitation of the Japanese style of greeting. Through the omission of the words which usually accompany the greeting ceremony, the pupil simply responds only to the word "soundless" in the master's question.

17.   In the demand to explain what it is "truly" like, the question entails a trap. Asked what it is "truly" like (i.e., its "essence"), the pupil has to answer that it is "truly" nothing ("mu"), for to define "truth" in positive terms is mere illusion. In his answer, the pupil rejects the master's demand to define the "ultimate truth" as something of illusory nature. If the pupil responded philosophically—for example, "everything exists, yet ultimately it is nothing"—he would be ridiculed by the master for the denial of existence.

18.   To define the "source" of things is similar to the definition of their "ultimate truth." The answer suggests that the emptiness (or void) of "mu" is the "source." The answer and the attached quotes express the mood of "mu" by using the symbols of far-extended time and space, serenity, and evenness.

B: *The Koan on Mu*   (pp. 51–54)

This version of the koan is recorded as the first koan in Master Mumon's (1183–1260) *Mumonkan* ("The Gateless Gate"). An earlier and larger version of this koan by Master Jōshū (778–897) is found in *Jōshūgoroku* ("The Sayings of Jōshū"). It seems that the shorter version has purposely been chosen for the koan teaching. Some of the master's questions in the discourse on this koan are related to points of doctrine discussed in the earlier version of the koan. However, the purpose of the koan in this book is not so much the problem of "Buddha-nature" (i.e., "dharma-nature"—the potentiality of self-realization or enlightenment) in its doctrinal aspect; as a point of doctrine, it is more or less expected that the question, whether a dog has Buddha-nature, be answered in the affirmative. And indeed, we find that in the fuller version of the koan, Jōshū *also* answers in the affirmative ("u") to the very same question. In the version of *Jōshūgoroku*, Jōshū explains his negation ("mu") and affirmation ("u") on doctrinal grounds.

The presentation of the koan in this book, the answer to the koan, and the discourse on it, make it evident that the point to be realized is not "Buddha-nature" in relation to the dog, but the nature of affirmation and negation. The monk expects an answer *either* in the affirmative *or* in the negative. But Jōshū's "mu" is neither "no" nor "yes." Like the "sound of the one hand," Jōshū's "mu" includes and at the same time excludes both "yes" and "no" (or "being" and nothing"). "Mu" is not a response to the contents of the question but to its logic.

It is perfectly legitimate to ask whether a dog has a tail. If the pupil says he would not answer the question about the tail because he does not recognize the dog (it is "nothing"), the master would stick the dog's tail into his mouth. Jōshū has nothing against the dog; it is actually the monk's enlightenment which is put into question. The monk may be well versed in Buddhist doctrine, but he knows little about dogs and still less about himself. With his "mu," Jōshū challenges the monk's logic and at the same time makes the utmost effort to kindly answer the "question" to the limit that language permits. Thus we would do best to read Jōshū's "mu" as "void" (in the sense of "null and void").

ANSWER

The pupil takes up Jōshū's answer, yelling "Mu——!" with all his might. In doing so, he adds to Jōshū's "mu" the urgency of "see! see!"

DISCOURSE

1–3. Similar to the corresponding questions and answers of the koan on the "one hand" (see p. 47).

4. As explained above, Jōshū's "mu" and the pupil's "Mu——!" are not the negative ("no"). In his answer, the pupil does not object to Jōshū's "u" (see below, note 6) but implies the rejection of the affirmative–negative mode of reasoning.

5. In "Mu——!" the pupil implies that he is not taken in by the distinction between the "karmic state" and the "enlightened state."

6. In the earlier version of the koan, when asked by the monk why he responded in the affirmative ("u") to the question on whether a dog has Buddha-nature, Jōshū answered, "Knowing yet trespassing." In the earlier version, this phrase could mean that the state of a dog is of the same karmic cycle as that of human beings (namely, it is of a self-conscious nature and therefore belongs to the realm of moral retribution). However, in our version of the

koan, it seems plausible that Jōshū's "knowing yet trespassing" should be understood as "knowing the truth of 'mu' yet purposely saying 'u.'" Namely, Jōshū admits that by answering in the affirmative he knowingly trespasses the "mu" (i.e., the negation of the affirmative–negative mode of reasoning). In this, Jōshū admits that his "u" answer is a trap intended to test if the monk is still taken in by the categories of "yes–no." Only if one takes Jōshū's "mu" as "no" does his "u" ("yes") appear as contradictory. The answer implies that the pupil is not taken in by the trap of interpreting Jōshū's "mu" as one of negation.

7. Master Mumon was given this koan by Master Getsurin. After six years, when he suddenly came to realization, he composed the "poem" that goes:

Mu! Mu! Mu! Mu! Mu!
Mu! Mu! Mu! Mu! Mu!
Mu! Mu! Mu! Mu! Mu!
Mu! Mu! Mu! Mu! Mu!

The pupil's answer (any quote consisting of twenty characters) implies that he is not taken in by "mu" in the sense of negation (nor in any other sense).

8. The pupil's action implies "it's me."

9. The concept of "working" is usually brought into relation with "essence." "Essence" is the "truth" of things, whereas "working" is the function or mode of operation. Having pointed at himself as the "essence" of "mu," the pupil implies that the working of "mu" is his own activity. In immediate response to the call of the moment, the activity of the (enlightened) self is not hampered by anything—it is absolutely free.

10. The pupil is tested whether he is taken in by the distinction between "enlightenment–non-enlightenment." In the description of a course taken from a certain place and back to that same place, the pupil implies that one ends up exactly where one has started from. He thus rejects the distinction between "holy" and "mundane."

11. The quotes simply refer to the course "to and back" of the previous answer.

12. Similar to the question and answer concerning the source of the one hand" (see p. 223, note 18).

The Way of the Takujū School

A: *The Koan on the Sound of the One Hand* (pp. 47–51)

There are only minor differences between the Inzan School and the Takujū School. In order to avoid repetition, I have refrained from including notes where the two schools are identical or similar in pattern. It should be noted, however, that the presentation of the koan on the one hand is made somewhat easier for the pupil through the addition of the word "soundless." It also appears that there is a greater tolerance in the Takujū School regarding the answer to the koan. The alternative verbal answer is not as sharp and clear as the answer of "thrusting one hand forward," but the reader may benefit from it if he is still in need of help in words.

DISCOURSE

5. Through this action the pupil implies "it's me," not taken in by the spatial aspect of the word "shape."

9. The pupil is not taken in by the seemingly paradoxical request to "grind the one hand into powder"; if the "one hand" may be "grasses, trees, cows, horses" (as in the alternative answer to the koan), it may as well be red pepper and noodles.

10. Having answered question 8 on the "Mt.-Fuji-summit-one-hand," this question is too simple a trap to be caught by.

11. The question is phrased so that it may be understood both as the "high-one-hand" (in contrast to "low" or "valueless") and as the "lifted-one-hand." The pupil is not taken in by the trap of "high–low" in the evaluative sense, and simply responds with an act of lifting the hand to the mouth the way traveling peddlers do when calling out their merchandise. The examples from everyday life also imply the rejection of the "high-one-hand" in the evaluative sense.

12. In question 9, "Grind into powder and swallow it," the master refers to a useful action that is indeed performed in everyday life. Here, however, the master's requirement is simply nonsensical and nothing more than a trap. The pupil sees through the trap and responds accordingly.

14. In the discourse of the Inzan School, the pupil responds to the question on the "source of the one hand" with an attempt

to answer verbally (see p. 223, note 18). However, such a question is better regarded as a trap. The pupil's response implies that he has seen through the trap and that the question does not deserve an answer.

16. The Zen monk is of course in no special position where the "one hand" is concerned. My "one hand" is to be writing this book, the reader's "one hand" is to be reading it.

18. The quote simply refers to the "one" of the "one hand."

B: *The Koan on Mu* (pp. 51–54)

DISCOURSE

1. The pupil is not taken in by affirmation–negation. But that does not mean that he transcends common sense. When something is not "no," it is simply "yes."

2. The response is simple and immediate. After all, the only distinction that can be made between "being" and "non-being" is that of "is" and "is not."

3. The pupil does not respond to the "u" and "mu" of the question. In his answer he simply refers to "how far." Instead of pointing out the "mixing of categories" in the master's question, he naively responds within the category that can be dealt with without trespassing common sense (i.e., distance).

9–13. The pupil implies that he has become "mu."

14. This question deals with the "essence" and "working" of things (similar to the Inzan School on the "essence" and "working" of "mu"—p. 225, note 9). "Knowing" a thing is simply seeing it. The "working" of a thing lies in its function or usage.

17. The question is nonsensical. The pupil naively responds to each of the master's demands without being bothered much about their meaning.

19. In the answer, the pupil simply responds to "selling articles" without being bothered about the distinction between "u" and "mu." The quotes imply that "u" and "mu" are of the same origin.

21. Another possible translation of the master's question can be: "Say Jōshū's 'mu' like this."

22. This original, striking question can, I believe, be considered an outstanding koan. It does not necessarily have to deal with Jōshū's "mu." The pattern of the question is: "What if . . . (any

fact) . . . had never happened?" The answer may, in any of the possible applications, be the same "mu——" (see note on the koan of "mu," Inzan School, pp. 223–224).

23. The one-footed Persian—Nata Taishi, a legendary figure in Buddhist folklore. Nata Taishi, having three faces and eight arms, symbolizes authority and freedom of action. It is difficult to make sense of Ryōfu's poem. The pupil, not taken aback by inconsistencies, naively responds to the parts of the poem without caring for its overall meaning. Note also how the pupil responds to the master's "Explain!" in the last part of the answer. If the master is not enlightened, he might attain enlightenment through the pupil's answer.

27. The answer would, of course, also be correct if the pupil said, "If you're 'mu' then I'm 'u.'" The point here is that the master asks for a "distinction" and the pupil provides him with one.

28. Identical to question 3 (see p. 227, note 3).

29–30. The pupil, not taken in by the demand to explain Zen, provides the master with an example of the correct usage of words.

31. The phrase "rush [or get into] this leather [or skin] bag" appears in the earlier version of the koan on "mu." When Jōshū answers in the affirmative to the question of whether a dog has Buddha-nature, the monk asks, "How did it [Buddha-nature] get into this skin bag [the dog's body]?" The pupil, who apparently knows the origin of the quote, implies in his answer that the skin bag (himself) holds everything.

32. In his answer, the pupil rejects the "source" question as a trap. The quotes however, hint at the "source" of mu. In the first and third quotes, we have a description of natural scenery; while the second quote speaks of "man's heart."

33. The answer sounds somewhat artificial. The pupil seems to imply "the essence of karma is karma" or simply, "karma is karma."

34–35. The reference to attachment in answer 34 does not necessarily imply non-enlightenment. Non-enlightenment does not lie in the karmic states themselves but, as mentioned in answer 35, in the making of a distinction between "u" and "mu."

36. The answer "u" implies, "Well, if you say Jōshū and 'u,' he must have said 'u'" or, "If you wish it to be 'u,' then let it be 'u.'"

37. The pupil implies that the view of things as "u" ("is," "existence") is the common sense view of the world. It should be noted that the answer does not entail any evaluation of this view.

38.   The state of "consciousness of one's deeds" is a state of freedom. Although one cannot escape the karmic consequences of one's deeds, one can *disregard* them. The first answer expresses the freedom which disregards the karmic consequences of one's deeds, whereas the second answer implies the absolute freedom that disregards the limitations of common sense.

NOTES TO PART TWO

Miscellaneous Koans

When the pupil has answered his first koan (either the "one hand" koan or the "mu" koan), the discourse on the koan (Part One) takes relatively little time. The pupil usually sees his master for "dokusan" (private meeting) twice a day. During "sesshin" (concentrated zazen practice usually taking a week), the pupil may meet his master three to six times a day. During each meeting, which lasts for about three minutes, the master asks the pupil one or two questions, more or less according to the order in this book. When the pupil is asked to attach a quote to his answer, he looks for a fitting quote (most of them from *Zenrinkushu*, a collection of Zen sayings) and presents it at the following meeting. When the pupil has answered all the questions of the "discourse" on his koan, the master presents the pupil with the "miscellaneous koans" of Part Two of this book. The koans in Part Two are presented to all pupils—that is, those who answered the "one hand" koan and those who answered the "mu" koan. As the "one hand" koan and the "mu" koan are ultimately the same thing, the "miscellaneous koans" do not differ much from the "discourse," but whereas the questions of the "discourse" are phrased in accordance with the language of the koan (either that of the "one hand" or that of "mu"), the miscellaneous koans are of a wider scope, not being restricted by any specific frame. In answering the "miscellaneous koans" the pupil demonstrates his ability to apply his realization of the first koan in thought and action in various situations.

The Koans

1. The question can also be translated as "your face before your father and mother were born." In his answer, the pupil implies "it's me," thus avoiding the trap of an unanswerable question.

2. The "body of truth" ("Dharma-body"; in Japanese,

"hosshin") is here referred to in the sense of "the body of enlightenment" or "the state of enlightenment." In ancient times ships were made of wood; "a metal ship floating on water" was considered a paradox. The metaphor hints at the quasi-paradoxical state of being enlightened yet still remaining in this world (of karmic existence). The pupil responds with "it's me"—identifying himself with "body of truth."

3. The question about the meaning of Bodhidharma, the founder of Zen, coming from the west (from India to China) is identical in meaning to the question, "What is the meaning of Buddhism?" or, "What is Zen?" Such a question is a "trap-question" for it should not and cannot be answered according to the phrasing of the question (i.e., in abstract terms). In his question, the master already hints at the futility of the question, presenting it as a "question in a dream." The pupil's answer disregards the question and responds only to "dream." When saying, "You think that answers it?" the master tries the same trap again. In the Japanese popular saying, there is a simple response to the word "sleep." Through the Chinese quote, the pupil distinguishes between the state of sound sleep in which no silly questions can be asked, and the state of awakening in which no questions remain, for everything has become clear.

4. If one is bothered with the thought of how to reach a destination, even a straight way is curved; free of delusion and doubt, the curved way is straight.

5. A more extreme version of the previous question. Jumping into the water without getting wet is similar to going straight in a curved way. If you do not care about the curves—you go straight; if you do not care about the water—you do not get wet.

6–7. The distinction between subject and object exists only as long as there is self-consciousness. When you forget yourself, you become one with the stone you are picking up. In such a state, even if the stone lies at the bottom of the sea, you pick it up without getting wet.

8–11. As in the case of the "curved mountain road" or the "stone," once you respond to a situation in an absolutely immediate way, you become the situation and the situation becomes you. Consciousness of movement exists only as long as there is consciousness of a static self. By becoming a boat you stop its movement, by joining the fight you stop the (consciousness of) quarrel, and by becoming the bell you stop the sound.

12. One cannot respond to four different sounds at once, but

by responding to each sound in its turn, ultimately all the sounds are one sound. This also answers the koan on the "sound of the one hand."

13. The pupil disregards the absurd request to exert influence over a distance of a "thousand miles" and simply responds by "blowing out" the lamp at home.

14. The pupil, disregarding the absurd request to draw out a mountain from the medicine case, presents the master with what is in the case—that is, medicine.

15–18. The pupil disregards the condition of "not using hands" and simply refers to his or the master's "getting up." He disregards "Mt. Fuji" and simply "walks"; he cannot "grind a mill in a duck egg" but he can do the grinding. The four questions are of the same pattern—demanding an action yet posing an absurd condition. The pupil performs only the desired action. Through the immediacy of his response, he makes the absurdities vanish.

19. The existence of legendary figures or even that of historical figures is not anything beyond one's self. This answer should not be interpreted idealistically. The pupil does not imply that "the world is consciousness"; like in the previous answers, he simply disregards the unanswerable and responds within the limits of his immediate knowledge.

20. In his answer the pupil rejects the theoretical systematization of "principles" or "virtues."

21. Being in a room the pupil cannot see the sky. Thus his answer can reach no further than where his eyes reach.

22–23. A somewhat artificial version of the "become one with the object" theme. In the popular saying, by referring to the woman's attachment to her lover, the pupil seems to be simply responding to the idea of "unity." These two questions and the saying may also refer to the absolute determination required of the novice in his pursuit of enlightenment.

24. The same pattern as questions 14–18. (See above.)

25. The pupil disregards the connotation of "blasphemy" in the question. In his answer, he becomes "Buddha" (which he actually is), and presents the commonplace situation of being shitted upon by a bird.

26–27. The pupil disregards the absurdities of "wooden cock crowing" and "straw dog barking" and simply responds to "cock" and "dog."

28.   A purposely grotesque presentation of the principle of "holding everything within oneself."

29.   The pupil disregards the peonies in China and simply refers to the peonies in front of his eyes.

30.   Disregarding the absurdity of walking in one day from India to China and back, the pupil simply "walks."

31.   This is another version of the koan on "the sound of the one hand." The master's quote suggests non-distinction between "u" (is) and "mu" (is not). It should be noted, however, that the answer does not imply the elimination of common sense. Repeating the master's quote, the pupil hits a piece of wood, which of course makes a sound, and hits the air, which of course makes no sound. There either is a sound or there is no sound; ultimately however, there is the "sound of the one hand." The pupil's answer equates all sounds (the sounding-sound of wood and the soundless-sound of air) with the "sound of the one hand."

32.   The pupil disregards the absurd condition and simply "holds the spade."

33.   The master poses the contradictory demand of "walking while riding." The first answer implies "walking," the second answer implies "riding," whereas the third answer (riding on the master-buffalo) turns the master into the victim of his own trap-question.

34.   After a series of trap-questions based on "contradiction," the master poses the trap of "simplicity." The pupil has proved sophisticated enough to react to "contradiction-questions" in a simple way. Now he proves that his mind is also simple enough to react to a simple question in a simple way.

35.   This is not a trap-question. The bridge stands still only in relation to water, whereas water flows on only in relation to the bridge. The attribution of qualities to things is done through the comparison of one thing to another. Seen beyond their relations, things are just what they are. A bridge is a bridge and water is water. The answer of pretending to be a "bridge" or "running water" is too dogmatic. This quote deserves a better response.

36.   The question is intended to test the pupil's attitude to magic as a means of "salvation." The Zen concept of "salvation" rejects magical and superstitious beliefs. The pupil, in his answer (imitation of a revengeful spirit) reacts naively to the master's story. In that, however, he does not answer the master's question. The master is asking for the pupil's reaction as a "Zen monk."

Therefore, the pupil's answer should perhaps better be interpreted as an ironical reaction to the question. That is, in making a farce of the master's story, the pupil ridicules "spirit–salvation" as nonsense.

37. In ordinary thinking, "space" or "void" is understood as an abstract concept and is distinguished from "matter" or "things." It is through this distinction that the differentiation between "u" ("being") and "mu" ("nothing") originates. As against this common sense distinction, the *Hannya-Shin-Gyo*—a summary of the *Prajñāpāramitā Sutras* ("the wisdom sutras," a group of sutras setting forth the doctrine of sūnyatā, kū, or "void")—argues "shikisokuzekū, kūsokuzeshiki"—"matter is void, void is matter." Therefore, by handing over any object to the master, the pupil at the same time also hands over "space" (or "void"). In this the pupil implies that his standpoint is one of non-distinction between "void" and "matter" (or "nothing" and "being").

38–39. More concrete implications of the previous problem. In accordance with the master's request, the pupil presents him with space in the form of "salad" and "powder."

40. Shōki—a god of Japanese folk religion who chases away the devils of sickness. The belief in this god originated in China. In fact, Shōki is neither one of the Shintō gods nor does he belong to Buddhist tradition. The pupil, through his answer, makes it clear that he is not taken in by superstitious beliefs.

41. The pupil suggests that his view of Buddhism does not entail the belief in magic and superstition. In Zen Buddhism, there is no reliance on external powers for "salvation." Enlightenment is entirely a matter of self-realization.

42. The pupil is not taken in by the historical situation. As far as he is concerned, his master is not the historical Buddha but the Zen master in front of him. The painting of Buddha's death expresses the deep sorrow of Buddha's followers. In contrast to the historical situation, the pupil presents the situation he would find himself in should his master pass away.

43. The pupil is not taken in by an abstract or supernatural interpretation of Buddha's entrance into nirvana. His answer simply suggests the state of death. The master's repeated question and the pupil's holding his breath is somewhat overdone.

44. There is indeed a cat in the painting referred to. However, the question, "Why is there a cat?" is a trap. There is a cat in the painting because the painter painted a cat. The problem is really

that of "why" and "because." In his answer the pupil demonstrates that his mind is clear enough (i.e., free from speculation) to avoid a "because" where "why" is nonsensical.

45–46. Similar to question 41. The pupil rejects the belief in mythological powers, implying that the "source" of everything is the self. The answers may also be interpreted as the pupil "becoming" the mythological figures. The meaning, however, is the same in as far as the mythological figures are not taken to be *external* powers.

47–48. Disregarding the myth of creation by external powers, the pupil simply responds to "give birth to a mountain," "give birth to a land."

49. The pupil disregards the "statue of Buddha" and implies that his concern is only with the "human Buddha."

50. In his answer to the master's story, the pupil disregards the absurdity of receiving fire as a gift, and simply responds to the situation of receiving a parting gift.

51. The tea ladle suffers no pain from heat and cold because it has "no-mind." The pupil's answer seems to suggest the "no-mind" state of the enlightened. "The mind of the moment"—"when hot, hot! when cold, cold!"—is, in effect, "no-mind" because it does not form a problem outside of the situation (i.e., it responds to the situation in an absolutely immediate way). Of course, this does not exclude the sensations of pain from heat or cold, only the mind's dwelling upon these sensations when the stimulus is over.

52. The pupil avoids the temptation to respond to the abstract "after death" and simply responds to "go."

53. Mt. Godai in China was a "holy" mountain. The metaphor of "clouds steaming rice" is employed for the poetical impact of the landscape description. The pupil's answer may suggest that the "rice-steaming clouds" are there because the monks of the monastery on Mt. Godai are cooking rice. It may also be read as a simple response to "rice." In either case, through the daily action of "cooking rice," the pupil implies that he is not taken in by the concept of "holiness."

54. As far as the dog is concerned, there is no difference between an old Buddhist temple and a telephone pole. Both are perfectly suitable to urinate on. The pupil's view is not much different from that of the dog.

55–56. The quotes of the master describe absurd situations.

The pupil responds only to those parts of the quotes that imply common situations ("fry" and "toss coins").

57–58.   The quotes suggest freedom from the common pattern of thinking in terms of "cause–effect." The pupil's response apparently implies freedom from the "subject–object" mode of thinking. The answer may, however, be interpreted as an ironical response to the master's quotes.

59.   It is no wonder that nothing is heard about the clay cows, for clay dissolves in water. The pupil's answer may simply imply "searching for" (the clay cows). This question–answer is not quite clear.

60.   Suiō and Tōrei were the disciples of Master Hakuin, who composed the koan on "the sound of the one hand." This trap-question is, of course, not to be answered and the pupil acts accordingly.

61.   By responding to the master's silly request to count the hairs of the nose, the pupil implies that he is not taken in by distinctions of value. As trivial and valueless as something may appear, one should not care about its "significance" and like a simpleton respond without hesitation.

62.   The master's question is an imitation of the story on Master Kyōgen's enlightenment upon hearing a piece of tile hit the bamboo. (The original version appears in *Kattōshū*, a collection of Zen stories on various masters. In this book it appears in Part Three, p. 164, koan 64, under the title SOUND).

The master changes the original version: (1) instead of Master Kyōgen, he speaks of "two young monks"; (2) the sound of the tile does not occur in a natural way, as in the original version, but is artificially performed by one young monk to "test" the other.

The pupil is not taken in by the seemingly "deep meaning" of the story; his reaction implies that he has seen through the trap.

63.   It is the reliance on "light" that puts one in the situation of "darkness." It is the clinging to the concept of "enlightenment" that makes one consider a "non-enlightened" state. In the first answer the pupil implies that all things are originally perfect the way they are—there is nothing wrong with "the maid's washing clothes at the well" and "the servant pissing in the field." Also, the alternative answers of "digging up the burdock root from the back field" and "pulling the cow out from the back shed" imply

everyday situations. The other two answers can be understood as a simple response to "darkness."

64.   Similar to question 49. (See p. 235, note 49.)

65.   If one responds to things in a simple and immediate way, there is no room for distinctions of value. All that can be said about excreta is "it stinks." There is nothing "unholy" about it. The same attitude is implied in the quote. The stupid person has his value as stupid, while the wise one has his value as wise.

66.   The pupil implies that he is not taken in by "might" or "authority" (in "lion" or "master") and simply does what he is told to do.

67.   The answer implies "here, now!"

68.   It seems that the master's question is better understood as a nonsensical trap-question. However, the pupil takes "pillar of the house" in its allegorical meaning as the "central figure."

69.   To "enter" the incense burner is of course nonsensical, but, by handling the incense burner in the way an incense burner is to be handled, the pupil in a sense "becomes" the incense burner.

70.   The pupil evades an abstract philosophical answer by simply responding to "come from" and "return."

71.   The pupil implies that he is not involved with problems that are not of his immediate concern. He does not know where the waters of the river go, but he knows where his own waters go.

72.   In popular belief, the bones of a saint (in Japanese, "shari") are given various magical qualities. As the master hints with the word "living," the pupil is expected to disregard the historical and legendary "Buddhas" and refer only to the "human Buddha" (see also p. 235, note 49; and above, note 64). In presenting the master with his own ear wax, the pupil himself becomes a Buddha. Reacting to the "body of a saint" through his own ear wax, the pupil also implies a disregard of the connotation of "holiness."

73.   The master's question is an artificial imitation of the Zen theme of "say it without words." However, "without words" does not necessarily mean "with your mouth shut." The pupil sees through the trap and in his witty response turns the master into the victim of his own question.

74.   The pupil disregards the theoretical "where would you start working on it?" by simply "working." His action also implies that he is not concerned with a situation far removed in time and space (an ancient bridge in China) but only with what is in front

of his eyes (the master). By quoting the popular saying concerning "beautiful" and "ugly," the pupil suggests that he is not taken in by distinctions of value (such as ancient China or present-day Japan, a stone bridge there, or a wooden bridge here).

75. Same pattern as question 74.

76. See p. 237, note 66.

77. A trap-question of the kind, "Have you stopped hitting your parents?" or, "Is the present king of France bald?" In answering such questions directly, you are bound to say the wrong thing. The pupil's answer also implies that he is not taken by metaphysical speculations.

78. Not being able to count the hairs in the back of his own head, the pupil simply counts the hairs of the master's head. For the significance of the counting see p. 236, note 61.

79. Same pattern as koans 37–39 (see p. 234). Through the popular saying, the pupil humorously combines "color" with "wind." The quotes simply refer to "color."

80. The pupil is not taken in by the speculative nature of the question and responds only to "rain." In the last alternative answer, the pupil disregards "rain" and simply responds to "where from," displaying the concrete attitude of common sense.

81. The quote is taken from *Hekiganroku* (No. 3). In the original, however, the stress is on negation ("mu" or "kū"— "void"). In contrast to the original, the pupil's answer seems to imply affirmation of all ways: "You can do it this way, you can do it the other way. This or that are all possible."

82. The "deliverance" of the ink stick is in using it.

83. The pupil is not taken in by the metaphysical problem of "life–death" and simply responds to "flower."

84–86. The same pattern as the questions on counting the hairs of the nose (koan 61), or of the head (koan 78). The master's demands are both silly and impossible. By naively responding to the silly and the impossible, the pupil proves what he is supposed to prove.

87. The pupil evades the trap of "why" and simply responds to "turtle."

88. By using the wine flask as a wine flask should be used, the pupil may be said to have "gone in and out" of the wine flask.

89. There is no clear answer as to which of the eight dragons of Indian–Buddhist mythology makes the rain fall. Even if there were, the pupil is not concerned with it. In his answer, the pupil

does just what the dragon does (i.e., "making the waters fall").

90. If you stand still against the wind, you "move" (i.e., your mind is taken in by the attitude of resistance). If you move *with* the wind, you really do not move (see p. 235, note 51).

91. The pupil disregards the nonsensical "bean curd" condition and simply acts as requested.

92. The pupil's answer implies "that's all I know" or "that's all I can see." Another possible answer to the same question may simply be, "Are you the elder or the younger sister?"

93. The question is similar to koan 88. The answer ("becoming a smoking pipe") is, however, somewhat artificial. It would be better to respond by using the smoking pipe.

94. The pupil rightly disregards the condition of "the day before yesterday." However, the answer ("becoming cigarette ashes") is overdone.

95. In Japan, gates are usually made of wood. The "stone gate" condition is brought in to exclude the possibility of breaking through by oneself. The pupil answers in the most obvious and natural way that can be thought of. It would, however, be a mistake to expect everybody to respond to this question in such a natural way. People who are taken in by speculative thinking often miss the most obvious.

96. Similar in pattern to Part One, Inzan School, the koan on "mu," discourse questions 8 and 9; and the Takujū School, the koan on "mu," discourse question 14. (See p. 225, notes 8 and 9; and p. 227, note 14.)

In this case, however, the definition of the "essence" of the wind as its blowing is not good. "Blowing" is the wind's function and should be put under "working."

97. In Zen, the concept of "reincarnation" is usually not taken in its literal sense (i.e., as a real happening), but rather used in a metaphorical sense for "spiritual" influence. The pupil is not taken in by the esoteric implication of the question. His response may mean "becoming" one with the masters of the past (in the spiritual sense), or it may simply imply that his concern with personal histories does not go beyond his own life.

98. The answer seems to refer to "kū" in the philosophical sense of "shikisokuzekū" ("the matter is void," see p. 234, note 37), but kū may simply imply the empty space of the room.

99. The pupil's first answer to the master's absurd request is a response to "tie up." Instead of tying up a "mountain" with a

"lamp wick," the pupil ties up his head with a "headband" the way Japanese (especially workers) do when going out. In the alternative answer, the pupil challenges the master himself to do the impossible.

100. Originally, Tokyo was a conglomeration of hundreds of towns and villages. It is, of course, impossible to see all of Tokyo through one's sleeve. In response, the pupil tells what *can* be seen when looking into the sleeve.

101. The answer may imply that Zen rejects the beliefs in magical powers of omniscience. However, it is better taken at its face value meaning, "There's no use speculating. To see what is inside the box you simply have to take its cover off and look."

102. Similar to koan 78. (See p. 238, note 78.)

103. The pupil disregards the metaphysical implications of the "after death" problem and simply responds to "meet."

104. The quote (taken from a collection of Zen sayings, *Kaisekiroku*) metaphorically refers to the spiritual power of the Zen master. The pupil's response to "turn heaven" by turning a somersault hints at the "turning" possibilities of humans, thus implying the rejection of the quote as an overstatement.

105. The pupil demonstrates a speculation-free attitude by responding simply to the phrases of the poem.

106. The pupil's answer may imply that he refuses to speculate on the concept of "the realm-of-no-thought" in its Buddhist meaning of "realm of enlightenment." Through the enumeration of personalities who passed away he suggests that the realm of "no-thought" is "death." In enumerating personalities from the secular world as well, the pupil may suggest that "the realm-of-no-thought" (this time in the sense of "enlightenment") is not restricted only to practitioners of religion.

107. In his answer, the pupil implies that he refuses to attribute supernatural or magical powers to the "greatly enlightened." The pupil's quote suggests the natural course of things. In the search for enlightenment and in the attainment of enlightenment, there is nothing transcendental.

108. The pupil wisely evades the question concerning the "ultimate truth." He agrees, however, with what has been suggested in the master's quote, that one achieves nothing through the search for the transcendental.

109. The answer may suggest that the simile is wrong because you cannot hit the sky the way you hit a drum (it affords no resis-

tance and therefore makes no sound). Such an answer is quite uncommon in its alertness to details. Most people would perhaps be taken in by the vast dimensions of the master's example and respond in a speculative, philosophical way.

110. The story appears in the collection of Zen stories, *Keitokudentōroku*. In his question concerning the wisdom of Buddhism, the emperor expects a metaphysical answer. In his response, Master Etchū ridicules the emperor's speculative frame of mind and aims at shocking him into enlightenment. Some may interpret the pupil's imitation of a floating cloud as a reference to "non-attachment" (to concepts). However, I think it is best taken simply as "a cloud is a cloud."

111. The story appears in *Keitokudentōroku*. It takes place in China. Monk Daiji (or Daijisanzō) was an Indian Buddhist who possessed the magical art of omniscience. The story does not imply a complete denial of Monk Daiji's mind-reading power. However, the final winner in this contest is Zen Master Etchū. Daiji can read Etchū's thoughts only as long as they are purposely brought forth in order to test Daiji. The pupil's answer suggests that where Etchū responds with the natural reaction of frustration and grudge, Daiji failed to read his mind. The simple and immediate reaction to a situation, whatever that reaction may be, is the "mind of the moment" or "no-mind" (see p. 235, note 51). Therefore Daiji can read Etchū's thoughts only where Etchū is not himself, but his powers do not reach to where Etchū is simply Etchū.

112. The quote implies that the moment one "inquires" (i.e., speculates) about a situation, one's mind is split into the "two halves" of "subject" and "object" or "active" and "passive." With the mind "broken into two halves," one misses the moment of spontaneous action. The pupil, in his answer, refers only to the actual happening—to where there is no doubt (the glittering of the sword). In this he implies a simple, immediate response to the situation.

113. In Buddhist legends, Monju (Manjusri) and Fugen (Samantabhadra) often appear as the attendants of Buddha. Monju, the left-hand attendant of Buddha, rides a lion; Fugen, the right-hand attendant, is mounted on a white elephant; whereas Buddha, in the center, is on foot. The pupil disregards history and mythology and through his answer suggests that the only Buddha he knows are those present (himself or the master).

114. As an alternative answer, the pupil could as well imitate

the form of a teapot, or, even better, demonstrate the correct usage of a teapot.

115. The answer implies "non-distinction." The attitude of an evenness of mind as to the distinctions between "nirvana" and "samsara," or "holy" and "mundane," answers the master's question.

116. The answer simply implies fulfilling one's duties when one is called upon. It relates to the theme of the previous question 115 in suggesting that along with the "religious" duties (meditation, sutra reading, etc.) there are the common everyday occupations, such as preparing food and managing household affairs.

117. Although the question may suggest the theme of question 115 in the philosophical sense of "the realm of light" (enlightenment) and "the realm of darkness" (non-enlightenment), it is better taken at its face value. The pupil evades the speculative suggestions of the question by simply describing what one does in the morning.

118. The phrase "know that there is" is a translation of "know 'u.'" This, however, does not mean that the racoons and the white oxen do not know "mu." One could "explain" the animals' "knowledge" through references to the "natural," "spontaneous," etc., but it would be better to leave this koan as it is.

119. The pupil's response to the quote may sound somewhat artificial, but it does strike a true note in reminding us that the nature of clouds and rivers is not the only "nature." Human life as it is, with its daily occupations and with its wars, is also "nature."

120. To carry a heavy weight and lightly float about is against the nature of human existence. This may be intended as a reminder to those seeking "liberation" from human bondage.

121. Almost identical to question 112. (See p. 241, note 112.)

122. The wisdom of the enlightened does not mean a disregard for worldly affairs, but the proper handling of them.

123. The quote is a saying of the Japanese Zen master Daitō-kotushi (from *Daitōkokushisantengo*); the same theme as koans 115 and 116. (See above, notes 115, 116.)

Instead of dealing with the "problem" of whether it is good or bad for a practitioner of Buddhism to be involved in social relations, the pupil simply points to the fact that *right now* he is in that situation.

124. The theme of non-distinction between samsara and

nirvana. In Zen, enlightenment is not, as in the Hinayana tradition, detachment from passions. Attachment is inevitable. One should not, however, be attached to one's attachment. The popular saying refers to the attachment of "love" in a melancholic mood typical of the Japanese mind.

125.   A wise paradox. Freedom of action does not only mean always hitting the center of the target. When absolutely free, one is also at liberty to miss the center of the target. The one who is free to do only "good" is not really free. Only when one is free to also do "bad" can one be said to be absolutely free.

Some may interpret the quote as suggesting that there is nothing absolutely perfect. I believe, however, that the above interpretation is more fitting. The pupil's response simply suggests "missing the center of the target."

126.   The same pattern as question 95 (see p. 239, note 95). For further reference, see question 51 (p. 235, note 51).

127.   The quote simply suggests that the teaching is the same although the techniques may be different. This is also suggested in the pupil's quotes. The reader should not be taken in by a value distinction between "milk" and "poison." As far as the snake is concerned, "poison" is perfectly all right.

128.   While this quote may originally imply philosophical idealism, the pupil's answer makes it perfectly clear that in the Zen context it is not meant to be interpreted in such a way. The pupil's response, rather than suggesting that the world is the *product* of consciousness, implies that human existence is centered around the common affairs of the human world. "Time" is, as far as we are concerned, our "yesterday, today, and tomorrow." "The Buddhas" are people around us, and "existence is the creation of mind" in so far as we plan our activity and act according to our intentions.

129.   The pupil is not taken in by the master's trap-suggestion to deny the distinctions between "high" and "low" in their physical sense.

130.   The quote implies—though it is ultimately "mu," it is to be admitted as "u." The answer is the same as in the discourse on koan 37 on "mu," Takujū School, (see p. 228, note 37). The world may ultimately be "nothing," but if you say a table is not a table, you are simply an idiot.

131.   A clever trap-question. The pupil's answer simply implies

that he has seen through the trap and refuses to speculate. I think, however, that the pupil also suggests that the "problem" is not in the sutra but in himself (and the master).

132. This quote does not differ in meaning from the quote of koan 130. Yet in suggesting that "knowledge" is not to be reached at through the senses, it puts a stronger stress on the "mu" aspect. The pupil's response is somewhat artificial.

133. The pupil wisely evades the philosophical problem of "time." In the first answer there is a simple response to "eating" (after all, people *do* eat). The alternative answer suggests the pragmatic conception of time as expressed in the framework of common activity (see p. 243, note 128).

134. "The mind does not dwell on any thought" does not mean that the mind is void of thought but means "the right thought at the right moment" (see p. 235, note 51). The pupil's answer suggests that a father acts in a fatherlike way, and a mother in a motherlike way. There is nothing wrong with that. It is only in a motherlike father and a fatherlike mother that there is no "true mind." The popular saying and the alternative answer suggest an immediate response to the situation.

135. The pupil simply responds to the poem without searching for its "deep meaning." Hakuin's "What do you hear?" may be understood as "What do you understand?" or, "In what way are you enlightened?" This is a trap intended to find out once and for all whether the pupil does not indeed attach a "meaning" to the poem. The pupil sees through the trap and responds to "hear" in its simple sense of hearing with one's ears.

NOTES TO PART THREE

The One Hundred Forty-Four Koans

The one hundred forty-four koans of Part Three are not intended for all the novices but only for those who aim to become Zen masters. In Japan, those who aim for the lower qualifications of a Zen priest end their monastic practice within a period of about three years. Usually such novices have to answer their first koan (the "one hand" koan or the koan on "mu"), the discourse on the first koan, and the miscellaneous koans. A novice who is quick in finding the answers may also receive a part of the koans of this chapter within the period of three years.

A simple priest of the Rinzai sect is supposed to live in one of the temples belonging to the sect, perform the religious duties of burial, say prayers for the dead on memorial days, and look after the temple and the burial grounds attached to it. In Japan, the temple is usually passed on through heredity. Correspondingly, most of the novices who train to become Zen priests are usually the sons of Zen priests.

However, in order to be qualified as a Zen master the novice has to stay in the monastery and practice under his master for many more years. The average period of training to become a master is about ten years. In order to be qualified as a master, the novice has to go through all the one hundred forty-four koans of this section. It is expected that once the pupil grasps the meaning of his first koan (including the discourse on it) and the miscellaneous koans, he will hit upon the answers to all the one hundred forty-four koans with relative ease. However, the time required for each koan depends, after all, on the personality of the pupil. Some may answer on the spot whereas others may "contemplate" one koan for a month or even more. Only someone who has become a Zen master is qualified to pass the koans on to a new generation of novices.

The original Chinese versions of the one hundred forty-four koans are to be found in *Mumonkan*, *Kattōshū*, *Hekiganroku*, and *Rinzairoku* (for the sources of each koan see Appendix A, "Sources to the Koans Part Three"). Some of the koans have been translated from Chinese into old or modern Japanese; there are also English translations of some of the koans of this section. The pupil is not supposed to look for sources, translations, interpretations, or historical commentaries. All this is absolutely beside the point. As most Japanese novices are not versed in Chinese, the master usually translates the koan into Japanese, thus presenting it (as far as the words are concerned) in such a way that the pupil does not have to do any further research into it.

In the translation of the koans, I have omitted many expressions which are not essential for the understanding of their meaning (such as the full Chinese names of Zen masters, honorific titles, names of places in China, etc.). I have also tried to make the translation of the Chinese Buddhist terms (such as the many expressions for "Buddha," "wisdom," "enlightenment," etc.) as simple as possible for the Western reader. Such a rendering of the koans is perfectly in accordance with the practice of koan teaching in Japan. Most of the Zen novices have little scholarly knowledge of Buddhist history or doctrine, and a good Zen master would avoid any reference to such matters as much as possible. In the notes, I have referred to matters of history or doctrine only where such comments seemed necessary for the understanding of the koans' meaning.

The pattern of most koans is that of a question or series of questions to which the Chinese Zen master answers in words or in action. The "answer" to the koan is thus already within the koan itself. However, as most of these "answers" seem strange and paradoxical, they are hard to understand without further clarification. The answer which the Japanese novice is supposed to provide is therefore, in most cases, no more than a clarification of what is already included in the koan. Such "answers" are by nature somewhat artificial. In some cases, the answer simply consists of a repetition of the essential phrase within the koan. In other cases, it adds a somewhat different variation of what is already implied in the koan. The best answers are those which through an unexpected phrase or action provide a flash of insight into the koan's meaning.

1. The Man up the Tree

It is plausible to assume that a man who holds onto a tree with his teeth would fall away. Answering or not answering the question is not his most urgent problem. What he needs is not philosophy, but somebody who is kind and courageous enough to help him down.

Commentaries by later masters are either: (1) criticisms of the koan or of the personalities appearing in the koan; (2) attempts to clarify the koan's meaning; or (3) in some cases simply implications of the mood of the later masters in relation to the koan. Setchō's quasi-paradoxical comment implies that the concrete problem of being caught up in a tree (i.e., being in danger) is not to be confused with abstract speculations about "the meaning of the founder of Zen (Bodhidharma) coming to China" (i.e., the meaning of Zen).

ANSWER

The answer is a simple response to the situation of being "on a tree" and its natural result (if one clings to a branch with one's teeth) of falling "under the tree."

2.   The Man in the Well

Shōkū's reaction to the question concerning the meaning of Zen ("getting a man out of a deep well without the use of a rope") suggests that the answer is no less impossible than the question. The monk, not satisfied with this, hints that monk Ō is superior to Shōkū and that *he* might be able to answer his question. Shōkū's reaction to this is quite natural.

Shōkū created the "problem" of the well and Kyōzan was caught up in it. Fortunately, Kyōzan's masters were kind enough to help him out. Tangen provided him with the "principle" (or "truth") in suggesting that there was no man in the well and therefore no one in need of being saved. Isan, by calling out "Kyōzan!" actually whisked Kyōzan out of the "well" he imagined himself to be in, thus providing Kyōzan with the "use" (or "working"). The general meaning is that we are all already enlightened, or at least quite perfect the way we are. However, let nobody be taken in by this.

ANSWER

The first and third answers (imitating the situation of having fallen into a well) miss the point. If the pupil responds with the second answer, he proves he has realized what Kyōzan did. Namely, that he is not in the "well," but right there in his master's room.

3. Why a Monk's Garment?

The trap in this koan lies in the word "wide." It is wrong to assume that to be free in this "wide" world means to exploit all the possibilities of life. To be free is to do what one is supposed to do without caring for what one could have done if. . . .

ANSWER

The answer suggests that a monk is free in being a monk-like monk. The quotes refer to the same idea, implying that if one answers the call of the moment without the slightest hesitation, there is no room to be unfree.

4. The World a Grain of Rice

This is on the same theme as, "Even though it is not a world, it is called a world" (Part Two, koan 130; see note on p. 243), and "Bind up space with a rope" (Part Two, koan 37; see note on p. 234). Seppō, with a touch of humor, drives the "mu" ("nothing," "void") aspect of the world ad absurdum.

ANSWER

Both the first answer with the attached quote and the alternative answer put the emphasis on "u" ("being," "matter"). Whatever the "ultimate truth" of the world may be, we are bound to live its common sense truth of "things are just what they are."

5. The Three Gates of Master Ōryū

Ōryū's questions are intended to test if Ryūkei is taken in by "mu." Should Ryūkei answer the question concerning his "origin" through the "mu" aspect, he would deny himself. Ryūkei thus refuses to speculate about his "origin" and presents himself as the "hungry monk" he actually is. He disregards the distinction between his own hand and that of Buddha and simply responds to "hand." In his answer to the third question, Ryūkei implies that though as far as "mu" is concerned all is the same ("a heron standing in the snow," i.e., both white), speaking "u"—Ōryū's foot is Ōryū's foot and a mule's foot is a mule's foot ("not of the same color"). It is noteworthy that Ryūkei resists the temptation to identify Ōryū with a mule. By "passing the gate and going straight on without caring for the gatekeeper," Ōryū implies that the "problem" of "u" and "mu" is answered not by solving it but by making it disappear.

ANSWER
As against, "Where is your origin?"

The first answer suggests "mu," whereas the alternative answers imply "u." To the question, "What are you?" the only reasonable answer would be to say what you *are* ("u") and not what you are not ("mu"). The quotes suggest the same attitude. In the poem on the bird and the monkey, however, we feel the undertone of "mu."
As against, "How is my hand when compared with that of Buddha?"

The first answer, humorously suggesting that "a leg is a leg," makes it perfectly clear that "a hand is a hand." The quotes are a simple response to "hand."
As against, "How are my feet when compared with those of a mule?"

Like in the above answer, through the example of "hand" the pupil suggests that "a foot is a foot." The quotes are a simple response to "foot."

6. *Where Do the Snowflakes Fall?*

In stating that "snowflakes do not fall on any particular place," Hōkoji suggests "mu" ("nothing," "void"). There is nothing really wrong with the monk's question; it is just that he sees the "u" of the snowflakes a little too naively. Hōkoji seems to be overly conceited where his insight of "mu" is concerned and his violent reaction to the monk's simplicity of mind is overdone. Hōkoji's understanding of the "mu" of snow is perhaps supreme, but there is something lacking in his understanding of the "u" of the monk. Setchō rightly suggests that the slapping and the scolding of the monk is unnecessary. If the monk is not conscious enough to the "truth" of snow, let him have some snow and he will understand.

ANSWER

The first answer and the quote on a snow landscape simply suggests "snow." The master's question as to the meaning of Hōkoji's remark actually requires an explanation concerning in what way "snow" is "non-snow." By slapping his master, the pupil reveals his attitude toward the master's demand to put "mu" into words. The last two questions of the master concern "hitting." The pupil refuses to speculate on the meaning of "hitting," suggesting that "to hit is to hit."

7. *Round Are the Lotus Leaves*

This poem is taken from a collection of poems by Zen Master Dai-e. It is fairly plausible to assume that the poem was not intended as a problem to be answered and has no special "meaning" besides what it says. The attempt to turn this poem into a koan is artificial and may only lead to unnecessary speculations which the Zen practitioner is supposed to avoid.

ANSWER

The master picks up the forms "round" and "pointed" and asks the pupil to apply them from the standpoints of "self-centeredness" and "other-centeredness." These concepts respectively imply the nature of Arhat (the ideal of sainthood in Hinayana Buddhism) and Bodhisattva (the ideal of sainthood in Mahayana Buddhism).

In his answer, the pupil points at himself for "self-centeredness" and at the "other" for "other-centeredness." In his reaction to the last phrase of the poem, the pupil contrasts his own situation, which is after all the only situation that concerns him, with the natural scenery described in the poem.

The first three answers under "according to another school" are somewhat less speculative. However the master's last question, asking the pupil to compare the phrases of the poem to the four social classes, is almost grotesque in its artificiality.

It is hard to imagine that the pupil can hit upon such far-fetched answers on his own. It is thus plausible to assume that the master provides the pupil with the traditional answer and passes on to the next koan. The high regard for tradition, so typical of the Japanese, may have its merits, but the preservation of such artificial "koans" is a sign of the stagnation of institutional Zen.

8. *The Sound of Rain*

The monk's answer to Kyōshō's "What is the sound outside?" is in itself quite natural. However, in Kyōshō's remark, "To put it into words is difficult," he may have suggested that there is still something wanting in the monk's answer.

The pupil, in his imitation of rain, probably suggests that the monk's answer of "It is the sound of rain" is perhaps correct, but that by words we do after all only comment *on* things. We should not confound "rain" with rain.

9.   The Three Questions of Master Tosō

1. This is a trap intended to tempt the pupil into explaining "mu" ("nothing," "void") using words.
2. Transcending "life" and "death" (or "u" and "mu") is fine as long as one is safe and sound. Yet, what becomes of the question of "life" and "death" when it is not just a matter of doctrine, but actually being on the brink of death?
3. The same trap as in (1) only here it is applied to the physical realm.

ANSWER

As against, "Now where is human nature?"

The pupil, in giving the pretense of searching, may be simply responding to "where." However, it may also suggest that "human nature" is everywhere (even in the situation of searching for it). The master's additional remark seems irrelevant. The aim of Tosō's question is to uproot the "philosophical disease" of searching for the abstract, whereas the master's remark can only direct the pupil's attention from the concrete to the search of the "self" in the abstract. "Searching for" is the common theme of all the attached quotes. Note that in all of the quotes the object of the "search" cannot be directly grasped.

As against, "On the brink of death."

The pupil's response and the quotes attached to it express the actual situation of being "on the brink of death." Through this response, the pupil suggests that "escaping from the circle of of life and death" does not imply that one can transcend death or the pain and horror involved in dying.

As against, "When the four elements are separated, where will you go?"

Through his response, the pupil simply implies that, being dead, one turns into a corpse. The attached quotes suggest that when a thing has fulfilled its function, nothing but its useless remains are left to be seen. The last answer ("with certain masters") on "gone away" and "return again," suggests that everything takes its natural course.

10. *The Sentence of Being and the Sentence of Nothing*

Ran-an's simile of "the wisteria vine twining around a tree" entails a trap. If the "wisteria vine" is distinguished from the "tree," one is inclined to distinguish "u" from "mu." Or rather, if one still distinguishes between "u" and "mu," one is bound to view the "wisteria vine" and the "tree" as separate. Sozan is caught up in the trap. He imagines the tree to "fall" and the wisteria vine to "wither," which makes Ran-an laugh. When Sozan implores with Ran-an to explain to him where he is wrong, Ran-an kindly enough hints that Sozan is taken in by "two" (i.e., dualistic thinking) and that he will not understand unless he becomes "single-eyed." When Sozan reports the discourse with Ran-an to Meishō, Meishō immediately sees what Ran-an saw and praises him ("Ran-an is a straight man from head to toe"). Meishō is kind enough not to "explain" to Sozan where he was wrong, upon which Sozan is enlightened.

Like Sozan, Dai-e too is caught in the same trap. His master, Engo, is patient enough to let Dai-e understand by himself. When Dai-e, absorbed in the chopsticks, forgets about the rice, Engo suggests that Dai-e's mind is still split. Chopsticks are there to be used for eating rice. This remark of Engo's is not unlike Ran-an's suggestion to Sozan to become "single-eyed." When Dai-e desperately implores Engo to enlighten him on the truth of Ran-an's simile of "u" and "mu," Engo suggests that Dai-e forget about the whole thing ("It is no use to make a sketch of it"), for it is all the same ("They come in succession"); upon this, Dai-e is enlightened.

ANSWER
The answer and the quotes imply that the "two" (the "tree" and the "wisteria vine," "u" and "mu") are "one."

11. *Subject, Object*

The shout "katsu" cannot be translated into words. When the master shouts "katsu" at his pupil, he is transmitting his satori (the Japanese term for "enlightenment" or "realization") to the pupil in a direct, immediate way. In some cases, the "working" of "katsu" can be compared to an electrical shock used in the treatments of psychotics, aimed at a sudden shaking up of the patient's whole constitution (see Part Three, koan 140, p. 214). The novice may sometimes "katsu" his master, and novices may "katsu" each other. "Katsu" is the concrete form with which one's mind, as if in a sudden burst, is turned inside out.

The two head monks shouted at each other at the same moment. This situation is used by the monk to question Rinzai on the relation of "host" (subject) and "guest" (object). The theme of "host–guest" is dealt with in many of the koans of Master Rinzai (see Part Three, koan 18, p. 124; and also koan 19, p. 126). Generally speaking, we may distinguish four possible relations between "host" and "guest":

1. The "guest" in the "host"—to create the concept of object" from the standpoint of the subjective (or "self").
2. The "host" in the "guest"—to create the concept of "subject" from the standpoint of the objective or "world").
3. The "guest" in the "guest"—there is no subject. The world (including one's own existence) is absolutely objectified.
4. The "host" in the "host"—there is no objective world; the subject is in complete unity with itself.

In states 1 and 2 there is a distinction between the "self" and the "other," whereas in states 3 and 4 this distinction has been eliminated. State 4 may be said to be that of a child acting spontaneously in perfect accordance with the movement of his will. The same is true for state 3; but whereas state 4 is a state of freedom of "self," state 3 is the "enlightened" freedom of "no-self." The difference between these two states should not, however, be overemphasized. In the final account, both are the same in as far as the distinction between "subject" and "object" does not exist. Zen satori is often defined as a state of "non-distinction" between "subject" and "object." However, in the actual situation of Zen training, any such verbal definition carries the danger of being turned into some kind of "truth" which the practitioner tries to understand or to realize in an overly conscious way. When one thinks of a situation in terms of "non-distinction" between subject and object, it only proves that one's mind is taken in by the "subject–object" mode of reasoning.

Rinzai is not concerned so much with the situation of the

two head monks who simultaneously shouted at each other. His answer is directed at the monk who raised the "subject–object" problem in relation to the situation. His answer is best understood within the framework of common sense. There certainly is the one who shouted (subject) and the one shouted at (object). How could it be otherwise? In giving this answer, Rinzai implies that in order to be free from "subject–object" distinctions, there is no use in trying to become "just subject" or "just object." One should freely move between the two in accordance with the situation. When shouting, one is the subject; when shouted at, the object.

ANSWER

The answer and the two quotes of the first section suggest acceptance of the natural order. Things are just what they are and it is only ridiculous to suggest that a "mountain is not a mountain." Things also stand in certain relation with each other. There is the "high" and the "low," the "green" and the "red," the "straight" and the "crooked." The two alternative answers are a more direct response to the problem of the koan. The pupil suggests that because there are master and pupil (or any two other related people), there is also naturally a subject–object relation between them. There is no use in denying the obvious.

12. *The Unrankable Being*

"The unrankable being" may be understood as "the undefinable being." In the realm of "u" ("being") things are rankable, whereas "mu" (nothing," "void") is unrankable. Rinzai may have referred to "mu" but it is better to take his remark at face value, as simply suggesting that the "self" cannot be defined. The "self" cannot be identified with the physical body, neither can it be separated from it. It has to be realized not through words but immediately ("See it! See it!"). In spite of Rinzai's warning, the monk still asks for a definition. In his reaction to the monk's stupidity, Rinzai suggests that whatever the "unrankable being" ("self") may be, in the case of the monk it is no more than "dry dung."

ANSWER

The answer of "placing one's hand on one's forehead" is a response to Rinzai's "See it!" This answer misses the point. The attached quotes simply suggest the theme of "seeing."

The same is true for the first answer under "according to another school." The pupil's dramatization of "See it!" ("fall down in surprise") only proves that he has misunderstood Rinzai. What Rinzai meant to be "seen" is nothing to be surprised at. The pupil's refusal to "say it" is perfectly in place.

13. *A Flower in Bloom*

The concept "pure body of truth" (in Japanese, "hosshin") stands for the absolute nature of the Buddha-mind—the supreme wisdom embodying all perfections. The monk's first question concerns the "essence" of the "body of truth," whereas his second question refers to its "working" or its form of appearance in the enlightened one. Ummon answers both questions using symbolic terms which suggest the "beautiful."

ANSWER

The pupil is not taken in by the suggestion of "beautiful" or "holy," and responds to both of Ummon's phrases by contrasting the "beautiful" with the so-called "ugly." Of course, the pupil does not imply that he prefers the ugly to the beautiful, but that his Buddha-mind is not taken in by the distinction between "beautiful–ugly" and "holy–mundane." The quotes suggest the same attitude through the enumeration of "ugly" or commonplace things together with "beautiful" things. The last answer (imitating a lion's roar) is simply a response to "lion," but it may have its merit in diverting the attention from the lion's "golden fur" to the lion's natural "working."

14. *Will IT Be Destroyed?*

"IT" refers to the "pure body of truth" (see note to koan 13, Part Three, above). The monk seems to be suffering from the "philosophical disease." He distinguishes the world and the self (in their "becoming" aspect) from the "eternal truth" or the "permanent essence." Faced with such a question, Daizui understands that the "problem" is not the nature of the world or of the self, but the monk's way of seeking for "salvation." Thus, whatever his view on the matter may be, Daizui is concerned above all with the "destruction" of the monk's dualistic thinking.

The answer may be understood as a simple demonstration of Daizui's words. However, I believe it also suggests the enlightened "no-mind" response to a situation (see Part Two, koan 51, note on p. 235).

15.   *Where Will ONE Return To?*

The monk has understood the "one in the many," but he does not understand the "many in the one." If we change the Taoist phrasing of the question into Buddhist terms, we may say that the monk realizes that all things are ultimately "mu" ("nothing," "void"), but he does not realize that "mu" is ultimately "u" ("existence," "the-many-things"). Jōshū directly answers the monk's question. By reminding himself (and the monk) of the very concrete fact of the "cotton dress weighing seven jin," Jōshū suggests that the "one" ("mu") returns to the "many" ("u"). When the pupil is taken in by "mu," it is the master's duty to remind him of "u." When the pupil is absorbed in "u," the master reminds him of "mu."

ANSWER

In an unoriginal, abstract way the pupil simply responds to Jōshū's phrases. The two quotes suggest that there is a relation between the "one" and the "many," whereas the popular saying implies the nature of this relation.

16.   *There Is No Such Thing as Holy*

The lessons implied in this koan are: (1) that one should not be taken in by "holy"; (2) that it is futile to try and define the "self."

ANSWER

In the first answer to "There is no such thing as holy," the pupil hints at himself. This might simply suggest an affirmation of the phrase, but it may also mean that the (enlightened) self holds everything in perfect evenness.

The alternative answer ("covered with mud, working") implies that there is "holiness" even in the most commonplace situation. The same is suggested in the attached quote through the

description of an everyday situation. In the remainder of the dialogue, the master tries to make the pupil answer what Daruma
himself refused to answer (What is the "self"?). The pupil is wise
enough to avoid the temptation of answering in terms of "mu"
("non-self"). He does not say he knows "nothing" (or "mu,"
which is a positive statement) but simply that he knows not. The
quotes attached to "I do not know" may suggest that that which
cannot be known is not of necessity non-existent.

17. *Words*

Jōshū suggests that the opposite of enlightenment is "choice"
(reasoning in terms of affirmation and negation). However, using
words does not necessarily imply that one is taken in by "choice."
The element of "choice" enters only where words are used to
speculate with. A non-speculative usage of words does not stand
in contradiction to "understanding" ("enlightenment"). Yet it is
not good to be conscious of one's "understanding." Such consciousness indicates that one is still taken in by "choice" (between
enlightenment and non-enlightenment). This is why Jōshū says
he is "not in the realm of understanding." The monk rightly suggests that if this were so, Jōshū would not be conscious of his
"not being in the realm of understanding"; for if Jōshū is "enlightened," why should he make a problem out of it? Jōshū wisely
enough says he does not know. Jōshū's "I do not know" is not only
a refusal to argue, but also an answer to the monk's question.
Namely, Jōshū's statement on "not being in the realm of understanding" might have been too speculative, but he is not taken in
by his own words. The monk takes Jōshū's "I do not know" as
merely a refusal to argue and presses Jōshū to explain himself. In
his answer, Jōshū suggests that being asked "words" he answers
"words"; that's all. The monk would do best to become less clever.

ANSWER

As against, "Reach the way."
   By pointing at himself, the pupil suggests that "the way" is
not anything exterior to the (enlightened) self.
As against, "Not difficult."
   The answer suggests that the "simplicity" of the way lies in
recognizing the world *as it is.*
As against, "The only setback is choice."

The answer ("What a pity! I want!. . . .") presents a state of "choice," but this "choice" is not to be confused with the "choice" Jōshū referred to (i.e., the "choice" of speculative thinking). The quote ("I only love to read . . . .") simply repeats the theme of the answer.

In response to the master's "I am not in the realm of understanding" (i.e., I am enlightened), the pupil simply accepts the master's statement and thanks him for his teaching. This answer should be contrasted with the skeptical attitude of the monk to Jōshū's enlightenment.

"Words reach from edge to edge" may seem to stand in contrast to what Jōshū says concerning "choice" in words. Yet Setchō's quote does not suggest "words" in their speculative function. What the quote implies is that in the enlightened state of mind (that is, when one is not overly conscious of one's enlightenment), "words" are used in a natural way and are therefore perfectly all right. If the pupil attempts to "explain" this quote, he would only prove that he is taken in by the "choice" (speculation) of words. His response in "Shut up!" is not unlike Jōshū's "I do not know." For the last quote ("*ONE* has many varieties, but *TWO* has got none") and its answer, see Part Three, koan 15, note on p. 256.

18. *The Four Ways of Master Rinzai*

"Man" stands for the subjective and "land" for the objective. These terms more or less correspond to "host" and "guest" in koan 11 of Part Three (see note on pp. 252–254). The four possible relations between "man" and "land" indicate four states of mind viewed from the standpoint of "subject–object" relations:

> 1. "Take away the man without taking the land"—to "take away" means to eliminate or to negate. This state refers to an attitude of mind in which the objective dominates the subjective.
> 2. "Take away the land without taking the man"—the emphasis is on the subjective; the objective world is negated.
> 3. "Take away both the land and the man"—the "emptiness" state (of meditation) from which both the subjective and the objective have been eliminated.

4. "Take away neither the land nor the man"—this is "the return to the common world" of Zen satori, in which both subject and object are recognized to be "just what they are."

ANSWER

The meaning of the answers should be clear from the above. Whereas the answers of the first school to the four states (using the hand as "land" and body as "man") simply consist of an abstract, symbolic demonstration, the answers of the second school express the four states in words. The quotes attached to the answers of both schools suggest, respectively, only "nature" ("object"), only "man" ("subject"); neither "nature" nor "man"; both "nature" and "man."

19.   The Three Sentences of Master Rinzai

This koan is unclear unless we understand what the monk is asking for and what Rinzai gives in reply. When the monk asks for Rinzai's "three sentences" he is in search of the "truth" (or contents) of Rinzai's teaching. Rinzai avoids reference to the contents (or meaning) of his teaching, and refers instead to the "working" (or function) of the Zen master. To say it in simpler words, the monk asks Rinzai, "Will you teach me the truth?" To this Rinzai answers, "Don't ask questions. Have trust in me and follow me."

Rinzai's first sentence on the seal and ink suggests that even though you may not be able to *read* the script, the "working" through which brings it into being is clear. The master's role is to "seal" ("host" or "subject"), whereas the pupil's role is to be "sealed" ("guest" or "object"). In his second phrase Rinzai suggests that one would do best not to be taken in by the "ideal" aspect ("essence" or "truth") of things; it is enough to know their "working." The third sentence implies that although it may not be clear to the onlooker, as in the puppet show, there is the one who "pulls" (the master) and the one that is "pulled" (the pupil).

ANSWER

The answers of both schools suggest that the meaning of the "three sentences" is exactly the same.

20. Before and After

Chimon's answers are contrary to truth. The lotus before it appears above water is a leaf. After it has appeared it is a flower. Zen satori is in a way a "return" to the world of common sense; yet although the "enlightened mind" admits common sense, it is not taken in by it. In order to "return" to common sense, it is necessary that one first "leave" it. Chimon's paradoxical phrases suggest the negation of common sense distinctions. Such "turning of the world upside down" is a teaching device of the Zen master used to make the pupil realize that distinctions can be played around with freely. However, if the pupil gets attached to such games, he falls into the trap of denying the natural order of the world. In the final account, the enlightened person is supposed to know what every child knows—namely, that the lotus is a leaf under water and a flower above water.

ANSWER
In his nonsensical answers the pupil suggests that he can play the same game. If one wishes to read deeper into the answers, they may be interpreted as also meaning "it is all the same."

21. To Beat the Drum

The quote on "mon," "rin," and "shin" is taken from the scripture Hōzōron, written by the Chinese Buddhist philosopher Sōjō (384–414). "Mon" suggests "study." "Rin" suggests coming near to "shin" ("truth" or "enlightenment") through the cutting off of study. Quite naturally the monk is, above all, curious about the meaning of "shin" ("truth"). He tries to make Kasan define "truth," which Kasan refuses to do. In his question on "the-mind-as-it-is-being-Buddha" (sokushinsokubutsu) and "no-mind-no-Buddha" (hishinhibutsu), the monk attempts to make Kasan speculate on the difference between these two concepts (both suggesting "enlightened mind") in relation to "truth" (see Part Three, koan 103 and koan 104). In answering "To be able to beat the drum" to all of the monk's questions, Kasan implies that he refuses to fall into the trap of defining "truth" (or "enlightenment"). This answer may also suggest the "working" of things (in contrast to their "essence").

By imitating the sound of the drum, the pupil suggests that he is "able to beat the drum." The attached quote suggests Kasan's thoroughness.

22.   No Great Masters?

In saying that "there are no more Zen masters in China," Obaku urges his pupils not to rely on others for enlightenment. By interpreting Ōbaku's remark as a reference to the condition of institutional Zen in China, the monk misses the point.

ANSWER

As against, "Do you know that there are no more Zen masters in China?"

By indicating his self-sufficiency, the pupil proves that he has understood the meaning of Ōbaku's saying. The quote suggests the power of one man.

As against, "I did not say there is no Zen anymore, only that there are no great masters!"

In his answer, the pupil may be taking the place of the monk. By "I was wrong," the "monk," as it were, admits that he has misunderstood Ōbaku's meaning. The attached quote suggests the theme of the power of one man.

In the answers "according to another school," the pupil naively responds to the phrases of the koan. However, in answering this way the pupil, like the monk, takes Ōbaku's words at their face value and thus misses their meaning.

23.   Where Did Nansen Go after His Death?

By making Shū ask Chōsa where Nansen went after his death, Sanshō sets a metaphysical trap for Chōsa. Chōsa's answer of Master Sekitō meeting Master Enō may be a historical fact, yet it has nothing to do with the question on Nansen. However, in answering this way, Chōsa does exactly what Shū has done. Namely, he mentions a fact of the past which bears no relation whatsoever to the present situation, and is nothing of the sort he or Shū have to occupy themselves with.

Shū misses the point of Chōsa's response and presses him to answer the question on Nansen, at which point Chōsa sends him to the right place to ask such a question. Shū's remark on the pine and the stalagmite is not quite clear. He may have meant to suggest that Chōsa's Zen, although unshakably strong, is not delicate enough; or that Chōsa's Zen may be perfect but it is not clear enough (or detailed enough) for the hearer to understand. At this, Chōsa is silent; he also keeps silent when Shū thanks him and Sanshō praises him. Silence is, after all, the only wise answer to the "after death" kind of metaphysical trap.

ANSWER

As against, "When Master Sekitō was a young priest he met Master Enō."

The quote deals with personalities who have already died. By mentioning the monk who has gone to buy bean curd, the pupil implies that he does not make any special distinction between "death" and "life" beyond the common distinction of regarding those who have died as dead and those alive as alive. His own concern is naturally with the living.

As against, "I didn't ask anything about Sekitō's young priesthood. I asked, 'Where did Nansen go after his death?'"

This answer suggests exactly the same thing as the previous answer above.

As against, "The master was still silent."

The pupil's silence and his "Shut up" have the same meaning as Chōsa's silence. He implies that the "after death" question is nonsensical and that the questioner had better shut up. All of the quotes attached to this answer suggest the natural course of the world, which goes quite a way toward answering the question on where one goes after death.

As against, "Go and ask Nansen!"

In "I wonder where he's gone," the pupil responds "naively" to the demand to go and search for the deceased Nansen. The first and the third quotes suggest the usual course of nature. If one insists on attaching meaning to the second quote, one may perhaps interpret it as suggesting a parallelism between the "life–death" states and the "dream–awakening" states. The popular saying simply refers to "searching for [Nansen]."

OR

(According to another school)

As against, "Where did Nansen go after his death?"

The answer, "I'm going to buy some sandals" disregards the "after death" part of the question and responds only to "go." Through the commonplace example of buying sandals, the pupil also suggests that there is not much difference between "going to buy sandals" and "going after death." Both are quite natural provided we regard them as such. As to the master's urging to forget the sandals, the pupil wisely responds with "paper." The quotes are a simple response to "where," suggesting "searching for."
As against, "When Master Sekitō was a young priest he met Master Enō."

The answer is unclear. Perhaps it is a simple response to "young."
As against, "Go and ask Nansen!"

The pupil suggests that he is not concerned with the non-existent (the deceased Nansen), but with the immediate occurrence as it presents itself moment after moment.

24. One, Two, Three

Sozan's question, "How much will you give the constructor?" is still within the commonplace situation of evaluating a piece of work and paying for it. The monk, instead of being concerned with the matter of construction, pays respect to his master. In response, Sozan fools the monk, embarrassing him with the "one, two, three" mon question. Rasan's nonsensical response to Sozan's question indicates that he has understood Sozan's mind. In dealing with daily affairs, one is certainly faced with distinctions and evaluations. However, this does not mean that one has to speculate beyond the actual situation as it presents itself. One has to pay the due price, that's all.

Sozan appreciates Rasan's answer and praises him for it. Yet, by "It is a December lotus flower" (i.e., out of season), he suggests that Rasan's phrases are perhaps superb but he would rather have the due answer at the right moment and forget about the whole matter. Rasan responds to the "December lotus flower" with the "hair of the tortoise" (the tortoise of course has no hair). By this he indicates that the whole matter (including Sozan's praise) is indeed outdated and even somewhat superfluous.

ANSWER
As against, "Which is the best thing to do—give the constructor three mon, or give him two mon, or just give him one mon?"

The pupil takes the place of the constructor and expresses his thanks for the money. By this he indicates that in paying a generous sum, one receives due thanks.

As against "An old Buddha is now radiating light which shines all the way to this place."

In contrast to Sozan's exquisite praise of Rasan, the answer suggests the commonplace.

As against (Rasan's), "If you give three mon, you will not have the monument built in your lifetime. If you give two mon, you will be both extending one hand. If you give one mon, you will both lose your eyebrows and beard."

The three pine trees differ in location and form but they are, after all, the same (in being pine trees). This answer indicates that, be it pine trees or money, one should not be taken in by "one," "two," "three"; when it comes time to pay, one simply pays.

As against, "A December lotus flower."

As against the "rare" and the "beautiful" the answer suggests the easy and the commonplace. This may refer both to the monk's not answering Sozan's question and to Rasan's answering it. The quote on the "many" and "one" provides a clue to the solution of the "one," "two," "three" problem. Once you realize the relations between the one (or "mu") and the many (or "u"), you simply stop speculating when things ought to be done.

OR

(According to another school)

By "Daruma does not know how to count," the pupil suggests that there is no need to speculate when counting. It is easy to count to three, or to seven, or to a million, provided you know what you are counting for. Ones does not need "special knowledge" for that.

As against, "The radiant light shines all the way to this place."

The pupil simply recites the phrase. Rather than attach "meaning" to this kind of answer, it would perhaps be better to consider what else the pupil could have done.

25. *An Iron Cow*

"If there is movement, there is no progress"—that is, if taken in by "u" ("existence," the world of "becoming") one loses sight of "mu" (the immutable aspect of "nothing," or "void"). There is thus "no progress" toward "enlightenment."

"If there is standstill, there is stagnation"—that is, taken in by the static aspect of "mu," one cannot move freely in the world of things ("u"). The "iron cow" stands for "no-movement" (being of iron), and "no-standstill" (being a cow). The problem Fuketsu raises in connection with "iron-cow-like-Buddha-mind" concerns the consciousness of "enlightenment." Being conscious of one's enlightenment (or of one's "iron cow" state of mind), can one really be said to be enlightened?

The monk declares that he is "enlightened" ("I hold: the working of the iron cow") and tells Fuketsu not to be bothered about it. By saying this, however, the monk only proves that he is too conscious of himself. In the example of the frog, Fuketsu suggests the narrowness of the monk's understanding. Fuketsu yells at the monk, hits him, and urges him to repeat what has just been said. When the monk opens his mouth to speak, Fuketsu hits him again. In thus treating the monk, Fuketsu draws out from the monk the consciousness of his own consciousness, and makes him return to what he originally is.

Bokushu's remark is an explanation of Fuketsu's "working" on the monk—when things get complicated and tangled up, there is a need to "cut." Fuketsu's getting down from his seat and leaving might simply mean what it says, but it is not unreasonable to assume that by leaving, Fuketsu "cuts" (the argument) for his own peace of mind.

ANSWER
As against, "Buddha-mind is like an iron cow."

A "stone mill" does indeed "not move a bit" as an object in itself, but its "working" is its movement. Through "stone mill" the pupil provides another, perhaps better, metaphor for the "no-movement-no-standstill" quality of Buddha-mind. The quotes attached to this answer suggest that the natural "working" of the mind means responding to the occasion as it presents itself.

As against, "If there is movement—there is no progress, if there is standstill—there is stagnation. This 'no-movement-no-standstill,' should one be mindful of it? Should one be unmindful of it?"

In his answer, the pupil indicates that he understands what the monk did not understand. Namely, that if one says one is "not mindful" of something it only proves that one is. By slapping his master, the pupil "cuts" through the entanglement of "consciousness of consciousness."

26.   *Similar to a Dream*

Rikkō is taken in by the Idealistic view that "the void is consciousness." (The quote expresses the standpoint of "idealistic monism" held by a group of the Yogācāra School philosophers). Nansen in his answer ridicules Idealism, suggesting that a flower is not a "dream" (the product of consciousness), but simply a flower.

ANSWER

The pupil's first two answers suggest that according to Rikkō's view a "flower is not a flower" (it is like a "mortar" or a "rice cake," everything being equally "dream stuff"), whereas Nansen regards the flower as a flower ("it has bloomed beautifully"). The following two answers concerning the "positions" of Rikkō and Nansen metaphorically suggest that Rikkō's standpoint is esoteric and metaphysical whereas Nansen's standpoint is that of common sense (or at least that which allows for common sense).

"To listen, to see, to learn, to know is not all," suggests that besides the subject there is the object as it is in itself; we do not "create" the things around us, we only perceive them. "The mountain and rivers should not be seen through a mirror" implies a rejection of the Idealistic standpoint which sees in the external world no more than its reflection on the "mirror of consciousness." In repeating the quote and demonstrating its meaning, the pupil misses the point. The pupil is not supposed to see things from Rikkō's standpoint but from Nansen's.

The master's following quote ("The moon is sinking from the frosty sky . . .") suggests solipsism (the inevitable result of Idealistic philosophy). This time, the pupil's reaction is in accordance with Nansen's view. He responds to the "being alone" suggestion of the quote as simply "there's no one to talk to." The pupil's (and Nansen's) standpoint is "realistic," both in the philosophical sense and in its ordinary sense ("I'll piss and go to bed"). However, philosophically speaking, it is not "naive realism." The last phrase of the attached quote—"But now, nothing but wild birds can be seen flying about"—suggests that along with the "u" aspect of things ("When Kōsen, king of Etsu . . . all over the spring palace like flowers") there is the "mu" ("nothing," "void"). It should be noted that my interpretation of the poem is not in accordance with the author's remark, which regards the poem as a representation of Rikkō's and Nansen's position. I find it hard to see what the author's interpretation is based upon. The quote on the donkey and the well suggests that "subject" and "object" are in harmony, interacting in accordance with the situation.

OR

(According to another school)

At first reading, the pupil's response to the phrases of the koan seems to represent the standpoint of Idealism. However, the pupil's quote on one wandering around without realizing he is already in the "peach paradise" (i.e., the "perfect" state), and his response ("guess I'll go to bed") to the Idealistically-mooded poem ("The moon is sinking from the frosty sky . . .") imply a rejection of the speculative attitude of the Idealistic mind.

Given this clue, we may interpret the answers to the first two "as against" phrases of the koan as suggesting "harmony with the world," not in the Idealistic sense (of the "world as consciousness"), but in the common sense of being "at peace" with the world. The pupil's reaction to the third "as against" phrase (pretending to be asleep) is a simple response to "dream," whereas in his answer to "to listen, to see, to learn, to know is not all," the pupil suggests that he understands that although all of these are functions of the "subject," this does not mean that the "subject" is the whole world. There is the act of seeing and there is the object seen, each in its own right. It is no use denying that the "object" of our mind is "out there," independent of the perceiver; the denial would estrange us from our surroundings and from the people we live with.

27. "Not Affected," "Not Deluded"

The old man fell into the state of a fox because he had sought his "enlightenment" in detachment from the natural order ("not affected by causality"). The "not affected" viewpoint is that of the old Theravada tradition, in which nirvana is regarded as a state of total liberation from (or "extinction" of) the natural process of cause and effect. Hyakujō suggests that everything is of necessity "affected" by causality. In his view, "enlightenment" does not mean freedom from the causal order but its total acceptance. In resisting the natural order, we are "deluded by causality." Zen satori consists not in the rejection of the world but in admitting it to be what it is. In the realization of this truth, the old man is delivered from his foxhood.

There is nothing wrong with Hyakujō's answer as far as Zen "doctrine" is concerned. The only flaw in the story is the suggestion that a "word" (or a "doctrine") carries much weight. Arguing on the difference between "affected" and "deluded" is futile no matter whether you side with "non-affected" or "non-deluded." The moment you are taken in by such speculations you become foxy anyway. Both Hyakujō and Ōbaku seem to have understood this. That Ōbaku understands we learn from his slapping of Hyakujō. That Hyakujō understands we learn from his paradoxical saying on the "red-bearded barbarian." The difference between "non-affected" and "non-deluded" suggests the saying, is more or less the same as between "it is a fine day today" and "today is a fine day." This does not necessarily mean that there is no difference, only that we had better forget about the whole argument.

ANSWER

As against, "Not affected by causality" and "not deluded by causality."

The pupil's answer suggests "it is all the same." However, if we interpret this answer as implying that there is no difference between "non-affected" and "non-deluded" we perhaps go too far. It would be better to take it as a refusal to argue about the matter. In his answer on the "fox" question, the pupil may suggest that in any Buddhist temple there is at least one silly monk who would never miss the opportunity to argue "Buddhist doctrine."

As against, "I only thought that the barbarian's beard was red, I never realized it was a red-bearded barbarian."

If the quote on "sweet" and "bitter" was carefully chosen, it might imply a warning not to interpret Hyakujō's saying on the "red-bearded barbarian" as suggesting that "not affected" and "not deluded" are exactly the same. After all, it makes some difference whether one tastes "sweet" or "bitter."

The answers of the second school are identical with those of the first school. In the answers of the third school, the pupil simply demonstrates the phrases of the koan. In answering thus, the pupil seems to have missed the point of the second half of the koan. However, such a response may also imply that the pupil takes a naive (non-speculative) attitude to the story.

28. *Where Thing Does Not Contradict Thing*

The philosophy of the Chinese Kegon school of thought was introduced to Japan around the middle of the eighth century. Although the doctrine of Kegon was widely studied in Japan, the sect did not prosper as a living religion. The philosophy of Kegon deals with the relation of the "world as a whole" to particular phenomena. The central concept of this philosophy is that every particle, no matter how infinitesimal, reflects the whole phenomenal world. In the answers, the Kegon philosophy on the "realms of existence" is given a Zen interpretation.

ANSWER
(The answers of the two schools are reviewed together)
As against, "The realm of truth."

If we consider the "truth" of the world ("mu" or "kū"—"nothingness" or "void") in itself, we lose sight of "u" ("existence" or "the particular thing"). The view of "truth" as "kū" or "mu" is a Zen interpretation of the quote. In the doctrine of Kegon, "truth" means the "law" (or "order" of) the phenomenal world.
As against, "The realm of things."

The answer of the first school seems to equate this realm with the realm "where thing does not contradict thing." Therefore, the difference between these two realms is better expressed in the answer of the second school—"to see the hand as a hand." "The realm of things" is the realm of "u" viewed in itself.
As against, "The realm where truth and things do not contradict each other."

This is the realm where "truth" and "things" are viewed as harmoniously interrelated; but where "mu" ("truth") and "u" ("things") are still distinguished as concepts. This is the realm where one "knows" that the particular and the whole are the same, however this knowledge has not yet been realized in fact.
As against, "The realm where thing does not contradict thing."

Whereas in the "realm of things" there is only the realization of a particular thing for what it is ("to see the hand as a hand"), in this realm each and every thing is realized for what it is. "Mu" and "u" are not only *thought* of as one, but indeed *become* one (in the "enlightened" mind). Note that the answer of the second school to this realm is identical with the answer of the Takujū School to the koan on the sound of the one hand.

29. *What Will You Call It?*

This koan is intended to test whether or not the pupil is taken in by speculations concerning the essence of things. The problem exists, of course, even if we disregard the Buddhist doctrine of rebirth—am I the same now as when I was a child, or a year ago, or a moment ago?

ANSWER

By simply giving his name, the pupil implies that he is concerned neither with existence in the past or future, nor with "essence." When asked, "Who are you?" one should give one's name; but when asked, "Who are you really?" one had better keep one's mouth shut.

30. *Stick!*

Shuzan suggests that, viewed as "mu" ("nothingness," "void"), a stick is not a stick, and viewed as "u," a stick is perhaps too much of a stick. But his question, "What will you call it?" is a trap. The realization of "mu" should not prevent one from calling things by their name. By breaking the stick and throwing it away, Sekken seems to imply that if Shuzan wants him to do away with the (word) "stick," he has to get rid of the stick. Shuzan's reaction ("Blind!") is unclear. It seems to me that Sekken answered the challenge in a perfect way and set a trap for Shuzan of his own. But as suggested in the answers, Shuzan seems to have expected the demonstration of the correct "usage" of the stick (as a proof of having transcended the problem of whether the stick is a "stick" or a "non-stick"). Therefore, Shuzan might have interpreted Sekken's act as implying the elimination of the stick (together with the word "stick"). Such an interpretation would suggest that in his insistence on "mu," Sekken is "blind" to "u" (of simply using the stick as a stick is to be used).

ANSWER

In the first school, the correct answer to the problem of the stick is "putting it away in the corner of the shelf" (where the stick of the Zen master is usually put). The same is implied in the second school by "stick it under the bathtub and burn it up." The rest of the discourse is a clarification of the aspect of "mu" and "u" concerning names of things. The last answer of the first school (turning a somersault) is somewhat artificial.

31. The Emperor and the Bowl

This koan may imply criticism of the story of Enō and his miraculous bowl. In lifting the bowl, the emperor does not act out of vanity. Through this act the emperor (and the composer of this koan) seem to suggest their ironical attitude to the supernatural.

ANSWER

The answers and the quotes are best understood from the position of Minister Ōzui. In the koan, Ōzui keeps silent. Whatever Ōzui's real attitude to Buddhism and its miracle-stories may be, as the emperor's minister he is supposed to serve his emperor and praise him. Those who feel inclined to interpret the minister's praise of the emperor as irony had better not serve under an emperor.

32. How Is Your Health?

According to Buddhist legendary folklore, Nichimenbutsu is the Buddha of the longest life term, whereas Getsumenbutsu is the Buddha of the shortest life term. However, it would be better not to attach too much meaning to the mentioning of these two Buddhas. Baso's answer suggests the transient nature of human life; or the mentioning of these two Buddhas may simply be a traditional prayer of the sick.

ANSWER

The answer of the first school implies that life is short-lived and nobody, not even Buddhas, can predict when one's term of life will be over. The master's quote suggests that one should not be carried away by bereavement when faced with the natural phenomenon of death. In the second school, the pupil's answer to the same quote simply suggests the pupil's position should his master die. The third answer ("Oh, the pain! The pain!") does not appear in the Japanese edition, but it is used with certain masters. This simple expression of the actual situation of a sick person in agony seems to me the best response to the koan. The answer was not told to me by any of the people mentioned in connection with the translation and notation of this book.

33. *The Gate!*

Suigan's "See if my eyebrows are still here" is based upon the popular saying that if one preaches too much Buddhism one's eyebrows will fall off. Hofuku, Chōkei, and Ummon were fellow pupils of Suigan. We may thus assume that this exchange of words did indeed take place. The meaning of these three masters' sayings is somewhat unclear. However, if we insist on interpreting them we may perhaps read them as:

HOFUKU: "Indeed, I am afraid you have talked too much."
CHŌKEI: "You are worried too much."
UMMON: [Don't come with these tricks] "Shut up!"

ANSWER

In both schools the pupil's answer to Chōkei's phrase and the accompanying quotes are a simple response to "growing." The answer to Hofuku's saying is no more than its repetition. The pupil's answer (second school) concerning "Suigan's feeling" suggests that Suigan is sure there is nothing wrong with him (for if he felt he had talked too much he would not have apologized for it). However, this answer may also be interpreted as suggesting Suigan's fear that in talking too much he has spoiled things.

The most important part is the answer to Ummon's "The gate!" In both schools, the pupil's quotes to Ummon's saying suggest that Ummon's way of rebuking Suigan is the perfect response to the situation. The answers of roaring "GAAATE!" and slapping the master (first school), as well as the longer phrase on "gate" (second school), all suggest: "From here on, not a single step further!" These "gate" answers, in implying that there is a natural limit to the use of words, have a similar effect to the "Mu——" answer of the koan on "mu" (see notes to the koan on "mu," Inzan School, pp. 223–224).

34. *Unforgivable*

Whether the historical Daruma (Bodhidharma—founder of Zen) should be "forgiven" or not is not the problem. What is put into question here is Zen. In fact, there is not much difference between "knowing" and "understanding." Both terms refer to thought and speech based upon abstract concepts. In as far as we cannot do without concepts, we should be "forgiven." But from the Zen point of view, our dependence upon them is "unforgivable."

The last quote suggests that "knowledge" and "understanding" are actually the same (just like a "good" courtier and a "faithful" one). The koan may thus be interpreted as "that we know is forgivable, that we know is unforgivable." In his "acceptance" of "knowledge" ("that's okay") the pupil implies that we cannot do without it. In his rejection of "knowledge" ("that's bad") he implies that there is nothing we can do with it. The quote on "cleverness" and "foolishness" indicates the Zen approach to the problem of "knowledge." It implies that it may be easy to be "clever" (to know), but it is difficult to be "foolish" (to not know).

35. *How Do You Say It?*

Kinzan lays a trap for Tokusan. He suggests that Tokusan's masters said "it" (their Zen) in a certain way, and he asks Tokusan to show him his own way of saying "it." Tokusan is not taken in. He refuses to define his Zen, and instead requires Kinzan to say "it." Whatever Kinzan may have intended to say, he deserves to be hit, for the problem here is not Zen but the "saying" of Zen. Gantō understands Tokusan's teaching but Kinzan, who is taken in by the insult of having been beaten, fails to understand.

ANSWER

The master lays the same trap of "say Zen" for the pupil. The pupil's answer suggests that by now he is only too familiar with this kind of trap-question.

36. *Discuss Buddhist Law*

In his story, Nansen implies that discussing Buddhist law is absolutely superfluous. It is not clear why Jōshū suggests that Nansen himself deserves a beating. He may have meant that the argument against arguments is itself a superfluous argument. Another possible interpretation of Jōshū's saying may be: "If it is so easy to solve all problems by beating, why don't we beat you too?"

The answers of both schools suggest the moral of Nansen's story. A discussion on Buddhist doctrine (or any other futile discussion) is likened to wandering thoughts at night (first school) and to irritating pain (second school), whereas the drastic "cutting off" of the discussion is likened to deep sleep and to relief from pain. The first quote may imply that, after all, Nansen too is guilty of futile discussion. The second quote suggests a state of evenness of mind in which all arguments pro and con have been eliminated.

37. Simultaneous Doubt and Enlightenment

In his statement on "simultaneous doubt and enlightenment," Nan-in suggests that it is not enough to know the interrelation between the pupil's question and the master's answer at the moment of enlightenment "as a thing in itself" (i.e., to know it in a theoretical way). By "not holding onto the mold" he implies that the correct "working" of "simultaneous doubt and enlightenment" should not be an overly conscious process. The monk who keeps on speculating about "simultaneous doubt and enlightenment" proves that he is too conscious of the matter, upon which Nan-in hits him. Still taken in by his problem, the monk searches for an answer at Ummon's place. A monk at Ummon's place understands and suggests that Nan-in's hitting *is* the "working" of "simultaneous doubt and enlightenment" ("Nan-in broke his stick"); at this the effect of Nan-in's stick is actualized and the monk is enlightened. In "At that time I was walking by the light of a lamp" the monk suggests that, before his realization, he was in need of an external aid to "see," whereas now he is free to see by himself.

In the first two answers, the pupil suggests that there should not be too much reliance on the master. As against "the application of simultaneous doubt and enlightenment" the pupil suggests that things take their natural course, and that one should not be too conscious of what one is doing.

38. Don't You Believe Me Now?

This koan is best understood if we do not overburden it with too many suggestions. In Zen, a witty mind is highly appreciated, provided the wit is not of a too speculative kind. If you want to convince people that a dog is a cat, just call "Hey, cat" and the "cat" will respond to the call.

The answers simply praise Chinsō's cleverness.

39. I Never Said a Word . . .

In "I never said a word about Zen," Kassan implies that he has never "preached" Zen. In reproving Kassan for his statement, the monk may have meant to suggest that the argument "I never argue" is also an argument. It is also possible to understand the monk's reproof of Kassan as implying that if Kassan "had never said a word" he has done nothing to teach the people. Of course, Kassan did not mean he had never taught Zen, only that he had never "spoken" Zen. In any case, by throwing Kassan off his seat, the monk implies that Kassan is not fit to be a teacher of the people. Kassan, who feels he does not deserve such a terrible verdict, challenges the monk to a duel. The monk, who has neither sufficient reason to kill Kassan nor enough wit to overcome the dilemma of having to die if he does not kill Kassan, is forced to sneak away.

ANSWER
In his answer, the pupil implies that no matter whether the monk is right in reproving Kassan or not, he would have done better had he not been taken in by Kassan's "pit-show."

40. Where in the World Are They?

Toku-un, in his philosophical saying, suggests that there are no distinctions of time and place in the "true" (enlightened) mind. In view of Toku-un's "philosophy," there is really no problem in Engo's question ("Where in the world are Toku-un and Zenzai?"). If all existence is included in "a simple thought," Toku-un and Zenzai could meet anywhere or nowhere and still be together. However, Engo's question is a trap. The pupil is not supposed to force "Buddhist philosophy" upon reality. In Zen, "deliverance" from the limitations of "time–space" does not mean to transcend time and space, but to eliminate "time–space" as a conceptual, abstract problem.

In his answer, the pupil suggests that in the common sphere of reality (what other sphere is there?) people simply *do* meet each other. Isn't he, in fact, meeting his master right now?

41. *A Bottle Is a Bottle*

Hyakujō's question is a trap. A bottle, of course, can only be called "bottle." The head monk is well aware of this, but only in theory. In his answer ("You cannot call it a wooden log") he suggests that "a bottle is a bottle," but his answer is still speculative. In making a statement on the obvious, the head monk takes an attitude that is too self-conscious. Isan, by simply kicking the bottle over, suggests "action" (as against "words"). It is not enough to "speak" common sense. Only through the natural and immediate response to the situation does ("enlightened") common sense reveal itself.

The quote suggests the natural movement of things. The head monk's answer does not fit the mood of the quote, whereas Isan's action does.

42. *A Silver Bowl Filled with Snow*

Daiba (Āryadeva) was the disciple of the philosopher Nāgārjuna (end of the second century A.D.), the originator of the Sunyata ("void") school of Buddhist thought. The term "Daiba sect" refers to one of the branches of the Sunyata School (a more common name of Chinese origin for this sect is "Sanron sect"). Zen, in its doctrinal aspect, is greatly influenced by Nāgārjuna's philosophy, whose essence is the rejection of the affirmative–negative mode of reasoning and the identification of samsara with nirvana (or "the world as it is" with "enlightenment"). The problem of this koan, however, is not the doctrine of the Daiba sect in itself but the monk's state of mind. The monk asks Haryō to express the "teaching" in words. In his answer, Haryō suggests that however "true" a doctrine may be, if it is viewed only in its verbal sphere it is of no use. Words ("snow"), even if put in the most perfect form ("silver bowl"), are bound to melt away.

In the answers of both schools, the pupil expresses his refusal to be taken in by doctrines (or mere forms). The quote suggests that the moment you open your mouth (to argue "truth") you betray yourself.

43. *Every Coral Branch Supports the Moon*

The monk's question on the "sharpest of all swords" suggests that he is searching for the one supreme "truth" or "enlightenment" that rules over all things. Haryō's saying implies that all things are one, and the one is all things. There is thus no need for any specific "truth."

By pretending to break the "sword" and throw it away (first school), the pupil implies that he is not taken in by any specific "truth." The pupil's answer in the second school implies that all ways are "the way" provided one does the right thing at the right moment. The quotes attached to this answer complete it, suggesting harmony with the natural state of things.

44. *An Open-eyed Man Falls into the Well*

The monk asking for "the Way" is one-track minded. He assumes that there is a method of clearly distinguishing between the "right" way and the "wrong" way in matters of enlightenment. Haryō's answer implies that by being conscious ("open-eyed") to "the way," one misses it ("falling into the well").

In his answer the pupil takes the monk's place and suggests his understanding of Haryō's warning.

45. *In Relation to One*

Ummon's "in relation to one" has the connotation of "monism," but such an outspoken philosophical statement would not be Zen-like. Zen scholars in Japan found it difficult to interpret Ummon's phrase, yet the answer makes its meaning quite clear.

ANSWER

In his answer the pupil suggests that "in relation to one" means to respond to the situation ("one by one") as it presents itself.

46. *In Opposition to One*

Buddha's real teaching is "in relation to one" (see Part Three, koan 45). Therefore, in "opposition to one" suggests "not Buddha's real teaching" or simply "not real" (or non-existent). What is "not right before the eyes" is in the abstract or the transcendental. But be it a "happening" or a "thing," it is all right here in front of us. Those who seek for the "truth" or "enlightenment" in the world beyond will not find it.

ANSWER

Instead of explaining the "meaning" of "in opposition to one" (or "not right before the eyes") the pupil, through the two quotes, suggests the human world and the world of nature (as it is "right before the eyes") with its loves and hates, flower blossoms, and chirping of birds. In his answer to "What is the transcendental?" ("A thing or a happening not right before the eyes"), the pupil simply repeats the question. Responding thus, he in a way disarms his master.

47. *Are You Alive?*

This koan deals with the relation between pupil and master (same theme as koan 37, see note on p. 274). If we change the metaphorical phrasing into everyday language we would get something like the following dialogue:

MONK: "I am looking for enlightenment. Will you teach me?"

MASTER: "Do you have enough energy (or will) of your own?"

MONK: "If I did not, I would not come here."

Kyōshō seems to be satisfied with the monk's attitude.

ANSWER

The answer suggests the reciprocal "working" of the pupil (the chick's "chirp") and the master (the hen's "peck").

48. The One-Piece Tower

The emperor seems to confuse Zen with the lectures he has been given by his Zen master. Regarding Zen as "teaching," he is concerned about his progress should his master die. Etchū says that when he dies the emperor should build a "one-piece tower." Every tower is, in fact, a combination of many "pieces." Taken in by the illusion that his enlightenment depends upon his Zen master, the emperor conceives himself as formed from several "pieces" stuck together. What Etchū suggests in his answer is that if the emperor understands that enlightenment is *self*-realization, he will become a "one-piece tower." Whether Etchū is alive or dead is nothing for the emperor to be concerned with. By "tower," the emperor seems to have understood a memorial tower for Etchū. Asking for the form of the "tower," he is actually asking for the form of his ("enlightened") self. In his silence, Etchū suggests that the emperor should restore his mind to where it originally is. The emperor, however, does not understand that the "tower" Etchū wants him to build is, besides being "formless," not Etchū's but solely his own.

ANSWER

As against, "To ask the master for the form of the tower."

The pupil's answer suggests that the form of the tower is that of oneself.

As against, "Etchū remained silent."

Through the quote the pupil suggests that Etchū's silence refers to the natural state of things. Everything is in its perfect state, not one thing trespasses on the other.

As against, "South of Shō, north of Tan."

There seem to be no such places, but even if there were, one is not supposed to be concerned with that. Wherever one happens to be is one's perfect place. Thus through "here is the shelf, here is the door," the pupil points to "right here, now!" Setchō's comment to the above quote may perhaps suggest "You have to do it yourself."

As against, "Within it overflows with gold."

The pupil suggests that he is not concerned with any marvelous sphere ("overflowing with gold") elsewhere, but only with where he happens to be and what he happens to see right in front of him. Setchō's comment to the quote may perhaps suggest "confusion" or "over-exaggeration."

As against, "Under a shadeless tree rests a ferryboat."

As against the fiction of the "shadeless tree," the pupil by sitting down suggests that his own "working" is the commonplace action of the real world. Setchō's comment on the quote may perhaps suggest "no movement."

As against, "There is an emerald palace that holds no Buddhist priest of fame."

This quote and the pupil's answer suggest that it is up to everyone to build his own "tower." The emperor (in his palace) is the emperor, whereas the Buddhist priest is the Buddhist priest. To combine the two would make a "double-piece tower." The emperor should know his own mind. Setchō rightly comments that by this statement Tangen "brought it right in front of the [emperor's] eyes."

49. *No Meaning*

Suibi and Rinzai rightly hit Ryūge for his question on the "meaning of Zen." Surprisingly enough Ryūge is neither dumbfounded nor "enlightened" by the "meaning" of Zen (as is the case in most koans of the same pattern), but categorically asserts that there *is* no meaning to Zen. Through Ryūge, Zen turns itself into an object of irony.

ANSWER

The pupil's suggestion (in the answer and in the attached quote) that throughout his Zen study he hasn't "gained" a bit is quite all right as far as Zen is concerned. Through such irony, Zen compliments itself.

50. *It Is Somewhat a Pity*

The meaning of this koan is not quite clear. In a somewhat forced interpretation it may be said that Hofuku, by mentioning the proper name of the mountain, is taken in by "u" ("existence" or "the world of things"). In "It is all right but it is somewhat a pity," Chōkei may be expressing his sorrow for Hofuku's state of mind, or (as Setchō suggests in his first comment) his sorrow for having taken Hofuku along with him. Setchō's second comment is unclear, whereas Kyōshō's comment suggests that if it were not for Chōkei, the situation would have been much worse.

ANSWER

As against, "That is the peak of Mt. Myōhō."

The pupil represents Hofuku's state of mind and suggests that Hofuku is exaggerating in his response to the landscape.

As against, "It is all right, but it is somewhat a pity."

In his answer, the pupil takes the position of Chōkei and suggests that it is no use dwelling upon a situation when it is time to move on. The attached quote on the parting of the soldier from his beloved general may refer to Hofuku's state of mind regarding the landscape.

51. *A Few Here, a Few There*

Mujaku seems to think that the state of the "teaching of Buddha" depends upon the number of monks and their degree of discipline (as to the monastic law). Being too conscious of the difference between "monk" and "layman," he is taken in by distinctions (between "south" and "north," "many" and "few"). Monju's answer ("The people and saints live together. Dragons and snakes mingle"), rather than indicating the state of Buddhism in the "south," suggests his own state of mind. Thus, whereas the Zen master Mujaku, in attaching great importance to the monastic order, takes a Hinayanic view of Buddhism, Monju represents the viewpoint of Zen. In his answer ("a few here, a few there") to the question on the number of monks, Monju suggests "it is all the same."

ANSWER

The quote given as an answer and the following attached quotes all suggest that no matter how hard you try to distinguish between one thing and another, ultimately all things are interrelated. Be it "front" or "back," "head" or "tail," you cannot consider the one without the other. Mujaku is looking for Buddhism in a particular place and with a particular group of people, but what is the use of hiding your "head" while exposing your "rear"? Head and bottom, monk and layman, each is where it is supposed to be. In the horse market there are only horses.

52. *Where Is the Mind?*

Similar to Part Two, koan 133. With the past no more, the future not yet, and the present no more than the borderline be-

(281)

tween past and future, how can anything "be"? The pupil is not supposed to provide an answer to this "philosophical trap" (who can?), but to disregard it. If we deny "existence" because we cannot rationally define it in terms of "time," what are we going to do with ourselves and the world around us?

In the first school, the answer and the quote suggest that things are perfectly all right where they are, the way they are. In the second school, by slapping his master and refusing to comment on "no existence," the pupil simply rejects the problem of "existence" as a trap. In the third school, as in the first school, the pupil points to "the world as it is." In reference to "Where is the mind?" the answers of the first and third schools suggest that the "mind" is right in the time–place situation one is in (in reference to the "mind-of-the-moment," see Part Two, koan 51, note on p. 235). The answer of the second school suggests that we had better not speculate about this matter.

53. A Speck of Dust

This koan is hard to understand. A possible, although somewhat forced, interpretation might regard Fuketsu's saying as dealing with "life" ("being") and "death" ("nothing"). This interpretation is also suggested in Setchō's comment. Whether a nation prospers or perishes certainly makes a great difference. In the same way, it is no less important for each individual whether he exists or not. Yet ultimately it does not really matter; no more than whether a speck of dust is raised ("u") or not ("mu"). Fuketsu may be suggesting that one should hold to both attitudes equally.

ANSWER

The poem on the two territories whose boundaries meet at the river, may suggest the relation between "u" and "mu."

54. Gya!

55. Nyan

In the older sources, these are combined into one koan. Here they are brought forth as two separate koans, apparently because each part was considered to deserve a separate answer. When Nansen holds up the cat, ready to cut it into two, he aims at driving the monks to their wits' end. Yet the monks, who are too conscious of the *master*, are taken in by speculation on the "meaning" of the situation and miss the point. What was it that Jōshū realized and the monks did not? Jōshū knew the *cat*. By putting his sandals on his head, Jōshū suggests turning things upside down. In his answer, the "human" turns into a "cat," the cat escapes Nansen, and the problem is solved. We may assume that had Jōshū been present, he would have snatched the cat away from Nansen. As for Nansen, no matter how important it is that monks be enlightened, he seems to be overdoing his Zen if he has to bother cats with it.

ANSWER

In speculating over the difference between life and death, philosophers are in danger of missing the point. The pupil's answers simply suggest the difference between the cat dying and the cat living.

56. *Come and Eat Your Rice*

There is nothing wrong with Kingyū feeding his pupils rice. It seems, however, that he is somewhat overly enthusiastic in trying to feed them his teaching.

ANSWER

In the first answer ("I'm full"), the pupil implies that he is in no need of Kingyū's teaching. The second answer, as against Setchō's comment ("The rice pot's empty"), suggests that Kingyū has nothing to feed his pupils with, and those who are tempted to respond to his noisy summons will return with an empty stomach. As against Chōkei's saying, the pupil recites a prayer which is usually said *after* meals, thus suggesting, as in the first answer, that he is already "full."

57. *Playing Ball on Rapid Water*

The Buddhist doctrine on the "person" views the psycho-physical organism as a complex interactive system of six senses—the five physical senses and the "mind" (or "thought") sense. The point of such an analysis is to do away with the concept of "self" (as a continuous "substance" above and beyond the incessant stream of personal events). Jōshū's answer implies that just as one cannot "play ball on rapid water" (there being no solid ground), there is no substratum ("self") uniting the flow of the personal events. Tōsu says the same thing in a direct way.

ANSWER

In imitating a baby, the pupil does nothing that can be interpreted as a refutation of the traditional "no-self" Buddhist doctrine. Yet his naive response to "baby" suggests the immediate, non-speculative Zen approach to reality.

58. *Playing with Mud*

In "What should one do to shoot the deer among deer?" the monk questions Yakusan as to his insight into the enlightenment of his pupils. By "Watch out for my arrow," Yakusan simply suggests "watch me" or "watch my working." However, in letting himself fall, the monk implies that it is *he* who is "the deer among deer." Being too self-satisfied ("he plays with mud") the monk has overplayed his game ("he knows no limits").

Setchō's comment implies that there was nothing wrong with the monk's first question (provided it was simply intended to ask for Yakusan's power of insight), yet with his second pose he doomed himself as a "useless corpse."

ANSWER

In his first answer (to "watch out for my arrow"), the pupil takes the position of the master. By "letting himself fall," he seems to be responding naively to the phrase, whereas in his last answer ("instead of the monk") he seems to assert himself by "shooting" his master.

59. *The Sturdy Body of Truth*

By "the sturdy body of truth" the monk asks for the permanent "essence" of things. In Buddhist philosophy, the "truth" or "essence" of existence is identified with "mu" ("nothingness"), or "kū" ("void"). The Sunyata ("void") school of Buddhist thought identifies "kū" or "mu" (the "essenceless essence" of things) with "u" ("existence" or "the world as it is"). In Zen this abstract philosophical principle is made actual and concrete in the "here–now" moment of satori (see Part Two, koans 37–39, notes on p. 234). Through the description of natural scenery, Tairyū suggests that "truth" is right where the physical body is.

ANSWER

In the first answer the pupil identifies his (enlightened) self with mountain flowers and a brook. He thus implies that he is making no distinctions between the material world and its "truth." The rest of the dialogue is centered around "rot and decay." If the "essence" (or "truth") of the world is the same as its "physical body," it is bound to rot and decay along with the myriad of things. The pupil's answers suggest that he is not overly concerned with the transient nature of existence. When things pass away, they are simply gone. What is the use of clinging to one state of nature ("life") while refusing to admit another ("death")?

60. *Put Together*

The "putting together" of a famous master with a pole suggests that every and all things are interrelated. It is no use regarding one thing as important and labeling the other as valueless. Ummon's saying on clouds and rain expresses the idea that all things become equally interrelated by turning the common sense "cause–effect" relations upside down. For the same theme see Part Two, koans 57 and 58 (notes on p. 236).

ANSWER

The answer and the first quote suggest the interrelation of all things in everyday life. In the second quote on the three schools of Taoism, Confucianism, and Buddhism, the same concept is applied to the "realm of ideas."

61. *"Say Nothing" and Nothing Said*

Monju only *says* one should be silent. Yuima *is* silent.

62. *Which Is Your Self?*

The koan suggests the theme of "subject" (the "internal") and "object" (the "external"). In taking medicine we certainly do use an external object to cure ourselves. However, should we regard "the world" as the medicine for "existential disease, we miss the point of being alive.

ANSWER

The answer "TURRNIP" to the question "Which is your self?" may be regarded (as the author implies in his comment) as the rejection of an unanswerable question through a nonsensical statement. At the same time, however, it may be an extremely concrete form of suggesting "non-distinction" between "self" and "other" (or "self" and "the whole earth"). The quotes express the same theme through the mood of harmony between man and nature.

63. *Blind, Deaf, Dumb*

Gensha's saying on the blind, deaf, and mute may be a suggestion that in grasping the "essence" of things, "kū" ("void") or "mu" ("nothingness"), there is no real need of the senses. However, Ummon's treatment of Gensha's saying suggests that we would do best to disregard the problem (of the "non-sensual" realm). As we actually *do* see, hear, and speak, why should we be concerned with the unseen, unheard, and unspoken in an overly conscious way?

ANSWER

In his answers, the pupil combines Gensha's words and Ummon's common sense Zen view into one phrase. The impact of this combination results in making Ummon's view the more acceptable. However, this does not necessarily mean that from the Zen point of view the combination of the two views entails contradiction. The attached quotes support Ummon's view through the description of the natural state of things in the world of the senses (colors, sounds, voices).

64. *Sound*

The koan need not be commented upon. It should be noted however that through the artificial imitation of Kyōgen's "enlightenment-situation" the answer misses the point (see Part Two, koan 62, note on p. 236).

65. *What Do You Understand by This?*

The simile of the cart is employed in some of the oldest Buddhist texts to illustrate the idea that things are without substance. True, if you take away all the parts of a cart, there is no cart any more; if you eliminate, one by one, all the physical and mental elements, there is no "person." But aren't there carts and people right here around us?

ANSWER

The pupil's answer suggests a non-speculative attitude. A cart is a cart; isn't he pushing one up the slope?

66. *Not Keeping Silent, Not Using Words*

"Not using words" does not necessarily mean "keeping silent." All it means is not using words *wrongly* (see also Part Two, koan 73, note on p. 237).

ANSWER

The man on the road "understands the way" (i.e., he is enlightened), he simply does not know the way to where he is going. In explaining the way to him there is of course no misuse of words.

67. *Taking a Bath*

Same theme as Part Three, koan 64, on Kyōgen's enlightenment upon hearing a piece of brick hit the bamboo. This koan has its merit in suggesting that the "taking a bath" situation is as good for the attainment of enlightenment, as any other situation. The answer, like the answer to koan 64, is superfluous for the same reason (see note 64, pp. 286–287).

68. *Without Cold, Without Heat*

This koan repeats the theme of Part Two, koan 51 (see note on p. 235).

69. *What Do You Have in Mind?*

In Zen, the circle is sometimes used to symbolize "mu," but it is best to regard Nansen's drawing of a circle as no more than a practical joke. Kisū and Mayoku seem to be taken in by the circle's "meaning" and interpret it as a place to sit in or as an object of worship.

ANSWER
The pupil's answer suggests a more naive attitude to the circle. It may be assumed that this answer would have satisfied Nansen.

70. *Don't Fancy*

No comment necessary.

71. *Buddha's Master*

The theme of non-distinction between "holy" and "mundane." It is to be expected that the "non-enlightened" pupil would tend to regard the Buddhas as realities of a "higher" sphere. By suggesting that the Buddhas are slaves of the common man, Hōen intends to shock the pupil into an evenness of mind.

72. *Swallow a River?!*

Hōkoji is looking for that which "transcends existence." It is, of course, impossible to satisfactorily answer this kind of search. Instead, Baso poses an impossible demand to Hōkoji ("swallow the waters of the river"). Hōkoji's poem suggests his realization that beyond existence there is "nothing."

ANSWER
The answer plays on the theme of "swallow." By simply "swallowing" his tea, the pupil stresses the natural as against the metaphysical.

73. *Thought of the Moment*

This phrase, given an abstract philosophical interpretation, may be viewed as an expression of the "monistic" thought of the Kegon School; it is not Zen-like to put the idea of the "self-holding-the-infinite-dimensions-of-the-time-space-within-itself" into words. The quote is therefore responded to through a Zen attitude of mind.

ANSWER

As against the first part of the quote the pupil suggests "unity," not with the "boundless world" as a whole, but with each situation as it presents itself in the natural course of events. As against the second part of the quote, the pupil suggests that "the-thought-of-the-moment-which-holds-the-happenings-of-past-and-present" is not anything beyond the commonplace; it is the human thought of hate, desire, love, or pain wherever and whenever it occurs. The two popular sayings at the end suggest that the "infinite dimensions" of the "thought of the moment" are its immediacy and thoroughness.

74. *Where Is My Rhino?*

The attendant cannot answer Enkan's paradoxical saying. The later masters—Tōsu, Sekisō, Shifuku, Hofuku—attempt to answer instead. Setchō comments on their answers. According to my translation, it is a fan with a drawing of a rhino on it. The Chinese phrase describing the fan can also be understood as referring to a fan made from a rhino's horn. However, this would not change the meaning of Enkan's saying. What Enkan is asking for is the "substance" of the fan. Namely, as the phenomenal fan "is broken," he wants the "fanness" of it—its "immutable essence."

Tōsu's saying implies that all there is are the things as they appear and change in the phenomenal world. Thus Enkan can get no more than the "broken" rhino. To this Setchō suggests that things are all right the way they are even though "imperfect" (i.e., changing, substanceless). It is no use distinguishing between a phenomenon and its essence.

Sekisō's saying implies that once the "essence" is endowed with form (in "giving" it to Enkan), it cannot be said to be the "essence" anymore. Setchō comments ("But the rhino is still there") that Sekisō is too concerned with the "perfection" of the rhino: perfect or not, a rhino is there.

In writing the word (character) "rhino," Shifuku suggests that what is unchangeable in the rhino is no more than the word (or concept) "rhino." Setchō's comment ("Why didn't you bring it out before?") may imply that even the word (or concept) is nothing substantial (i.e., beyond time–space limitations), for it comes into being only through the occasion of its employment.

Hofuku suggests that the problem lies in Enkan's searching for "essence." Enkan appears to be no more than an old man in his dotage. In his last saying, Setchō ironically concludes the argument expressing "sorrow" that "all efforts [to find the 'essence'] are in vain."

ANSWER

As against, "Give me back my rhino."

The pupil's answer implies that the "essence" Enkan is looking for is gone with the fan.

As against, "I want imperfect head and horn."

If all there is is only the "imperfect" aspect of things, then the "essence" of things is their appearance. By the example of a commonplace object ("a piece of silk for sixty-five cents") the pupil suggests that one thing is as good as the other.

As against, "Why didn't you bring it out before?"

The pupil suggests that nothing *is* before it appears. By their very nature, things are there when they are, and are not there when they are not.

As against, "All efforts are in vain."

Setchō's saying is best taken as ironical. The pupil's response ("weeping") may be said to be largely exaggerated. The attached quote, however, is an excellent piece of irony on the futile search for "essence."

75. *Ōbaku's Stick*

When Rinzai became a Zen master, his Zen came to be known as "stick-Zen," for he never missed the opportunity to beat pupils and masters alike. This koan on his experience as a novice makes it quite clear that Rinzai's own enlightenment was the "working" of the stick. We may take this koan at face value if we keep in mind: (1) that beating on the right occasion is the master's way of enlightening the pupil, and the pupil's way of demonstrating his enlightenment to the master; and (2) that curses often mean praise.

Kyōzan, in his saying on the tiger, means that once enlightened, Rinzai is in full control of the situation. That is, in "riding the tiger's head and holding onto the tiger's tail," Kyōzan suggests that from now on Rinzai can handle both Ōbaku and Daigu.

ANSWER

In his answer, the pupil praises Ōbaku's "stick-Zen." The quote suggests the master's favor toward the pupil.

76.   The Three Sentences of Master Rinzai

In the sources (*Rinzairoku* and *Kattōshū*) this koan is connected to koan 19, also entitled, "The Three Sentences of Master Rinzai" (p. 126). As explained in the note to koan 19 (p. 259), Rinzai deals with the "working" of the master. This koan may refer to the "working" of things in general. It implies that the "working" (or function) of things has many aspects, that it is subtle and to be judged in accordance with the situation.

ANSWER

In the answer, the fan is used as a concrete symbol to demonstrate the variety of functions of one thing.

77.   On an Isolated Peak; At the Crossroads

Rinzai's saying suggests that one should not be taken in by extremes. The fact that Yuima meditated in an isolated place and that Fudaishi was involved in worldly affairs should not be taken to mean that Yuima lost contact with the world or that Fudaishi was so involved with the world that he could not possibly be enlightened. Both the way of Yuima and that of Fudaishi are perfectly all right as long as we do not misconceive of them by forming too rigid a distinction between "detachment" and "involvement." One may be on a peak of an isolated mountain while still being involved with the world; one may be at the crossroads yet still not "seeing" what is in front of one's eyes. It does not really matter *where* one is, but *how* one is.

ANSWER

The first answer refers to the Arhat "isolation" (or "detachment") way of religious practice with a touch of criticism, whereas the second answer refers to the Bodhisattva "involvement" state in a favorable mood. The combined answer of the second school seems to suggest the "involvement" state ("the old man, old-man-like; the old woman, old-woman-like"), but it may also be interpreted as meaning that all ways (both at the "mountain" and at the "river") are perfect as long as they fit in with the nature of the situation.

78.   *Why Can't the Tail Go Through?*

This striking paradox seems to imply that "enlightenment" is not to be measured by common logic. Once enlightened, one is in danger of deceiving oneself that one is absolutely and completely "through." Yet although one may be "through" where it is difficult and painstaking to pass, it is at the easiest, most taken-for-granted place where one fails.

ANSWER

The pupil identifies the "cow" with his own (enlightened) "self." He implies that his "self" is not (in view of the "mu" aspect) to be conceived in terms of personal history (birthdate and birthplace); his "form" is the actual form of the situation as it presents itself. The novice being a male, the cow too is a "male cow." The pupil also suggests that his "working" lies in his relation with his master. Yet when asked, "Why can't the tail go through?" (why is enlightenment not perfect), he identifies the "cow" with his master, suggesting that as far as (the imperfection of) enlightenment is concerned, masters fare no better than pupils.

The answers of the second school do not differ much in meaning. It seems, however, that the pupil is getting somewhat too "cowish."

79.   *What Is Jōshū?*

The Chinese cities of ancient times had gates in all four directions. Jōshū, faced with the unanswerable question concerning the essence of his "self," suggests through the gate simile that one may enter (Jōshū) from wherever one wishes. In view of "mu," it is perhaps permissible to interpret Jōshū's simile as a suggestion that Jōshū has no "self" (this is also what the answer to the koan seems to suggest). However, this does not result in saying that there is no Jōshū.

80. A Shell Holding Moonlight

Chimon's metaphor on the "essence" and "working" of the "supreme wisdom" refer to "kū" or "mu" ("void" or "nothingness"—the essenceless essence of things). Moonlight is (according to this simile) nothing in itself. Yet through its reflection on the shell, it becomes an inseparable "aspect" of the shell. In the same way, "kū" cannot be conceived as a substance in itself but only through its "reflection" in things. The same simile is employed to explain the "working" (or function) of "kū."

In China and Japan, the form on the moon's face is not a man (as in some Western cultures) but a rabbit. Thus, the "working" of "kū" (its active aspect) in things is compared to the moonlit shell bearing the child of the rabbit in the moon. As far as the simile is concerned, whether the moon shines upon the shell or not, it does not change the shell in itself (provided of course we accept the assumption inherent in the simile that light is no-thing in itself). But we would overstretch the simile if we interpreted it as suggesting that the "supreme wisdom" (or "kū") is of a fictitious nature.

ANSWER

In his answer, the pupil points at himself as the "essence of the supreme wisdom" (or enlightenment) and identifies his activity with its "working."

81. It Is Your Hearts That Move

The statement, "It is your hearts that move" is not to be interpreted as "philosophical idealism." Enō does not mean to suggest that the banner, the wind, and everything else is "mind-stuff." The "heart moves" because the monks indulge in futile argument. As the answer to the koan suggests, the solution to the monks' problem is simply, "a banner fluttering in the wind is a banner fluttering in the wind."

82. The Immovable Cloak

The historical background of this koan centers around the division of Zen into the northern and the southern sects during the seventh century A.D. Zen chronicles written on the process that led to the split report various dramatic events which assert the superiority of Enō (638–713) over his rival and fellow novice Jinshū (606?–706), the founder of the northern sect. The purpose of this legend is apparently to assert Enō as the legitimate successor of his master, Gunin (602–674). It is less clear what its function as a koan is supposed to be. The pupil's stereotyped repetition of the central phrase only strengthens the impression that the story has no "koan effect."

83. *What the Old Woman Meant*

The old woman's "Go straight ahead" and her "This one too is no different from the others" sound very suggestive. The monk is taken in by the "meaning" of the old woman's words.

ANSWER

The first answer ("the strong one beneath the porch") is unclear, whereas the answer of the second school (repetition of the old woman's words) and that of the third school (imitation of Jōshū's "going") are clear in themselves but they do not aid much in understanding the situation. The last answer ("with certain masters") is not in the Japanese edition of the book, but I have added it into the text because it seems to be the best one. This answer implies that what Jōshū understood is extemely simple. It is so simple that neither the Chinese monk (of the koan) nor the Japanese masters (who composed the first three answers to the koan) understood it. Jōshū understood that there was "a wrinkled-faced old woman" who had said what she had said; that's all there was and is to it.

84. *The Tortoise Is a Turtle*

In "What is the lamp in the room?" the monk asks for the standard of absolute certainty (or "truth"). Kōrinon in his answer suggests there is no such thing.

ANSWER

The first answer suggests that a name does not indicate the nature of a person (or any other thing), whereas the second answer ridicules the distinctions people try to create through names. Whatever you *call* a straw mat, it is after all simply what it is. The quote on the "stains on the lapels" may have meant to suggest the uncertainty concerning the real nature of things.

85. *Cut!*

In asking the monk from the western capital, "Can you still get a sword?" Gantō means, "Is there Zen in the western capital?" (or which comes to equally mean, "are you enlightened?"). When the monk answers that he "can get a sword," he stretches the simile of the sword too far, for Zen (or "enlightenment") is nothing you can get hold of. In his "cut-show," Gantō ridicules the monk's "sword" conception of Zen. Seppō, by beating the monk, proves that he understands what Gantō found lacking in the monk.

ANSWER
In his first answer, the pupil suggests that, unlike the monk, he is not taken in by Gantō's trap. The second answer and the answer "according to another school" suggest that Zen is not like a sword which one may "get."

86. *When the Sail Is Hoisted*

"When the sail is not yet hoisted" refers to the state of mind before "enlightenment"; "when the sail is hoisted" refers to the enlightened state of mind. The same dialogue is repeated twice but the meaning is the same. When striving for it, "enlightenment" is conceived as something supermundane beyond the boundaries of common logic; yet, being enlightened, things are simply what they are.

ANSWER
The first answer seems to suggest a ship standing still. In such a state, the ship does not fulfill its function of sailing, for there is no movement. The second answer echoes the mood of "the donkey eating grass" and "the river flowing northward" by suggesting the natural course of things, only this time the pupil refers to his own situation.

87. Why Don't People In Know about Out?

Kempō's saying on the "self" is too doctrinaire. Ummon, dissatisfied with such an approach, suggests that rather than speculating on Buddhist doctrine it would be better to known more about the world as it is ("outside of the hermitage"). Kempō laughs his consent at this and praises Ummon. Ummon agrees he deserves the praise and thus in an indirect way praises Kempō for his understanding.

ANSWER

The pupil's response to Kempō's saying ("scornful laugh") may be interpreted as, "[Being enlightened] I know better," but it is best taken as a suggestion that the saying is too doctrinaire. If we read the answer in the first meaning, the rest of the dialogue on Kempō's saying may suggest the difficult way one has to pass "before enlightenment." However, viewed as a criticism of Kempō's saying, it seems to suggest, "Beware, there is a trap in Kempō's words."

The pupil's response to Ummon's "outside of the hermitage" suggests that it is indeed necessary to know what is going on in the world, yet ("he slams the door shut") a monk should not forget that a monastery is a monastery. In his response to the "holy body" (of "truth") the pupil refuses to be taken in by metaphysics and simply refers to his physical body.

In the answers of the two other schools the pupil provides a doctrinaire interpretation to "three kinds of diseases" and "two kinds of light." Thus he seems to miss the point of Ummon's criticism.

88. Where Is the Old Man Going?

By "Tokusan does not know the last sentence," Gantō is laying a metaphysical trap for both Tokusan and Seppō. Actually there was nothing wrong in Tokusan's coming to the dining hall before mealtime. The old man was simply hungry.

ANSWER

The pupil suggests that "Tokusan's returning to his room" is simply Tokusan returning to his room. In reporting the affair to Gantō, Seppō apparently did not intend to imply that the old master was lacking in "knowledge." Therefore, the pupil ("instead of Seppō") rebukes Gantō for his far-fetched criticism of Tokusan and suggests that the idea of the "last sentence" (ultimate truth) is no more than useless talk. It is not quite clear what Gantō in his whisper "revealed" to Tokusan. But it is a fair guess that he told Tokusan that his remark on the "last sentence" was no more than a trap. In the last section, the pupil ridicules Gantō's "prophecy" concerning the life term of Tokusan. Tokusan may indeed have died after three years, but people's life term is not something that can be predicted.

89. *Yet I Should Not Be Rash*

In view of "mu," what is the use of "acting with proper dignity and ceremony"; but in view of "u," why should one not do what one is expected to do? As Setchō suggests ("He has got it!"), Tokusan understands both "mu" and "u" and is not taken in by either. When Tokusan calls out "Master!" Isan reaches for his stick to hit Tokusan if he says a word too much. Tokusan responds with "Katsu" and thus, in an instant, the two seem to be on common ground. Later Isan praises Tokusan, to which Setchō comments that there is no need to overburden the obvious with so many words ("to add frost on snow").

ANSWER
In the first two quotes ("bitter to the root" and "sweet clear through"), the pupil suggests Tokusan's thorough understanding of "mu" and "u." "Bitter" and "sweet" should not be taken in an evaluative sense. The last quote seems to suggest an agreement with Setchō that there is no use in saying the obvious.

90. *Every Day Is a Good Day*

Ummon asks for the nature of the enlightened state of mind, and answers, "Every day is a good day." As the answers to the koan suggest, however, one ought to be aware of a double trap. Taken in by the distinction between "before enlightenment," "after enlightenment," and "the moment of enlightenment," one is deluded to believe that one's "enlightened" view may change things, but the world is just what it is. Taken in by "good" in opposition to "bad," one is deluded to believe that through "enlightenment" one may relieve oneself from suffering and death. "Every day is a good day" means that having attained "evenness" of mind, "every day is as good as the other."

91. *Without Caring, Go Straight*

This koan deals with the theme of solitary practice as against organized monastic religion. The "goton" sound of the stick (first answer) suggests that the solution of this dilemma is in the moment of enlightenment. Like the people of olden times (before the formation of organized religion) one should not rely too much on "others" (i.e., masters) for guidance of "the way." But as suggested in the answers, through solitary practice ("dropping your bottom steadfast into the evenness of the plane of enlightenment") it is impossible to "lead the masses to salvation." Thus, with an independent spirit and without abhorring the vicissitudes of fate, be a *monk*.

92. *Seven*

"The six things" refer to the six senses (the five physical senses and the mind sense). According to Buddhist doctrine the "person" (i.e., the psycho-physical organism) is formed through the functional interaction of the six senses (on the "six senses," see Part Three, koan 57, note on pp. 283–284). Ummon's statement of the "true self not holding six things" should not be interpreted as there being a "self" above and beyond the six senses. Ummon only suggests that one should not be taken in by the "six-sense doctrine."

ANSWER

By counting to seven, the pupil simply suggests that he is not taken in by "six" (nor by "seven"). "To say it in reference to the other," means to say it (the "self") from the objective point of view. As the "six" belongs to the "subject," the objective is not bound by "six." The pupil thus simply describes various things according to their conventional numerical definition as they appear in the objective world.

93.   I Have a Lot of Things to Do

In his fish-and-net question, Sanshō asks Seppō to explain to him the "subtle working" of the enlightened mind. But in viewing the enlightened person as "fish" and enlightenment as a "net," Sanshō splits into two what is in fact one. By asking Sanshō to bring forth the "net," Seppō ridicules the inappropriate simile. Sanshō, who does not understand the irony of Seppō's answer, is still conceited with his "clever" question, at which Seppō hints that he would appreciate it if Sanshō took his leave.

ANSWER

The answer suggests that the "working" of the enlightened mind is nothing mysterious. It consists of doing the right thing at the right moment.

94.   Rice in a Bowl, Water in a Bucket

The monk, in his philosophical Kegon-styled question, asks for the "mysterious essence" of the smallest particle. He is apparently deluding himself into thinking that through such "knowledge" he will understand the world. But one does not have to be an expert in molecular physics to know that things are what they are. Ummon's saying is of the same logical pattern as the answer the monk is expecting (in x is y), yet it deals with the commonplace objects of the ordinary world.

95.   I Have a Headache Today

What the monk is actually asking of Baso is to say "the meaning of Zen" without words. He seems to have missed the point of Baso's answer ("I am tired today") and poses the same unanswerable question to Chizō and Ekai, who likewise reject him. Baso's remark on Chizō and Ekai implies "be it white or black, it is the same head." In this he praises the two, suggesting that they have behaved as a Zen-like Zen master is supposed to behave. If the reader is not taken in by a derogatory interpretation of "shit dropper" and "bed wetter," he will understand that the pupil's answer means exactly the same as Baso's.

96. "All Over"; "Throughout"

The many eyes and hands of Kannon Buddha symbolize Kannon's all-encompassing compassion. Ungan's question as to the "meaning" of the many eyes and hands is intended to test if Dōgo is taken in by esotericism. Through the description of a commonplace situation, Dōgo avoids the trap, implying (as the pupil's answer to Dōgo's phrase suggests) that "a hand is a hand." When Ungan declares that he understands the meaning of Dōgo's answer, Dōgo in his turn plays a practical joke on Ungan. Ungan's phrase (using the word "throughout") of course means exactly the same thing. However, once such a difference is pointed out, it is not easy to be simple enough to disregard it.

97. Why Is That Thing Not You?

This koan is hard to understand. As the last phrase suggests, its general meaning is that the functions of seeing and knowing are an integral part of the subject. The subject can thus "see" (or know) things only as they appear from the subject's point of view. As the quote attached to the answer suggests, our world is to a large extent a reflection of our moods and feelings. However, an overly Idealistic interpretation that the world is "mind-stuff" would be reading too much into the text.

98. Go and Have Some Tea

Buddhists often use the argument that the Buddha revealed his "real" doctrine only to the initiated, whereas to the laymen he preached in accordance with their understanding (in Japanese— "hōben"). Chōkei rejects this "double language" argument, also suggesting that the often-used argument of Buddha (or Zen) having "no language" (i.e., is not to be transmitted through words) is wrong. Naturally enough, Hofuku asks for the "one language" of Buddha. In his paradoxical answer that the deaf can hear, Chōkei seems to suggest something of the sort of a "no-language-language" (or "non-conceptual language"). Chōkei may be right but he says it in a too roundabout way. Hofuku in turn gives a more direct answer ("Go and have some tea") through the actual usage of the language of the common world.

ANSWER

It seems that the pupil, instead of repeating Chōkei's phrase, would do better if he took up Hofuku's pattern of stating the commonplace. However, the attached quotes, in describing the world of nature and man in everyday situations, echo Hofuku's way of saying it.

99. *Made a Fool Of*

The quote from the Diamond Sutra interprets the karmic state of adversity as caused by past sins, yet at the same time holding within itself the factor of redemption and deliverance.

ANSWER

As a point of doctrine, the statement of the Diamond Sutra is not rejected. However, the sutra's wording suggests an overly conscious attitude toward the karmic causality of one's present state. The pupil's answers and the attached quotes suggest an immediate response to the situation without questioning the causes or caring for the consequences of one's deeds.

100. *"Wrong!"*

It is not clear whether Tenpyō includes himself among those who "do not understand the teaching of Buddha"; in any case, his statement is too categorical. If he does not include himself among those who do not understand, he is conceited with pride; if he does, he is conceited with humbleness. Saiin gives Tenpyō a thorough shakeup. Looking up when called by his name, Tenpyō is "wrong." Moving two or three steps—Tenpyō is "wrong." Tenpyō in admitting he was wrong—is "wrong" again. Thus Saiin drives Tenpyō out of Tenpyō. Setchō adds a blow of his own, saying that what Tenpyō thought about his being wrong is "wrong," whereas the pupil in his answer to the koan concludes that if Setchō thinks he is right in his "wrong," he is "wrong." This koan is a good lesson for those who think there is something they can teach others. However, we should not forget that in their imperfectness all are quite perfect the way they are.

101. *Tread on the Head of Buddha*

The meaning of Etchū's two sayings is made clear through the answer to the koan. To say that one is Buddha is perfectly all right. It would be wrong, however, to conclude that just because one is Buddha one is "pure." The right conclusion should be that one's "bowels being filled with piss and shit"—Buddha is "dirty."

102. *The Body Emits Autumn Wind*

The monk is concerned about the decline and decay of things. Ummon suggests that decay is a natural process no less than birth and growth. If one accepts spring and summer, one has to accept autumn too. The answer to the koan suggests that though it is part of human nature to long for the past times of youth and vigor, the flow of time–space takes its natural course. It is a futile daydream to imagine the time–space situation of the past in the present.

103. *The Mind as It Is*

No comment necessary.

104. *No Mind, No Buddha*

Baso's two sayings mean exactly the same thing. The enlightened "mind of the moment" may be termed "mind" because of its consciousness of events, but it is "no mind" in as far as it does not dwell on anything beyond the bare fact of the moment. (For the same theme see Part Two, koan 51, note on p. 235; and Part Three, koan 73, note on pp. 288–289.)

105. *One*

The phrases of the koan suggest the philosophical concept of "one" (according to the Kegon School), in which everything contains the whole. As against this metaphysical "one," the pupil simply responds with the "one" of everyday language. The answer also suggests to "cut out" philosophical speculation and have a cup of tea.

106. *Take Care!*

Kanzan's saying, if interpreted according to Buddhist doctrine, suggests that one should at any moment be aware of the karmic consequences of one's deeds. In the answers, however, this "warning" is interpreted as a trap. The pupil suggests that "deliverance" from karma is not a matter of being "pure" from the worldly defilements (being "naked") but of a total immersion into the karmic process moment by moment as it presents itself. For the same theme see Part Three, koan 90, note on pp. 297–298.

107. *What Will You Do after Three or Four Shouts?*

The shout ("Katsu") is good if it comes at the right moment—then it sweeps away everything and leaves nothing behind (or takes away nothing and leaves everything as it is). But if it is employed only as a means to draw attention to oneself, it does not differ from a dog's bark. Bokushū hits the monk simply to silence him. The answer to the koan and the author's interpretation of the answer as showing the "simultaneous working of the stick and the shout" seem to miss the point. This koan is better regarded as Zen self-irony. (For a real example of the "simultaneous working of the stick and the shout" see Part Three, koan 89, note on p. 297.)

108. *Non-Attachment*

Rinzai's lecture is of the nature of a Zen sermon preached by the master on certain fixed dates to all the novices. The answer to the koan consists of the pupil demonstrating his understanding of the sermon in more concrete terms.

109. *Calamity! Calamity!*

Note that the monk poses his question just as Rinzai is going to use "words" (in his lecture). In "to be under the threat of the blade," the monk suggests a situation where, driven into the corner, one is at the end of one's wit. Rinzai's "Calamity! Calamity!" and the answers to the koan imply an immediate, spontaneous response to the situation. The quotes attached to the answer echo the mood of "calamity," yet the "simpleton" who remains indifferent to the catastrophic events suggests evenness of mind.

110. Use the Air as Paper

This koan is the same in pattern and theme as koan 109, Part Two (see note on pp. 240–241). Only the first answer ("the wily old fox") seems to be a suitable response to the master's "metaphysical trap."

111. What Is Your Feeling at This Moment?

As the answers to the koan suggest, the hermit fails for two reasons: (1) he does not see through the trap the old woman set for him; (2) he does not have enough "warmth" in his heart to see the girl in her own situation. The koan would be more difficult to answer had the girl been attracted to the hermit, seeking his love of her own will. It must not be automatically assumed that a Zen monk must reject a woman seeking his love. Zen has altered the traditional Buddhist monastic prohibition. For example, the "Zen law" says that one may drink wine but one should not be "drunk" (i.e., taken in) by it. The same I suppose may be true for sexual relations. Nowadays in Japan, Zen priests and even Zen masters are allowed to marry.

112. Of a Different Color

All humans are subjected to the natural course of life ("the snow covers a thousand hills"); why should the "enlightened" one be different ("why is only the one peak not white")? Sōzan admits the "difference" yet at the same time terms it "the absurdity of absurdities."

ANSWER

The answers of both schools suggest the natural course of life. In the first school the "peak" is likened to the head. When reaching the "age of white hair," every head ("enlightened" or not) turns white. In the first answer of the second school, the "peak" (head) is "not white," not because of some supernatural quality but simply because one shakes the snowflakes from the hair. The second answer suggests that when it is cold, everybody is cold. Only the popular saying suggests the uniqueness of the "one" ("one branch looks especially green"), but this too is within the natural framework of causality ("the monkey jumping"). The point of the koan is in admitting the uniqueness of the enlightened, yet at the same time equating it with all the rest.

113. *Beard*

According to tradition, Bodhidharma *had* a beard. The point of Wakuan's paradoxical question is the relation between "is" ("u") and "is not" ("mu"). If the pupil answers directly to the question (for example, "That is false, Bodhidharma had a beard"), he is taken in by the "u–mu" mode of reasoning. In view of "u," Bodhidharma *had* a beard; whereas in view of "mu," it is ultimately wrong to state that x is y. Therefore, what is the use of making categorical statements? In all the answers to the koan, the pupil solves this dilemma through the naive response to "beard"— when unshaved there "is" a beard, when shaved there is "no" beard. That's all there is to it.

A more speculative approach to this koan may interpret Wakuan's saying as a suggestion that Bodhidharma is totally "purified" from the karmic process, and the pupil's answers as the rejection of the idea that through "enlightenment" one is unaffected by natural causality.

114. *It Is Here*

Kenpō's and Ummon's sayings suggest the rejection of the other-worldly approach to "'enlightenment." The question "where is enlightenment?" should not be answered in the first place (the pupil slapping his master), but if answered—anything is as good as another. In this "Buddha-world" there are no two things that are not related to each other ("strike the carp of the eastern sea and rain will come down"); you may draw a line in the air or throw up your fan—there is enlightenment.

115. *Is There? Is There?*

As a historical fact, there might have been a good reason for Jōshū to reject one master's fist and accept the other's. Jōshū's phrase on the second master's fist suggests thoroughness. However, all *we* know about it is simply that Jōshū did not stay in the first place and wanted to stay in the second. If one is taken in by the "difference" between the two fists, one is in a trap. The answer to the koan is a stereotyped repetition of the last phrase, but the quotes suggest that although there might be slight differences, things are ultimately the same; it is no use choosing too much.

116. *Where Do You Come From?*

Hōgen's and Enmei's criticism of Tokusan seems to suggest that his warning the pupils not to ask questions lest they be hit was in place, yet his explaining to the monk of Shinra the "working" of his stick was superfluous. Setchō disagrees with Hōgen's and Enmei's criticism of Tokusan. His comment seems to suggest that Tokusan knew what the monk was in need of and handled the situation in a perfect manner. The answers to the koan suggest a naive approach to the "working" of the stick; whether in beating or being beaten, it is no good speculating too much about the matter. If one is too conscious of one's "stick," one had better throw it away (last answer).

117. *One Got It, One Missed It*

Same theme as Part Three, koan 115 (note on pp. 305–306). Whatever Hōgen might have seen, *we* should not be taken in by the difference between the two monks. The answer to the koan is a simple, non-speculative response to Hōgen's saying.

118. *Yes*

As the first answer suggests, the attendant has done Etchū "wrong" in not responding attendantlike. This does not mean that the attendant's response was not humble enough. The attendant-monk does Etchū "wrong" not because he serves Etchū badly, but because he has not realized Etchū's Zen of "when called as an attendant, answer as an attendant." The pupil's answer in the second school seems to demonstrate the "attendantlike" reply.

119. *Three Pounds of Flax*

The theme and the pattern of this koan are the same as in koan 15, Part Three (note on p. 256).

120. *Even Up Till Now*

As the answer to the koan suggests, the "deep meaning" of Zen is simply to realize that things are just what they are. To say it in an extreme form—*Zen has no "meaning."* For the same theme, see koan 49, Part Three (note on p. 280).

Another possible, though less Zen-like interpretation of the koan, would be to regard the saying on Bibashi Buddha as a suggestion that no matter how hard or how long one practices, one never reaches a state of absolute perfection. Under such an interpretation, the answer may suggest the various phases of "the way."

121. *One Finger*

The koan can be viewed as a version of the koan on the "one hand." The answers to the koan appear in the same working as in the discourse on the "one hand" koan.

122. *It Is Important That the World Be in Peace*

The koan as a whole stresses the worldly as against the transcendental. In his saying on the legend of Buddha's birth, Ummon suggests the principle of "self-realization" (in Japanese, "jiriki") as against "divine-salvation" ("tariki"). Rōyakaku's comment adds to Ummon's view the Bodhisattva ideal of self-sacrifice. As the second answer and the attached quote suggest, "the world in peace" is a state in which all things take their natural course.

123. *Mother and Father*

The legend on Prince Nata implies the idea of self-sacrifice and filial piety. The first answer, through the imitation of the pilgrim, seems to suggest selflessness. The second answer ("with certain masters"), which is not in the Japanese edition, suggests the simple and natural way of fulfilling one's filial duties.

124.   The Eastern Mountain Walks on Water

If the question concerning "the place of origin of Buddha" refers to the historical Buddha, it is irrelevant and unimportant. If the monk refers to Buddhahood, his question is a metaphysical trap. Through his nonsensical answer, Ummon ridicules the monk and rejects the question in both senses.

The first reply answers the monk's question in suggesting the the living Buddha right here, now. In the second, the pupil seems to identify himself with the "mountain walking on water," perhaps implying that the origin of Buddha is in oneself.

125.   Youngsters Like You Never Know of That

This koan should be taken at face value. For a change, the Zen master is simply a teacher in the good sense of the term. If one takes this koan lightly, one has perhaps become too "enlightened."

126.   The Guy Understands This Time

A possible interpretation of this koan could be the suggestion that the same words carry a different weight depending on whether they are said before "enlightenment" or after "enlightenment." It would be better, however, to regard the suggestion that there is a difference between Kassan's two sayings as a trap. Read thus, the koan is similar in pattern and meaning to koan 115, Part Three (note on pp. 305–306) and to koan 117, Part Three (note on p. 306). The answers to the koan suggest that the "formless" and the "blemish-free" is the world *as it is.*

127.   How Can We Go Through Without Interfering?

The monk asks an important and penetrating question to which Fuketsu answers directly in a serious and delicate way. It would thus be best to concentrate on the koan itself and disregard the somewhat clumsy "answers" to it.

128. Peach Blossoms

Reiun's moment of enlightenment recalls Fuketsu's saying in the previous koan (127). Isan, Reiun's master, affirms Reiun's enlightenment, whereas the comments of Gensha, Ummon, and Daisen suggest criticism. Their criticism seems to refer to the mood of self-confidence in Reiun's poem and implies a warning not to be too preoccupied with any specific enlightenment experience.

129. I Have Nothing to Hide from You

Maidō, through the quote from Confucius, suggests that in "enlightenment" there is nothing mysterious; it is the bare moment as it is—don't we smell the fragrance of flowers right here, now? Through his question on "after death," Maidō sweeps away metaphysical delusions and awakens Sankoku's mind to the actual moment of the present. The pupil in his answer to the koan, disregards the "metaphysical" meeting (after death) and simply responds to "meeting."

130. Bamboo Shoots Sprout Sideways under a Rock

Kidō's "bamboo shoots will sprout sideways under a rock and flowers will grow down on an overhanging cliff" suggests the natural harmony between Nansen and the monk. Unrestricted, absolutely free, Nansen and the monk are like-minded. Kidō's poem implies that in the hustle and bustle of everyday life, people are acting in perfect concert with each other. The quote-answers to the koan refer to Nansen's longing after the monk.

131. Not Enter Nirvana, Not Fall into Hell

Whereas the old school (Hinayana) created a dichotomy between the "unconditioned" state of nirvana and the "conditioned" events of the samsaric world, Mahayana thought, and especially the Zen school, assumes the "unity of samsara and nirvana." According to the latter view, once the barrier of conceptual thought has been removed, the unity of samsara and nirvana is realized; there is no longer any distinction between impure and mundane, and the pure and holy. One does not "leave" the samsaric world for it has lost its samsaric nature. The answers of both schools suggest elimination of all such distinctions. Void of differentiations of category and value, the world is just what it is. Whether you call it "heaven" or "hell," it is the same Buddha-world with its thieves, roosters, farmers, dogs, artisans, nightingales, merchants, dragonflies, winters and springs, everything in its perfect condition.

132. *High Rank, Low Rank*

The theme of this koan is similar to that of koan 131 (see previous note). Monju's inability to arouse the woman from her contemplation may be interpreted as irony towards the "transcendental." As the answers to the koan suggest, Monju dwells in the "higher spheres" above and beyond the "trivialities" of the natural realm of cause and effect. Although the "high-ranked" Monju and the "low-ranked" Mōmyō are "the same" in being "enlightened," it is after all Mōmyō and not Monju whose enlightenment is of real "working."

133. *The Oak Tree in the Front Garden*

The "oak tree in the front garden" may have been the object Jōshū happened to see when asked about the "meaning of Zen." A similar pattern of answer we find in Part Three, koan 15 (note on p. 256) and koan 119 (note on p. 307). The monk suggests that Jōshū is taken in by his object of sight; Jōshū denies this and his disciple echoes Jōshū's denial, saying that Jōshū "had never said anything about an oak tree." If Jōshū insisted on "oak tree" beyond the "oak tree situation," the monk would be right in accusing him of being taken in by "u"; yet Jōshū's answer was simply *that* moment's situation. At another time, in another place, it might be a "pen" (right now in my hand), "the rice bowl," or any other "here-now."

The answers to the koan are in part a simple response to "oak tree"; however, the first three quotes (first school) and the answer, as against the "root [or origin] of the oak tree," echo "mu."

134. *That Is Still Not Enough*

The same theme as koan 34, Part Three (see note on pp. 272–273), and koan 49, Part Three (see note on p. 280). The answer to the koan is best taken as ironical.

135. *Give, Grab*

As implied in the last answer to the koan, Basho's saying refers to "thoroughness." It may, however, also suggest the attitude of total acceptance of the state of affairs as it is.

136. *The Three Sentences of Master Busshō*

The answers to the koan point to the trap in each of Busshō's sentences. The first sentence suggests the distinction between "heaven" and "hell." The answer rejects the notion that in the "Buddha-world" there is an "upward way" and a "downward way." There is only the straight one. If one does what one is supposed to do, one is right on "the way." The comments on Niso and Gensha in the second sentence are unclear (that might also be the reason why they are not referred to in the answer to the koan). The denial of a historical fact ("Daruma did not come to China") sounds "clever" (viewed "mu") but one should "take care" not to be taken in by such paradoxes; after all, Daruma *did* go to China. The third sentence on the "void" may tempt one to conceive of "enlightenment" as something transcendental. As against this metaphysical trap the pupil suggests the Zen conception of "enlightenment" as being "right now, right here."

137. *Which One Is Real?*

This koan contains the "body-spirit metaphysical trap." Hōen is asking which is the "real" aspect of human existence. Against this search for the "real," the answer to the koan points to the actual states as they reveal themselves in human life. The "real" is not to be found in any abstract concept ("body" or "spirit") but in the bare events of existence. This naked reality may be termed both "samsara" and "nirvana" (or "body" and "spirit"), or neither "samsara" nor "nirvana"—names do not change things.

138. Only There Is a Word that Is Not Very Proper

The moment-situation of Eimei's enlightenment echoes Kyō-gen's enlightenment upon hearing a piece of brick hit the bamboo (Part Three, koan 64, note on pp. 286–287), and Reiun's enlightenment upon seeing the peach blossoms (Part Three, koan 128, note on p. 309). Kidō's critical comment seems to follow the same pattern as the criticism on Reiun's enlightenment. In Eimei's experience, it is not so much "a *word* that is not proper" but Eimei himself. Yet why should one be perfectly proper?

In his answer to the koan, the pupil points at his master as "not proper" (or "not perfect"). There is nothing wrong with the master's nose. The Japanese, when indicating themselves or others, always point with the finger at the nose. The answer of pointing at the master as "imperfect" seems better than the unnecessary humbleness of pointing at oneself.

139. Functions Like Theft

As the answers to the koan suggest, Kanzan's saying should be interpreted as a praise of the thoroughness and nimble effectiveness of Jōshū's "oak tree" answer (see Part Three, koan 133, note on p. 310).

140. The Four Shouts of Master Rinzai

For "Katsu," see note to koan 11, pp. 252–253. The first three "Katsus" suggest the various moods of the "shout situation," whereas the last—"a shout that does not function as a shout"—is the most natural and spontaneous of all. The pupil's first answer implies that he is not taken in by the distinction between the various "Katsus," whereas the second answer suggests the thoroughness of the "no-shout-shout."

141. First, Second, Third

This koan is a trap intended to test if the pupil is taken in by the distinctions in degrees of "truth" (or "enlightenment"). The answer suggests that there is no such distinction as "first truth" and "second truth"; a beautiful woman may *appear* somewhat different in this or that situation but ultimately she is just what she is. In the same way, "truth" (or "enlightenment") may have various functions but it does not have two faces.

142. *Host and Guest*

Mayoku asks Rinzai for the "absolute truth" ("the eye proper"), at which Rinzai throws the same question back at Mayoku and urges him to answer quickly. Mayoku asserts himself through action and Rinzai swiftly responds through action. Through this exchange, the problem of "truth" (or "essence") may not have been solved but the relation (or "working") of the two as "host" (subject) and "guest" (object) is made clear. On "host–guest" and the meaning of the koan's answer, see Part Three, koan 11 (note on pp. 252–253) and koan 19 (note on p. 259).

143. *The Dragon Bitten by a Snake*

Butsugen's saying symbolically implies that the "perfect dragon" (i.e., enlightened monk) should not by its nature be affected by worldly causes ("the snake's bite"). Ungo does not fall into the trap and suggests that being enlightened does not exclude one from the order of nature. It is a mistaken concept of "enlightenment" to conceive of it as deliverance from suffering and pain.

144. *Zen*

No comment needed, not even this.

Sources to the Koans of Part Three

Note that the titles of the koans in this book are those of the translator. The abbreviations of the sources are as follows:

Kattōshū	=	KT	*Hekiganroku* =	HG
Mumonkan	=	MK	*Rinzairoku* =	RR

1.	KT, MK (5)	33.	HG (8)	63.	HG (88)
2.	KT	34.	KT	64.	KT
3.	KT, MK (16)	35.	KT	65.	MK (8)
4.	HG (5)	36.	KT	66.	MK (36), KT
5.	KT	37.	KT	67.	HG (78)
6.	HG (42)	38.	KT	68.	HG (43)
7.	——	39.	KT	69.	HG (69)
8.	HG (46)	40.	KT	70.	KT
9.	KT, MK (47)	41.	MK (40)	71.	KT, MK (45)
10.	KT	42.	HG (13)	72.	KT
11.	RR, KT	43.	HG (100)	73.	KT
12.	RR, KT	44.	KT	74.	HG (91)
13.	HG (39)	45.	HG (14)	75.	KT, RR
14.	HG (29)	46.	HG (15)	76.	KT, RR
15.	HG (45)	47.	HG (16)	77.	KT, RR
16.	HG (1)	48.	HG (18)	78.	KT, MK (38)
17.	HG (2)	49.	HG (20)	79.	HG (9)
18.	RR, KT	50.	HG (23)	80.	HG (90)
19.	RR, KT	51.	HG (35)	81.	KT, MK (29)
20.	HG (21)	52.	HG (37)	82.	KT, MK (23)
21.	HG (44)	53.	HG (61)	83.	MK (31)
22.	HG (11)	54.	HG (63),	84.	KT
23.	KT		MK (14)	85.	HG (66)
24.	KT	55.	HG (64),	86.	KT
25.	HG (38)		MK (14)	87.	KT
26.	HG (40)	56.	HG (74)	88.	KT, MK (13)
27.	KT, MK (2)	57.	HG (80)	89.	HG (4)
28.	KT	58.	HG (81)	90.	HG (6)
29.	KT	59.	HG (82)	91.	HG (25)
30.	KT, MK (42)	60.	HG (83)	92.	HG (47)
31.	KT	61.	HG (84)	93.	HG (49)
32.	HG (3)	62.	HG (87)	94.	HG (50)

95. HG (73)
96. HG (89)
97. HG (94)
98. HG (95)
99. HG (97)
100. HG (98)
101. HG (99)
102. HG (27)
103. MK (30), KT
104. MK (33)
105. RR
106. KT
107. HG (10)
108. RR
109. RR
110. KT
111. KT
112. KT
113. KT, MK (4)
114. MK (48)
115. KT, MK (11)
116. KT
117. MK (26)
118. MK (17)
119. HG (12), MK (18)
120. KT
121. HG (19), MK (3)
122. KT
123. KT
124. KT
125. KT
126. KT
127. MK (24)
128. KT
129. KT
130. KT
131. KT
132. MK (42)
133. KT, MK (37)
134. KT
135. KT, MK (44)
136. KT
137. KT, MK (35)
138. KT
139. KT
140. KT, RR
141. KT, RR
142. RR
143. KT
144. KT

BIBLIOGRAPHY
BY BEN-AMI SCHARFSTEIN

A full bibliography on Zen Buddhism would be impracticably large. I have therefore concentrated on the scholarly books that have so extended our knowledge of Zen in recent years. Except for the translations of Nagarjuna and the accounts of the influence of Zen on Japanese culture, the books cited in the bibliography have all been used in the preparation of my introduction (see pp. 5–37). I have made a particular point of including books that I have quoted or paraphrased extensively. Not all the books listed here are of the highest scholarly standards, but I think they all make a genuine addition to our knowledge of Zen. I should particularly like to mention Holmes Welch's *The Practice of Chinese Buddhism*, which gives a full and honest report on the life of Zen monks in China, and from which I have drawn long quotations. I have listed a number of German and French books which were helpful to me, as well as the articles of which I have made direct use.

There is no ideal way to provide background knowledge, but I have tried to suggest a reasonable minimum. The bibliography also includes the books I have drawn on for the sake of the comparisons with Zen. Page numbers have been added only in the few cases in which my information or my quotations seem to me both important for my text and difficult to locate without exact references. The books are arranged by categories and, under each of these, by dates of publication. The category called Comparisons is an exception in that the books are arranged in the alphabetical order of their authors' names.

1. Mysticism

Scharfstein, B.-A. *Mystical Experience*. Indianapolis/New York: Bobbs-Merrill; and London: Blackwell, 1973.

Staal, F. *Exploring Mysticism*. Harmondsworth: Penguin Books, 1975.

2. History of Buddhism

Lamotte, E. *Histoire du Bouddhisme Indien*. Louvain: Publications Universitaires/Insitut Orientaliste, 1958, pp. 685–86 (on the origin of the debate between exponents of gradual and sudden enlightenment).

Conze, E. *Buddhist Thought in India*. London: Allen & Unwin, 1962.

Robinson, R. H. *The Buddhist Religion: A Historical Introduction*. Belmont, California: Dickenson Publishing Co., 1970.

3. Sutras (Scriptures)

Suzuki, D. T. *The Lankavatara Sutra*. London: Routledge, 1932.

Conze, E. *Buddhist Wisdom Books*. London: Allen & Unwin, 1958.

Hakeda, Y. S. *The Awakening of Faith, Attributed to Aśvaghosha*. New York: Columbia University Press, 1967.

Yampolsky, P. B. *The Platform Sutra of the Sixth Patriarch*. New York: Columbia University Press, 1967.

Conze, E. *The Large Sutra on Perfect Wisdom*. Berkeley: University of California Press, 1975. The first part was published by Luzac, in 1961, under the same title.

4. Taoism

a. History

Fung Yu-lan. *A History of Chinese Philosophy*. Princeton: Princeton University Press, Vol. 1, 1952; Vol. 2, 1953.

————. *A Short History of Chinese Philosophy*. New York: Macmillan, 1964, esp. chaps. 19, 20.

b. Texts

Lau, D. C. *Lao Tzu, Tao Te Ching*. Harmondsworth: Penguin Books, 1963.

Chan, Wing-tsit. *A Source Book in Chinese Philosophy*. Princeton: Princeton University Press, 1963, esp. p. 186.

Watson, B. *The Complete Works of Chuang-tzu*. New York/London: Columbia University Press, 1968, esp. pp. 35, 39.

Graham, A. C. "Chuang-tzu's Essay on Seeing Things as Equal," in *History of Religions*, Vol. 9, Nos. 2–3, November and February 1969–70. A careful discussion and translation of the second chapter of Chuang-tzu, from which all but one of my Chuang-tzu quotations come. A single quotation from this chapter is taken from Chan's *Source Book*, and another, from the first chapter, from Watson's translation.

5. *Madhyamika Philosophy* (of Emptiness)

a. History and Exposition

Murti, T. R. V. *The Central Philosophy of Buddhism*. London: Allen & Unwin, 1955.

Chang, G. C. C. *The Buddhist Teaching of Totality*. University Park, Pa.: Pennsylvania State University Press, 1971.

b. Translations

Stcherbatsky, T. *The Conception of Buddhist Nirvana*. Reprint. The Hague: Mouton, 1965.

Ramanan, K. Venkata. *Nagarjuna's Philosophy as Presented in the Maha-Prajnaparamita-S'astra*. Rutland, Vt. Tokyo: Tuttle Press, for the Harvard-Yenching Institute. Paraphrase with explanation.

Streng, F. *Emptiness: A Study in Religious Meaning*. Nashville/New York: Abingdon Press, 1967.

Inada, K. K. *Nagarjuna: A Translation of his Mulamadhyamikakarika*. Tokyo: The Hokuseido Press, 1970.

6. *Transfer of Madhyamika to China*

Robinson, R. H. *Early Madhyamika in India and China*. Madison, Wis.: University of Wisconsin Press, 1967.

7.   Chinese Buddhism

a. History

Wright, A. F. *Buddhism in Chinese History.* Stanford: Stanford University Press, 1959.

Ch'en, K. S. *Buddhism in China.* Princeton: Princeton University Press, 1964.

de Bary, W. T. "Individualism and Humanitarianism in Late Ming Thought." In *Self and Society in Ming Thought,* edited by W. T. de Bary. New York: Columbia University Press, 1970.

Hurvitz, L. "Chu-hung's One Mind of Pure Land and Ch'an Buddhism." In *Self and Society.*

Okada, T. "Wang Chi and the Rise of Existentialism." In *Self and Society.*

Ch'en, K. S. *The Chinese Transformation of Buddhism.* Princeton: Princeton University Press, 1973.

Chung-yuan Chang, "'The Essential Source of Identity' in Wang Lung-ch'i's Philosophy." *Philosophy East and West* 23 (January/April, 1973).

Okada, T. "The Chu Hsi and Wang Yang-ming Schools at the End of the Ming and Tokugawa Periods," in *Philosophy East and West* 23 (January/April, 1973).

b. Translations

de Bary, W. T. *Sources of Chinese Tradition.* New York: Columbia University Press, 1960.

8.   History of Japanese Religion

Anesaki, M. *History of Japanese Religion.* London: Kegan Paul, 1930.

9.   History of Zen

Dumoulin, H. *A History of Zen Buddhism.* London: Faber & Faber, 1963.

10.   History and Nature of Koan Meditation

Suzuki, D. T. *Essays in Zen Buddhism. Second Series.* London: Rider & Co., 1953.

Miura, I. and Sasaki, R. F. *Zen Dust: The History of the Koan and Koan Study in Rinzai (Lin-chi) Zen* (parts 1, 2, 3 originally published under the title *The Zen Koan*). New York: Harcourt, Brace & World, 1966.

11. Translations of Zen Classics

de Bary, W. T., ed. *Sources of Japanese Tradition*. New York: Columbia University Press, 1958.

Blofield, J. *The Zen Teaching of Huang Po*. New York: Grove Press, 1959.

Gundert, W. *Bi-yän-lu: Meister Yüan-wu's Niederschrift von der Smaragdenen Felswand*. Munich: Hanser, 1960.

Luk, C. *Ch'an and Zen Teaching*. Series 2. London: Rider, 1961.

Blofield, J. *The Zen Teaching of Hui Hai*. London: Rider, 1962.

Blyth, R. H. *Mumonkan*. Zen and Zen Classics, Vol. 4. Tokyo: Hokuseido Press, 1966.

Chang, Chung-yuan. *Original Teachings of Ch'an Buddhism, Selected from The Transmission of the Lamp*. New York: Pantheon Books, 1969.

Sasaki, R. F., Iriya, Y., and Fraser, D. S. *The Recorded Sayings of Layman P'ang*. New York/Tokyo: Weatherhill, 1971.

Yampolsky, P. B. *The Zen Master Hakuin: Selected Writings*. New York: Columbia University Press, 1971.

Demiéville, P. *Entretiens de Lin-tsi*. Paris: Fayard, 1972.

Masunaga, R. *A Primer of Soto Zen: A Translation of Dogen's Shobogenzo Zuimonki*. London: Routledge & Kegan Paul, 1972.

12. Life of Zen Monks

a. In China

Welch, H. *The Practice of Chinese Buddhism, 1900–1950*. Cambridge, Mass.: Harvard University Press, 1967, esp. pp. 55, 62–71, 80–88.

b. In Japan

Kuzunishi, S. and Sato, K. *Zen Life*. New York/Tokyo/Kyoto: Weatherhill/Tankosha, 1972.

Shibata, M. *Dans les monastères Zen au Japon*. Paris: Hachette, 1972.

13. *Influence of Zen on Japanese Culture*

a. General

de Bary, W. T., ed. *Sources of Japanese Tradition.* New York: Columbia University Press, 1958.

Suzuki, D. T. *Zen and Japanese Culture.* Princeton: Princeton University Press, 1959. See chapters on Zen and Confucianism, Samurai, Swordsmanship, Haiku, and the Art of Tea.

b. The Tea Cult

Hayashiya, T., Nakamura, M., and Hayashiya, S. *Japanese Arts and Tea Ceremony.* New York/Tokyo: Weatherhill/Heibonsha, 1974.

c. Gardens

Hayakawa, M. *The Garden Art of Japan.* New York/Tokyo: Weatherhill/Heibonsha, 1973.

d. Painting

Fontein, J. and Hickman, M. L. *Zen Painting and Calligraphy.* Boston: Museum of Fine Arts, 1970.

Awakawa, Y. *Zen Painting.* Tokyo: Kodansha, 1970.

Suzuki, D. T. *Sengai the Zen Master.* London: Faber & Faber, 1971.

Tanaka, I. *Japanese Ink Painting: Shubun to Sesshu.* Rev. ed. New York/Tokyo: Weatherhill/Heibonsha, 1974.

Matsushita, T. *Ink Painting.* New York/Tokyo: Weatherhill/Shibundo, 1974.

14. *Comparisons*

Alexandre, P. "Riddles." In *Dictionary of Black African Civilization*, edited by G. Balandier and J. Maquet. New York: Leon Amiel, 1974.

Bambrough, R. "How to Read Wittgenstein," in *Understanding Wittgenstein*, Royal Institute of Philosophy Lectures, Vol. 7, 1972–1973. London: Macmillan, 1974, esp. pp. 121–25.

Bascom, W. "African Dilemma Tales: An Introduction." In *African Folklore*, edited by R. A. Dorson. New York: Doubleday/Anchor, 1972, p. 150.

Boswell, James. *Life of Johnson*. London: Oxford University Press, 1953, p. 333.

Bowler, B. *The Word as Image*. London: Studio Vista, 1970.

Brouwer, L. E. J. *Collected Works*. Vol. 1: Philosophy and Foundations of Mathematics, edited by A. Heyting. Amsterdam/Oxford: North-Holland Publishing Co., 1975, p. 108.

Feldman, S. *African Myths and Tales*. New York: Dell, 1963, pp. 201–202.

Freud, Sigmund, "Analysis Terminable and Interminable." In *The Complete Psychological Works of Sigmund Freud*, ed. J. Strachey, Vol. 23 (London: Hogarth Press, 1955).

Moore, G. E. *Philosophical Papers*. London: Allen & Unwin, 1959, pp. 145–46.

Watts, H., ed. *Three Painter-Poets: Arp, Schwitters, Klee, Selected Poems*. Harmondsworth: Penguin Books, 1974.

Wisdom, J. *Philosophy and Psycho-Analysis*. Oxford: Blackwell, 1953, p. 37.

15. *Zen Logic*

Cheng, Chung-ying, "On Zen (Ch'an) Language and Zen Paradoxes." In *Journal of Chinese Philosophy* 1 (1973): 77–102.

HANDBOOK

OF

BIBLE LANDS

by

Guy P. Duffield, S.T.D., D.D.

G/L
REGAL
BOOKS
TM

A Division of G/L Publications
Glendale, California, U.S.A.

Published by
Regal Division G/L Publications
Glendale, California, U.S.A.

Library of Congress Catalog Card No. 77-80446

CONTENTS

LIST OF MAPS

LIST OF ILLUSTRATIONS

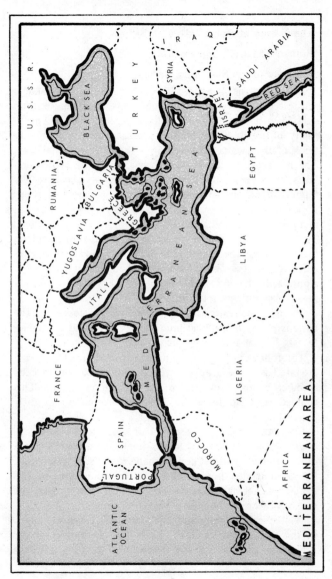

MEDITERRANEAN AREA

1

FOREWORD

A trip to the Lands of the Bible can be one of the greatest experiences in a Christian's life. Reading, or even studying the Bible without definite reference to the geography of the lands referred to, results in a tendency to think of the events described in a vague, impersonal way. The names and locations of rivers, mountains, cities and lakes mean very little. Distances have no significance. The topography of the countries does not assume its proper importance. The Bible appears to be only a book of lessons and people unrelated to places and things.

Of course, nothing is better than actually to stand on the sites mentioned, and view with your own eyes scenes described in the Word of God. Then, the whole Book, along with the individual incidents takes on an entirely new and significant meaning.

On my first trip to the Holy Land, as we stopped at the various places of Biblical interest, people would continually ask, "What took place here?"

The following year, in planning my first directed tour, I prepared a mimeographed syllabus and gave one to each member of the tour before the date of departure. This enabled them to have the Biblical information at their fingertips.

Since then many ministers and tour leaders have requested copies of the syllabus. Realizing the need for a more complete and yet concise handbook the original work has been tripled in size and now comes to you in this handy pocket-sized form. The helpful maps, and the pictures taken by the author have been added.

Well over one thousand Scripture references are given in this Handbook. A few places, not mentioned in the Bible are included in the descriptions because of their

2

close association with important characters or events. Over five hundred and fifty Biblical locations have been indexed. Where the name of a place has been changed, due to occupation by various nations during its history, each name is given. Eleven countries in which Bible events took place are included in the descriptive material.

Whether you be the fortunate tourist, a student or a teacher of the Bible, I trust that this Handbook will make your experience with the Book more meaningful and blessed.

Guy P. Duffield

CYPRUS

.

The island of Cyprus is located 60 miles west of Syria in the eastern end of the Mediterranean Sea. It is the third largest island in the Mediterranean, 148 miles long and from 15 to 45 miles wide. It is shaped like a fist with the forefinger pointing toward Antioch in Syria. Cyprus comprises about 3,572 square miles of land. Its population in 1962 was 590,000. It became an independent republic August 16, 1960 and a member of the United Nations on September of the same year. Its capital is Nicosia with a population of 103,000. There are 1,000 mils in one Cyprus pound, valued at $2.40 U.S. dollars. It was the birthplace of Barnabas.

Cyprus is first mentioned in the New Testament as one of those areas, along with "Phenice ... and Antioch," to which Christians fled as a result of the persecution which took the life of Stephen. They preached the Gospel to the Jews wherever they went (Acts 11:19-21). It is also noted that some who came to Antioch from Cyprus and Cyrene (a city of Libya in North Africa) preached also to the Greeks.

In the year 45 A.D. Barnabas and Paul set sail for Cyprus on their first missionary journey (Acts 13:1,2). They landed at Salamis the largest city on the island at that time. It was then some 3 miles from the present city of Famagusta. It had a fine harbor which today is filled with silt. There was a large population of Jews in the city as evidenced by there being several synagogues in which Paul and Barnabas preached (Acts 13:5). Tradition says Barnabas later suffered martyrdom in Salamis. A church in his memory was built there.

Leaving Salamis, Paul and Barnabas passed through the island to Paphos, now called Baffo, on the western shore of

4

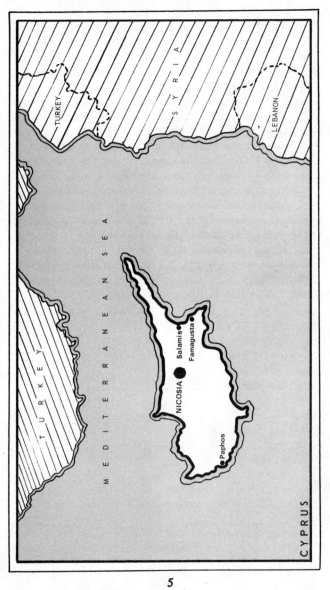

the island. It was then the capital of the Roman province of Cyprus and site of the temple of Aphrodite, Greek goddess of love and war. Here Paul preached to the proconsul whose name was Sergius Paulus. A Jewish ocultist, by the name of Bar-Jesus or Elymas, withstood the message but was sternly rebuked by Paul and smitten blind. This miracle led to the conversion of Sergius Paulus the proconsul (Acts 13:6-13). From here Paul and Barnabas sailed to Perga in Pamphylia (Acts 13:14), and then to Antioch in Pisidia. Both of these are located in Asia Minor.

Because of a disagreement over John Mark, who had left them at Perga on their first missionary journey, Paul and Barnabas did not travel together on the subsequent missions. Barnabas, with Mark, went back to Cyprus, while Paul chose Silas as his companion and returned to Asia Minor overland (Acts 15:36-41). Cyprus became a stronghold of the Christian Church. This is shown by the fact that they were able to send three bishops to the Council of Nicaea in 325 A.D.

Presidential Palace of the Archbishop and the Folk Museum at Nicosia, Cyprus.

Ledra Street, main business avenue of Nicosia, capital of Cyprus.

EGYPT

The land of Egypt is one of the most fascinating countries of the Middle East. Side by side with modern development, you see people living, dressing and working virtually as they did 3,000 years ago. No nation ever had such a prolonged era of greatness. Beginning about 3,000 B.C., when Upper and Lower Egypt were combined into a single nation, Egypt was the world's most magnificent civilization for the next 2,000 years. The spade of the archaeologist continues to reveal the marvels of those great days.

Egypt is entirely situated around, or along, the Nile River, 4,145 miles in length and vying with the Mississippi as the world's longest. It is one of the few large rivers in the world which flows north. The northern section of the country is composed of the huge delta formed by the many mouths of the river. It is about 125 miles south to north and 100 miles east to west, comprising about 8,500 square miles in area. Below the delta Egypt is mainly a strip of green along the banks of the Nile, varying in width from 13 miles to only 1 mile at places and extending some 500 miles south. Egypt has been well called "the gift of the river." Its total area is 386,200 square miles. Only 4% is permanently settled.

The Nile's summer floods, from June through September, enrich Egypt's soil making it ideal for plowing and planting. These floods, which for generations were at the whim and fancy of nature, are now controlled by the dams at Aswan. The height of the river's flood has been recorded annually, as the chief event of the year, since at least 3,600 years B.C. One can still stand with one foot on fertile ground and the other foot on the desert. The

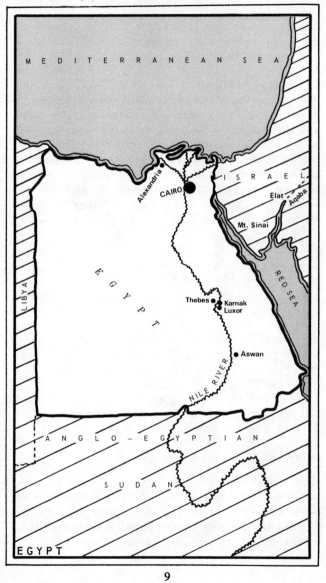

country possessed natural defenses, being bound by water on the north and almost impassable deserts on either side.

Because the visitor will hear constant reference made to events in its past, we present here a very brief outline of Egypt's colorful history.

In ancient history two Egypts have always been recognized: Lower Egypt, comprising the delta to the north, and Upper Egypt to the south, extending along the banks of the river to the first cataract at Aswan. About 3,000 years B.C. these two were combined under an all-powerful god-king Menes who founded the first of the 30 dynasties which ruled Egypt until its conquest by Alexander the Great in 332 B.C. Egypt's history, to that point, largely centers around three Kingdoms with two Intermediary Periods.

Outline of Egypt's History

Early Dynastic Period 3000-2700 B.C.

Dynasty I and II—Capital at Memphis—Biblical Noph (Isaiah 19:13; Jeremiah 2:16; 46:14,19; Ezekiel 30:13, 16.)

Old Kingdom—2700-2200 B.C.

Dynasty III to VI

During this time the great pyramids were constructed.

First Intermediary Period 2200-2000 B.C.

Dynasty VII to X

Middle Kingdom—2000-1800 B.C.

Dynasty XI and XII

Capital moved to Thebes—Biblical No (Jeremiah 46:25; Ezekiel 30:14-16; Nahum 3:8).

This was the time of the artistic decorations of the tombs.

Steppe Pyramid of King Djoser at Sakkara, south of Cairo. The oldest monument of cut stone in the world.

Queen Hatshepsut's Funerary Temple, Deir-el-Bahari, at ancient Thebes, across the Nile from Luxor, Egypt.

Second Intermediary Period 1800-1600 B.C.

Dynasty XIII to XVII

The Hyksos, Asian overlords, ruled from 1674-1567 B.C. During the XV to XVII Dynasties.

New Kingdom—1600-1100 B.C.

Dynasty XVIII to XX

The age of Egypt's supreme power and wealth.

During this time the Children of Israel were in Egypt and the Exodus took place.

Post Empire Period 1100-300 B.C.

Dynasty XXI to XXX

During Dynasty XXII Shishak ruled (I Kings 11:40; 14:25-27; II Chronicles 12:2-12).

During Dynasty XXVI Pharaoh Necho ruled. (II Kings 23:28-30, 33-35; II Chronicles 35:20-24; 36:4; Jeremiah 46:2).

Persian Rule 525-332 B.C.

Ptolemaic Period 300-30 B.C.

Alexander the Great 332-323 B.C.

Ptolemy I-XII 304-51 B.C.

Cleopatra 51-30 B.C.

Roman or Byzantine Period 30 B.C.-392 A.D.

Conquered by the Arabs 600 A.D.

Mameluk Period 1250-1517 A.D.

Ottoman Period-Turkish 1517-1800 A.D.

1805 A.D. Mohammed Ali appointed governor. Egypt began its period of modernization.

1882-1936 A.D. Egypt occupied by the British.

1952 A.D. King Farouk, the last of the dynasty founded by Mohammed Ali, abdicated.

1953 Egypt became a Republic.

1954 Gamel Abdel Nasser elected president of the United Arab Republic.

1956 Suez Canal nationalized by Egypt.

Mizraim (Genesis 10:6,13; 1 Chronicles 1:8,11), refers to ancient Egypt. Isaiah, Jeremiah and Ezekiel have extended references to Egypt in their prophecies. The country occupies an important place in the history of the Bible through its influence upon the children of Israel and its special relationship to four men:

Abraham went to Egypt during the famine not long after his migration to the land of Canaan (Genesis 12:10-20). Only the goodness of God protected his wife from being taken by Pharaoh. Abraham came out of Egypt with great riches in cattle.

Joseph was sold as a slave into Egypt (Genesis 37:36). He served as slave in the house of Potiphar (Genesis 39:1-20). He experienced imprisonment (Genesis 39:21-40:23). He was exalted by Egypt's ruler (Genesis 41). He revealed himself to his brethren after his dreams had been amazingly fulfilled (Genesis 42-45). Jacob and his family moved to Egypt where he spent his last 17 years in the land of Goshen, located at the southeastern edge of the Nile Delta (Genesis 46,47). Joseph gave commandments concerning the carrying of his bones out of Egypt (Genesis 50:22-26; Exodus 13:19; Joshua 24:32; Hebrews 11:22).

Moses was born in Egypt during the oppression—usually believed to be during the long reign of Ramses II. He was marvelously preserved and prepared for the work God had for him to do. After forty years on the desert of Sinai he was called to lead the Children of Israel out of Egypt (Exodus 1-14).

Jesus was taken by Mary and Joseph to Egypt, in response to the visitation of an angel of the Lord, that He might escape the wrath of Herod (Matthew 2:13-15) and also that Scripture might be fulfilled (Hosea 11:1). Visitors to Old Cairo are shown the cave under the Church of St. Sargius, an old Coptic Orthodox church built in the 5th century, where it is said the Holy Family lived while in Egypt. The angel of the Lord visited them and directed them back to the land of Israel where they settled in Nazareth (Matthew 2:19-23).

Places of Interest

Memphis—about 14 miles south of Cairo, is the oldest capital of Egypt, and its capital during most of its earliest history. It dates back to 4000 B.C. It has long since been buried. However, interesting items are being unearthed by the spade of the archaeologist, including the alabaster sphinx and the huge image of Ramses II. Memphis is Biblical "Noph" (Isaiah 19:13; Jeremiah 2:16; 46-14,19; Ezekiel 30:13,16).

Sakkara—the mortuary temple complex of King Djoser. A 37 acre wall enclosure centered around the Steppe Pyramid of Djoser, the oldest of known pyramids dating back to 2700 B.C. In this vast area are the graves of more than 20 kings and hundreds of nobles. The Steppe Pyramid is probably the oldest free-standing building of cut stone in the world.

The **Serapeum**—tombs of the sacred Apis bulls which were worshiped at Memphis. The Serapeum is 35 feet underground, 15 feet wide and some 1,200 feet long in the form of a semicircle. The granite sarcophagi of 24 of these sacred bulls were found here.

The **Pyramids of Giza**—The three largest are those of Cheops, his son Chephrun and his son Mycerinus. Cheops, the largest of all was one of the seven wonders of the ancient world. It now stands 455 feet high, though once it was 481. It is 750 feet long on each side, built exactly east west, north and south. There are approximately 250,000 blocks of stone weighing from 3 to 10 tons each—a total of some 5,400,000 tons. The base covers between 13 and 14 acres. It was the burial place of King Cheops.

The **Sphinx**—189 feet long, carved out of the natural cliff. Close to the pyramids at Giza.

Valley of the Kings at Thebes. 450 miles south from Cairo is the second oldest capital of Egypt. It is called "No" in the Bible (Jeremiah 46:25; Ezekiel 30:14-16; Nahum 3:8). It is now known as Luxor. On the west side of the Nile is the most famous burial grounds of all Egypt. It is the "city of the dead." 64 tombs have been found here. Only one has been discovered before its treasures were robbed. In 1922 English archaeologist Howard Carter broke through into the tomb of Tutankhamen and was amazed at the treasures before his eyes. These may be seen in the Egyptian museum at Cairo.

Deir-el-Bahari—funerary temple of Queen Hatshepsut. One of the first women rulers of the world. Believed by some to be the queen who reared Moses (Exodus 2:5-10).

Karnak—a short distance north of Luxor. Another of the seven wonders of the ancient world, are three temples originally covering an area of 100 acres. The oldest buildings date from 2300 to 2000 B.C. The great Hypostyle Hall, called the Forest of Columns, contains 134 columns 75 feet high and 12 feet in diameter. It is said that 100 men could stand on the top of each. These columns are lavishly carved with the stories of the conquests of the Egyptian kings.

Cairo with its mosques, bazaar, museum and general appearance is a fascinating experience to behold. The CITY OF THE DEAD, with its 15 square miles of buildings in which only the spirits of men are supposed to live is an unusual sight. In Old Cairo the Bible student will enjoy a visit to the CHURCH OF SAINT SARGIUS. This is the oldest church in Egypt—a Coptic Orthodox church built in the 5th century. Under its altar is a cave believed to have housed Mary and Joseph and Jesus during their stay in Egypt (Matthew 2:13-15).

GREECE

Greece occupies the southern tip of the Balkan peninsula in the Eastern Mediterranean. It is bounded on the north by Albania, Yugoslavia and Bulgaria, on the east by the Aegean Sea and Turkey and on the west by the Ionian Sea. It comprises 51,123 square miles, slightly smaller than the British Isles or the State of Florida. Its population in 1964 numbered 8,560,000. The capital city is Athens with a metropolitan population of about 2,000,000. 98% of the people are members of the Eastern Greek Orthodox Church. Complete religious freedom is recognized, but proselytizing from and interference with the Greek Orthodox Church is forbidden.

The unit of currency is the drachma. There are 100 leptae in a drachma. $1.00 in U.S. currency equals 30 drachmae.

The Bible student is particularly interested in Greece for its associations with the missionary journeys and ministry of the Apostle Paul. He and his party first came to Greece on his second missionary journey, in response to the night vision Paul had while in Troas. He saw a "man of Macedonia . . . saying, Come over into Macedonia, and help us" (Acts 16:9). Macedonia is now the northern part of Greece. Paul first visited Philippi where he and Silas were cruelly beaten. He then traveled along the Egnatian Way, famous military and commercial highway, 33 miles southwest to Amphipolis—now Neochori. Twenty-eight miles farther southwest he stopped briefly at Apolonia—modern Pollina. An additional journey of 40 miles along the Egnatian Way brought the party to Thessalonica—now Salonika. .After ministering here and meeting much opposition, the evangelists traveled 50 miles south to Berea—modern Verria. From here Paul was conducted to Athens and thence to minister in Corinth. He later returned to Greece on a subsequent missionary journey.

Athens—Athens is in the southern part of Greece known as Achaia, the Roman name for Greece. In Paul's day Corinth was the capital and chief city of Achaia although Athens was the cultural center, being the seat of learning for the world. The world's greatest university was here. Athens is two miles from its seaport at Piraeus. In early days the two were connected by two long parallel walls built two hundred yards apart. Along these walls, and throughout the city, were countless altars and shrines. It has been said that there were almost more gods than men in Athens. Among its altars Paul saw one dedicated to the "Unknown God." He used this later as the basis for his sermon on Mars Hill.

The city of Athens is built around the Acropolis, a rocky prominence five hundred feet high, on which are built numerous temples. Visitors may see the famous Parthenon, the Erechtheum with its famous porch of the maidens, the temple of Wingless Victory and other ruins of the glory of Athen's past.

North of the Acropolis was the agora or market place. Here Socrates taught and was forced to drink the deadly hemlock. In the agora the Athenians met to transact business and argue philosophy (Acts 17:17). It was here Paul entered into the discussions and "preached unto them Jesus, and the resurrection" (Acts 17:18).

At the northwestern approach to the Acropolis is Mars Hill or the Areopagus, so named because it was here the city court of Athens, called the Areopagus, met to decide matters concerning the city. It is a rocky hill 377 feet high. Paul was brought here that the council might hear more of the doctrine he preached. His great address, recorded in Acts 17:22-34, was delivered on this rocky hill. It stresses

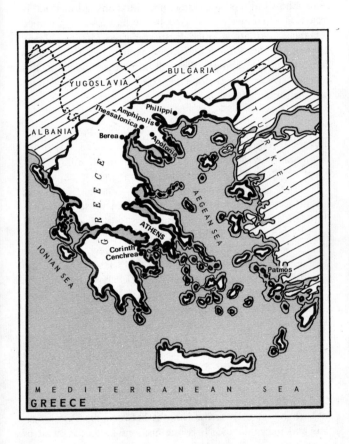

the facts that God is Creator, Sovereign and yet near to each one. He will judge all men by Jesus, Whom He raised from the dead. As usual, this great sermon had conflicting reactions: "Dionysius, the Areopagite and a woman named Damaris and others with them (believed)" (Acts 17:34). As for the rest of the council some mocked while others procrastinated saying, "We will hear thee again of this matter" (Acts 17:32). Paul departed from them and went to Corinth.

Berea—After the uproar at Thessalonica Paul was sent by the brethren from that city. He traveled down the Egnatian Way to the city of Berea, about 50 miles south-west of Thessalonica. The city, with a present population of about 15,000, is known today as Verria. Here Paul found a group of Jews "more noble than those in Thessalonica, in that they received the word with all readiness of mind, and searched the scriptures daily, whether those things were so." Because of this many Jew and Gentile women accepted the gospel (Acts 17:10-14). Christian Bible study classes throughout the world have adopted the name "Berean" from the attitude of these people. Jews from Thessalonica came down and stirred up the unbelievers so that it was necessary for the brethren to send Paul away. He was brought to Athens. He, no doubt, revisited the church in Berea on his later trips through Macedonia (Acts 20:1-5).

Corinth—The city of Corinth is situated 40 miles west of Athens on the narrow isthmus between the Peloponnesus and the mainland. It is one and one-half miles west of the Corinthian Canal. It had two harbors: Cenchrea (Acts 18:18; Romans 16:1) on the Saronic Gulf, an arm of the Aegean Sea, and Lechaeum on the Gulf of Corinth, an arm of the Ionian Sea. Ships from the East, Asia Minor and

The Propylaea, gateway to the Parthenon on the Acropolis at Athens, Greece.

Part of the extensive ruins of Old Corinth showing the Temple of Apollo.

21

Egypt, used the former while the latter was the gateway to Italy and the Western Mediterranean.

In Paul's day there was no canal across the isthmus, although Nero, in 66 A.D., attempted to dig one, turning the first soil with a golden spade. It was a 200 mile journey around Cape Malea, with its treacherous and feared winds, and mariners found it less expensive to transfer their cargo across the 4 mile neck of land. Boats that were not too large were taken bodily out of the water and hauled across the isthmus on a roller-like skid structure, while cargos in boats that were too heavy for this operation were taken across the four miles, and then reloaded into trustworthy sea-going vessels. Corinth prospered greatly from its strategic position in the center of all this trade. In 1881-1893 the project of cutting the canal through the four miles of the isthmus, at its narrowest point, was completed. The ancient city lies just a short distance from New Corinth. This is a small city compared to the 500,000 people who lived in Corinth during Paul's days. It was the capital of what is now southern Greece, called Achaia.

Above the city and to its south rises the high rock—Acro-Corinthus. It is 1,886 feet above sea level and 1,500 feet above the city. Atop this was the temple of Aphrodite, the goddess of love. The temple was served by more than 1,000 religious prostitutes who lodged in luxurious quarters surrounding the shrine. A large percentage of those who lived in Corinth were given over to the vicious and voluptuous practices of the worship of this goddess. Thus Corinth was the most notorious seat of immorality in the Roman empire. "To live like a Corinthian," became synonymous with a life of luxury and licentiousness.

The Apostle Paul went to Corinth from Athens probably about 50 A.D. (Acts 18:1-11). It was then the most thriving, as well as the most sinful, city in Greece. Here Paul met Priscilla and Aquila who had come to Corinth because Claudius had expelled all Jews from Rome. Like Paul, they were tentmakers. The first preaching was in the Jewish synagogue. Crispus, the chief ruler of the synagogue, and his family were converted. Meeting severe opposition, Paul turned to the Gentiles, shaking his raiment as a testimony against the Jews (Matthew 10:14; Acts 13:51). He then preached in the house of Justus. He ministered in this city for a year and a half. The judgment seat—Bema —is shown to the visitor today (Acts 18:12-17). Gallio was a brother of the stoic philosopher Seneca. Paul's first epistle to the Thessalonians was written from Corinth. The two epistles to the Corinthian church are unique in their extensive instructive and corrective material concerning church decorum as well as the spiritual gifts and ministry.

Patmos, Island of—The bare, rocky island of Patmos is in the Aegean Sea about 70 miles southwest of Ephesus— 37 miles from Miletus. It is about 8 miles long by six miles wide and comprises approximately 22 square miles. It was used by the Roman government as a place for the banishment of criminals, who were forced to work the island's mines. The Apostle John was sent here by the Emperor Domitian in 95 A.D. and it was while in exile on Patmos he received the visions recorded in the Book of the Revelation (Revelation 1:9, 10). The monastery of St. John on a rocky hill commemorates this event. Patmos belongs to Greece.

Philippi—Philippi was located about 10 miles from the Aegean Sea and its port city of Neapolis (modern Kavalla) (Acts 16:11). It was in the province of Macedonia, north of Greece. Macedonia was the home of Alexander the Great. The town was named after Philip of Macedon, father of Alexander. It became a Roman colony after the victory of Octavius (later emperor Augustus) and Antony over Brutus and Cassius on the plains outside the city. It was on the famous Egnatian Way. Ruins of the uninhabited site date from the 2nd century. The actual city of St. Paul has not come to light. The site today is called Felibedjik.

Paul and Silas came to Philippi on the second missionary journey in response to the call of the "man of Macedonia" (Acts 16:9). However, the first convert in Europe was not a man but a woman. Because there was no synagogue in the city, the Jews who lived in Philippi, met for worship on the sabbath day beside the Gangites River. Lydia, a business woman from Thyatira, who sold purple cloth, accepted the message of salvation, was baptized along with her household, and opened her home for the members of Paul's party. Thus the first Christian church in Europe was established in Philippi.

As a result of casting out a spirit of divination from a young lady who daily cried after them, Paul and Silas were cruelly beaten and imprisoned (Acts 16:16-24). Miraculously delivered from their bonds, the apostles baptized the jailor and his household (Acts 16:25-34). The authorities of Philippi were deeply disturbed when they found they had inflicted violence on a Roman citizen (Acts 16:35-40). Paul left Philippi for Amphipolis, Apollonia and Thessalonica (Acts 17:1).

Paul returned to Philippi on his third missionary journey as he returned to Jerusalem (Acts 20:3-6). The Philippian Church was especially generous to Paul (II Corinthians 8:1-6; 11:9; Philippians 4:16-18). Paul's epistle to the church at Philippi was written from Rome while the apostle was imprisoned.

Thessalonica—Thessalonica, now known as Salonika, capital of the province of Macedonia, is located at the head of the Gulf of Salonika. It is the principal seaport of southeast Europe. It is about 100 miles southwest of Philippi on the Egnatian Way which connected Rome with the cities of northern Greece. The city has a population of about 250,000. It was named by Cassander after his wife, who was a sister of Alexander the Great.

The Christian church was founded by Paul after he left Philippi (Acts 17:1-9). Here, in the synagogue of the Jews he preached for some three weeks. Some Jews, many Greeks and a good number of "the chief women" believed. However the Jews who did not believe influenced a base element to stir up a great disorder. They assaulted the house of Jason where the apostle was staying. They accused Paul and his company of disloyalty to Caesar, accusing them of "saying that there is another king, one Jesus." It was here the well-known expression, "These that have turned the world upside down are come hither also," was used. Paul was immediately sent by the brethren away from the city. He proceeded to Berea. Paul probably visited Thessalonica again, perhaps twice (Acts 20:1-4). He addressed the earliest of his epistles to the church here.

IRAN

Prior to 1935 we knew this country as Persia. It is one of the world's oldest empires. It has been called the "land of Sunshine, Roses and Poetry." It is the farthest east of the lands of the Old Testament. It occupies the western half of the Iranian Plateau which extends from the Indus River on the east to the Tigris River on the west. Iran is bounded by Russia and the Caspian Sea on the north, by Afghanistan and Baluchistan on the east, by the Persian Gulf on the south and by Iraq on the west. The average height of the plateau country is 4,000 feet above sea level. The central part is a vast desert.

The capital of Iran is Tehran with a population of about 2,700,600. The total population of the country is about 26,000,000. It has an area of 636,293 square miles—three times the size of France. The monetary unit is the rial with a fluctuating exchange rate of about 75.75 rials to the United States dollar. A better rate can often be legally obtained. Religiously, the country is almost unanimously devoted to the Shia sect of Islam—Mohammedanism.

The name of the country was changed from Persia to Iran by official action of the Persian government in 1935. Iran means "the (land) of the Aryans." The Medes and the Persians were the two Aryan tribes which came into the greatest prominence. The Medes occupied the northwest portion with their capital at Ecbatana (modern Hamadan). The Persians lived in the southeastern area. Cyrus built their capital at Pasargadae but it was soon moved by Darius to Persepolis in the south central part of the country. The other Aryan tribe, the Elamites, lived in the southwestern area of present Iran with their capital at Biblical Shushan.

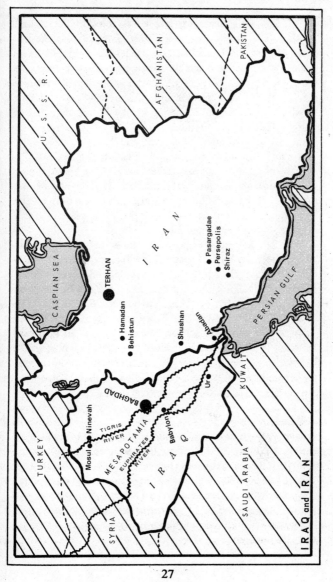

IRAQ and IRAN

27

The following Scripture references refer to Persia and Media: II Chronicles 36:21,22,23; Ezra 1:1-4; Esther 1:3,14,18; 10:2; Daniel 8:20; 10:1,13,20; 11:1,2. The places described here which are in Iran are interesting to the Bible student because of their relation to the Achaemenian clan: Cyrus, Darius and Ahasuerus (Xerxes). Other cities of importance are Abadan on the Island of the same name which is at the mouth of the Shatt al Arab—the name of the combined Euphrates and Tigris Rivers which join about 100 miles north of the Persian Gulf. Abadan is notable because of its extensive facilities for the shipping of oil throughout the world. Shiraz, the capital of the province of Fars, is quite modern in comparison to the ancient cities of Iran. It is noted as the burial place of Iran's two great poets: Sa'di and Hafiz.

One of the most important events to take place in Tehran in recent years was the conference between President Franklin D. Roosevelt of the United States, Prime Minister Winston Churchill of Great Britain and Joseph Stalin of the U.S.S.R. from November 28, 1943 to December 1. At this four day conference plans were agreed upon for an all-out attack on Hitler's "European Fortress" to bring World War II to a speedy end. They planned to defeat the German armies by land, their U boats by sea and their war plants from the air.

Behistun—Behistun, or Besitun as it is called, is a village at the foot of a precipitous peak, 1,700 feet high, in the Zagros Mountains. The old caravan road between Ecbatana (Hamadan) and Babylon passes at the foot of this cliff. Some 500 feet above the spring at the base of the rock Darius had inscribed an impressive autobiography of his conquests. One of his victories was accomplished near here in 516 B.C. The carvings depict the king lording it over his enemies.

Beautiful detail of a huge mosque at Isfahan in Iran.
Photo courtesy of Pan American Airways.

Typical Iranian Mohammedan mosque located at Isfahan,
Iran. Photo courtesy of Pan American Airways.

The inscription is written in three languages: Old Persian, Elamite and Akkadian. It was this trilingual inscription which enabled scholars to unlock the cuneiform script just as the trilingual Rosetta Stone provided the key to the Egyptian hieroglyphs.

Hamadan—Hamadan is the Achmetha of the Bible (Ezra 6:1,2), where Darius found the record of Cyrus' decree allowing the Jews to rebuild the Temple at Jerusalem. The classical name of this city through much of its important history has been Ecbatana.

Ecbatana was the capital of Northern Media. Cyrus the Great held his court here.

Pasargadae—Pasargadae is a city of ancient Persia situated in the modern Plain of Murghab some 30 miles northeast of the ruins of Persepolis. It was built by Cyrus to celebrate the victory which made him king of Media as well as Persia. Here he built his palace and the tomb in which he is buried. Darius later moved the capital to Persepolis.

Persepolis—Persepolis is the ancient capital of Persia built by Darius I 40 miles northeast of Shiraz. The site is marked by a large terrace on which are a number of colossal ruins including many huge pillars still erect.

This city was captured and partially destroyed by Alexander the Great. These ruins used to be called "Sad-Sutun," meaning "the 100 columns." They are now known as Takht-i-Jamshid. Here are found the tombs of Artaxerxes II and III. Not far from the ruins of Persepolis, at Nakshi-i-Rustrum, are the tombs of Darius, Xerxes I, Artaxerxes I and Darius II.

Shushan—Susa, as it is called today, was the capital of the province of Elam. It is located east of Babylonia, on the Karkheh River, 150 miles north of the Persian Gulf.

We read of Chedorlaomer, king of Elam, in the days of Abraham. He was one of the kings who fought against Sodom and other cities and took Lot captive (Genesis 14:1-11). There were Jews from Elam present in Jerusalem on the day of Pentecost (Acts 2:9).

Susa was called Shushan in the Bible during the time it was part of the Persian Empire (Nehemiah 1:1; Esther 1:2). Shushan was the royal winter residence of Darius the Great and was one of the three capitals of the Persian Empire. The great palace covered 20 acres.

The dramatic events of the Book of Esther took place at Shushan. Here Haman built the gallows on which he hoped to destroy Mordecai, but on which he himself was executed (Esther 5:14; 7:9,10). The great deliverance which was achieved by the Jews through the intervention of Queen Esther, herself a Jewess, is celebrated each year by the Jews at the Feast of Purim (Esther 9:20-32). The Ahasuerus of the Book of Esther is the great Persian king Xerxes of secular history.

One of the most important discoveries to be unearthed at Susa is a black basalt pillar on which is inscribed the famous law code of the Babylonian king Hammurabi. Also to be seen at the site are the outline, and some of the beautiful glazed bricks of the splendid Persian royal palace begun by Darius I and enlarged and adorned by later kings.

Muslim tradition says that the tomb of the prophet Daniel lay in the bed of the Karkheh River not far from Susa. A mosque was built on the bank opposite the supposed spot.

IRAQ

The modern country of Iraq, which was taken from Turkey during World War I, became a sovereign state at the end of the British mandate in 1932. It is made up principally of the land between the Tigris and Euphrates Rivers which was known anciently as Mesopotamia. "Mesopotamia" comes from two words meaning "between the rivers" (Genesis 24:10; Acts 7:2). It is bounded on the north by Turkey, east by Iran (formerly Persia), south by Kuwait and the Persian Gulf and southwest by Saudi Arabia. The population of Iraq is about 7,000,000. Its capital city is Baghdad with a population of over 1,500,-000. It is situated on the Tigris River. Baghdad is not mentioned in the Bible, being only about 1,200 years old. It is the city of the medieval caliphs, and known to the West through the "Arabian Nights."

The Tigris River is about 1,150 miles in length. It has its rise in the highlands of Armenia in Asia Minor (now Turkey), and flows in a southwestward direction to join the Euphrates about 100 miles from the Persian Gulf. The combined stream is called Shatt al Arab. The Tigris, though narrower than the Euphrates, is swifter and carries much more water. The great Assyrian cities of Ashur and Nineveh were on its banks. The ancient capitals at Babylon and Nineveh were once the greatest cities of the world. Opposite the site of old Nineveh, in northern Iraq, is Mosul, center of extensive oil deposits. The Tigris is called Hiddekel in Genesis 2:14 and Daniel 10:4.

The Euphrates River has its source in the Anti-Taurus range of Eastern Turkey near the Black Sea. It flows through Syria, then southeastward through Mesopotamia to join the Tigris at Basra, 100 miles from the Persian

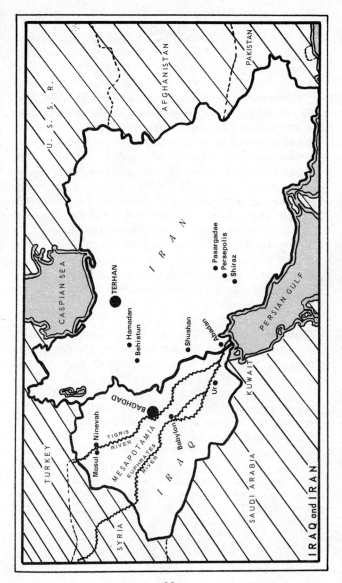

Gulf. The Euphrates is about 1,675 miles in length and is navigable for 1,000 miles.

The Euphrates is first mentioned in the Bible in Genesis 2:14. It was "the river" (Exodus 23:31; Deuteronomy 11:24) and "the great river" (Genesis 15:18; Deuteronomy 1:7). Thus God promised it was to be the northeastern boundary of the land given to Abraham and his seed. Only for a short period of time, during the reigns of David and Solomon, did Israel possess this extensive territory (II Samuel 8:3; 10:16; I Kings 4:24). During the reign of Jehoiachin of Judah the Euphrates served as the dividing line between the spheres of influence of Babylonia and Egypt (II Kings 24:7). The delta of the Euphrates ends at Hit, 400 miles upstream. At this place the elevation is still less than 100 feet above sea level. Thus the flatness of the area can be realized.

The Bible particularly mentions the cities of Ur and Babylon which were in what is now Iraq.

Babylon—The first reference to Babylon is no doubt the story of the Tower of Babel (Genesis 11:1-6). This tower, which the people of that day thought to build to heaven, may have been similar to the characteristic building of the Mesopotamia area called a ziggurat. This is a huge artificial mound made out of sun dried bricks. There being no timber or rock on the alluvial plain of Babylonia, the people devised the brick for their construction. Genesis 11:3 states, "Go to, let us make brick, and burn them throughly. And they had brick for stone and slime (bitumen) had they for mortar." More than two dozen of these mounds have been found in this plain. Some were mounds of clay well tamped down and buttressed on the outside by brick and bitumen. These were built in step-like stages. There were usually three stages with a temple to one of their gods on top. As many as eight stages have been built.

Ruins of Babylon, Iraq.

The Tower of Babel, which may or may not have been a ziggurat, was probably built prior to 4000 B.C. Perhaps the others were copies of it.

"Babylon" comes from the Hebrew root meaning "to confound." Its original founding is attributed to Nimrod, "a mighty hunter before the Lord" (Genesis 10:8-10). The city began to rise in prominence about 1830 B.C., but did not reach the height of its glory until the reign of Nebuchadnezzar II (605-562 B.C.). He built huge fortifications, great streets which were laid out at right angles to each other, canals, temples, a ziggurat and the famous hanging gardens. These were huge terraces on which were planted full grown trees. The inner and outer walls of the city were said to be over 13 miles long on each side, 250 to 300 feet high and at least 80 feet thick. The city was square with the Euphrates River running through it. There were 100 gates, 25 on each side.

Babylon was more than a city. It was also a great empire which extended from the Persian Gulf to Syria and Palestine. It was the first of the great Gentile world kingdoms represented by the image of Nebuchadnezzar's dream (Daniel 2:31-38). It was Nebuchadnezzar, king of Babylon, who destroyed the beautiful temple at Jerusalem, built by Solomon, and who carried Judah away to Babylon in captivity (II Kings 24:11-25:21). The city of Babylon fell to the Medes and Persians (539 B.C.) as Belshazzar desecrated the sacred vessels taken from the temple in Jerusalem (Daniel 5).

Because of its iniquity God prophesied total and permanent destruction to the city of Babylon. Probably no other city of its prominence has suffered a more total extinction. Note the drastic judgments in these prophecies: Isaiah 13:19-22; 47; Jeremiah 50, 51.

Alexander the Great died at Babylon June 13, 323 B.C. after a short illness.

In the Book of Revelation Babylon represents apostate

Famous Ishtar Gate reconstructed in blue tile on the site of ancient Babylon on the Euphrates River in Iraq.

Huge building made of cane. Typical construction in ancient Mesopotamia, Iraq.

Christendom or ecclesiastical Babylon, the great harlot. It also seems to represent the consummation of political power (Revelation 17, 18).

Nineveh—Nineveh was the great capital city of Assyria. Assyria proper extended from the Mountains of Armenia in the north to the lower Zab River in the south. Media was its east boundary and it extended somewhat into Mesopotamia on the west bank of the Tigris. At one time it was expanded to control the territory from the Persian Gulf to the Mediterranean Sea, including Egypt. The city of Nineveh was located on the banks of the Tigris River about 200 miles north of Babylon.

To this great city Jonah was instructed to go. After his experience in the great fish, he obeyed (Jonah 1:1,2; 3:1-10). The city with its environs was very extensive. It is called "that great city," and "an exceeding great city" (Jonah 1:2; 3:2,3; 4:11). It apparently took Jonah three days to cover its territory (Jonah 3:3,4). Jonah 4:11 would seem to indicate that there were 120,000 who were too young to tell their right hand from their left, thus giving some idea of the total population.

Because of its repentance, Jesus said Nineveh was a sign to His unrepentant generation (Matthew 11:41; Luke 11:32). He also spoke of Himself being a sign as Jonah was (Matthew 12:40; Luke 11:30). Though Nineveh repented at Jonah's preaching it was later destroyed in 612 B.C. by the combined forces of the Medes and the Babylonians. The prophecy of Nahum is concerned with the destruction of Nineveh. The following references are most expressive (Nahum 1:8; 2:6; 3:13,15).

The city of Samaria fell before the Assyrians in 722 B.C. and Israel, the Northern Kingdom, was carried captive to their land (II Kings 17:3-6,23). A later king of Assyria, Sennacherib, was not quite as successful in his campaign against Judah. During the reign of Hezekiah, king of Judah, he conquered much of Judah's territory but his forces were destroyed by the angel of the Lord as they had surrounded the city of Jerusalem (II Kings 18:13-19:37; II Chronicles 32:1-21; Isaiah 36,37).

Ur—"Ur of the Chaldees" (Genesis 11:28,31; 15:7; Nehemiah 9:7; Acts 7:4) was located on the Euphrates River in what is now Iraq. In ancient times it was the capital of the land of Sumer—called in the Bible Shinar (Genesis 11:2). Sumer once encompassed the territory from the Persian Gulf to above Baghdad. Sumer was forgotten until about 100 years ago. Now thousands upon thousands of clay tablets have been unearthed bearing man's oldest form of writing. This is called cuneiform, from Latin "cuneus" meaning "wedge." The letters are wedge shaped. These tablets bear stories of man's creation and of a great flood inundating all mankind except one good man.

Ur was the capital of earth's first great civilization. Here the Bible, as well as history itself, began. There were chariots in those days, which go back to 3500 B.C. The wheel was in use in Sumer 1500 years before it was introduced to Egypt by the Hyksos intruders. The Sumerians produced the sexagesimal system—numbering by sixties—which is still used in reckoning time, and in the measurement of a circle. For example: the sixty seconds in a minute and sixty minutes in an hour, also the 360 degrees in a circle.

King Ur-Nammu, who founded the last great dynasty of Ur, is famous for having drawn up the oldest code of laws yet known to man—4,000 years ago. The great Hammurabi borrowed from him. Sumer was conquered by Hammurabi about 1750 B.C. He came from the northern city of Babylon and with his sword and laws overcame Sumer. At Ur may be seen one of the finest remains of a ziggurat—similar, no doubt, to the tower of Babel.

ISRAEL

The nation of Israel is located at the extreme eastern end of the Mediterranean Sea. It is bounded on the north by Lebanon and on the east by Syria and the Hashemite Kingdom of Jordan. It has always been a sort of land bridge between the north, Mesopotamia and Egypt. Since June 1967 Israel has enlarged its occupied area from 8,000 square miles to 26,000 square miles. Its population, since June 1967, is about 4,030,000. Jerusalem is its capital.

Israeli currency is based on the pound, called lira (plural lirot), 'divided into 100 agorot (singular agora). Three and one-half Israeli pounds is equal to one U.S. dollar.

The nation of Israel is a young nation having been established as late as May 14, 1948. Its founding is full of drama and apprehension. In 1947 the British government announced that it was giving up its mandate over Palestine in May of 1948. As a result of this, in 1947, the United Nations established a Special Committee on Palestine to look into the problem. After considerable study they recommended that the country be partitioned into two states, one Jewish and one Arab. Jerusalem was to become an international city. The Jews accepted the plan but the Arabs refused to do so, indicating that partition meant war. However, on November 29, 1947, the United Nations Assembly approved the recommendation. The Arab states were against the idea. Seven Arab nations surrounded the little Jewish area. To combat the combined armies of these nations Israel had only 35,000 partially trained troops equipped with a few thousand rifles, a few hundred machine guns, home-made Sten-guns and a few dozen anti-aircraft guns and mortars.

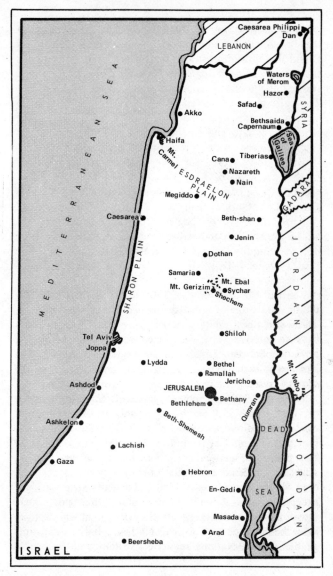

As the day of May 14, 1948 approached the members of the "National Administration," under the leadership of David Ben Gurion, searched their hearts and contemplated the wisdom of declaring a Jewish state. Their underground warned them of the impending attacks by land and air. The cities were defenseless and wide open to air attack. In face of all this, less than forty-eight hours before the British Mandate ended, the majority of the council of thirty-seven members representing all political groups within the country, voted for Independence. At four o'clock in the afternoon of May 14, 1948, a few hours before the British had withdrawn, the ceremony began in which David Ben Gurion read the 979-word Declaration of Independence, while people throughout Israel and the world gathered around radios to listen. A nation was born out of antiquity after 1,878 years. That night Egyptian planes bombed Tel Aviv and the Arab armies marched into Israel.

The story of the "War of Liberation," as it is called by the Israeli, is one of unbelievable dedication—and miracle. The world's best military leaders gave Israel four to seven days to survive. The war raged for a year before an armistice between Israel and Jordan was arranged. The Arab peoples have never recognized the existence of the state of Israel. They refer to it as "Occupied Palestine."

The year 1956 saw another climax of increasing tensions between Israel and her Arab neighbors. Any hopes of calmer conditions were shattered by Egyptian nationalization of the Suez Canal on July 26, 1956. On October 29 Israeli troops, recognizing their main foe was Egypt, attacked the Sinai peninsula and, by November 5, occupied all the peninsula, including the Gaza strip with the exception of a ten-mile cordon along the Suez Canal. Great Britain and France attacked Egypt in an effort to keep the canal open. This invasion lasted only a brief time as the United Nations requested Britain and France to

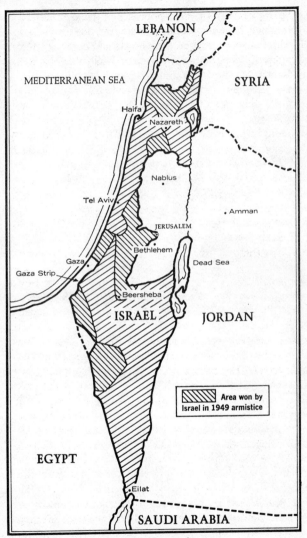

Israel before the six day war.

43

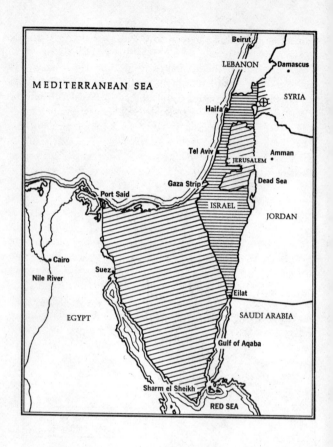

Cease Fire Lines—"War's Aftermath" Israel said war
in the Middle East had wiped out past armistic pacts
and indicated borders would have to change. Area over-
run by Israeli forces is shown in light shading. Cease-fire
in the Syrian area (cross) was accepted.

44

withdraw. Israel also agreed to withdraw her troops to the 1949 Armistice lines.

As a result of the six-day war in June 1967 Israel has extended her territory to include all of the Sinai Peninsula to the banks of the Suez canal, the entire Western Bank of the Jordan River and the Golan Heights east of the Sea of Galilee. Most important of all, the City of Jerusalem has been united under Israeli government. Thus, three times within the brief twenty years of her existence, Israeli has fought three wars. What will the outcome eventually be?

Outline History of the Holy Land

The visitor to the Holy Land, unless he has made a detailed study of the history of the Middle East, will soon become confused as different periods in the long and varied past which this land has known are referred to. The following outline traces the main periods, with approximate dates, and will help the average person to better relate places and events to each other and to the whole amazing movement that has been transpiring for centuries past.

Pre-Biblical Period 9000-2000 B.C.

Archaeologists tell us that the Holy Land was occupied as early as 9000 B.C.—the oldest known communities on earth. During the last millenium of that time, 3000-2000 B.C., Palestine was in close contact with Egypt.

Biblical Period - Beginning with Abraham.

1900 B.C. Abraham arrived in Canaan from Mesopotamia. Palestine held by the Hyksos (Shepherd Kings) of Egypt until 1479 when defeated by Thothmes III at Megiddo. Palestine was part of Egypt for the next 400 years.

1630 B.C. Jacob and his family went to Egypt, during the great famine, to be with Joseph.

1250 B.C. Joshua crossed the Jordan and conquered Palestine, dividing it among the 12 tribes.

1200 B.C. The Philistines' invasion from Crete.

1100 B.C. They occupied all Palestine by 1050 B.C. Samson killed.

1064 B.C. Saul crowned the first king of Israel. He was slain at Mt. Gilboa 1004 B.C.

1004-965 B.C. David's reign.

965-922 B.C. Solomon's reign. The Temple was dedicated about 953 B.C.

930 B.C. Israel divided into Northern and Southern Kingdoms—Israel and Judah.

721 B.C. Assyrians capture Samaria and take Israel—ten Northern Tribes—into captivity, marking the end of that kingdom.

Babylonian Period 605-562 B.C.

587 B.C. Nebuchadnezzar captures and destroys Jerusalem, carrying Judah into captivity to Babylon.

Persian Period 549-332 B.C.

539 B.C. Cyrus, Persian conqueror of the Babylonian Empire, allows Jews to return to Jerusalem.

Greek Period 334-63 B.C.

334 B.C. Conquest by Alexander the Great. Palestine controlled by the Ptolemies of Egypt.

198 B.C. Antiochus III of Syria defeated the Egyptians at Paneas (Caesarea Philippi) and Palestine passed into the hands of the Seleucides.

175 B.C. Antiochus IV—"Epiphanes"—became king. Abolished worship of Jehovah. Installed statue of the Olympian Zeus in the Temple as the object of worship and offered swine on the Temple altar.

Hasmonean Period 166-63 B.C.

Jewish revolt against the Seleucides led by an aged priest, Mattathias, and his sons Judas Maccabaeus ("The Hammer"), Jonathan, Simon and their successors.

Roman Period 63 B.C.-330 A.D.

63 B.C. Roman conquest of Palestine by Pompey.

40 B.C. Parthians surprised Romans and took the land.

39 B.C. Herod the Great expelled the Parthians and reigned until 4 B.C.

36-26 B.C. Pontius Pilate procurator of Judea.

30 A.D. Crucifixion of Jesus.

66 A.D. First Jewish Revolt under the Zealots.

70 A.D. Jerusalem destroyed by Titus, son of Vespasian.

132-135 A.D. Second Jewish Revolt under leadership of Bar-Kokhba. Hadrian rebuilt Jerusalem as a Roman city. Under penalty of death, no Jew was to approach its environs. He called it Aelia Capitolina. He also changed name of country from Judea to Syria Palestina—Syria of the Philistines—hence the name "Palestine."

Byzantine Period (Roman) 330-634 A.D.

Constantinople, or Byzantium as it was called, was made capital of the Eastern half of the Roman Empire. Christianity spread rapidly after conversion of Emperor Constantine. Churches built and Palestine flourished.

Second Persian Period 607-629 A.D.

On May 20, 614, Jerusalem taken. 33,877 people slain. Christian churches destroyed. The work of 300 years' construction obliterated.

Arab Period 634-1099 A.D.

570 A.D. Muhammad born in Mecca. At age 43 he received a series of revelations later gathered and pub-

lished as the Koran. Died in 632 but the faith of Islam had by then welded together the Arab tribes.

636 A.D. All Palestine under Arab control. Jerusalem became Islam's third sacred city next to Mecca and Medina.

1009 A.D. Fatimid Calif Hakim ordered destruction of Church of the Holy Sepulchre. 30,000 Christian buildings are said to have been destroyed in Asia Minor. These atrocities sparked the Crusades.

Crusader Period 1099-1268 A.D.

1098-99 A.D. First Crusade.

1099 A.D. Jerusalem taken by Crusaders and Latin Kingdom of Jerusalem formed.

1187 A.D. Saladin, a Muslim prince from Egypt, gained control of Egypt, Syria and Mesopotamia and then unitedly marched on Palestine. The Crusaders were routed at the Horns of Hattin in Galiee. October 2, 1187, Jerusalem capitulated. Later the Crusaders controlled Jerusalem for a short time in 1229 and in 1241 A.D. Mongol tribes from Central Asia took Jerusalem with a terrible slaughter in early 13th century.

Mameluk Period 1263-1516 A.D.

1263 A.D. the Mameluk Sultan Baybers of Egypt captured the remaining Crusader strongholds. They held the coastal cities intermittently for next 250 years.

1400 A.D. Another Mongol invasion under Tamerlane.

Turkish Period 1517-1917 A.D.

1517 A.D. Palestine conquered by the Turkish Ottoman Empire and held for 400 years.

1799 A.D. Napoleon made an unsuccessful attempt to add Palestine to his empire. He captured Jaffa (Joppa), then marched on Acre but, because his navy had been defeated by the Ottomans and the British at the Battle of the Nile, the French were unable to land their seige guns and Napoleon retreated to Egypt.

1917 A.D. Jerusalem taken by the Allies in World War I under General Allenby.

Modern Period 1917—

1917 A.D. Balfour Declaration.

1922 A.D. British Mandate over Palestine.

1948 A.D. British Mandate ended.

May 14, 1948 A.D. Jewish National Council established the State of Israel. Jewish-Arab War.

July 18, 1948. The fighting ended officially. Palestine partitioned between Israel and Jordan by the United Nations.

June 5, 1967 A.D. Sparked by Gamal Abdel Nasser's closing of the Gulf of Aqaba to Israeli shipping, war began between Israel and the Arab nations. Six days later it was concluded with Israel occupying the entire Sinai Peninsula to the Suez Canal, the Golan Heights east of the Sea of Galilee and the West Bank of the River Jordan. The Old and New cities of Jerusalem became one. The Jews had access to the Western Wall—Wailing Wall—for the first time since 1948.

Absalom's Pillar—On the east slope of the Kidron Valley, just opposite the southern portion of the Temple area, is a prominent stone pillar known as Absalom's Pillar. Sometimes it is referred to as Absalom's Tomb, but his body is probably not buried there. This may be the pillar spoken of in II Samuel 18:17,18. Adjacent to this pillar are sepulchres believed to be the tombs of St. James, Zachariah father of John the Baptist, and Jehoshaphat. It was customary for the Jews to whitewash their tombs each year and it has been suggested that Jesus was referring to these very tombs in the Valley of Kidron when He

49

accused the hypocritical Pharisees of being like whited sepulchres—beautiful on the outside but inside full of dead men's bones (Matthew 23:27).

Aceldama—The Potter's Field-The Field of Blood—On the southern side of the Valley of Hinnom, where it meets the Kidron Valley at the foot of the hill Ophel, is the Potter's Field, called Aceldama, "The Field of Blood." This is the field of which Zechariah prophesied (11:12,13). It was purchased by the high priests with the 30 pieces of silver Judas threw down in the Temple after he realized the enormity of his crime of betraying Jesus (Matthew 27:3-10; Acts 1:18,19). The field was to be a place in which to bury strangers.

Acre—Accho-Ptolemais-Akko—is one of the oldest cities in the world. It was known in the Old Testament times as Accho (Judges 1:31). It is nine miles to the north of Haifa and at the northern tip of a huge crescent-shaped bay. It was assigned to the tribe of Asher but was not taken by them at that time (Joshua 19:24-31; Judges 1:31). It was later called Ptolemais after the Ptolemies of Egypt. Paul stopped here briefly on his final trip to Jerusalem (Acts 21:7). It was a most important port because of an excellent harbor and ease of access to the interior by way of the Plain of Esdraelon, to the east, and to the north via the narrow pass, The Ladder of Tyre. During the Crusades Acre was their capital for 100 years. The city is famous for the remains of Crusader construction as well as those of the Turks. It was the last place held by the Crusaders in Palestine, being taken from them by the Saracens in 1291. Napoleon's unsuccessful attempt to capture Acre, after a two months' seige in 1799, marked the end of his dream of an Easter Empire. The town is now known as Akko.

Antipatris—North of Lydda (Lod) on the fertile plain of Sharon is the town called Antipatris. It is mentioned in

Absalom's Pillar by the Kidron Valley.

House of Simon the Tanner at Joppa where Peter prayed on the housetop.

Acts 23:31 as the place where the soldiers, taking Paul from Jerusalem to Caesarea, stopped for the night. It was built about 35 B.C. by Herod and named after his father Antipater. There is some authority for believing it was built on the site of ancient Aphek, mentioned as the place of battle to which Israel brought the ark of God from Shiloh and where it was captured by the Philistines (I Samuel 4:1-11).

Arad—The new city of Arad is being built near the site of the ancient city, about 17 miles south of Hebron. It is the tenth to be built here. Arad is mentioned in the earliest accounts of the efforts of the children of Israel to penetrate into the Promised Land from the south. The men of Arad took some of the children of Israel prisoners and Israel vowed to destroy this and other cities associated with them (Numbers 21:1,2; 33:40; Joshua 12:14; Judges 1:16).

Ashdod—One of the five great cities of the Philistines. Here was a temple built in honor of their god Dagon. It is first mentioned as one of the homes of the giant Anakims (Joshua 11:22). It was included in the portion of land given to Judah but not occupied by Judah until the time of Uzziah (II Chronicles 26:6; Joshua 13:3; 15:46,47). It was the first city to which the Philistines brought the ark of God after they had taken it from Israel. The next morning the image of the god Dagon was found fallen on its face before the ark (I Samuel 5:1-7). Several prophets prophesied against Ashdod for its enmity to Israel (Amos 1:8; Zephaniah 2:4). These calamities were fulfilled when Sargon and the Assyrians took the city (Isaiah 20:1).

Nehemiah sternly rebuked the Jews who had intermarried with the women of Ashdod (Nehemiah 13:23-27). The ancient city of Ashdod was located about 3 miles south of the present new city of the same name, which is being developed into a great port. After Philip the Evangelist

52

left the revival at Samaria to minister to the Ethiopian eunuch, he was found at Azotus—a place believed to be the same as ancient Ashdod (Acts 8:26-40).

Ashdod is being developed today to be Israel's largest seaport.

Ashkelon—Askelon—Ashkelon was one of the five most important Philistine cities (Gaza, Ashkelon, Ekron, Ashdod and Gath). It was the only one built on the coast with a harbor. It was mentioned by Joshua (Joshua 13:3) and taken by the tribe of Judah (Judges 1:18).

Here Samson slew thirty men and took their clothes and possessions to pay off those who had discovered his riddle (Judges 14:19). When King Saul was killed, David cried, "Tell it not in Gath, publish it not in the streets of Askelon; lest the daughters of the Philistines rejoice, lest the daughters of the uncircumcised triumph" (II Samuel 1:20). The Philistines were among Israel's fiercest enemies and several of the prophets spoke against their cities, including Ashkelon (Jeremiah 25:20; 47:6,7; Amos 1:8; Zephaniah 2:4,7). In relation to this last reference it is interesting to note that the main thoroughfare in modern Ashkelon is named Zephaniah Boulevard. Askelon is believed to be the birthplace of Herod the Great.

Beersheba—Beer-shev'a—It is interesting to note that Beersheba, in the days of the patriarchs Abraham, Isaac and Jacob, was neither a city nor a fortress. It was simply a cluster of wells in the open desert. It means "Well of the Oath" (Genesis 21:27-31). It probably served as a small wayside station for caravans traveling between Canaan and Egypt and the Arabian Peninsula.

Excavations have revealed that as far back as 5,000 years ago people lived in the area in underground villages. Subterranean homes have been found complete with furniture and domestic appurtenances.

After the days of Abraham it became a village of some size. However at the beginning of this century there was nothing there, having been abandoned hundreds of years before. The Turkish rulers built a small administrative and marketing center for the Bedouin near the spot where the ancient city stood. During the First World War in 1917, Beersheba was the first town to be captured from the Turks by General Allenby. It was a wind-swept desert village of barely 2,000 population. When it fell to the Israel Army in 1948 it numbered only about 3,000. Today, as a result of the efforts and energy of the nation of Israel, it boasts some 30,000 inhabitants and is the capital of the Negev from which the entire southern part of the country is administered. It is Israel's southern railhead and road transport center.

Beersheba was the southernmost city of Israel in Old Testament times, while Dan was the most northern. Hence the frequently found expression, "from Dan even to Beersheba" (Judges 20:1; I Samuel 3:20, etc.), Abraham lived for some time at Beersheba (Genesis 22:19). It was here he met Abimelech, king of the Philistines, and they made a covenant together (Genesis 21:22-34). Later Abraham's son Isaac dwelt here and built an altar to God Who revealed Himself to him. He also dug a well and made a covenant with the king of the Philistines (Genesis 26:23-33).

The Lord appeared to Hagar in the wilderness of Beersheba after she had been sent from Abraham's home (Genesis 21:9-20). From Beersheba Jacob began his journey to Haran in flight from the anger of his brother Esau (Genesis 28:10). Jacob stopped and offered sacrifices to God at Beersheba on his journey into Egypt to live with Joseph during the great seven-year famine (Genesis 46:1-5). Beersheba was part of the inheritance of the tribe of Simeon within the portion alloted to Judah (Joshua 19:1, 2). It was in this vicinity that Elijah, during his flight from the threats of Jezebel, sat under the juniper tree and wished that he might die. Here the angel of the Lord served him the food, in the strength of which he went 40 days and nights to Mt. Horeb (I Kings 19:1-8). Samuel's two unworthy sons were judges at Beersheba (I Samuel 8:1-3).

Bethany—The village of Bethany is located 15 furlongs —1¾ miles from Jerusalem on the eastern slope of the Mount of Olives. It is on the road to Jericho. Here was the home of Mary, Martha and Lazarus (John 11:1), as well as that of Simon the leper (Mark 14:3). Jesus seemed to have made Bethany His home in Judea as He did Capernaum in Galilee (Matthew 21:17; Mark 11:11). No doubt this was because of the love He had for Mary, Martha and Lazarus (John 11:5).

It was undoubtedly in Bethany that Mary sat at Jesus' feet while Martha was "cumbered about much serving" (Luke 10:38-42). Here occurred the great miracle of the raising of Lazarus from the dead after he had laid in the grave four days (John 11:1-44). It was at supper in the house of Simon the leper that Mary anointed Jesus with the precious spikenard and Judas complained of the waste of such costly ointment (Matthew 26:6-13; Mark 14:3-9; John 12:1-8).

From the vicinity of Bethany Jesus sent two of His disciples to get the donkey on which He rode into Jerusalem on Palm Sunday (Mark 11:1-11; Luke 19:29-40). While returning to Jerusalem from Bethany one morning Jesus cursed the barren fig tree (Mark 11:12-14; Matthew 21:17-22).

Christ's ascension from the Mount of Olives must have been close to the village of Bethany (Luke 24:50,51).

Bethel—"The House of God"—Beitin—Bethel was one of the royal cities of the Canaanites (Joshua 12:16) and was allotted to Benjamin (Joshua 18:22), although it was the house of Joseph who took it from the Canaanites (Judges 1:22-26). It was originally called Luz (Genesis 28:19).

It is located eleven miles north of Jerusalem. Here Abraham built his second altar when he came into the land of Canaan from Ur of the Chaldees (Genesis 12:8). He returned here after the famine which took him into Egypt (Genesis 13:3,4). Abraham and Lot then separated because of strife between their herdsmen (Genesis 13:5-12).

It was at Bethel Jacob spent the first night on his flight from the anger of his brother Esau (Genesis 28:11-22). On this night he saw the vision of the ladder set up on earth and the angels ascending and descending. When the Lord called Jacob back to Canaan, twenty years later, He spoke of Himself as "the God of Bethel" (Genesis 31:13), and it was to this spot Jacob returned with his family and his flocks (Genesis 35:1-15), at which time God renewed to Jacob the covenant concerning the land which He had previously made with Abraham and Isaac.

Samuel made a yearly circuit, in his ministry as judge and prophet, which included Bethel, Gilgal and Mizpah (I Samuel 7:16). It seemed to be an important center of worship. (I Samuel 10:3. Also see I Kings 13.)

At the time of the secession of the ten tribes and the formation of the northern kingdom of Israel, Jeroboam was afraid the people would return their allegiance to Judah when they made the annual pilgrimage to Jerusalem at the feast time. To forestall this he made two golden calves and announced to the ten tribes, "Behold thy gods, O Israel, which brought thee up out of the land of Egypt." One of these was placed at Bethel, the other to the north in Dan. Priests were ordained and sacrifices made to these idols. This is the sin for which Jeroboam was known (I Kings 12:26-33). (Note Jeremiah 48:13.) Amos, the herdsman prophet, was forbidden by Jeroboam from prophesying in Bethel because he foretold the death of the king and the captivity of Israel (Amos 7:10-17). King Josiah destroyed this altar and high place and slew the priests who ministered there at the time of the great revival during his reign (II Kings 23:4,15-20).

Bethel was the first stop on Elijah's journey toward his translation. Elisha accompanied him (II Kings 2:2,3). On his return to Bethel from Elijah's translation Elisha was mocked by a group of little children, "Go up, thou bald head." He turned and cursed them in the name of the Lord and two she bears came and killed the children (II Kings 2:23,24).

Little may be seen in Bethel today in the way of archaeological findings for the excavations have been filled in so that the land may be used by the present inhabitants of the village.

Bethlehem—As the birthplace of the Lord Jesus, Bethlehem is one of the most picturesque and heart-touching places in the Holy Land. It lies about 5 miles south of Jerusalem and is built on the terraced hillside. It is first mentioned in the Bible as the place where Jacob's wife, Rachel, died while giving birth to Benjamin (Genesis 35:16-20; 48:7). Rachel's Tomb is pointed out today just a little north of the city. (Note I Samuel 10:2.) Ibzan, the tenth judge in Israel was from Bethlehem (Judges 12:8-10).

The beautiful story of the Book of Ruth centers in Bethlehem. It was from here Elimelech and Naomi went to Moab with their two sons at a time of famine (Ruth 1:1, 2). After the death of her sons Naomi, with Ruth her daughter-in-law, returned to Bethlehem (Ruth 1:19-22). Ruth's marriage to Boaz is a fitting climax to this lovely story. She became the great grandmother of David, king of

Israel (Ruth 4:17; I Samuel 17:12). Thus Bethlehem is the original home of the Davidic family. This is the reason Joseph of Nazareth came here to pay his taxes (Luke 2:4-7), and thus it became the place where Jesus was born. The fields of Boaz where Ruth gleaned and met her lover are pointed out today.

It was at Bethlehem that Samuel the prophet anointed the boy David to be king of Israel in Saul's place (I Samuel 16:4, 11-13). On the hills and fields of Bethlehem David tended his father's sheep (I Samuel 17:15), and perhaps here experienced God's delivering power from the lion and the bear (I Samuel 17:34-37).

The Philistines were occupying Bethlehem when David, becoming a little homesick, longed for a drink from the well of his boyhood town. Three of his mighty men broke through the ranks of the enemy and brought the water, but David refused to drink it, pouring it out as an offering to the Lord (II Samuel 23:14-16; I Chronicles 11:16-19).

Micah designated Bethlehem as the place where Israel's Messiah would be born (Micah 5:2; Matthew 2:4-6; John 7:42). This prophecy was fulfilled (Luke 2:4-7). Here the shepherds worshiped (Luke 2:15,16), and the wise men presented their gifts (Matthew 2:7-11). Herod the Great slew the innocent babes of Bethlehem endeavoring to destroy the One born King of the Jews (Matthew 2:16-18; Jeremiah 31:15).

The Church of the Nativity in Bethlehem is the oldest church in Christendom. Built over the cave where it is believed Jesus was born, the church was originally constructed by Constantine about 326 A.D. Marking the traditional birthplace is a silver star inscribed in Latin: "Here of the Virgin Mary, Christ was born."

Bethphage—The site of Bethphage is on the slopes of the Mount of Olives between Bethany and the city of Jerusa-

Dome of the Rock on Mount Moriah, the ancient Temple area.

Church of the Nativity, Bethlehem.

lem. It was from here the Triumphal Entry began (Matthew 21:1-11; Mark 11:1-11; Luke 19:29-40).

Bethsaida—Bethsaida means, "the place of catching" and apparently refers to its association with the fishing industry. Peter, Andrew and probably Philip, disciples of Christ, were from this village and were fishermen (John 1:44). The location of the city, called "Bethsaida Julius," was at the place where the Jordan River enters the Sea of Galilee. It was another community, along with Capernaum and Chorazin, that experienced the woes of Jesus because of its unbelief and failure to repent (Matthew 11:21; Luke 10:13). No doubt it was because of the unrepentance of its inhabitants that Jesus took the blind man out of the city before He healed him (Mark 8:22-26). The "desert place" to which Jesus took His disciples after their first preaching experience, and where He fed the 5,000, was near Bethsaida (Luke 9:10). It is most significant that the three cities upon which the woes were pronounced are gone today while Tiberias, which received no word of judgment from Jesus, is flourishing.

Beth-shan—Beth-shean—Beit-shean—About 17 miles due south of the Sea of Galilee is the city of Beit-shean, located where the Valley of Jezreel meets the Valley of the Jordan. It was inhabited as long ago as 3,000 years B.C. The Tell el-Hosn, as it is called, contains eighteen levels of ancient settlements. It was on the main caravan route from Egypt to Mesopotamia. Thus it often fell to rival armies who passed this way. Later it became a wealthy Greek center, the leading member of the Decapolis, the league of ten cities, and the only one west of the Jordan River. It declined under the Moslems and remained no more than a village to our day. The Jews are endeavoring to revive it now. It is called both Beth-shan and Beth-shean in the

Bible. It was part of the inheritance of the tribe of Manasseh (Joshua 17:11), but the men of Manasseh were never able to subdue the Canaanites there (Judges 1:27) because of their chariots of iron (Joshua 17:16). Beit-shean is at the foot of Mt. Gilboa where Saul and Jonathan were slain. When their bodies were found the Philistines fastened them to the wall of Beth-shan. Valiant men from Jabesh-gilead came by night and took the bodies down from the wall and buried them (I Samuel 31:8-13). These were later recovered by David and buried in the country of Benjamin (II Samuel 21:12-14).

Archaeologic excavations have unearthed six temples, two of which date to the time of the Philistine rule and are believed to be those associated with the death of Saul.

Beth-shemesh—Beit-shemesh—About 20 miles west of Jerusalem are the excavated ruins of Beth-shemesh on a hill near Zorah where Samson was born (Judges 13:2-25). It was to Beth-shemesh the Ark of the Covenant was borne by the two "milch kine" after it had brought so much distress to the Philistines during the seven months they kept it. The people of Beth-shemesh rejoiced when they saw the sacred ark coming and they offered the kine as a sacrifice unto the Lord. They made the serious mistake, however, of lifting the golden mercy seat and looking into the ark, thus exposing the two tables of the law. A great number of them were slain. The people of Beth-shemesh sent to Kirjath-jearim asking the men of that place to come and take the ark to their city (I Samuel 6:7-21).

Bireh—Bireh is situated 15 miles north of Jerusalem, adjacent to the town of Ramallah. They virtually form one community. Bireh was the first stopping place for caravans going from Jerusalem to Galilee. It is therefore thought to be the place where Mary and Joseph first missed the boy

61

named Jesus, as they were returning from Jerusalem, when He was 12 years of age (Luke 2:41-45).

Caesarea—Located on the Mediterranean coast about midway between the city of Haifa and Tel Aviv. It was first called "Strato's Tower" by the Phoenicians who built a small anchorage here about 250 B.C. The city of Caesarea itself was founded in 22 B.C. and built by Herod the Great. It was the capital of the Roman government in Palestine. He named it in honor of Caesar Augustus. Its palace, theatre, hippodrome, aqueduct and circular breakwater were famous. It is first mentioned in the New Testament as the most northern city of Philip's evangelistic endeavors after his encounter with the Ethiopian eunuch (Acts 8:40).

Caesarea was the home of the godly centurion Cornelius whose prayers were answered in the remarkable incidents relative to Peter's vision on the housetop at Joppa, and his being sent to preach the gospel in this Gentile's home (Acts 10:1-33). Here the opening of the door of the gospel to the Gentiles was manifest by the outpouring of the Holy Spirit as on the day of Pentecost (Acts 10:44-48).

Herod Agrippa I died at Caesarea, being "eaten of worms." He had just delivered such a notable speech that the people said, "It is the voice of a god, and not of man." Herod did not give God the glory and was smitten by the angel of the Lord (Acts 12:19-23).

Caesarea is mentioned on a number of occasions in relation to the experiences of the apostle Paul. He sailed from here to Tarsus after his first visit to Jerusalem following his conversion (Acts 9:30). Traveling from Ephesus to Jerusalem he stopped at Caesarea on the occasion described in Acts 18:22. When making his final journey to the Holy City Paul and his company landed at Caesarea where he stayed a number of days in the house of Philip the evangelist, who was one of the seven chosen to oversee the ministry to the widows (Acts 6:3-6), and whom God used to bring the Gospel to the city of Samaria (Acts 8:5-8). While Paul was in Caesarea at this time, Agabus prophesied that if Paul went to Jerusalem he would be bound and delivered to the Gentiles. The apostle refused to be persuaded not to go (Acts 21:10-13).

After Paul was taken into custody in Jerusalem it was discovered that forty men were determined to kill him, and he was taken by a group of soldiers to Caesarea (Acts 23:23-33). Three times he made his defense in outstanding addresses while here. The first was before Felix the governor of Judea, while Ananias the high priest and an orator named Tertullus accused him (Acts 24:1-22). Felix listened to Paul on many occasions (Acts 24:23-27). After two years in Caesarea Paul was then brought before Festus, the governor who succeeded Felix, and was moved to appeal his case, as a Roman citizen, to Caesar (Acts 25:1-12). The third time Paul was allowed to speak in his own behalf, while at Caesarea, was before King Agrippa—Herod Agrippa II and brother-in-law to Felix (Acts 26).

The Great Jewish War, which ended four years later with the fall of Jerusalem, was begun by the Jews here in Caesarea in 66 A.D. In the 3rd century A.D. the celebrated Christian scholar Origenes established the school of Caesarea as a center of Christian learning. Eusebius was bishop of Caesarea and carried on the tradition of the school in the early part of the 4th century. Imposing Crusader fortifications were built here by Louis XIV of France in 1251 A.D. After these were captured by the Turks in 1265 the city was abandoned and buried by sand dunes.

Excavations and important findings at Caesarea have been quite extensive. These have uncovered the great aqueduct along the sea shore which brought water to the city from the mountains some 12 miles away. The imposing ruins of the Crusader fortifications are very impressive as is the Roman theatre, used now each year for musical productions.

Here the first archaeological evidence of Pontius Pilate, under whom Jesus was crucified, has been unearthed. It is an inscription bearing the names of Emperor Tiberius and Pontius Pilate.

Caesarea Philippi—Banias—Caesarea Philippi is situated at the base of Mount Hermon northeast of the Sea of Galilee. It was probably the point farthest north to which Jesus traveled. It was originally called Panias because it was the center of the pagan worship of the Greek fertility-god Pan. From a cave—Mugharet Ras en-Neba— nearby there flows a spring which is one of the principle sources of the Jordan River.

At the death of Herod the Great the region north and east of the Sea of Galilee was given to his son Philip. He rebuilt and enlarged the town and gave it the name of Caesarea in honor of the then-reigning emperor, Caesar Tiberius. The name Philippi was added to honor its builder, Philip, and to distinguish it from Caesarea on the coast midway between Haifa and the present city of Tel Aviv. The old name is still used with a slight variation as the town is now called Banias.

Mount Hermon, 9,101 feet above sea level, is by far the highest mountain in or near Palestine. It was sacred to the worshipers of the Canaanite deities and was the religious center of primeval Syria. Its Baal sanctuaries were well known before the Exodus. It is mentioned in Joshua 11:17 and Joshua 12:1. It was sometimes called Baal-Hermon (Judges 3:3).

Because of these close associations with pagan worship it is significant that Jesus should have chosen Caesarea Philippi as the place where He asked His disciples,

"Whom do men say that I, the Son of man, am?" And here He elicited from Peter, through the revelation of the Father, the glorious confession, "Thou art the Christ, the Son of the living God." This was a great testimony in the heart of paganism (Matthew 16:13-16; Mark 8:27-30; Luke 9:18-21).

Because of its great height Mount Hermon, rather than Mount Tabor (1,850 feet high), is believed to be the "high mountain" of Matthew 17:1; Mark 9:2 and Luke 9:28, where Jesus was transfigured before Peter, James and John. The fact of Hermon's proximity to Caesarea Philippi, and that the account of the transfiguration follows Peter's great confession, adds to this theory but no positive proof can be offered.

Cana—Kefer-Kanna—lies about four miles northeast of Nazareth on the road to Tiberias. Here Jesus performed His first miracle—the changing of water into wine at the wedding feast (John 2:1-11). A Franciscan church has been built upon the remains of what is believed to be the house where the miracle occurred. Stone waterpots, similar to those used in Christ's time, are shown. It was also at Cana that Jesus healed, at a distance, the nobleman's son in Capernaum (John 4:46-54). Cana was the home of Nathanael, one of the twelve disciples (John 21:2).

Capernaum—The city of Capernaum was located along the northwest shore of the Sea of Galilee, about 2½ miles from where the Jordan River enters the lake. It lay along the great trade route from Damascus to the Mediterranean coast and Egypt. Tolls were collected by the Roman government on this traffic and it was from the office of the Capernaum toll house that Jesus called Matthew (Levi) to be His disciple (Matthew 9:9; Mark 2:14; Luke 5:27-29). Here also Jesus paid the tribute money with the coin Peter took from the fish's mouth (Matthew 17:24-27). Capernaum was also an important military center for we learn of the Roman centurion who was stationed there. Some have estimated that Capernaum may have had as many as 10,000 inhabitants in Jesus' day. He made it His headquarters (Matthew 4:13-16). It is called "His own city" (Matthew 9:1). More of Christ's miracles were performed here than in any other city. These include: Peter's mother-in-law (Matthew 8:14,15; Mark 1:29,31; Luke 4:38,39), the centurion's servant (Matthew 8:5-13; Luke 7:1-10), the palsied man let down through the roof (Matthew 9:1-8; Mark 2:1-12; Luke 5:18-26), a demoniac in the synagogue (Mark 1:21-27; Luke 4:31-36), the nobleman's son (John 4:46-54), probably the healing of the woman with the issue of blood (Matthew 9:20-22; Mark 5:25-34; Luke 8:43-48), the raising from the dead the daughter of Jairus (Matthew 9:18,19,23-26; Mark 5:21-24, 35-43; Luke 8:41,42,49-56), the healing of the two blind men (Matthew 9:27-30), and the deliverance of the dumb demoniac (Matthew 9:32-34). In addition to these specific cases great multitudes were brought and were healed (Matthew 8:16,17). Christ's great discourse on the bread of life, as well as others, was delivered in Capernaum (John 6:24-71; Mark 9:33-50).

In spite of all these miracles Capernaum failed to repent of her sin and came under Christ's woes of judgment (Matthew 11:23,24; Luke 10:15). This judgment was fulfilled and Capernaum is no more. Excavations have yielded ruins of one of the finest limestone synagogues in the Holy Land. Some have thought it might be the one built by the kindly centurion (Luke 7:1-5), and thus be the one in which Jesus preached. Experts believe, though, it was built in the 2nd century A.D. However, there is every probability that it stands on the same spot amidst a grove of eucalyptus trees. Remains of the old stone quay can also be seen along the water front.

Carmel, Mount—Carmel, roughly triangular in shape, is a beautifully wooded range running for about 13 miles in a southeasterly direction from the promontory which drops to the Mediterranean near Haifa. In the language of Scripture it is often pictured as the symbol of beauty and fruitfulness, or majesty and prosperity (II Chronicles 26:10; Song of Solomon 7:5; Isaiah 35:2; Jeremiah 46:18; 50:19). When Carmel is said to languish it is an indication of God's judgment upon the land (Nahum 1:4; Amos 1:2; Isaiah 33:9).

From earliest times its heights were the site of altars to many strange gods. There are many remains of Canaanite shrines and caves where hermits found solitude. "Though they hide themselves in the top of Carmel," cried the prophet Amos, "I will search and take them out hence . . ." (Amos 9:3). An ancient altar to Jehovah also stood here (I Kings 18:30). Thus it is not strange that Elijah should have chosen this place for the great contest with the prophets of Baal (I Kings 18:19-39). The traditional site of this confrontation is where the Carmelite Monastery of St. Elijah now stands, about 500 feet above sea level. At the foot of the slope of Carmel, at the brook Kishon, Elijah slew all the prophets of Baal (I Kings 18:40). On the top of Carmel, Elijah interceded until the three and one-half year drought ended and from here he ran before the chariot of Ahab until he came to Jezreel, some 18-20 miles away (I Kings 18:42-46). At the foot of Carmel in the "Cave of Elijah," is where that prophet is believed to have taken refuge on one of his flights from the anger of Ahab.

Chorazin—The ancient site of Chorazin is two miles north of Capernaum. It was one of the cities against which Jesus pronounced judgment because it refused to repent in spite of His ministry (Matthew 11:21-23; Luke 10:13-15). Ruins of an old synagogue of the third or fourth century have been uncovered there. The stones and pillars were made of black volcanic basalt.

Dan—Dan is a very familiar name in the Old Testament in that it was the city which marks the northern limit of the land of Israel, while Beersheba was its southern extremity. The expression "from Dan even to Beersheba" is used in many places (Judges 20:1; I Samuel 3:20; etc.). It is at the foot of Mount Hermon near one of the sources of the Jordan River.

It is first mentioned in the Bible as the location to which Abraham and his servants pursued the army of Chedorlaomer, and the three kings associated with him, in order to rescue Lot and his family and goods. The battle was continued until Abraham gained victory at Hobah, north of Damascus (Genesis 14:14-16).

The city was originally a Phoenician city called Laish (Judges 18:27-29). It was also called Leshem (Joshua 19:47). Apparently the tribe of Dan was not satisfied with the inheritance allotted to them in the province of Judea (Joshua 19:40-47), much of it being occupied by the Philistines. So they sent an army of 600 men to capture Laish, far to the north, which they rebuilt and called Dan. The 18th chapter of Judges tells the dramatic story of this invasion and the setting up of a graven image which the tribe worshiped instead of going to Shiloh where the Tabernacle had been set up.

When Jeroboam and the ten tribes revolted from Rehoboam and the house of Judah, after the death of Solomon, he set up his own kingdom known as Israel (I Kings 12:16-20; II Chronicles 10:12-19). Being afraid that, if his people returned to Jerusalem to worship at the great Temple, their hearts would return to Judah and they would rebel against him, Jeroboam set up two places where his people could worship. He made two golden calves, putting one in Bethel, to the south of his territory, and the other in Dan, the northern extremity. He told Israel, "Behold thy gods, O Israel, which brought thee out of the land of Egypt" (I Kings 12:26-33). Thus the Northern Kingdom fell a prey to idolatrous pollution, and this great sin in leading Israel astray was associated with the name of Jeroboam forever. He is almost always referred to after this, as "Jeroboam, the son of Nebat, who made Israel to sin" (I Kings 22:52; II Kings 3:3; II Kings 10:29; etc.).

During the war between Asa, king of Judah, and Baasha, king of Israel, the former hired Benhadad, king of Syria, to assist him and he smote the city of Dan (I Kings 15:16-20; II Chronicles 16:1-4). It was regained by Jeroboam II (II Kings 14:25) but shared Israel's fate at the hands of Tiglath-pileser, being carried captive to Assyria (II Kings 15:29).

Dead Sea—The Dead Sea is formed by the waters of the Jordan River and other small streams. In the Bible it is known as the Salt Sea (Genesis 14:3; Numbers 34:3, 12; Joshua 15:2, 5; 18:19), also the Sea of the Plain (Deuteronomy 3:17; Joshua 3:16; 12:3). It is the only place in the world where you can fly in an airplane more than 1,000 feet below sea level, being just about 1,300 feet below the normal level of the world's seas and oceans. Near its northern end it is about 1,300 feet deep, making its bottom 2,600 feet below sea level. It is approximately 50 miles long and averages about 10 miles wide.

There is no outlet but upward, by means of evaporation —at an average rate of something like seven million tons per day. Only fresh water escapes this way, so the salinity and mineral content of the water are constantly increasing. The water is 27% mineral. This is five times saltier than the ocean which is only 5% solid material. Consequently it is impossible to sink in its waters. They are not only salty but bitter. It is estimated that these waters contain about 45 billion tons of valuable chemicals: mainly sodium, chlorine, sulphur, potassium, calcium, magnesiun and bromine. Their commercial value is almost beyond computation. The cities of Sodom and Gomorrah are believed to have been toward the lower end of the Dead Sea, possibly on a shallow extension called "The Tongue."

Dothan—Dothain—Tell Dotha—Dothan is about 14 miles north of Sebastia. It was here Joseph found his brethren and their flocks when his father sent him out of Hebron to look for them. His brethren conspired against him, cast him in a pit at Dothan and then sold him to the Ishmaelite merchantmen for 20 pieces of silver (Genesis 37:13-28).

Dothan was also the city where the Syrian army surrounded Elisha and his servant. When the servant was filled with fear the following morning, the prophet prayed "Lord, I pray thee, open his eyes that he may see" and he saw the mountain "full of horses and chariots of fire round about Elisha" (II Kings 6:13-23).

The Tell, or mound, of Dothan covers about 25 acres. It was a very important city on the caravan routes in early days. Very few people live there now.

Elah, Valley of—Somewhat over 20 miles west and a little south of Jerusalem is the Valley of Elah where David, the shepherd boy, killed Goliath the Philistine giant (I Samuel 17:1-52). The Philistines occupied the hills to the one side while Saul and the army of Israel were encamped on the hills opposite. The Valley of Elah crosses the Shephelah south of the valley of Sorek.

Elath—Elat—Ezion-geber—Eilat—At the head of the Gulf of Aqaba, an arm of the Red Sea, is modern Elath or

Elat or Eilat. It is located on the western side of the gulf in Israel, while the town of Aqaba is on the eastern side of the head of the gulf in the Kingdom of Jordan. Both of these communities are near the Biblical site of Elath and Ezion-geber, a short distance to the north. These last two mentioned places are spoken of as on the route of the Children of Israel's journey from Egypt to Canaan (Deuteronomy 2:8). It is also in this area that King Solomon, in the middle of the 10th century B.C., "made a navy of ships in Ezion-geber, which is beside Eloth, on the shore of the Red sea, in the land of Edom" (I Kings 9:26). This is the part of the country which certainly fulfills the prediction made to Israel that the Promised Land was "a land whose stones are iron, and out of whose hills thou mayest dig brass (copper)" (Deuteronomy 8:9). Sixteen miles to the north lies Timna where a large new copper mining plant has been set up since Israel became a state in 1948. Here stand two russet-colored projections of rock called Solomon's Pillars.

Dr. Nelson Glueck, American archaeologist, made some astounding discoveries when he carried out an extensive excavation at Ezion-geber. He found that Solomon had done more than build a navy there. He had turned Ezion-geber into an industrial city with huge smelters and workshops. The smelters were ingeniously designed and located to take advantage of the constant north winds which blow off the gulf. These fanned the flames of the furnaces and kept them blazing at maximum heat all the time. Glueck says, "No hand-bellows system was necessary, because with brilliant calculation, Solomon's engineers had harnassed the winds to furnish natural draught. The Bessemer principle of forced-air draught, discovered less than a century ago, was, in essence, already familiar three millenia back." The mines, furnaces, slag heaps and the ruins of the enclosure Solomon built to keep his slave labor from escaping, are visible today.

Emmaus—Emmaus is the village toward which Cleopas and another disciple were walking when Jesus joined them after His resurrection. He talked with them and opened to them the Scriptures though they did not know Him. He accepted their invitation to dine with them, and as He broke the bread their eyes were opened and they recognized Him. He then vanished from their sight (Luke 24:13-35). Luke says that Emmaus was "from Jerusalem about three-score furlongs"—about 7½ miles.

Three villages are pointed out as the most probable locations of ancient Emmaus. One is Qubeibeh about 7 miles west of Jerusalem. Another, due mainly to the writings of Eusebius and Jerome, is Amwas, about 20 miles west of Jerusalem. Obviously the distance does not fit Luke's account, though much Roman Catholic tradition supports it. The Crusaders believed that Emmaus was where the Arab village of Abu Ghosh now stands.

Endor—'Ein-Dor—On the north side of the Valley of Jezreel (Esdraelon) near Mt. Tabor is the city of Endor, the dwelling place of the witch to whom Saul went on the eve of his final battle with the Philistines (I Samuel 28:7-25). It is also mentioned as the place where some of Sisera's army perished (Psalm 83:9,10).

En-gedi—'Ein-Gedi—En-gedi is situated on the west shore of the Dead Sea about midway between its north and south ends. It is about 10½ miles north of Masada. In Bible days it was also known as Hazazon-tamar (II Chronicles 20:2). It was one of the cities in the inheritance of Judah (Joshua 15:62). The precipitous cliffs rise some 2,000 feet and are filled with caves. In these David and his men took refuge from King Saul (I Samuel 23:29). It was here David spared Saul's life, after cutting off part of his garments while Saul slept, because he was the Lord's anointed (I Samuel 24). En-gedi was famous for its verdure

72

and fruitful vineyards made possible by immense springs of water which come out of the limestone cliffs. The fruitfulness of the area is extolled in the Song of Solomon 1:14. One wonders if Ezekiel's prophecy (Ezekiel 47:9,10) does not look forward to a time when the waters of the Dead Sea will be fresh enough for fish to exist in as the river, of which the prophet speaks, flows through it.

Esdraelon, Plain of—Valley of Jezreel—This is the largest valley in Israel and cuts in two the central ridge of mountains dividing the mountains of Galilee in the north and those of Samaria to the south. It has always been a sort of land bridge over which invading armies have marched through history in their almost endless wars between the Euphrates and the Nile. The Pharaohs of Egypt, the Hittites, Israelites, Philistines, Assyrians, Syrians, Persians, Greeks, Romans, Crusaders, Turks and even the British under Lord Allenby during the first World War in 1918, have marched and fought on its plains. John speaks of it as the site of the last great battle of this age—the battle of Armageddon (Revelation 16:13-16).

The Plain of Esdraelon is also referred to as the Valley of Jezreel. This expression is used more commonly in the Bible of the valley running eastward between Mount Gilboa and the Hill of Moreh, now known as Giv'at Hamore. In this valley Gideon and his 300 soldiers routed the hosts of the Midianites (Judges 6:33; Chapter 7). Here also Sisera and his army were defeated by Israel under the leadership of Deborah and Barek (Judges 4). See also "Megiddo." Down this valley, some 20 miles from Mount Carmel to Jezreel, Elijah ran before the chariot of Ahab (I Kings 18:46).

In spite of all the sin, and tragedy and judgment that came upon Israel in the valley of Jezreel, the prophet Hosea prophecies great blessing upon the nation in this very place (Hosea 1:10,11). This, no doubt, looks forward to their millennial blessing after the battle of Armageddon (Hosea 2:21-23).

Galilee, The Sea of—Perhaps the supreme adventure in any visit to the Holy Land is to be at the Sea of Galilee. The ancient Rabbis used to say that "Jehovah hath created seven seas, but the Sea of Galilee is His delight." Josephus called it "The Ambition of Nature."

This beautiful body of water, which played such an important role in the ministry of our Lord, is known by five different designations. In the Old Testament it is called "the sea of Chinnereth" (Numbers 34:11; Joshua 12:3; 13:27, etc.). The modern name, Lake Kinneret is the same, meaning "harp." Possibly because the lake is shaped like a harp. Later it was called "the lake of Gennesaret" (Luke 5:1) from the fertile plain on its northwest shore. When Herod Antipas built Tiberias and made it his capital, the lake became known as "the Sea of Tiberias" (John 6:1,23; 21:1). The name by which is is best known is "the Sea of Galilee" (Matthew 4:18; 15:29; Mark 1:16; 7:31; John 6:1). It is 13 miles long and about 7½ miles wide at its northern end and 32 miles in circumference. It lies almost 700 feet below sea level. Its greatest depth is 200 feet. The lake abounds in fish as it must have in Christ's day. On its north shore Jesus called Peter and Andrew, James and John who were fishermen by trade (Matthew 4:18-22).

In Jesus' day the west shore from Tiberias to the Jordan River at the north end must have been an almost continuous series of cities. Actually there were nine cities. Today only Tiberias remains. Magdala (Matthew 15:39), the home of Mary Magdalene (Luke 8:2; Mark 16:9), was situated three miles north of Tiberias. The Plain of Gennesaret (Matthew 14:34; Mark 6:53) is just beyond Magdala. It is one of the most fertile areas of this part of the country.

North of Magdala, and before you come to Capernaum, is Tabgha and its Church of the Multiplication. This was built to mark the place of the miracle of the feeding of the five thousand with the five loaves and two fishes (Matthew 14:13-21; Mark 6:32-44; Luke 9:10-17; John 6:1-14). However, this miracle probably took place on the opposite side of the Sea of Galilee in the wilderness near Bethsaida. Thus the church at Tabgha merely commemorates this marvelous event.

Above the Plain of Gennesaret rises the Mount of the Beatitudes where it is believed Jesus spoke those wonderful principles of the blessed life (Matthew 5:1-12), and the Sermon on the Mount (Matthew 5:7). In one of the sheltered coves, which form a natural amphitheatre, Jesus borrowed Peter's boat and from it spoke to the multitude (Luke 5:1-3).

Galilee yielded two remarkable catches of fish in response to obedience to Jesus' command (Luke 5:4-11; John 21:6-8). Sudden and violent storms often rush down on the lake from the high peaks of Hermon and the Lebanon mountains not far to the north. Two of these storms revealed the omnipotence of Jesus—even over the powers of nature. In one storm Jesus was in the boat with the disciples (Matthew 8:23-27; Mark 4:35-41; Luke 8:22-25). In the other Jesus came walking on the stormy water to the disciples in the boat (Matthew 14:22-33; Mark 6:45-52; John 6:15-21).

On the eastern side of the lake the cliffs rise as much as 2,000 feet above the shore. Down one of these cliffs the 2,000 head of swine plunged into the sea after Jesus had cast the demons out of the demoniac and permitted them to enter the herd of swine (Matthew 8:28-34; Mark 5:1-21; Luke 8:26-40).

Before His crucifixion Jesus promised His disciples He would meet them in Galilee following His resurrection (Mark 14:28). Reiterated by the angel at the tomb (Mark

16:7), this was fulfilled at the early morning breakfast meeting by the shore of Galilee (John 21).

Gaza—Gaza is situated about 40 miles south of Jaffa (Joppa). It was one of the five principle cities of the Philistines and probably the oldest. It has always been important for it lies at the southern end of the Fertile Crescent joining Assyria and Egypt. It has been conquered by every world power which has held sway in the Middle East.

Joshua reached Gaza (Joshua 10:41) but it is doubtful if he ever conquered it (Joshua 11:22). The tribe of Judah captured the city (Judges 1:18) but probably did not hold it long for it was a Philistine city in the days of Samson, whose exploits have made it famous. To escape being killed by the Philistines, Samson carried off the gates of the city on his shoulders and deposited them in Hebron about 40 miles away (Judges 16:1-3). It was to Gaza that Samson was taken after the Philistines had captured him following his seduction by Delilah. The Philistines put out his eyes and made him grind in the prison house (Judges 16:21). He met his death in Gaza when he pulled down the pillars of the house of Dagan, taking 3,000 Philistines to death with him (Judges 16:23-30).

Various of the Hebrew prophets spoke against Gaza (Amos 1:7; Zephaniah 2:4). It is only mentioned once in the New Testament, when Philip was directed by the angel of the Lord to go from Jerusalem to Gaza, where he met and baptized the Ethiopian eunuch (Acts 8:26).

Geba—Geba was a town on the border of the inheritance of the tribe of Benjamin (Joshua 18:24), 6 miles north of Jerusalem, across the valley to the south from Michmash. It was one of the cities given to the Levites (Joshua

76

21:17; I Chronicles 6:60). Its modern name is Jeba. It was on the northern boundary of the kingdom of Judah. The expression, "from Geba to Beersheba," marked the whole extent of the kingdom of Judah (II Kings 23:8).

In the second year of his reign King Saul undertook to drive the Philistines from his realm. Jonathan, his son, struck the first blow at Geba (I Samuel 13:3). This was followed up by Jonathan and his armorbearer's almost impossible feat as they climbed up the rocky gorge toward Michmash and smote the Philistines. This, certainly with the help of the Lord, put the enemy to confusion and flight (I Samuel 14:1-23).

Geba was among the cities reoccupied by Judah after the 70 year exile in Babylon (Ezra 2:26; Nehemiah 11:31).

Gerar—Gerar was an ancient Philistine city on the border between Palestine and Egypt (Genesis 10:19). It seems definitely to be associated with Tell el-Jemmel, which has been partly excavated by Sir Flinders Petrie. It is located 8 miles southeast of Gaza on the way to Beersheba.

It was at Gerar that Abraham very foolishly repeated his act of calling Sarah his sister rather than his wife (Genesis 12:11-20; Genesis 20). Only God's intervention in each of these instances hindered disgrace to Sarah and confusion with regard to God's plans concerning Abraham's seed. Strangely enough, Isaac repeated his father's folly at the same place many years later (Genesis 26:6-11). One feels like saying, "Like father; like son." Excavations lead us to believe that Gerar controlled a rich caravan trade in spices and incense between Arabia and Palestine and the West.

Gethsemane, Garden of—Gethsemane probably means "oil press." John 18:1 speaks of it as a garden across the Kidron from Jerusalem, and Luke 22:39 tells us it was on

Mount across the Kidron from the Golden Gate of Jerusalem. It was a place where Jesus often went to pray (Luke 22:39). Judas seemed to know where he could find Jesus to betray Him to the priests in the absence of the populace (Luke 22:6). It was the place of Jesus' agony, His betrayal and arrest (Matthew 26:36-56; Mark 14:32-52; Luke 22:39-53; John 18:1-14).

The original area of Gethsemane must have been much larger for Jesus and His disciples to have found solitude there. The present garden is maintained by the Franciscans, and contains 8 ancient olive trees. It is doubtful if these are the same trees which were there in the time of Christ, for Josephus tells us Titus cut down all the trees in the environs of Jeruslaem during his siege of the city in 70 A.D. Because of the nature of olive trees it is possible that these eight may have grown from the roots of those under which Jesus prayed on that memorable night.

Adjacent to the Garden is the Church of All Nations in which is said to be the very rock by which Jesus prayed. The church is so named because sixteen nations contributed to its construction: Argentina, Australia, Belgium, Brazil, Britain, Canada, Chile, France, Germany, Hungary, Ireland, Italy, Mexico, Poland, Spain and the United States.

Gibeah—Gabaath—Tel el-Ful—In the hill country, about four miles north of Jerusalem, and east of the road to Ramallah is the site of king Saul's hometown, sometimes called in the Bible Gibeah of Benjamin and sometimes Gibeah of Saul (I Samuel 11:4; 13:16; 15:34). It is now known as Tel el-Ful. Excavations point to four great fortresses having been built one on another. The first points back to the destruction by fire referred to in Judges 20:40. On the ruins of this was built what was probably the fortress of Saul's time. Its remains measure 170 by 155 feet and its sloping walls were 6 feet thick. Later two other smaller fortresses were built on top of these.

The sordid story of the abuse heaped upon the Levite and his concubine, which led to the civil war that almost exterminated the tribe of Benjamin, took place at Gibeah (Judges 19:12-30; 20:1-48).

After Saul had been crowned as the first king of Israel, he returned to his home in Gibeah accompanied by a "band of men whose hearts God had touched" (I Samuel 10:26). It was from here Saul came to the aid of the men of Jabesh-gilead in their conflict with Nabash and the Ammonites (I Samuel 11:4). Saul and Jonathan made Gibeah the headquarters of their army in the battle with the Philistines described in I Samuel 13 and 14. It was at Gibeah of Saul that the bodies of the seven sons of Saul were hung up by the men of Gibeon (II Samuel 21:6) because Saul had transgressed the covenant made with them by Joshua (Joshua 9).

Gibeon—El-Jib—About 8 miles northwest of Jerusalem is the village of El-Jib, which has been identified as Gibeon, where the sun stood still in the days of Joshua (Joshua 10:12,13). Prior to this the inhabitants of Gibeon, hearing what Israel had done to Jericho and Ai, had tricked Joshua into making a league with them (Joshua 9:3-27). When they heard of this covenant, five kings of the Amorites joined together to fight against Gibeon. The Gibeonites immediately called to Joshua for help. He marched all night to come to their aid and in the great battle which ensued God sent hailstones from heaven destroying more of the enemy than the Israelites killed. In order to finish the destruction of the enemy and not to be hampered by darkness, Joshua commanded the sun and moon to stand still at Gibeon and in the nearby Valley of Ajalon. The five defeated kings hid in a cave at Makkedah near Azekah and were subsequently slain by Joshua (Joshua 10:1-27). Gibeon was the only city that made peace with the Israelites in their conquest of Canaan, and they were made servants to Israel (Joshua 11:19). Gibeon became part of the territory of the tribe of Benjamin and was given to the Levites as one of their cities (Joshua 21:17). Gibeon on one spectacular occasion was called Helkath-hazzurim —"The Field of Swords."

Here an attempt was made to settle a quarrel between the army of Ishbosheth, under Abner, and of David, under Joab, by having 12 men from each side fight. The plan failed because the 24 killed each other at the pool. Gibeon has a most spectacular water system. Cut entirely from solid rock, it includes a pool 82 feet deep, 37 feet in diameter, equipped with a circular stairway of 79 steps. Beyond the pool there is a tunnel, again carved from solid rock a distance of 167 feet, leading to a spring outside the ancient city. This unusual contest of arms probably took place beside this great pool (II Samuel 2:12-16).

King Saul failed to honor the ancient covenant with the Gibeonites and slew a number of them. Later, during the reign of David, the Lord sent three years' famine on Israel as a judgment for Saul's deeds. The Gibeonites refused to accept a settlement of silver or gold and were only appeased when they had hanged seven of Saul's sons whom they insisted should be delivered to them (II Samuel 21:1-9).

When David brought the ark of God back to Jerusalem (II Samuel 6:12; I Chronicles 15:1, 25-29), it seems that the tabernacle of the congregation was situated at Gibeon (II Chronicles 1:3-6). Here Solomon offered one thousand burnt offerings. That night, in a vision, Solomon was given a choice of anything he might ask of God. He prayed for a wise and understanding heart to enable him to govern Israel. God was pleased and promised him also riches (I Kings 3:4-15; II Chronicles 1:2-17).

Gilboa, Mount—Mt. Gilboa rises on the eastern edge of the Plain of Esdraelon. It was the site of the defeat and death of Israel's first king, Saul, and his sons, Jonathan, Abinadab and Melchishua (I Samuel 28:4; I Samuel 31:1-6; II Samuel 1:5-10; I Chronicles 10:1-7). The death of Saul and Jonathan called forth the eloquent and heart-rending lament from the soul of David, wherein he prays that no dew will ever fall again on Mt. Gilboa (II Samuel 1:19-27). The River Kishon takes its rise on the slopes of Mt. Gilboa.

Harod, Well of—'Ein Harod—At the foot of Mt. Gilboa is the spring at which Gideon gathered the people of Israel to fight against Midian (Judges 7:1). Here the diminished host of 10,000 was made to drink, and God chose to deliver the Midianites into the hands of the 300 who lapped the water (Judges 7:4-7).

Hazor—Hazor is located nine miles north of the Sea of Galilee. It was a city of importance in earliest ages. It is mentioned as early as the 19th century B.C. in documents from Egypt. The first city was built more than 4,500 years ago. In the 18th century B.C. it was the largest city in the country and one of the largest in the middle east. It was a frequent point of attack and was destroyed and rebuilt on a number of occasions through the centuries.

When Joshua and the children of Israel invaded the country Jabin, king of Hazor, gathered together all the kings of that region to fight against them. God encouraged Joshua, and Israel won a great victory over their combined might. He took the city of Hazor and burned it to the ground (Joshua 11:1-13). When Israel did evil in the sight of the Lord after the death of Ehud, the second judge, "the

Lord sold them into the hand of Jabin king of Canaan."
He apparently is a later Jabin who had recovered Hazor,
for he was reigning there. He was noted for having 900
iron chariots and he held dominion over Israel for 20
years. The captain of his army was Sisera. Under the
inspiration of Deborah, a prophetess, Barak led the children of Israel to a great victory over Sisera and his hosts
in the Esdraelon Valley (Judges 4:1-24).

Solomon, during his reign, rebuilt Hazor, Megiddo and
Gezer, three cities which dominated the plains of Huleh,
Jezreel and Ajalon respectively (I Kings 9:15). Hazor was
conquered by the Assyrian king Tiglath Pileser in 732 B.C.
Archaeologists began a four seasons' dig at the Tell of
Hazor and the rectangular plateau to its immediate north
in the year 1955.

Hebron—Hebron lies about 19 miles in a southwesterly
direction from Jerusalem. In ancient times it was known as
Kirjath-arba (Joshua 14:15; 20:7). In Arabic, Hebron is
called El Khalil—"the friend"—after Abraham. (II Chronicles 20:7; Isaiah 41:8; James 2:23). After his separation from Lot, Abraham came and dwelt here. He built his
fourth altar "in the plain of Mamre, which is in Hebron"
(Genesis 13:18). Hebron, as a city, did not exist in Abraham's day. It was founded about 1700 B.C. (Numbers
13:22). The terraced hills were famous for their olive
groves and fig trees. It was from this area that the spies
took back to Kadesh Barnea "a branch with one cluster of
grapes, and they bare it between two upon a staff"
(Numbers 13:22,23). This was the part of the country
where the sons of Anak, the giants, lived.

It was in this Hebron area that God appeared to
Abraham in the form of three men and reconfirmed His
promise of the birth of Isaac (Genesis 18:1-15). Here also

Abraham made intercession for Sodom and Gomorrah (Genesis 18:16-33). The oak at Mamre, under which it is believed Abraham had pitched his tent, is shown today. Its heavy branches are supported by steel beams and it is carefully surrounded by a high iron fence.

Abraham's wife, Sarah, died at Hebron and was buried in the cave of Machpelah, which Abraham purchased from the sons of Heth (Genesis 23). It was the only portion of Canaan that Abraham actually owned, though God had promised him the whole land. Later Abraham was buried beside her, as were also Isaac, Rebecca, Jacob and Leah, in the years that followed. A huge mosque is built over the cave. Cenotaphs in the mosque commemorate those who are buried below. A limited view of the cave may be had through a small opening, but no one is allowed to enter it. To the Moslems, Abraham was the first Moslem. Because of its association with Abraham, Hebron is regarded as one of the four sacred cities of Islam. From Hebron Abraham went out to rescue Lot (Genesis 14:13-16). Isaac lived here for a time (Genesis 35:27). Jacob lived here after the death of Rachel (Genesis 37:14).

Joseph's journey from Hebron to Dothan in search of his brothers and their sheep (Genesis 37:13-19).

Hebron was taken by Joshua in his conquest of the land of Canaan (Joshua 10:36,37). It was given to Caleb as his inheritance because of his faithfulness in following the Lord (Joshua 14:10-15). It was designated one of the six cities of refuge (Joshua 20:7; 21:13). At the gate of Hebron Joab treacherously killed Abner, who had been Saul's general, and paved the way for his master, David, to be king of all Israel (II Samuel 3:27-39). After the death of Saul, David was crowned king of Judah at Hebron (II Samuel 2:1-4). David reigned here 7½ years before he was made king of all Israel (II Samuel 2:11; I Kings 2:11). Absalom made Hebron his headquarters in his revolt against his father David (II Samuel 15:7-12).

The Herodium—Three or four miles southeast of Bethlehem is a gigantic pile of dirt built by Herod the Great in a colossal earth-moving operation. It is called the Herodium. At its foot were palaces, terraced gardens and pools. Two hundred white marble steps led to the towers of the citadel on top. It served as a place of retreat for Herod as well as another in the series of fortresses he built throughout the land, including the Alexandrium in the Jordan Valley and Masada. The Herodium was chosen by Herod as the place for his tomb. He died in his summer palace at Jericho in 4 B.C. and his body was taken to the Herodium. It is significant that his burial place was not far from Bethlehem, where he had ordered the slaying of the infants at the time of the birth of Jesus.

Hinnom, Valley of—West of Mount Zion and running around the southern side of the walled city of Jerusalem to the Kidron Valley, south of the hill Ophel, is the Valley of Hinnom. It is also called "valley of the son of Hinnom" (Joshua 15:8; II Chronicles 28:3; 33:6, etc.), and "valley of the children of Hinnom" (II Kings 23:10). Located in this valley was Topheth, "the place of burning" Jeremiah 7:31). During the reign of Ahaz and of Manasseh, idolatrous practices were carried on in this valley. Children were offered as burnt sacrifices to abominable heathen gods (II Chronicles 28:3; 33:6). During his great revival, Josiah is said to have "defiled Topheth, which is in the valley of the children of Hinnom" that no more horrible sacrifices might be made there (II Kings 23:10). Because of the evil practices conducted in the valley, Jeremiah announced a change of its name to "the valley of Slaughter" (Jeremiah 7:31-33). The valley became a place for burial until there was no more room and the bodies were just cast into it to be consumed by dogs and vultures. Fires were kept burning continually to consume the rubbish of the city. Jesus used the word "Gehenna"—taken from the Aramaic "Ge-Hin-nom"—to signify eternal hell (Matthew 5:22,29,30; 10:28; 18:9; 23:15,33; Mark 9:43,45.47; Luke 12:5; James 3:6).

Jenin—Thirteen miles north of Dothan is the town of Jenin—ancient En-gannim (Joshua 15:34; 19:21; 21:29). According to tradition, it was here that Jesus healed the ten lepers, only one of whom returned to give Him thanks (Luke 17:11-19).

Jericho—Located in a very fertile plain north of the Dead Sea and west of the Jordan River, about 17 miles from Jerusalem. Called "The City of Palm Trees" (Deuteronomy 34:3; II Chronicles 28:15), Mark Anthony once gave it to his friend Cleopatra. Herod the Great built a luxurious palace here and made Jericho his winter capital. He died here in 4 B.C.

Jericho is specially known as the first city Joshua and the children of Israel took in their conquest of the land of Canaan. Here the spies were received and protected by Rahab (Joshua 2), and there the walls of the city fell down after the people of Israel had encircled them a total of thirteen times (Joshua 6). Joshua pronounced a curse against anyone who would attempt to rebuild the city (Joshua 6:26). I Kings 16:34 tells of one man who tried to do so and of the judgment he endured. Jericho was one of the places to which Elisha followed Elijah on the journey that led to Elijah's translation (II Kings 2:4,5).

Spring of Elisha—From the mound of ancient Jericho known as Tell es-Sultan, one looks down on the Spring of Elisha whose waters were made sweet as he put salt in them (II Kings 2:18-22). The women still come with their waterpots, or modern five gallon oil cans, to draw the family's supply of water.

Extensive excavations have been made at Jericho since early in the twentieth century. Claims have been made that the ruined walls of Joshua's time have been uncovered, but none of these are apparent today. This may be because some of the earliest archaeologists tore apart a section of the ancient city so that it is lost to scientific study. Other unearthed ruins have been destroyed by the elements. However, extensive ruins have been uncovered which date back to 7000 B.C. and earn for Jericho the distinction of being probably "the oldest walled city in the world." Outstanding is a huge defense system and an old tower 35 feet thick.

The modern city of Jericho is located to the east of the ancient site. It was outside modern Jericho that Jesus healed blind Bartimaeus (Matthew 20:29-34; Mark 10:46-52; Luke 18:35-43). He encountered Zacchaeus sitting in one of the sycamore trees that were abundant here (Luke 19:1-10). The road from Jericho to Jerusalem was the scene of Christ's story of the Good Samaritan (Luke 10:30-37).

West of Jericho, and overlooking the Jordan valley, the hills of the western highlands rise abruptly. Just a mile from Jericho is the 1,500 foot high ridge known as Jebel Kuruntul. Here the spies who were protected by Rahab hid for three days before returning to Joshua (Joshua 2:15-23). It is believed that this is the mountain to which the Holy Spirit led Jesus, immediately after His baptism in Jordan, to be tempted of the devil. Here He fasted for forty days and nights and then triumphed over Satan with the three simple but direct quotations from the book of Deuteronomy—"It is written" (Matthew 4:1-11; Mark 1:12,13; Luke 4:1-13).

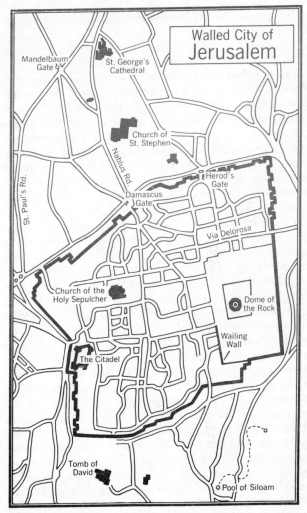

Walled City of Jerusalem

Mandelbaum Gate

St. George's Cathedral

Nablus Rd.

St. Paul's Rd.

Church of St. Stephen

Herod's Gate

Damascus Gate

Via Delorosa

Church of the Holy Sepulcher

Dome of the Rock

Wailing Wall

The Citadel

Tomb of David

Pool of Siloam

Map of the Old City. June 1967 there is no longer a No Man's Land separating this sector from modern Jerusalem.

Jerusalem

The most important place in the Holy Land is the city of Jerusalem: because of its place of antiquity, because of its association with the many vital events in the life of our Lord, and because of its future significance during the coming kingdom age. The City of Jerusalem might well be called the world's most hated city, for though its name means "peace," more wars have been fought at its gates than at any other city in the world. But Jerusalem is also the world's most loved city for it is sacred to the three great religions of the world: Christianity, Mohammedanism and Judaism. Pilgrims by the tens of thousands come each year to walk her streets and worship at her memorable places. It is situated on a rocky prominence about 2,500 feet above the Mediterranean and 3,800 feet above the Dead Sea. It is 33 miles east of the Mediterranean Sea and 14 miles west of the Dead Sea.

Its history goes back into the hazy past, at least to the 15th century B.C. It was called "Urusalimu" in Egyptian and Babylonish literature. Hence its present name. Jerusalem is first mentioned in the Bible during the time of Abraham under the name of Salem, which means "Peace" —city of Melchisedek "the priest of the most high God" (Genesis 14:18). When the Israelites conquered Canaan, Jerusalem was known as Jebus and its inhabitants Jebusites (Judges 19:10,11; I Chronicles 11:4). The strong city which the Jebusites had built on the hill was considered impregnable, but David and his men took it against the taunts of the inhabitants (II Samuel 5:6-9; I Chronicles 11:4-7). It was called "Zion"—also "the City of David." David made Jerusalem his capital and brought the Ark of the Covenant there (II Samuel 6:12-17; I Chronicles 15).

The city which David captured was on the hill Ophel,

St. Stephen's Gate in old wall of Jerusalem. Here Stephen was martyred while Saul of Tarsus stood by.

City of Jerusalem as seen from the Mount of Olives.

south of the walls of the present city, with the Kidron Valley on the east and the Valley of Hinnom to the south. It was probably not more than 8 acres in size. Solomon built the beautiful temple on Mount Moriah immediately to the north.

Nebuchadnezzar, king of Babylon, destroyed the city in 586 B.C. and carried the Jews into captivity (II Kings 25:1-21; II Chronicles 36:15-21; Jeremiah 39:9-14). In all, the city has been captured some 26 times in its history. Nehemiah rebuilt the walls after Cyrus the Persian monarch gave permission (Ezra 11:1-11; 6:1-3; Nehemiah 2:4-20; 6:15,16). Other conquerors included Alexander the Great in 332 B.C. and Antiochus Epiphanes in 168 B.C. It has been totally destroyed at least five times.

At the time of Jesus, the city had been greatly enlarged, particularly as the result of the building activities of Herod the Great. The city spread to the north and west of the original location on the hill Ophel. The present walls of the Old City were built in 1542 during the reign of the Turkish Sultan Suleiman—called "The Magnificent." In it there are 8 gates and 34 towers. They are 2½ miles around. The modern city, capital of the State of Israel, sprawls far beyond the walls to the northwest.

In accordance with the prophecy of Jesus (Luke 19:41-44; Luke 21:20-24), Jerusalem was destroyed in 70 A.D. by the Roman legions under Titus. At least nine times since then its control has passed from one religion to another. Emperor Hadrian built a pagan city on this site which he called Aelia Capitolina. Since then it has been held by Christians (3rd century), the Persians (7th century), Arabs, the Crusaders, Arabs under Saladin and the Ottoman Turks from 1517 A.D. until the Allied troops under Allenby entered its gates in 1917. After World War I Jerusalem and Palestine were placed under British Mandate. This was given up in 1948. The War of Liberation resulted in a United Nations Armistice, partitioning the city between Israel and Jordan. During the six day war of 1967 Israel took the Old City and united Jerusalem with free access to each section for all.

Points of interest in Jerusalem center around:

The Via Dolorosa—This is the traditional pathway Jesus took from Pilate's judgment hall to Calvary. It begins at the site of Herod's great fortress the Antonia. Here Paul made his speech to the people of Jerusalem (Acts 21:35-40). Here also was the tower of Hananeel in Nehemiah's day (Nehemiah 3:1; 12:39; Jeremiah 31:38; Zechariah 14:10). The "Ecce Homo Arch" commemorates the words of Pilate "Behold the Man" (John 19:5). Some feet below the present roadway, under the convent of the Sisters of Zion, may be seen the pavement upon which Jesus walked as He went out of the judgment hall (John 19:13). It is called the Lithostrotos—Hebrew Gabbatha. You will also be shown the prison cell of Barabbas as well as the one occupied by Christ. The Church of the Holy Sepulchre has been built over what is believed to be the site of Calvary and the tomb of Joseph of Arimathaea. The church is a round building with the tomb in the center. Some distance away and 14 feet higher is a chapel built over what is thought to have been the hill of Calvary. There are three main shrines, plus many others split up between six churches: the Latin (Roman), Eastern Orthodox, Arminian, Coptic, Syrian and Abyssinian. It is usually a disappointing place to evangelical Christians. Gordon's Calvary and the Garden Tomb, located outside the walls of the Old City, are held by many to be the true location of these sacred places. Whatever may be said for or against either location, the latter certainly gives one a clearer picture of what these places must have looked like in the time of our Lord.

The Golden Gate—or Eastern Gate—of the city of Jerusalem is on the east side of the city facing the Mount of Olives. This is the gate built on the place where it is believed Jesus entered on the occasion of His Triumphal Entry. This gate was closed by the Turkish governor of Jerusalem in 1530 in the hope of postponing the day of judgment and the end of the world. Legend had it that this would be the spot where the trumpet would sound and the dead would be raised. Many Christians believe that when Jesus comes again, the gate will be opened and He will once again enter the Holy City (Ezekiel 44:1-3). If the gate were open it would be the only gate that would lead directly into the temple area.

St. Stephen's Gate—Also on the east side of the city, St. Stephen's Gate is the site of the martyrdom of Stephen while Saul of Tarsus was looking on (Acts 7:57-60). It is also called the Sheep Gate, and sometimes the Lions' Gate because of figures of lions on the gate.

The Dome of the Rock—To the left and to the south as you enter Jerusalem by St. Stephen's Gate, is the great area surrounding Al-Haramesh-Sharif—the Dome of the Rock. This stands on what is believed to be Mount Moriah, where Abraham took his son to offer to God in obedience to His command (Genesis 22:1,2). This was also the threshing floor of Ornan the Jebusite (Araunah, II Samuel) which David bought as a place of sacrifice to Jehovah that the plague might be stayed (II Samuel 24:18-25; I Chronicles 21:18-30). On this site Solomon built the first great temple (II Chronicles 3:1,2). This beautiful building was destroyed in 586 B.C. by Nebuchadnezzar (II Kings 25:9; II Chronicles 36:18,19). The second temple was built by Zerubbabel (Ezra 3:8-13; 4:23,24; 5:1-5; 6:15-18). This was rebuilt and enlarged by Herod the Great about 20 B.C. This was the temple in existence in the time of Christ and to which His disciples called His attention (Matthew 24:1,2; Mark 13:1,2; Luke 21:5,6).

The golden-domed octagonal shaped mosque with its

brilliant blue Persian tiles, stands today where the Jewish temples were erected. The present building was built in the last part of the 7th century. It is built over and around an immense rough-hewn rock about 40 by 52 feet which rises 7 feet above the level of the temple area. It formed the base of the Jewish Altar of Burnt Offering. There are grooves in the Rock with a hole in the middle through which the blood and refuse were taken down and out of the temple and through the Dung Gate of the city to the valley below. It is from this area, of the Dome of the Rock, Mohammed is supposed to have gone to heaven on his winged steed, el-Baruk, meaning "Lightning." The Rock is considered second only in sanctity to Mecca and Medina as a Moslem shrine.

The Wailing Wall—A portion of the western wall of Herod's temple was preserved by the Romans when they destroyed the city in 70 A.D. to show how formidable they were. This fragment of wall is revered by the Jews and called The Wailing Wall. It is about 50 yards long and 60 feet high. One stone is 16½ feet long and 13 feet wide. Here the Jews gather to wail the loss of their temple. It was the goal of the Israeli soldiers who conquered the Old City during the six-day war of 1967.

The Pool of Bethesda—This may be seen on the grounds of the Church of St. Anne just inside St. Stephen's Gate to the right as you enter the gate. It is very much below the surface of the present city streets, as are all places from the time of Christ, due to the many times the city has been destroyed and rebuilt on top of the rubble. It was here Jesus healed the impotent man who had lain so long on one of the five porches waiting for the angel to trouble the water (John 5:2-15).

The Church of St. Anne was built by the Crusaders on what was believed to have been the site of the home of

Anne and Joachim, parents of the virgin Mary, and the place where she was born.

Solomon's Quarries—Just north of Herod's Gate, between that and the Damascus Gate, is a seven foot fissure in the natural rock on which the wall of the city of Jerusalem is built. This opening was discovered almost 100 years ago and found to lead into a vast underground cavern—the famous quarries from which the stone was cut for the building of Solomon's Temple. Thus we read in I Kings 6:7, "And the house, when it was in building, was built of stone made ready before it was brought thither: so that there was neither hammer nor axe nor any tool of iron heard in the house, while it was in building." Being deep underground all sound was cut off during the cutting. In 1948 the Jordanians closed the quarries because they feared its passages might lead to the Israeli side of Jerusalem. Since the uniting of the city this fear is no more and visitors will be permitted to view them. This will be of special interest to the Masonic Lodge. Masons regard the first 3,600 overseers, who put the people to work on the stones for the temple, as the first Freemasons. Blocks hewn from the virgin rock have been shipped to many countries for use as foundation stones in Masonic Lodges.

Solomon's Stables—When Herod the Great was rebuilding and enlarging the temple in Jerusalem, he desired to make the temple area much more expansive. In order to do this he built up the hill to the southeast of the temple by a series of arches which today are popularly called "Solomon's Stables," though all agree they had nothing to do with the time of Solomon. Thus a huge platform was made to expand the desired area. There are some 88 pillars in these fascinating underground vaults. Holes in the stone pillars indicate that at some time, possibly Herod's or that of the Crusaders, horses were kept here. Because of this huge platform, the southeastern corner of the temple area was lifted 170 feet above the gorge of the Kidron. This corner is called "the pinnacle of the Temple" (Matthew 4:5; Luke 4:9).

Jezreel, City of—Yizre'el—For Valley of Jezreel see Esdraelon—Near modern Yizre'el in the eastern portion of the Valley of Jezreel is the site of the city of Jezreel where Ahab, king of Israel, built one of his palaces (I Kings 21:1). After the miracle of the fire falling on Mt. Carmel and his destruction of the prophets of Baal, Elijah ran before the chariots of Ahab from Carmel to Jezreel a distance of some 20 miles (I Kings 18:46).

Next to Ahab's palace was a vineyard owned by Naboth which the king desired in order to make of it a garden of herbs. Naboth did not want to part with the inheritance of his fathers, but the wicked queen Jezebel arranged a plot to accuse Naboth of blaspheming God and the king and had him stoned to death. Thus Ahab could take the vineyard (I Kings 21:1-16). However, God sent Elijah the prophet to announce that the dogs would lick the blood of Ahab in the same spot where they had licked Naboth's blood. He also predicted that Jezebel would be eaten by dogs by the wall of Jezreel (I Kings 21:17-25). The fulfillment of the prophecy concerning Ahab is recorded in I Kings 22:38. That concerning Jezebel is told in II Kings 9:30-37.

The many acts of judgment executed by Jehu, the furious-driving king of Israel, against the house of Ahab took place in and about the city of Jezreel (II Kings 9:14-37; 10:6-11, etc.).

Joppa—Jaffa—Yafo—Joppa, the Greek name for this city, is immediately south and adjacent to the modern city of Tel Aviv. They are now one municipality. It has a recorded history of 3,500 years.

Joppa was known in Joshua's time as Japho (Joshua

19:46), and was part of the inheritance of the tribe of Dan. During the time of Solomon's reign it became the chief seaport of Jerusalem. The famous cedars of Lebanon were floated down from that country to Joppa for overland transportation to Jerusalem for the building of the temple. Later, during the time of Ezra, additional cedars were brought here for the rebuilding of the temple by Zerubbabel (Ezra 3:7). Joppa was the port from which Jonah sailed in a vain endeavor to go to Tarshish rather than obey the call of God to go warn the wicked city of Nineveh (Jonah 1:3).

Joppa was the home of Dorcas, who seems to have become the mother of the Women's Missionary Movements throughout the Christian church. She died and the disciples sent to Lydda, about 11 miles to the southeast, for Peter. After coming, Peter prayed and said, "Tabitha, arise," and the woman arose immediately, and many believed on the Lord (Acts 9:36-42). Peter remained in Joppa at the house of Simon, the tanner, which was by the sea (Acts 9:43). While praying on the housetop at noon he saw the vision of the great sheet let down from heaven containing all manner of animals. The Lord showed him that He was no respecter of persons (Acts 10:9-16). This led to Peter's ministry to the Gentiles of the house of Cornelius at Caesarea (Acts 10:17-48).

The first Zionist pioneers of the 19th century entered the Promised Land through Jaffa harbor. Jews from Jaffa moved a few miles north and founded the city of Tel Aviv in 1909. It is now Israel's largest city.

Jordan River—The Jordan is the only river in the world which flows for most of its course below sea level. It has its source in a grove on the side of Mount Hermon, about 1,700 feet above sea level. In a distance of about 12 miles it drops nearly to sea level at Lake Hulah, or "The Waters of

Merom." This area, which was very marshy, has now been drained except for a small wild fowl sanctuary. Much valuable agricultural land has been reclaimed and millions of gallons of water, which previously seeped into the ground, have been saved.

The descent continues another six miles until it enters the Sea of Galilee which lies 682 feet below the level of the sea. From the lower end of Galilee, 13 miles farther south, it begins its winding course down to the Dead Sea, almost 1,300 feet below sea level. Though the distance from Galilee to the Dead Sea is only 65 air miles, the river twists and turns so that it is about 200 miles in length. The river is but 100 to 200 feet wide except at flood time when it overflows its banks.

The River Jordan has witnessed many miracles of God's power. Three times in history its waters have been miraculously stopped. The first was to enable Joshua and the Children of Israel to pass over into Canaan (Joshua 3:13-17). This was when the river was at flood tide (Joshua 3:15; 4:18). Twelve stones were set up in the bed of the river and twelve were taken from the bottom of the stream and set up at Gilgal as a memorial of what God had so marvelously done for His people (Joshua 4:1-9, 20-24). The second occasion was when Elijah smote the waters so that he and Elisha might pass over (II Kings 2:6-8). The third was when Elisha wished to return after the translation of Elijah (II Kings 2:12-15). This became a sign to those who viewed it that the spirit of Elijah rested upon Elisha. It was in the River Jordan that Naaman dipped seven times and was healed of his leprosy (II Kings 5:10-14). In these same waters Elisha caused the axe head to "swim" (II Kings 6:4-7).

John the Baptist ministered to the multitudes that came from Jerusalem and all Judea at the River Jordan. Because Gabriel foretold that John the Baptist would go before the Messiah "in the spirit and power of Elias" (Luke 1:17), it is believed the place John chose to baptize was the same as that where Elijah and Elisha miraculously crossed the river on dry ground. Indeed the traditional place from which Elijah was translated is pointed out about one mile east of the baptismal spot where our Lord came to be baptized. Here, near Bethabara, John baptized those who repented of their sins and here he prophesied of the coming of One Who "shall baptize you with the Holy Ghost" (Matthew 3:11). John baptized Jesus at His request and insistence. Seeing the Spirit of God descending upon Him as a dove, John presented Jesus to the multitude with the unique introduction, "Behold the Lamb of God, which taketh away the sin of the world" (John 1:29-34).

Kidron, Valley of, Brook—Cedron—The Valley of Kidron is about 2¾ miles long. It is immediately east of the wall of Jerusalem between the city and the Mount of Olives. It seems to have been a favorite burying place and one in which undesirable things were disposed. During the reforms and revivals under some of Israel's godly kings, idols and other materials used in pagan worship were disposed of in the Brook Kidron. Note the following: Asa burnt his mother's idol here (I Kings 15:13; II Chronicles 15:16); Josiah destroyed the vessels made for Baal and the grove which had been erected in the house of the Lord, also the heathen altars made by Ahaz and Manasseh in the temple court (II Kings 23:4,6,12); Hezekiah ordered the priests to carry all the "uncleanness that they found in the temple of the Lord" to the Brook Kidron (II Chronicles 29:16), also the heathen altars that were in Jerusalem (II Chronicles 30:14).

When Absalom led the rebellion against his father David, the people who were loyal to the king wept as he passed over the Brook Kidron, thus abandoning the city of Jerusalem to his rebellious son (II Samuel 15:23). How different as we read of our Lord crossing this brook on His way to Gethsemane (John 18:1)! The Valley of Kidron is sometimes called the Valley of Jehoshaphat and is associated with the great day of the judgment of the nations (Joel 3:2,12).

Kirjath-Jearim—Abu Ghosh—A flourishing Arab village about nine miles west of Jerusalem. It was one of the four cities of the Gibeonites which was spared because of the league which Joshua made with them (Joshua 9:17).

Here on the top of a hill is the site of the house of Abinadab who kept the Ark of the Covenant for twenty years after the Philistines sent it back from their territory, and before David carried it up to Jerusalem (I Samuel 7:1, 2; II Samuel 6; I Chronicles 15:25-29). The place today is called Abu Ghosh and the site of the house of Abinadab is marked by a huge statue of Mary carrying the baby Jesus in her arms. A French monastery was built there in 1924 called "Notre Dame de L'arche d'Alliance"—"Our Lady of the Ark of the Covenant."

Pious Jewish pilgrims used to rend their garments at this spot in mourning over the destruction of the temple. It was believed by the Crusaders to be the site of the village of Emmaus (Luke 24:13). See "Emmaus."

Kishon, River—Having its rise on Mt. Gilboa, the River Kishon flows west through the Plain of Esdraelon. At the base of Mt. Tabor the chariots of Sisera were mired in the mud, contributing to their defeat by the forces of Israel under Deborah and Barak (Judges 4:7,13; 5:21). By this river, as it flowed by the foot of Mt. Carmel, Elijah killed the 450 prophets of Baal after the Lord had answered by fire (I Kings 18:40).

Lachish—Twenty miles inland from Ashkelon is the site of the Biblical city of Lachish. It was important because it guarded the approaches to the Judean hills and Jerusalem to the north and Egypt to the south. Joshua completely destroyed the inhabitants of Lachish in his campaign through the southern part of Canaan (Joshua 10:31-33). Archaeologists have found the ruins of this city. David made it a provincial administrative center. His grandson Rehoboam strengthened its defenses about 920 B.C. (II Chronicles 11:5-12). It was destroyed by Sennacherib in 701 B.C. as he found his way to Egypt blocked. One hundred years later the reconstructed city was destroyed by Nebuchadnezzar in 587 B.C. It was resettled by some of the Jews on their return from the Babylonish captivity (Nehemiah 11:30). After the fourth century B.C. Lachish declined when the administrative center was moved to nearby Mareshah. It is merely a Tell today. Mareshah (II Chronicles 11:8) is a conspicuous Tell some 3 miles northeast of Lachish.

Lubban—About 17 miles north of Jerusalem, in an imposing valley, is the village of Lubban. This marks the traditional frontier between Judea and Samaria. This city has been identified with Lebonah mentioned in Judges 21:19.

Lydda—Lod—The modern city of Lod is located about 11 miles southeast of Jaffa, or Joppa, and is known in the New Testament as Lydda. It was here Peter healed Aeneas who had been bedridden with palsy for eight years (Acts 9:32-35). The city was known as Lod in Old Testament times (I Chronicles 8:12; Ezra 2:33; Nehemiah 7:37; 11:35). It is the site of Israel's largest airport.

Tradition says that St. George, the patron saint of England, was born at Lod and that in 303 A.D. he was martyred here for tearing down the anti-Christian edicts of the Roman emperor. He was buried here. The Church of St. George commemorates his exploits.

Magdala—Magdala was situated three miles north of Tiberias on the western shore of the Sea of Galilee (Matthew 15:39). It was the home of Mary Magdalene, out of whom Jesus cast seven devils (Luke 8:2; Mark 16:9). Magdala is mentioned prominently in the writings of Josephus by its Greek name, Taricheae. It would appear to have been a town of considerable size in the 1st century A.D. It was one of the sites which Josephus fortified when he was Governor of Galilee—before his defection to the Romans. The city fell to Titus during the 66-70 A.D. struggle of the Jews against the Romans. 6,700 Jews were killed, 6,000 of the strongest sent to Nero to dig the Corinthian Canal and 30,400 were auctioned off as slaves.

Masada—Metsada—Masada is an immense brown crag about 2½ miles from the western shore of the Dead Sea in the wilderness of Judah. In Hebrew it means "Fortress." It is half a mile long and 220 yards wide. Some scholars think that Masada is referred to in the story of David's flight from King Saul. In I Samuel 24:22 and I Chronicles 12:8 the word translated "hold" is the Hebrew "Metsada." Herod the Great made a great fortification out of this huge plateau, surrounding the top with a high wall interspersed with great defense towers. He also constructed an elaborate palace on the northeastern corner. The top was used for cultivation and great cisterns and cellars were hewn out of the rock for the storage of water and food. It was designed to withstand any seige and was considered impregnable.

When Jerusalem fell to the Romans under Titus in 70 A.D. a band of Jewish patriots, under the leadership of

Eliezer Ben Yair, determined to continue the fight for freedom and made their way to Masada. For three years the Romans sought unsuccessfully to storm the fortress. Eventually they built a huge earth ramp up to its walls and set fire to the inner wall of wood which the defenders had built. As the fire burned through the night the besiegers withdrew. The next morning they launched their attack but were met with complete silence from within. Finally two women emerged from hiding to tell the story. Eliezer had warned the remaining defenders of the torture they and their families would receive if they were captured, challenging them to die by their own hand rather than to surrender. Josephus describes the heroic end of Masada in his "History of the Jewish Wars":

"For at the very moment when with streaming eyes they embraced and caressed their wives, and taking their children in their arms pressed upon them the last, lingering kisses, hands other than their own seemed to assist them and they carried out their purpose, the thought of the agonies they would suffer at the hands of the enemy, consoling them for the necessity of killing them. In the end not a man failed to carry out his terrible resolve, but one and all disposed of their entire families. Oh! victims of cruel necessity, who with their own hands murdered their wives and children and felt it to be the lightest of evils! Unable to endure any longer the horror of what they had done, and thinking they would be wronging the dead if they outlived them a moment longer, they quickly made a heap of all they possessed and set it on fire; and when ten of them had been chosen by lot to be the executioners of the rest, every man lay down beside his wife and children where they lay, flung his arms round them, and exposed his throat to those who must perform the painful office. These unflinchingly slaughtered them all, then agreed on the same for each other, so that the one who drew the lot should kill the nine and last of all himself: such perfect confidence they all had

Fortress of Masada showing Roman ramp and Herod's three-level palace.

One level of Herod's palace at Masada.

in each other that neither in doing nor in suffering would one differ from another. So finally the nine presented their throats, and the one man left till last first surveyed the serried ranks of the dead, in case amidst all the slaughter someone was still left in need of his hand; then finding that all had been dispatched, set the palace blazing fiercely, and summoning all his strength drove his sword right through his body and fell down by the side of his family." The tragedy was enacted on the 15th of April, 73 A.D. 960 men, women and children perished.

Masada has become a shrine and a symbol to the new nation of Israel. "Masada shall not fall again!" is the proud oath which cadets swear during the impressive graduation ceremony of Israel's military academy.

From 1963-65, under the leadership of Yigael Yadin, professor of archaeology at the Hebrew University, a great expedition labored at Masada unearthing and restoring much of the massive fortifications, storehouses, palaces, churches, etc. What they found supports Josephus' reports. Uncovered, also, were portions of Scripture from Deuteronomy, Ezekiel and a part of Psalms 81-85. The remarkable and thrilling thing is that these portions correspond almost word for word with the present Hebrew Masoretic text. Thus another link is provided in the testimony of the unerring character of the Word of God.

Megiddo—The Tell of Megiddo lies on the southern edge of the Plain of Esdraelon, the most famous battlefield in the world. The mound, which has been extensively excavated, covers some 13 acres and reveals 20 cities built one upon the ruins of another. One of the reasons for its importance as a military stronghold was its water system which dates back 2,800 years. A shaft 120 feet deep connects with the spring outside the city walls by a tunnel 215 feet long.

It was one of the royal cities of the Canaanites, the king of which was slain by Joshua (Joshua 12:21). Sisera and his army were defeated "by the waters of Megiddo" (Judges 5:19). During Solomon's reign Megiddo was well fortified as one of the important defense posts of his kingdom (I Kings 9:15). It was one of his "cities for chariots" (I Kings 10:26). Excavations have revealed stables capable of taking care of 450 horses and 150 chariots. Here Ahaziah king of Israel was slain (II Kings 9:27). Josiah unwisely fought with Pharaoh Necoh and the Egyptian army at Megiddo and was slain (II Chronicles 35:20-24). The last great battle of this age will be fought at Armageddon—Har Mageddon, Mount of Megiddo (Revelation 16:13-16).

Michmash—Michmash is a town in the inheritance of Benjamin which lies east of Bethel and seven miles north of Jerusalem. Its modern name is Mukhmas. It lay across the valley to the north from Geba. Israel's great victory over the Philistines in the early days of Saul's reign began here (I Samuel 14:1-23). This was sparked by the courage and faith of Jonathan and his armorbearer. These two warriors took advantage of the narrow, precipitous pass which alone offered access to Michmash. The peculiarity of the terrain is taken into account as Isaiah describes the approach of the Assyrian and his army as he makes his way to Jerusalem. When he comes to Michmash the prophet says he must lay up his carriages—store his baggage—because of the narrowness of the passage (Isaiah 10:28). Michmash is among the towns which Judah resettled as they returned from their captivity in Babylon (Ezra 2:27; Nehemiah 7:31).

Mizpah or **Mizpeh**—The Hebrew permits both spellings. It was a town in the territory of Benjamin (Joshua

18:26). It seems to have been a prominent religious center particularly in the time of Samuel the prophet. Here the men of Israel were gathered together to deal with Benjamin after the incident of the Levite and his concubine (Judges 21:1-8). Samuel called Israel to Mizpeh for prayer and re-dedication (I Samuel 7:5-7). While here they were attacked by the Philistines. In Mizpeh Saul, the son of Kish, was proclaimed the first king of Israel (I Samuel 10:17-24). Other references to this place are: I Kings 15:22; II Chronicles 16:6; II Kings 25:23; Nehemiah 3:7,15,19; Jeremiah 40:8; 41:10.

There seems to be disagreement among the scholars regarding the exact location of Mizpeh. Some hold to Tel en-Nasbeh, 7 miles north of Jerusalem. Others believe it to be Nebi Samwil, "the prophet Samuel," 4½ miles north-west of Jerusalem, which is the traditional home and burying place of Samuel.

Moreh, Hill of—Hill of More—Giv'at Hamore—This hill is mentioned in the account of Gideon's battle with the Midianites in the Valley of Jezreel (Judges 7:1). It rises abruptly from the northern edge of the valley. It used to be called "Little Hermon," but is now known as Giv'at Hamore.

Nain—Na'im—At the foot of the Hill of Moreh, to the north is the village of Nain. Here Jesus raised from the dead the widow's only son as he was being taken out of the gate of the city for burial (Luke 7:11-18). A small church has been erected to commemorate this miracle.

Nazareth—The city of Nazareth lies in the hills of southern Galilee about midway between the Sea of Galilee and the Mediterranean. It is first mentioned in the Bible at

One of the main streets of Nazareth. The tower of the Church of the Annunciation can be seen at right.

Virgin's Fountain in Nazareth.

the time of the Annunciation (Luke 1:26). It was a rather obscure village, off the regular trade routes. Nathanael's words, "Can any good thing come out of Nazareth?" (John 1:46), indicates its lack of reputation. Joseph the carpenter lived here and from Nazareth he took his wife, Mary, to Bethlehem where Jesus was born (Luke 2:1-7). After their return from the flight into Egypt, to escape the ire of Herod, Mary and Joseph, with Jesus, took up residence in Nazareth (Matthew 2:19-23; Luke 2:39,40), where the years of Christ's boyhood and young manhood were spent (Luke 2:51,52).

After His Baptism and Temptation, Jesus came to minister in Nazareth. Here He preached His first recorded sermon. However the opposition to Him in the synagogue there was so violent that He may never have returned (Luke 4:16-30). The mountain from which the people sought to cast Him is called today "The Mount of Precipitation." Some believe that Matthew 13:53-58 and Mark 6:1-6 indicate one later visit. In these passages it is stated that He could do no mighty works there "because of their unbelief."

Visitors today are shown the traditional Grotto of the Annunciation, where it is believed Gabriel visited Mary (Luke 1:26-38). Here may be seen two granite pillars, one called the "Column of Gabriel," and the other the "Column of Mary." Also shown is the traditional cave where the home and carpenter shop of Joseph and Mary was located.

The Church of the Annunciation is built over the former and the Church of St. Joseph is built over the carpenter shop home. Of particular interest is Mary's Well, or the Virgin's Fountain, as it is sometimes called. It is fed from the only spring in Nazareth and most certainly is the same from which Mary obtained water at the time of our Lord. The name Nazarene was applied to Jesus both by His friends and enemies (Matthew 21:11; Acts 2:22; 10:38).

Olives, Mount of—Due east of the city of Jerusalem, across the Kidron Valley, is the Mount of Olives. Its height reaches 2,641 feet above the Mediterranean Sea, making it considerably higher than Jerusalem itself. From its summit one is afforded the most inspiring view of the city as well as the Jordan valley to the east. It is associated with some of the most important events in the life of our Lord. The northern of the two main summits, which is 2,723 feet above sea level, is known as Viri Galilaei. The chief hill of Olivet is just south of that and is marked by the Tower of the Ascension of the Russian Orthodox Church, which is visible for miles. The next elevation to the south is called "The Prophets" because of the presence of ancient tombs, believed by some to be those of Absalom, James and Zachariah, the father of John the Baptist. The southernmost elevation is called the Mount of Offense, being associated with the places of idolatrous worship which Solomon built through the influence of his heathen wives (I Kings 11:4-8; II Kings 23:13).

References to the Mount of Olives in the Old Testament are very few. David, fleeing from the city of Jerusalem at the time of Absalom's rebellion, crossed the Kidron and worshiped atop the Mount of Olives (II Samuel 15:30-32). Just past the summit of the hill, David was met by Ziba, the servant of Mephibosheth, who presented him with asses to ride on and bread, raisins, fruit and wine to sustain him on his flight (II Samuel 16:1,2).

With but few exceptions (John 8:1 and the possible giving of the Lord's Prayer) all the recorded incidents associating Jesus with this mount belong in the Passion week. Of course the incidents described in relation to Bethany took place on the Mount of Olives inasmuch as Bethany is on the eastern slope of the hill.

From Bethphage Jesus began His Triumphal Entry going down the slopes of Olivet, across the Kidron and through the Golden Gate into Jerusalem (Mark 11:1; Matthew

21:1; Luke 19:29). Somewhere on Olivet, as the city lay spread out before His gaze, Jesus wept over Jerusalem (Luke 19:41-44). Near, and above, the Garden of Gethsemane, a little church named Dominus Flevit has been erected to commemorate this event in the life of Jesus.

During this week He taught in the temple through the day and "at night he went out, and abode in the mount that is called the mount of Olives" (Luke 21:37). The particular part of the mount was Bethany (Matthew 21:17; Mark 11:11). Somewhere between Bethany and Jerusalem He cursed the fig tree on which He found no fruit and the tree withered away. This He used as a sign to the disciples of the power of faith unmingled with any doubt (Matthew 21:18-22; Mark 11:12-14, 20-24).

As Jesus sat upon the Mount of Olives His disciples asked the three great questions which drew forth from Jesus the Olivet Discourse, outlining the destruction of the temple and events leading up to His second coming (Matthew 24 and 25; Mark 13; Luke 21:5-35).

After eating the Passover with His disciples in the upper room, Jesus established the Communion Service and then they went out to the Mount of Olives (Matthew 26:30; Mark 14:26; Luke 22:39), where under the old olive trees in the Garden of Gethsemane Jesus agonized in prayer while the disciples slept (Matthew 26:36-46; Mark 14:32-42; Luke 22:39-46; John 18:1). Here he was betrayed by Judas Iscariot and arrested by the soldiers (Matthew 26:47-56; Mark 14:43-52; Luke 22:47-54; John 18:2-13).

In the vicinity of Bethany, rather than on the traditional spot, Jesus gave the great promise of the Holy Spirit's power, lifted up His hands and blessed His disciples, and was carried up into heaven (Luke 24:50,51). Then appeared the two in white apparel who spoke of the Lord's return in the same manner in which He went away (Acts 1:8-11). Zechariah describes the Second Coming of Jesus, when "His feet shall stand in that day upon the mount of Olives" at which time the mount will cleave in the midst forming "a very great valley" (Zechariah 14:4).

Although the Scripture does not so state, tradition has it that it was on the Mount of Olives Jesus taught His disciples to pray. The Pater Noster Church has been built on this supposed spot. On the walls of the church are tiles inscribed with the Lord's Prayer in 44 languages.

Petah-Tikva—The Door of Hope—East of Tel Aviv is the oldest Jewish agricultural settlement in Israel—Petah-Tikva, founded in 1878. It is named from Hosea's prophecy, "I will give her her vineyards from thence, and the valley of Achor for a door of hope" (Hosea 2:15). The valley of Achor, which is in the Jordan plain near Jericho, is the place where Achan was executed as the result of stealing some of the spoils from the conquest of Jericho (Joshua 7). This settlement, near Tel Aviv is named from this event.

Philip's Spring—South of Solomon's Pools on the road to Hebron is a spring of water traditionally associated with Philip the Evangelist and his encounter with the Ethiopian eunuch from the court of Candace, Queen of Ethiopia. Philip was led by the Holy Spirit to leave the revival at Samaria and go south from Jerusalem to Gaza. He met the eunuch reading the prophecy of Isaiah and pointed him to Christ. This spring is on one of the old caravan routes that led from the east through Gaza and it is said that this was the place where Philip baptized this new convert (Acts 8:26-40).

Qumran—At the northwest corner of the Dead Sea lies the site of Qumran, made famous by "the greatest archaeological find of the twentieth century"—the Dead Sea

111

Scrolls. One hot day in 1947 a young Bedouin goatherder, Muhammad Adh-Dhib, was amusing himself tossing stones across a wadi—a valley—into a cave. He was startled to hear a sound as though pottery was breaking. Investigating, he found a number of pottery jars containing rolled up scrolls of leather. He took them home and kept them for a time, then spoke of them to a merchant in Bethlehem. The merchant brought them to the American School of Oriental Research in Jerusalem. Other caves in the Qumran area were searched and many more scrolls were found. Eventually a number of these were purchased for the State of Israel and the Hebrew University. They may be seen at The Shrine of the Book in Jerusalem, Israel.

The story of the Dead Sea Scrolls centers around a monastic sect called the Essenes who lived here at Qumran. They apparently believed it their responsibility to copy the Sacred Scriptures in addition to their Manual of Discipline and an account of the "War Between the Children of Light and Darkness." The most significant parchment is of the complete text of Isaiah, 24 feet long and 10 feet high. This manuscript is 1,000 years older than any known previously. Portions of all other Old Testament books, with the exception of Esther, have been found. These were copied between 170 B.C. and the early part of the first century A.D. The Scriptural text is amazingly similar to the accepted Hebrew text. It is believed that the Essenes, hearing of the approach of the Roman legions in 68 A.D., put their precious scrolls in pottery jars and hid them in caves in the nearby hills, intending to come back for them. The Essenes were probably killed by the Romans.

The uncovered ruins at Qumran show every evidence of a detailed communal type of living. Outstanding are the cisterns, a store house, community kitchen, dining room, workshops, a pantry in which hundreds of bowls, dishes and jugs were found stacked in piles against the wall, and the Scriptorium, where the scrolls were copied, containing

Qumran, showing the large Scriptorium where the Dead Sea Scrolls were copied.

Cave Number 4 at Qumran. More scrolls were found here than in any other cave.

long tables and benches and even two ink wells. The Dead Sea Scrolls have done much to offset some of the criticisms of skeptical scholars.

Safad—Zefat—This city is located ten miles northeast of the Sea of Galilee. Prior to the occupation of the Western Bank in June of 1967, it was the highest town in Israel, being 2,660 feet above sea level. Nearby are the twin peaks of Har (Mount) Meiron, the highest point in Israel, 4,199 feet above sea level. Safad stands on the ancient highway from Damascus in Syria to Acre on Israel's Mediterranean coast. The view of Palestine is superb from here. Though it is not mentioned in the Bible, many believe this was the city to which Jesus referred when He spoke of a "city set on a hill cannot be hid." It can be seen from the Mount of Beatitudes from where these words were spoken (Matthew 5:14). Safad is the Arabic name while the Israeli name is Zefat. The four cities held sacred by the Jews are Jerusalem, Hebron, Tiberias and Zefat.

Saint Peter in Gallicantu—The Palace of Caiaphas— South of the Dung Gate and on the eastern slope of the hill overlooking the Valley of Kidron, is the site of the Palace of Caiaphas, who was high priest at the time of Jesus' arrest and crucifixion. It was here the Lord was taken immediately after the soldiers laid hold of Him in the Garden of Gethsemane. This was the scene of His first trial (Matthew 26:57-63; Mark 14:53-65; Luke 22:54, 63-71; John 18:12-14, 19-24). This was the place where Peter denied his Lord three times before the cock had crowed twice in fulfillment of Christ's words (Matthew 26:34, 69-75; Mark 14:66-72; Luke 22:54-62; John 18:15-18, 25-27).

114

Beautiful columned street of Samaria, capital of the Northern Kingdom of Israel. Now called Sebaste.

Solomon's Stables at Megiddo, fortress city by the Valley of Esdraelon.

The Assumptionist Fathers have built a church on this site which they call "St. Peter Gallicantu," meaning "At the crowing of the cock." Here are shown the steps which may well be the oldest street in Jerusalem, up which Jesus was led from Gethsemane. You will also see the courtyard where Peter warmed himself, the servants quarters where the maid who questioned Peter must have lived, and the cell in which Jesus was kept that memorable night. There is also another cell which could have been the place where the apostles were imprisoned by the Sanhedrin (Acts 4:3; 5:17-23).

Samaria—Sebaste—Sebastiyeh—Nine miles north of Nablus is the city of Sebaste—modern Sebastiyeh—known in the Bible as Samaria. According to I Kings 16:24, Omri, king of Israel, bought an imposing hill from Shemer for two talents of silver and began to build a beautiful capital city. He lived here only six years when he died and his son Ahab reigned in his place. Here Ahab built his beautiful ivory palace. Ahab's wife was the infamous Jezebel, who induced her husband to build a temple to Baal right in the capital city (I Kings 16:31-33). His son Jehoram, put away the image of Baal (II Kings 3:2). Jehu later destroyed all semblance of Baal worship and killed all the priests of Baal (II Kings 10:17-28). Jehu also destroyed all of the house of Ahab, including his 70 sons who lived at Samaria (II Kings 10:1-11). Samaria was the burial place for the kings of Israel—the Northern Kingdom: Omri (I Kings 16:28; Ahab (22:37); Jehu (II Kings 10:35); Jehoahaz (13:9); Joash (13:13); Jehoash (14:16).

It was to Samaria that Naaman came to be healed of his leprosy (II Kings 5:3-5). Elisha led the blinded Syrian army, which had surrounded him at Dothan, into the city of Samaria, Israel's capital (II Kings 6:18-23). Following this came the great seige of Samaria, the terrible famine, and the marvelous deliverance of God which was discovered by the four leprous men who found that the Syrian army had fled (II Kings 6:24-33; 7:1-16).

Samaria continued to be the capital of the Northern Kingdom of Israel until 722 B.C. when the King of Assyria carried the ten tribes of Israel into captivity (II Kings 17:3-6,23). Shalmaneser began the siege but died before the city fell. Sargon, one of his generals, actually took the city and carried the inhabitants away captive. Later the territory was occupied by the Babylonians, Persians, Greeks and Romans. After the Roman conquest the town was rebuilt by Pompey. Later Augustus gave it to Herod the Great who called it "Sebaste"—Greek for "Augustus."

It was at Samaria that Philip the evangelist was used to bring great revival, and here the Holy Spirit was outpoured through the ministry of Peter and John (Acts 8:5-25).

Shechem—Nablus—Shechem, or Sichem, sits in a pleasant valley between Mt. Gerizim and Mt. Ebal. This place witnessed many important events in Bible history. It was the site of Abraham's first altar when he came from Haran to the land of Canaan (Genesis 12:6,7). It was under an oak tree near here that Jacob, on his way back to Bethel to worship God, buried the idols that his family had brought with them from Padan Aram (Genesis 35:1-4).

Joseph went to Shechem to seek his brethren who were feeding their flocks (Genesis 37:13,14). On this journey he was sold by his brothers to the Ishmaelite traders who took him to Egypt. Subsequently Joseph gave commandments to his brethren not to bury him in Egypt but to carry his bones back to Canaan (Genesis 50:25). The twelve tribes carried his coffin with them through all the forty years of their wilderness wanderings. They buried him at Shechem in a plot of ground which Jacob had, many years before, purchased from Hamor (Genesis 33:18,19; Joshua 24:32).

117

Moses had commanded the children of Israel that, when they had entered the Land of Promise, they should gather before Mt. Gerizim and Mt. Ebal. The blessings of obedience to God were to be read from the former, while the curses were read from the latter (Deuteronomy 11:26-30; 27:9-26; chapter 28). This Joshua did (Joshua 8:30-35).

Here, in the natural amphitheatre formed by Mt. Gerizim and Mt. Ebal, Joshua, toward the end of his life, assembled the tribes of Israel to commemorate the victories God had given and to enter into a solemn covenant that they would continue to serve the Lord (Joshua 24:1-28).

Shechem was one of the six Cities of Refuge (Joshua 20:7; 21:21).

Abimelech, the son of Gideon by a concubine, endeavored to establish himself head over all Israel at Shechem. He slew 70 of his brothers, allowing only one to escape. Abimelech reigned 3½ years in Shechem, but God brought judgment against him and he was slain (Judges 9).

Rehoboam, one of Solomon's sons, went to Shechem to be crowned king of all the twelve tribes (I Kings 12:1). Jeroboam, his brother, led a successful revolt against him and became king of the northern ten tribes. He made Shechem his capital city (I Kings 12:3-25). This was later moved to Tirzah (I Kings 14:17; 15:21), and then to Samaria (I Kings 16:24).

The modern Arab name for this community is Nablus. The present city, one of the largest in this area, is a little to the northwest of the old site of Shechem. Nablus is of special interest to Bible students because here is located the Samaritan Synagogue. The present building is a new one replacing the ancient one which was destroyed by earthquake in 1927. In it is the ancient Samaritan Pentateuch which is reputed to be the original copy of the words of Moses—the oldest copy in existence. Modern scholars, however, date the oldest parts of this document no earlier than the 10th or 11th centuries A.D.

The Samaritans were remnants of the northern tribes who were left in their land when the Assyrians carried the majority into captivity in 721 B.C. (II Kings 17:6,23). These remnants intermarried with colonists settled in Samaria by the Assyrians (II Kings 17:24). The Jews, coming back from the Babylonish captivity, believed the blood of those who claimed to be their brethren was tainted and refused to recognize them. Thus a bitter quarrel and hatred began which led to the erection of this rival temple on Mt. Gerizim. The Samaritans claimed that this mountain fitted Abraham's description better than Mt. Moriah in Jerusalem. When Nehemiah rebuilt the walls of Jerusalem after the captivity in Babylon, the Samaritans represented by Sanballat, greatly hindered the work (Nehemiah 2:19, 20; 4:1-9; 6:1-14). The Samaritan temple was destroyed by John Hyrcanus about 125 B.C., but the Samaritans still celebrate the Passover feast every year on Mt. Gerizim on the evening before the full moon of Nisan (April).

Shiloh—Seilun—Shiloh may be called the first capital of Israel for here the Tabernacle was set up and the Ark of the Covenant was kept during the long period of the rule of the judges (Joshua 18:1). Shiloh is in a very central location and was the rallying point for the tribes of Israel for almost three and one half centuries before its fall (Joshua 22:12; Judges 21:19; I Samuel 1:3). Here Joshua divided the land of Canaan among the tribes (Joshua 18:2-10; 19:51; 21:1-3).

A yearly sacrifice was made by the people at Shiloh, and Elkannah came with his wife Hannah. She prayed for a son and dedicated him to the Lord before his birth. Later she brought Samuel and it was here he grew up in the service of the Lord under the high priest Eli (I Samuel 1). The Lord called Samuel in the night and told him of the judgment that was to fall on the house of Eli (I Samuel 3).

The wife of King Jeroboam disguised herself and came to the blind prophet, Ahijah, at Shiloh to inquire concerning their sick son. She learned of the judgments of God upon the house of Jeroboam (I Kings 14:1-18).

A yearly feast was held at Shiloh, at which time the young women danced by the vineyards. During the civil war which came about because of the sin of the men of Gibeah, the tribe of Benjamin was virtually exterminated. There were no wives for the men who remained and the other tribes had sworn that they would not give their daughters to the Benjamites. However, the men of Benjamin were encouraged to hide in the vineyards and catch each one a bride from among the young dancers of Shiloh (Judges 21:16-23).

It appears from history and archaeology that Shiloh was destroyed by the Philistines about 1050 B.C. after they had taken the Ark of the Covenant (I Samuel 4). Jeremiah refers to this as a judgment of God because of Israel's sins and uses it as an example of what He would do to Jerusalem and the nation at the time he prophesied, four and a half centuries later (Jeremiah 7:12-15; 26:6,7).

Shunem—Solem—Sulam—Shunem lies toward the eastern section of the Valley of Jezreel, south of Mt. Tabor. It was the place where the Philistines gathered their forces prior to the battle with Saul and his army who faced them across the valley from the south at Mt. Gilboa (I Samuel 28:4). Here lived the "great woman" who made "a little chamber" for the prophet Elisha to use on his frequent journeys in that area. The son, whom Elisha promised should be born to this woman because of her kindness, died but was raised from the dead as Elisha placed himself upon the child (II Kings 4:8-37).

Siloam, Pool of—The Pool of Siloam is located south of

the hill Ophel where the Valley of Hinnom runs into the Kidron Valley. It was originally constructed by King Hezekiah as a reservoir at the southern end of his great conduit. Jerusalem's main supply of water was the Gihon Spring which was outside the wall in the Kidron Valley just below the hill of Ophel, thus exposed to an attacking enemy. In 701 B.C. Sennacherib, king of Assyria, invaded Palestine and besieged Jerusalem. To strengthen the city against the siege, Hezekiah had a conduit 1,777 feet long cut through the solid rock to carry the waters from the Gihon Spring to the Pool of Siloam (II Kings 20:20; II Chronicles 32:30). The Gihon Spring was then covered over from the outside. "Why should the kings of Assyria come and find much water?" the people said (II Chronicles 32:2-4). Workmen began at either end of the tunnel with hand picks and accomplished a remarkable engineering feat. The tunnel averages 6 feet high. When the two excavating parties finally met, an inscription was carved in the wall of the tunnel commemorating the event. In 1880 it was accidentally discovered, 19 feet from the Siloam end of the aqueduct, by a boy wading in the pool. It is translated as follows:

The boring is completed. Now this is the story of the boring through. While the workmen were still lifting pick to pick, each toward his neighbor, and while three cubits remained to be cut through, each heard the voice of the other who called his neighbor, since there was a crevice in the rock on the right side. And on the day of the boring through the stone-cutters struck, each to meet his fellow, pick to pick; and there flowed the waters to the pool for a thousand and two hundred cubits, and a hundred cubits was the height of the rock above the heads of the stone-cutters.

This inscription was later cut out and placed in the

Museum of the Ancient Orient at Istanbul. It is one of the very few examples of Hebrew writing that has been preserved from the period prior to 700 B.C.

The blind man was instructed by Jesus to wash in the Pool of Siloam and he came seeing (John 9:7-11). It is believed to be the same as "the pool of Siloah by the king's garden" (Nehemiah 3:15) and "the waters of Shiloah that go softly" (Isaiah 8:6).

Sinai, Mount—Horeb—The Sinai Peninsula is a huge triangle, 260 miles long and 150 miles wide at the north, situated between the Gulf of Suez and the Gulf of Aqaba. At the southern end of the peninsula is a mass of granite mountains, some of which are 8,000 feet above sea level. The chief peak is Jebel Musa, "Mountain of Moses." This mountain reaches a height of 7,519 feet. Part way up its slope is the 1,400-year-old Monastery of St. Catherine. It is named after a 4th century martyr whose bones were supposed to be carried here by angels after her death. Legend has it that she was a beautiful girl, daughter of the King of Alexandria in the third century. She renounced the religion of her father and embraced Christianity. Catherine upbraided the Emperor Maximinus for his cruelties and adjured him to give up the worship of false gods. The angry tyrant ordered her scourged and imprisoned. She performed many miracles, not least of which was her return to life fifteen times when her father's servants repeatedly put her to death. Only when decapitated did she remain dead. Hundreds of years later her body was found on Mount Sinai and brought to the monastery which from then on bore the name of this saint.

It is the oldest monastery of the Greek Orthodox Church. Christian hermits came to Sinai in the third century, seeking escape from Roman persecution and to lives of seclusion as did Elijah and John the Baptist. In the sixth century Emperor Justinian ordered this monastery built (527 A.D.) so these hermits might have a place of shelter from continued attacks of the Bedouin. The monastery holds a great library of 2,000 matchless icons and manuscripts. It was here, in 1844, the German scholar Konstantin von Tischendorf found the fourth-century Codex Sinaiticus, one of the oldest Greek manuscripts of the New Testament. It is now in the British Museum.

Mount Sinai is also called Horeb in many passages of Scripture, particularly the Book of Deuteronomy. It is first brought to our attention as the place to which Moses led the flock of Jethro, his father-in-law, the priest of Midian. It is called "the mountain of God." Here God appeared to Moses in the bush that burned but was not consumed, to commission him to go to Egypt and lead the children of Israel from bondage to the Promised Land (Exodus 3:1; 4:27). It was promised to Moses, as a special token of God's direction, that he would bring the delivered people to this very mountain (Exodus 3:12). This was fulfilled after the Passover night (Exodus 19:1,2).

Sinai is best known by the fact that it was here God gave the children of Israel the Ten Commandments (Exodus 20:1-17; Deuteronomy 5:1-27). Special precautions were ordered so that no one would touch the mountain when God came down (Exodus 19:1-13). For one year the people of Israel camped before the mount. Here those who had been but a disorganized group of slaves were moulded into a nation. Laws and ordinances were given to cover every phase of their life as individuals and as a nation. Here also Moses received directions from God for the building of the Tabernacle. From the offerings of the people this highly significant place of sacrifice and worship was erected. Chapters 32-34 of Exodus tell the tragic failure of Israel in their worship of the golden calf as they became impatient with Moses' long stay—40 days—up in the mountain. However, God heard Moses' intercession and, although some 3,000 of the people were slain (Exodus 32:28), God spared the remainder. Moses, in his dismay, had broken the two stone tables upon which the Decalogue was written (Exodus 32:19), but God called him back to receive the other two tablets (Exodus 34:1-4).

Sinai is also associated with the great prophet Elijah. After his mighty triumph over the prophets of Baal at Mt. Carmel (I Kings 18:17-41), Elijah was frightened by the threats of King Ahab's wife, Jezebel (I Kings 19:1,2), and fled southward some 100 miles to Beersheba. Near here he rested and was refreshed by the angel and, in the strength of the meal that was given, he journeyed all the way to Mt. Sinai another 250 miles (I Kings 19:3-8). It was here God sent the wind, the earthquake, the fire and then the still small voice (I Kings 19:9-18).

In the New Testament Mount Sinai is used by Paul (Galatians 4:21-31) to refer to a life of bondage to the law, typified by Ishmael, Abraham's son by the Egyptian bond-woman Hagar. It is in contrast to one born after the Spirit. Paul is showing the difference between being under law, as a means of salvation, and under grace. Again, in Hebrews 12:18-24, Mount Sinai and Mount Sion are set in contrast to show the difference between the covenant of the law under Moses, and the covenant of grace under Jesus Christ.

Solomon's Pools—Two miles south of Bethlehem, on the road to Hebron, are three large reservoirs known as Solomon's Pools. Most authorities are agreed that they are misnamed, in that they were built by Pontius Pilate, as part of his aqueduct system to supply water for Jerusalem, rather than by King Solomon. There is some conjecture, however, that Solomon had beautiful gardens here and that this may be the spot to which he refers in Ecclesiastes 2:4-6. These huge basins gather the water that drains from the hills and springs in this area and are still used as a source of water for Jerusalem.

Sorek, Valley of—Sorek is one of the narrow valleys which cross the Shephelah, a rocky plateau east of the coastal plain and which runs from the valley of Ajalon southward toward Gaza. The valley of Sorek parallels the valley of Ajalon to the north and the valley of Elah to the south. This is the area where Samson and his parents lived and where he met and succumbed to the enticements of Delilah (Judges 16:4-21). Eshtaol and Zorah (Judges 13:25) were on the north side of the valley while Timnath, where Samson sought a wife (Judges 14:1,2), is located farther southwest, near the mouth of the valley.

Sychar—Askar—Jacob's Well—In Genesis 33:18-20, we learn that Jacob and his family lived for a time near Shechem. It was probably at this time that he dug the well that has become so famous since New Testament times (John 4:5,6,12). It is not mentioned in the Old Testament. The well is about 75 feet deep. The conversation which took place there between Jesus and the sinful Samaritan woman is one of the choice insights into Jesus' marvelous method of dealing with needy individuals (John 4:3-42). Sychar is about one-half mile northwest of Jacob's well, at the foot of Mt. Ebal.

Mt. Gerizim—In her conversation with Jesus at Jacob's well, the Samaritan woman sought to engage Jesus in the age-old argument between the Jews and Samaritans: "Our fathers worshipped in this mountain; and ye say, that in Jerusalem is the place where men ought to worship" (John 4:20). She was referring to the fact that the Samaritans had

built a temple on top of Mt. Gerizim and annually kept
the feasts of the Passover, Pentecost and Tabernacles there
rather than in Jerusalem.

Tabor, Mount—Cone shaped and quite symmetrical,
Mount Tabor rises on the northeastern area of the Plain of
Esdraelon, or Jezreel as it is sometimes called. It is about
5½ miles southeast of Nazareth and 12 miles north of Mt.
Gilboa. It rises 1,843 feet above sea level. Tabor is men-
tioned as a boundary between Issachar and Zebulun
(Joshua 19:22).

It was on the summit and slopes of this mountain that
Deborah, Israel's only judge, inspired Barak to gather an
army from the tribes of Issachar, Zebulun, and Naphtali.
From here they swept down the slopes to battle Sisera and
the Canaanite hosts in the great valley of Esdraelon. A
heavy rainstorm caused the River Kishon to overflow and
in the mud Sisera's chariots became useless, if not a real
liability (Judges 4:4-16). It was also at Tabor that the brothers of Gideon were slain by Zebah and Zalmunna (Judges
8:18-21).

As most mountains and high places were the scenes of
heathen worship, Tabor is mentioned as the site of ensnar-
ing rituals (Hosea 5:1). The mountain is also referred to in
Psalm 89:12 and Jeremiah 46:18. It has been the ground of
many battles as various conquerors have swept over Palestine.

As early as the 4th century A.D., tradition has placed
the scenes of the Transfiguration of Christ on Mount
Tabor. Thus a succession of churches and monasteries
have been erected on this mountain. The Roman and
Greek Catholic churches have substantial buildings there
now. However, inasmuch as there is good reason to believe
a town was on top of the mountain in Jesus' time, it seems
improbable that He could find a spot secluded enough to fit

the description, "a high mountain apart, by themselves," at Tabor (Matthew 17:1; Mark 9:2; Luke 9:28). Many believe a better location would be found somewhere on the slopes of Mount Hermon, the highest mountain in the vicinity of northern Palestine.

Tekoa—Tell Tequ'a—The old city of Tekoa is identified by the Tell Tequ'a located 6 miles south of Bethlehem. It is of particular interest to Bible students because it was the home of the prophet Amos (Amos 1:1), who was a "herdman and a gatherer of sycamore fruit" (Amos 7:14)—a small fig. There are none of these trees in this area now. Josephus wrote that the tomb of Amos was located here. Pilgrims used to come to the area to visit it.

Rehoboam fortified many of the cities of Judah when he became king and Tekoa is mentioned as one of these (II Chronicles 11:6). From here came the "wise woman" brought by Joab in his attempt to make a reconciliation between David and Absalom after Absalom had slain his brother Ammon because of his wrong to Tamar their sister (II Samuel 14:1-24).

The Tell covers an area of 4 or 5 acres. Not much remains on the surface to suggest the former importance of the city. Arab Bedouins live here but in underground caves. Shepherds still tend their sheep in the area as did Amos of old.

Tiberias—Tiberias is situated on the west shore of the Sea of Galilee about ten miles south of Capernaum. It is the only city of any size on the lake. It gave its name to the lake (John 6:1; 21:1). The city was built around 20 A.D. by Herod Antipas as his new capital. He named it after the then-ruling emperor of Rome, Tiberius. There is no record that Jesus ever visited Tiberias though it is referred to in

John 6:23. The area is noted for its therapeutic hot springs which may account for so many sick people coming to Jesus for healing during His Galilean ministry. Capernaum, Bethsaida, and Chorazin came under the judgment of Christ. Tiberias did not. They are gone. It remains.

After the the destruction of Jerusalem by the Romans in 70 A.D., Tiberias became the seat of Jewish learning and the home of the great sages. Here the Palestinian Talmud, popularly called the Jerusalem Talmud, was compiled.

Zion, Mount of—Mount Zion is the height which rises close to the southwest corner of the old walled city. It was once within the walls of ancient Jerusalem. It is held to be one of the most sacred places in Israel because here is located the traditional tomb of King David. Above it is an upper room believed to be on the site of that upper room in which Jesus and His disciples ate the last Passover together and where He established the Communion Service (Mark 14:12-16; Luke 22:7-13). The room is called Coenaculum, which is Latin for "dining hall." This upper room has also been considered to be the place where the 120 disciples were gathered when the Holy Spirit came upon them on the Day of Pentecost (Acts 1:12-15; 2:1-4).

On Mount Zion may also be seen the large buildings of the Dormitian Monastery which marks the spot where it is believed Mary, the mother of Jesus, died. Roman Catholic dogma asserts that from this place, after her death, she was taken into heaven body and soul. This is known as the Assumption.

A very heart-touching memorial to the 6,000,000 Jews, slain in Germany during World War II, is found in one of the buildings and courtyards on Mt. Zion. It has been called the "Chamber of Destruction."

ITALY

Italy occupies the familiar boot-shaped peninsula extending from the Alps into the Mediterranean Sea. On the north the land frontiers with France, Switzerland, Austria and Yugoslavia. Its peninsular coastline is about 2,600 miles. The whole country is about 725 miles long and between 80 and 135 miles wide except at the north where it is 375 miles wide. Its population is nearly 53,500,000. Its capital is Rome, with about 2,600,000 residents. 99% of the population are members of the Roman Catholic Church, though freedom of religion is constitutionally guaranteed.

The monetary unit is the lira which is divided into 100 centesimi. $1.00 U.S. funds equals 620 lira.

Italy is important from a Bible standpoint because of the influence its Roman conquerors had upon Bible lands and Christian believers. It was an edict of Rome which sent Joseph and Mary from Nazareth to Bethlehem so that Jesus might be born where it was prophesied He should (Micah 5:2; Luke 2:1-7). It was during the comparatively short two or three hundred years that Judea was under the rulership of Rome that Christ came to earth. Thus when He was condemned to death He was crucified as the Scripture had foretold (Isaiah 53; Psalm 22). Crucifixion was a Roman form of punishment. The Jewish custom of capital punishment was stoning. This could not be the means of Christ's death for the Scripture said, "a bone of him shall not be broken" (John 19:36; Psalm 34:20).

The closing years of the ministry of the Apostle Paul were spent in this land. After suffering shipwreck on the Island of Melita—Malta (Acts 28:1)—he was brought first to Syracuse, on the eastern coast of the island of Sicily, and then to Rhegium on the Italian mainland. It is now called

Reggio. Then the ship sailed to Puteoli in the Bay of Naples. The city is now known as Pozzuoli. It was the best harbor nearest to Rome. From here Paul was brought up the Appian Way to the city of Rome (Acts 28:11-16). Paul was kept a prisoner but was allowed to see friends, and minister to them (Acts 28:17-21). It is believed he suffered martyrdom here in Rome.

Rome—The traditional date for the founding of the city of Rome is 753 B.C. Romulus was its first king. He and his brother Remus were preserved, when cast out by cruel relatives, by a wolf and a shepherd's wife. Thus the symbol of Rome is the she wolf. The city is by the Tiber River some 17 miles from the Mediterranean into which the river flows. The city is said to be "the city of the seven hills," though the highest of these, the Capitoline, is only 174 feet high. The lowest, the Esquiline is 100 feet high. Originally the city was confined to the Palatine hill. As the settlement grew the other six were added in this order: Capitoline, Quirinal, Caelian, Aventine, Esquiline, and the Viminal. These are all on the east side of the Tiber.

In Paul's day Rome was the greatest city in the world, with a population of over 1,000,000. Today it boasts of 2,700,000 residents. It is the seat of the government of Italy. Actually it is the seat of two governments, for Vatican City, comprising no more than 110 acres, and known as the "state within a city," is the capital of Roman Catholicism. It is the smallest independent state in the world, having a population of about 1,000. It has its own postoffice and stamps, its own railway station, newspaper, radio station, cemeteries and small jail. It issues its own passports. It is the largest owner of capital in Italy, with resources in the billions, yet it pays no taxes to the Italian government. Some sixty-five nations maintain embassies or legations to the Holy See distinct from their missions to the

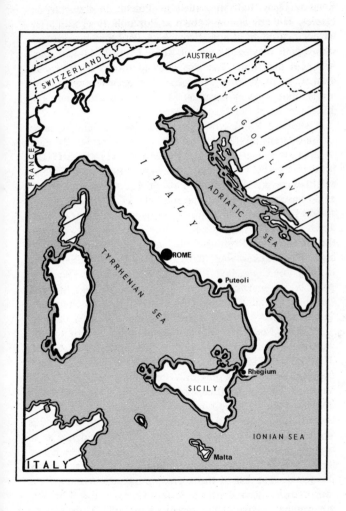

government of Italy. It is the site of St. Peter's, the largest church in Christendom. The Vatican Library is a quarter of a mile long. Among its hundreds of thousands of volumes is Codex Vaticanus—one of the oldest manuscripts of the Bible. The Sistine Chapel, the Pope's private chapel, is noted for its famous paintings executed on the walls and ceiling by the great Michelangelo. Outstanding is his depiction of the final judgment.

Visitors to Rome will want to see the sites and remains of the following: The APPIAN WAY over which Paul walked as he came to Rome; the MAMERTINE PRISON, where it is believed Paul spent some time; the CATACOMBS, sacred burial grounds of Christians and where they took refuge from persecution, ST. PAUL'S OUTSIDE-THE-WALLS, believed to be where he was martyred; the FORUM, which lies in a valley between the Capitoline and Palatine hills, containing many famous buildings, arches and temples; the PANTHEON; the ARCH OF CONSTANTINE; the SCALA SANTA, Holy Steps where Martin Luther accepted the truth that "the just shall live by faith"; ST. PETER-IN-CHAINS, in which is the original of Michelangelo's famous MOSES; the PALAZZO VENEZIA, where Mussolini held forth on the balcony; the huge monument to VICTOR IMMANUEL II; the SPANISH STEPS; the TREVI FOUNTAIN, made famous by "Three Coins in a Fountain"; the COLOSSEUM, not built until after Paul's time; the CIRCUS MAXIMUS, seating 250,000 in Nero's time, etc.

The time of the introduction of Christianity to Rome is entirely uncertain, nor is there any positive evidence as to who was used to do so. It has been suggested that it was brought here by Jews who were in Jerusalem on the day of Pentecost. The list of those present includes "strangers of (lit. "from") Rome" (Acts 2:10). There was a Christian church here when Paul arrived (Acts. 28:15). In fact he had addressed his epistle to them a few years before

The Colosseum at Rome.

The Forum at Rome.

(Romans 1:7). That Peter established the church here is more than tradition. Paul was permitted to preach while he was in custody (Acts 28:17-24,30,31; Philippians 1:12, 13).

At first Christians were not distinguished from Jews by the Roman officials. However, after Nero set fire to the city and accused the Christians of doing so, persecutions began. Sometime after this it became unlawful even to be a Christian. Persecutions of the Christian church were carried on intermittently until Constantine issued the Edict of Milan in 313 establishing toleration and restoring the property of the church.

JORDAN

The Hashemite Kingdom of Jordan (previously Trans-jordan) came into being officially in 1947. In 1950 it was enlarged to include the district of Samaria and part of Judea. The country is bounded by Syria on the north, Iraq on the northeast, Saudi Arabia on the east and south and Israel on the west. The total area was 37,500 square miles. Since the six-day war of June 1967 this has been reduced by 2,165 square miles west of the Jordan River. The country extends south to its only seaport at Aqaba on the Gulf of Aqaba. The population is estimated at 1,250,000. The capital city is Amman, known in the past as Philadel-phia. It has a population of over 400,000.

The currency is based on the Jordanian dinar, worth $2.80 in U.S. dollars. There are 1,000 fils in a dinar.

In Biblical times the area consisted of, from south to north, Edom, Moab, Ammon, and Gilead. The Children of Israel traversed this area as they came up the eastern side of the Dead Sea before crossing the Jordan River into Canaan. The Edomites refused to allow the people of Israel to pass through their land (Numbers 20:14-21; 21:4). This is a reflection of the ancient strife between Jacob, father of the Israelites and Esau his brother, father of the Edomites. Moab was occupied by the Moabites, descendents of Lot's older surviving daughter who bore a son to him (Genesis 19:30-37). The people of Moab also refused to let Israel pass through their borders, so they had to go around (Deuteronomy 2:9-11; Judges 11:17,18). Ammon was the son of Lot by the younger of his two surviving daughters (Genesis 19:38). Moab was the country to which Naomi and her husband went during the famine. Ruth was a native of Moab (Ruth 1:1-4). The country of the Ammon-ites extended from the brook Arnon on the south to the

Jabbok on the north. Sihon, king of the Amorites who lived west of the Jordan, had taken much of the territory of the Ammonites including Gilead to the north. Joshua fought against him as well as Og king of Bashan, north of Gilead, conquering both (Numbers 21:21-35; Deuteronomy 2:24-3:11; Judges 11:19-23). Their land was part of the inheritance given to the children of Israel—specifically the tribes of Reuben, Gad and one half of Manasseh (Deuteronomy 3:12-20; Joshua 1:12-18;22).

Amman—Amman is the capital of the Hashemite Kingdom of Jordan. It was once the capital city of the Ammonites—about the year 1200 B.C. It was called Rabbath Ammon. In the Bible it is associated with the dishonorable act of King David in taking Bathsheba while he arranged for the murder of her husband, Uriah the Hittite (II Samuel 11). David had intended to befriend Hanan the king of the Ammonites, sending ambassadors of good will to comfort him at the death of his father. Their purpose was misunderstood and the Ammonites insulted David's men by cutting off half their beards and one half of their clothes. This led to the war between the Israelites and the Ammonites (II Samuel 10:1-19).

The huge Roman Theatre, seating 6,000, is one of the best preserved antiquities in all of Jordan. It was built in the 2nd or 3rd century A.D. and is still used today. The city has a population of about 400,000.

Aqaba—The port of Aqaba, Jordan, is located at the northeast end of the Gulf of Aqaba, an arm of the Red Sea. It is at the southern end of the Arabah, the fascinating desert chasm which is the southern extension of the Jordan Rift. It contains many awesome rock formations. The Wadi Ram, northeast of Aqaba, is said to equal, in many

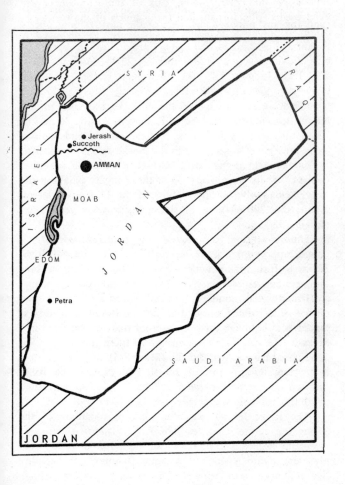

JORDAN

ways, the beauty of the Grand Canyon. Aqaba is a resort and Jordans' only seaport. One of the most famous guests to disembark here was no doubt the Queen of Sheba (I Kings 10:1-13). Aqaba is about two miles south of Ezion-Geber.

Jerash—Gerasa—One of the cities east of the Jordan River known as the Decapolis. Damascus was the largest of these and Jerash was second. It is the most complete ruins of a provincial Roman city in the world. It has been called "The Pompeii of the East," and "The city of a thousand pillars." There were over 600 of these stately pillars in the city. Seventy-five of them still line the long main street. Altogether 200 of these still stand. Excavations were begun in the 1920's.

These inspiring ruins reveal: the triple-arched gate, a huge hippodrome, a theatre seating 6,000, the only oval Roman forum surrounded by 56 Ionic columns, plus tremendous temples, baths and public buildings.

The Revised Standard Version connects Mark 5:1 and Luke 8:26 with Gerasa, but it is believed that this is incorrect. Although there is no proof that Jesus ever visited Jerash, He was certainly well known there (Matthew 4:25) and could have visited the city (Mark 7:31).

A few miles south of Jerash one crosses the River Jabbok. It was by this river at Penuel, that Jacob wrestled with the heavenly visitor (Genesis 32:22-31).

The River Jabbok was the northern boundary of the Kingdom of the Amorites. The River Arnon, which flows into the eastern side of the Dead Sea marked its southern border, adjoining Moab to the south (Numbers 21:21-24).

Nebo, Mount—East of the Dead Sea, in what was the land of Moab, and in line with the north end of the sea, is Mount Nebo, from which Moses viewed the Promised

Stage and few seats of Roman Theatre seating over 6,000 at Amman, capital of Jordan.

Entrance to the Siq, narrow defile leading into Rose Red City of Petra, Jordan.

Land and in a valley of which he died and was buried
(Numbers 33:47; Deuteronomy 32:49-52; 34:1-8). From
here, on a clear day, the entire land of Canaan can be seen
inasmuch as it is so small—150 miles from Dan to
Beersheba and an average of 40 miles from the Jordan
River to the Mediterranean. Mount Nebo was the summit
of Mount Pisgah.

Penuel—Penuel was located somewhere east of the Jordan and north of the River Jabbok. Its exact location has
not yet been identified, but it must not have been far from
Succoth. After his remarkable encounter with the heavenly
visitor Jacob called the place "Peniel" which means "the
face of God" (Genesis 32:21-31). Years later a city with a
strong tower stood upon the spot. It was in the line of
Gideon's pursuit of the Midianites. Because of the churlish-
ness of the inhabitants, Gideon returned and destroyed the
tower (Judges 8:8,9,17). After his rebellion and the
separation of the Northern Kingdom from that of the
South, Jeroboam built and fortified Penuel in Gad (I Kings
12:25).

Petra—About 166 miles south of Amman, Jordan, about
halfway between the southern end of the Dead Sea and
the Gulf of Aqaba, is the fabulous rose-red city of Petra.
On the way south to Petra one passes Ma'an believed by
some to be the scene of the healing of the children of Israel
by the miracle of the brazen serpent (Numbers 21:4-9;
John 3:14). A few miles north of Petra is 'Ain Mussa,
accepted by the Moslems as the place where Moses struck
the rock and the water came forth (Numbers 20:8-13).
Today the water still flows generously in an otherwise arid
wilderness.

Petra is surrounded by the rugged mountains of Edom.
On one of these, Mt. Hor, Aaron died and was buried

(Numbers 20:23-29). Petra was probably the land of the Biblical Horites around 2000 B.C. (Genesis 14:6; 36:20, 21,29). Then Esau, the brother of Jacob, migrated to this area and was the ancestor of the Edomites. They incurred the displeasure of God for refusing passage to the children of Israel through their land (Numbers 20:14-21; Obadiah 10; Amos 1:11; Ezekiel 25:12-14). It could be that the expression, "thou that dwellest in the clefts of the rock," refers to ancient Petra (Jeremiah 49:16,17; Obadiah 3). In II Kings 14:7 is the account of the conquest of Edom by King Amaziah of Judah. "Selah" is Petra. See Isaiah 16:1.

About 800 B.C. the Nabateans from North Africa settled in Petra. They plundered the caravans that carried luxuries over the route between Arabia, Syria and Egypt. The stolen goods were hidden in the caves of Petra. Later they abandoned their plundering but exacted high toll for safe passage of the caravans through the valley. With their wealth they embellished Petra with temples, houses and tombs.

The Romans conquered Petra in 106 A.D. and added many buildings: temples, baths, shops, market places and a huge amphitheatre seating 3,000 to 5,000 people.

The valley is entered by the Siq—a narrow defile in the red sandstone cliffs which rise 200 to 300 feet. At some places this narrow entrance is only 8 feet wide. It is something less than 2 miles long.

Petra was lost to the world for hundreds of years until, in 1812, John Burckhardt, posing as a Moslem who had vowed to sacrifice a goat at the altar of Aaron, looked with wonder into the valley. The huge temples and altars are an amazing exhibition of artistic and engineering skill.

Succoth—Succoth is believed to have been at the location known today as Tell Deir 'Alla. It is on a highland somewhat over a mile north of the Brook Jabbok and 4 miles east of the Jordan River in the territory allotted to Gad. Upon his return from Padan Aram, and after being reconciled with his brother Esau, Jacob journeyed to Succoth and here built a house for his family and booths for his cattle (Genesis 33:17; Joshua 13:27). The place took its name from these booths. Succoth means "booths."

After his great victory over the Midianites, Gideon and his three hundred men sought bread from the men of Succoth as they were faint from pursuing the two kings of Midian, Zebah and Zalmunna. They were refused, but after capturing these two kings Gideon and his army returned to punish the people of Succoth (Judges 8:5-7, 15,16).

On the plain of Jordan were rich deposits of clay especially suitable for making molds in which to cast bronze. It was here that Solomon cast an abundance of vessels to be used in the worship at the temple in Jerusalem (I Kings 7:46; II Chronicles 4:17).

Succoth is referred to in Psalm 60:6 and 108:7. It is not to be confused with the first stopping place of the children of Israel on the night of the Exodus (Exodus 12:37; 13:20; Numbers 33:5).

LEBANON

The modern State of Lebanon was created after 1918, first under French mandate, and then as an independent territory in 1941. It occupies a strip of land, 4,015 square miles in area, at the east end of the Mediterranean Sea. It is bordered by Syria on the north and east and Israel on the south. It has a population of about 2,500,000, half of whom live in the capital city of Beirut. Religiously, half the population is Christian and the rest are Muslims and Druses. The country is dominated by the Lebanon mountains to the west side and the Ante Lebanons to the east. Between these two ranges is the beautiful Bekaa Valley, 10 miles wide and 70 to 80 miles long. It is a most fertile plain, and was once called the "bread basket of Rome." Lebanon has the highest level of education of all countries of the Middle East.

Lebanon is first mentioned in the Scripture in Deuteronomy 1:7; 11:24, where it is spoken of as one of the borders of the land God promised to Israel. Lebanon is noted for its beautiful scenery and Bible writers often used its beauty and fruitfulness to suggest blessings, both natural and spiritual (Psalm 72:16; 104:16-18; Song of Solomon 4:15; Isaiah 2:13; 35:2; 60:13; Hosea 14:5). It was noted for its cedars which were used in the construction of Solomon's beautiful temple at Jerusalem. These famous trees may still be seen on the upper slopes of the Lebanon range, though only a few over 400 still exist today (I Kings 5:8-11).

The Lebanese unit of currency is the pound. There are 100 piasters in the pound. Approximately three Lebanese pounds comprise the U.S. dollar.

In Bible days what is now Lebanon was called Phoenicia (Acts 11:19; 15:3; 21:2).

143

Baalbek, Lebanon—Running north and south through the center of the country of Lebanon, with the Lebanon range to the west and the Ante Lebanons to the east, is the great fertile valley of Bekaa. It was once said to be "the bread basket of Rome." Toward the northern end of the valley, and at its narrowest point, stand the ruins of the famous temples of Baalbek. It is interesting to note that Baal was worshiped as a triadic deity. Jupiter Heliopolitanus consisted also of a triad: Jupiter, the father; Venus, the mother; Bacchus or Mercury, the son. At Baalbek are the three temples to Jupiter, Bacchus and Venus.

These were planned and built by the Romans to outshine all other existing temples of the Empire. They are thought by many to be Rome's great attempt to impress the kingdoms of the east and to stabilize their Empire against the advances of Christianity. They were perhaps Satan's last great attempt to overpower the spread of the Gospel. Certainly here was the greatest concentration of pagan worship anywhere in the world. They contain the tallest columns ever built, the largest stone blocks ever used by man, and have been said to be the boldest architectural engineering feat ever carried out by man. The temples were begun under Emperor Augustus and construction was carried on for 250 years.

The temple was entered by a great central stairway, 150 feet wide containing 51 steps. The first court was built in the form of a hexagon 212 feet in diameter. It was fronted by 30 red granite columns. Granite for these and hundreds of others was brought from Aswan, Egypt, some 1,200 miles away. Beyond the hexagonal court was the Great Court 400 feet long and 385 feet wide. A double row of red granite columns 25 feet high, 128 in all, surrounded the inside of the court. The Great Altar towered 57 feet high.

Above and beyond the Great Court were the 54 massive

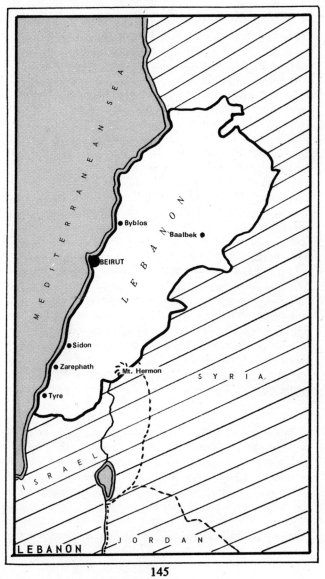

MEDITERRANEAN SEA

LEBANON

• Byblos
Baalbek •

BEIRUT

• Sidon

• Zarephath

Tyre •

Mt. Hermon

SYRIA

ISRAEL

JORDAN

LEBANON

145

columns of the Temple of Jupiter—only six of these remain. They are 65 feet high and composed of three drums of granite from 12 to 25 feet high each, held together with bronze and iron dowels packed with lead. The base of the temple of Jupiter contains the three largest stones ever handled by man, called the Trilithon. They are 14 feet six inches high, 12 feet thick and average 64 feet in length. They each weigh approximately 800 tons.

To the west of the Temple of Jupiter is the smaller but more ornate Temple of Bacchus. It is one of the most beautiful and best preserved Corinthian temples in antiquity. Twenty-four of the original 46 beautifully fluted Corinthian columns, 57 feet high, still stand today. This room is the most pretentious scheme of interior decoration ever produced in limestone. The carvings in the limestone of the entire temples are beyond comparison. The still smaller temple of Venus is mostly in ruins.

In 306 A.D. Constantine recognized Christianity and later embraced it, making it the state religion. The rapid spread of Christianity resulted in the closing of the temples at Baalbek and the outlawing of the cult of Jupiter and Venus. The heathen statues were destroyed and the temples of Baalbek were converted into Christian churches. Later it became an Arab fortress. It was disastrously shaken by a series of earthquakes in 1158 and almost destroyed. Recently they are being strengthened and partially rebuilt.

Byblos—Gebal—The city of Byblos in Lebanon is located on the Mediterranean coast 25 miles north of Beirut. In Bible times it was known as Gebal. The Revised Version of Joshua 13:5 reads, "land of the Gebalites and all Lebanon." (Authorized Version, "Giblites.") From Byblos the famous cedars of Lebanon were shipped to David and Solomon. The Revised Version, as well as others, adds "and the Gebalites" to "Solomon's builders and Hiram's

146

Crusader Castle by the Sea at Sidon on the Mediterranean coast of Lebanon.

Pillars of the Temple of Jupiter at Baalbek, Lebanon.

builders" in I Kings 5:18, indicating that the people from ancient Byblos aided in preparing timber and stone for the building of the temple at Jerusalem. Psalm 83:7 mentions Gebal and Ezekiel 27:9 indicates that the workmen of Gebal assisted in the building of ships for the famous voyagers of Tyre.

Byblos is recognized as one of the oldest cities in the world. Its ancient walls date back to 2900 B.C. The Phoenicians manufactured papyrus. From this city comes the name of our Bible, for when the Greeks imported papyrus from Byblos they called the material "byblos" after the name of the city of its origin. Writings on this material were called "biblia." Thus our Bible, meaning literally "Book of books," comes from this city. It was at Byblos that the linear alphabet was originated, thus it is also the home of our alphabet. It was called "the book town," because so many manuscripts were published here.

Sidon—Zidon—Sidon is about 30 miles south of Beirut in Lebanon—ancient Phoenicia. It is the oldest of the Phoenician cities, rich and famous long before Tyre was built. It is mentioned as the most northern of the cities of the Canaanites (Genesis 10:19). Joshua refers to it as "great Zidon" (Joshua 11:8). Judges 10:12 apparently claims that Sidon oppressed the children of Israel. Its sailors were famous for their maritime endeavors, being the first to sail beyond sight of land, and to sail at night guiding themselves by the stars (Isaiah 23:4).

Ahab, king of Israel, added to his other sins by taking Jezebel, "daughter of Ethbaal, king of the Zidonians" as his wife. Thus the curse of Baal worship was introduced into Israel (I Kings 16:31-33). Jesus made dramatic reference to the sinfulness of Sidon and also Tyre (Matthew 11:21-24; Luke 10:13,14).

God, through the prophet Ezekiel, uttered grave prophecies against the wicked city of Sidon (Ezekiel 28:21-24). Sidon, though not destroyed as was Tyre, has seen much bloodshed in her streets. In 351 B.C. the Persians attacked the city and, rather than surrender, the inhabitants set fire to it and 40,000 are said to have perished.

On one occasion Jesus visited as far north as "the coasts of Tyre and Sidon" (Matthew 15:21; Mark 7:24), and here healed the daughter of the Syrophenician woman. Herod received a delegation from Tyre and Sidon at Caesarea (Acts 12:20). Paul, as a prisoner of Rome, was permitted to visit his friends in Sidon (Acts 27:3).

Tyre—Tyre is situated on the coast of the beautiful blue Mediterranean, 30 miles south of Sidon, Lebanon. It was once the most splendid city of the world. It was built partly on the mainland and partly on an island about ¾ mile out in the sea. Joshua 19:29 refers to "the strong city of Tyre." It was attacked many times through its history but was always able to resist because its ships controlled the sea. Nebuchadnezzar from Babylon once laid seige to it for 13 years. He destroyed the mainland city but was not able to take the island.

A remarkable series of prophecies against Tyre are found in Ezekiel 26—28:19. Here the famous Phoenician merchant fleet sailing the seas of the world, her pride in her island fortress and the invasion of Nebuchadnezzar, etc. are set forth. See also Isaiah 23. Ezekiel 28:12-19 is taken by many to refer to Lucifer, Satan—"the anointed cherub that covereth"—before his fall. The amazing prediction, "I will also scrape her dust from her, and make her like the top of a rock," (Ezekiel 26:4), was fulfilled when Alexander the Great scraped the debris of the destroyed city on the mainland into the sea to form a causeway out to the island city. He was then able to capture and destroy

149

Tyre, killing 10,000 and taking 30,000 men, women, and children captive and selling them as slaves.

Ezekiel 26:14 states plainly that this city is to "be built no more." Visitors to present day Tyre may wonder about the fulfillment of that prophecy. If one looks at an aerial view of Tyre he will find that, by the action of the sea, the causeway built by Alexander the Great has become a wide peninsula between the mainland and the former island. The prophecy of Ezekiel was spoken concerning the mainland city. The island and peninsula area have been built many times and there is a thriving city of 14,000 on it now. But the mainland, where the principal city used to be, has never been rebuilt.

Hiram, king of Tyre, provided cedars of Lebanon for Solomon with which to build the temple at Jerusalem (I Kings 5:1-12). Solomon also engaged skilled workers in brass from Tyre (I Kings 7:13,14).

Jesus visited the area of Tyre (Matthew 15:21; Mark 7:24), where He healed the Syrophenician woman's daughter. The people from this area came to hear Him and to be healed (Mark 3:8; Luke 6:17). The sins of Tyre and its sister city Sidon were well known—akin to that of Sodom (Matthew 11:21-24; Luke 10:13,14). Acts 12:20 mentions Herod's displeasure with the people of Tyre. It was at Tyre that Paul stopped and stayed seven days on his last journey to Jerusalem. The disciples here warned him not to go to Jerusalem. Before his departure they all gathered for prayer on the seashore (Acts 21:2-6).

Zarephath—Sarepta—Sarafend—Zarephath lies on the Mediterranean coast about midway between Tyre on the south and Sidon on the north. It is called Sarafend today. "Sarepta," used in the New Testament is the Greek of the Hebrew Zarephath. This is the place to which Elijah was sent to be sustained by the widow woman during the latter days of the three and one-half year famine. She and her son were also provided for through the miracle of the barrel of meal that did not waste and the cruse of oil which did not fail (I Kings 17:8-16; Luke 4:25,26). Here also Elijah raised the widow's son to life again (I Kings 17:17-24). Zarephath is also mentioned in Obadiah 20.

The first Gentile to whom Jesus ministered was a Syrophenician in the "coasts of Tyre and Sidon." He delivered her daughter from a demonic affliction, calling attention to her great faith (Matthew 15:21-28; Mark 7:24-30). It is believed the woman was from Zarephath.

SYRIA

Before 1918 "Syria" was a term rather loosely applied to the whole of the territory now forming modern Syria, Lebanon, Israel and Jordan. In other words, in Bible times it had extended from the Euphrates to the Mediterranean. Now it is much more confined with most of its borders arbitrarily determined. It comprises 74,000 squares miles. Its population is about 5,200,000. Syria borders on Turkey to the north, Iraq on the east and southeast, Jordan to the south, Israel to the southwest and Lebanon on the west. Its Mediterranean coastline stretches for 200 miles.

The Old Testament records many battles between Israel and the Syrians. There are also times when Syria was an ally of either Israel or Judah. Places of particular Bible interest are Damascus, Antioch and Seleucia. See articles on each of these cities.

The Syrian pound, divided into 100 piasters, is valued at 4 to the U.S. dollar.

Damascus—Damascus, capital of Syria, is the oldest continuously inhabited city in the world, dating back 6,000 years. It has a population of 600,000 people. In an area dominated by desert, Damascus has always been a garden spot for travelers over the ancient Fertile Crescent. It was a free city and a member of the Decapolis—that chain of ten autonomous cities which included Beth-shan (Scythopolis) on the west side of Jordan and Pella, Dion, Kanatha, Raphana, Hypos, Gadara, Philadelphia (Amman), Damascus and Gerasa (Jerash) on the east side of the Jordan.

The city is referred to a number of times in the Old Testament. In Genesis 14:15 we read of Abraham pursuing the kings, who captured Lot at Sodom, and recovering his

nephew and his goods at Hobah "which is on the left (north) of Damascus." In Genesis 15:2 Abraham complains that he has no heir except the steward of his house, "this Eliezer of Damascus." The kings of Damascus were a constant problem to some of the kings of Israel: David (II Samuel 8:5), Solomon (I Kings 11:23-25). Asa, king of Judah, paid Ben-Hadad large tribute money to attack Baasha, king of Israel, and thus relieve the pressure on his forces (I Kings 15:16-20). Ahab, king of Israel, was greatly harassed by Ben-Hadad, king of Syria (I Kings 20). When King Ahaz of Judah was attacked by the kings of Syria and Israel he sent to Tiglath-pileser, king of Assyria, silver and treasure, enlisting his assistance. This led to the overthrow of Damascus by the king of Assyria (II Kings 16:5-9), a fate which was soon to befall the city of Samaria and the king of Israel.

Damascus is of principle interest to the Christian because of its association with the conversion and the very early ministry of the Apostle Paul. It was following the martyrdom of Stephen that Paul (then called Saul), armed with written authority to persecute the Christians, was on his way from Jerusalem to Damascus. This was a journey of about six days. Nearing the city walls, at the hour of midday, Paul was smitten to the ground by a light from heaven and dramatically converted to Christ (Acts 9:1-19. See also Acts 22:1-16; 26:9-18). Being blinded, he was led into the city where, after three days, he was healed, filled with the Spirit and baptized in water through the ministry of Ananias.

After his conversion Paul spent part of three years in Arabia and then returned to Damascus (Galatians 1:17, 18). In order to avoid arrest, he was let down through a window in the wall in order that he might escape (Acts 9:22-25; II Corinthians 11:32,33).

Places of interest in Damascus for the Christian today include: The Street Called Straight, on which was the

St. Paul's window in the wall of Damascus, Syria.

Beautiful inner courtyard of home in Damascus in Syria.

house of Judas where Paul stayed (Acts 9:11). It still bisects the city from east to west. The house of Ananias, an underground chapel. The window in the city wall where it is believed Paul made his escape. The Church of John the Baptist, now the huge Omayad Mosque. The tomb of Saladin who defeated the Crusaders and conquered Palestine in 1187 A.D. Also, the fabulous covered bazaars.

Flowing through the city of Damascus is the River Abana to which Naaman referred when he did not care to follow Elisha's directions to dip seven times in the River Jordan to be cured of his leprosy (II Kings 5:12). The River Pharpar is a few miles south of the city.

Palmyra—Palmyra is the Latin and Greek for a famous city of the East located about 150 miles northeast of Damascus. Palmyra is called Tadmor in the Bible, where we learn that King Solomon built Tadmor as a commercial outpost (II Chronicles 8:3,4). This gives some idea of the extent of the kingdom of Israel under Solomon.

Tadmor was very prosperous as indicated by its extensive ruins. It was an oasis in the Syrian desert where the great trade routes from the Phoenician ports to the Persian Gulf and those coming up from Petra and South Arabia met. The city collected a duty on all imports and exports. They also enriched themselves by guaranteeing safe passage of caravans through robber infested areas.

The city was in existence many hundreds of years before Christ, but it was not until the last half of the 1st century B.C. that it came into real prominence. The imposing central avenue, 1,240 yards long, consisted of no less than 750 columns 55 feet high. The time of the city's greatest splendor was 130-270 A.D. During the Parthian wars of the 3rd century Palmyra became the mistress of the Roman East. The city actually extended its sway over Syria, Arabia and Egypt. Because of its revolt against Rome, the populace of Palmyra was killed and the city destroyed in 272 A.D. The city walls and its Temple of the Sun were restored but Palmyra never recovered its greatness.

The Christian Church made considerable progress in this city. The city of Palmyra sent its bishop to the Council of Nicaea in 325 A.D. It was still a wealthy place as late as the 14th century, but in the general decline of the East and the change in trade routes it finally sank to be only a poor group of hovels in the courtyard of the Temple of the Sun. The town called Tudmur on the Iraq-Tripoli oil pipelines lies about one half mile from the ruins of old Palmyra.

TURKEY

Except for a comparatively small area which lies south of Bulgaria and east of Greece on the European continent, Turkey is in Asia. It occupies the peninsula of Asia Minor with seas on three sides: the Aegean on the west, the Black Sea to the north, and the Mediterranean on the south. Mountain ranges are on its east, bordering Russia, Iran, Iraq and Syria. It is 880 miles long and 390 miles wide, comprising 301,381 square miles—a little larger than Texas. In many ways Turkey may be called a passage land between Europe and Asia. Its population is about 31,400,-000. Over 2,250,000 live in Istanbul, which was formerly called Constantinople, and before that Byzantium. Istanbul lies mostly in Europe, but part of the city is across the Bosphorus in Asia. The capital of Turkey is Ankara, with a population of almost 1,100,000. 98% of the people in Turkey are Moslems. There are about 500 mosques, many of them former churches, in Istanbul alone.

The monetary unit is the lira, which contains 100 kurus. The United States dollar is worth 9 lira.

Turkey is very significant to the Christian student because of the many places of Biblical import which are within its borders: Mount Ararat, where Noah's Ark came to rest (Genesis 8:4). Haran, to which Abraham journeyed with his father when they left Ur of the Chaldees (Genesis 11:31,32). Most of the cities where Paul preached in Asia, as well as Tarsus where he was born. These include Antioch and Seleucia (then in Syria), Attalia, Perga, Antioch in Pisidia, Iconium, Lystra, Derbe, Miletus, and Troas. All of the seven churches mentioned in Revelation 2,3 which are: Ephesus, Smyrna, Pergamos, Thyatira, Sardis, Philadelphia and Laodicea.

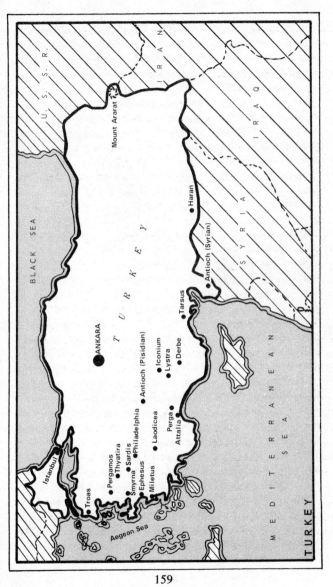

Antioch—Antakya—Antioch in Syria is now known as Antakya and is in modern Turkey. In Paul's day it was the capital of the province of Syria. It is located on the south bank of the Orontes River about 21 miles up from the river's mouth at the Mediterranean. It is some 300 miles north of Jerusalem. In Roman times it had a population of 500,000 being third largest in the Roman Empire. It was known as "the Queen of the East." A terrible earthquake shook Antioch in 526 A.D., causing the death of 250,000 people in the province and completely destroying the city.

Syrian Antioch was a very important place in the early history of Christianity. It seems there was a considerable Jewish population in the city. At the time of the persecutions of the Christians that took place following the stoning of Stephen, believers fled from Jerusalem. One of the chief places to which they went was Antioch in Syria (Acts 11:19). The Gospel was preached here, not only to the Jews but to the Gentiles also. It seems that the church at Antioch pioneered in this departure from tradition. Such was the result that tidings of the revival came to Jerusalem and Barnabas was sent there from the home base at Jerusalem. He later went to Tarsus and brought Paul to Antioch to assist in the work. It was here the name "Christians" was first applied to the followers of Jesus (Acts 11:20-26). Nicolas, a proselyte of Antioch, was one of the first deacons of the church at Jerusalem (Acts 6:5). Peter was in Antioch for a while (Galatians 2:11-14).

The Church at Antioch sent relief to the saints in Judea during the famine in the days of Claudius Caesar (Acts 11:27-30). Antioch became the center of the missionary endeavors of the early church. It was Paul's starting point for his three missionary journeys (Acts 13:1-3; 15:36-41; 18:22,23), and it was here he returned after the first two (Acts 14:26-28; 18:22). The church here instigated the Council at Jerusalem whose decision relieved Gentile Christians of the burden of the Jewish law (Acts 15). It is famous as the birthplace of Chrysostom in 347 B.C. who led the church to its most flourishing period. Archaeologists have uncovered the ruins of more than a score of Christian churches in Antioch.

Antioch in Pisidia—In Paul's day Pisidia was a part of the Roman province of Galatia, district of Phrygia. It was the capital of Southern Galatia. Around 6 B.C. it was made a Roman colony, its citizens thus being awarded Roman citizenship. Ruins of the ancient city are located a mile northeast of the village of Yalvac, 155 miles northeast of Antalya. The University of Michigan has uncovered several buildings of old Antioch.

At the close of their ministry on the island of Cyprus, during the early days of their first missionary journey, Paul and Barnabas sailed from Paphos to Perga in Pamphylia and from thence made their way to Antioch in Pisidia (Acts 13:13,14). It must have been a tortuous journey over the rugged mountains which were notably infested with robbers. Many have thought Paul had this journey in mind when he later referred to having been "in perils of robbers" (II Corinthians 11:26). Here, in the Jewish synagogue, Paul preached the first of the three great sermons recorded in the Book of Acts (Acts 13:14-43). The other two are: on Mars Hill at Athens (Acts 17:22-31), and at Miletus to the elders of the church at Ephesus (Acts 20:17-35).

The city was moved by Paul's message, but the envious Jews opposed him (Acts 13:44,45). Paul and Barnabas gave public testimony that they were turning to the Gentiles and many of them believed, "and the word of the Lord was published throughout all the region" (Acts 13:46-49).

Widespread and official persecution was stirred up against the apostles. So they went down to Iconium (Acts 13:50-52; II Timothy 3:11). Paul and Barnabas returned to Antioch to strengthen the Christians and to ordain elders in the church, before setting sail for Antioch in Syria, thus concluding their first missionary journey (Acts 14:21-26). Paul probably again visited the church in Pisidian Antioch on his second missionary journey (Acts 16:6) and perhaps on his third (Acts 18:23).

Attalia—Antalya—Attalia was a large port on the south coast of Pamphylia in Asia Minor. This was where Paul and Barnabas landed when they came from Cyprus toward the beginning of their first missionary journey. They proceeded from here to preach in Perga, Antioch, Iconium, Lystra and Derbe. Retracing their steps they sailed from Attalia (Acts 14:25,26) back to Antioch in Syria from whence their journey started (Acts 13:1-3).

Derbe—Derbe was the farthest point reached by Paul and Barnabas on their first missionary journey (Acts 14:20, 21). It was the last town in Roman territory on the road running through southern Galatia to the East. There is considerable uncertainty regarding the site of ancient Derbe. It has been presumed to be 16 miles southeast of Lystra in Lycaonia. Recent opinion, because of the discovery of a column, which is now in Konya, is that the location is about 12 miles north of the village of Karaman which is 66 miles southeast of Konya. The location is called Kerti Huyuk.

Among the many converts at Derbe may have been Gaius (Acts 20:4; Romans 16:23). Rather than making the comparatively short trip from Derbe, through the Cilician Gates to Tarsus and thence to Antioch in Syria, Paul and Barnabas chose to retrace their steps and again visit Lystra, Iconium and Pisidian Antioch. This gave them the opportunity to strengthen the churches and appoint qualified leaders over them (Acts 14:21-23). Paul also came through Derbe on his second missionary journey (Acts 16:1).

Ephesus—Selcuk—In Paul's day Ephesus was the capital of proconsular Asia—the Roman province in the western part of Asia Minor. It was one of the three most important cities of the East—along with Alexandria in Egypt and Antioch in Syria. It is midway between Smyrna (Izmir) and Miletus—about 40 miles south of Smyrna. It was built on the Cayster River about three miles from the Aegean Sea. There have actually been five cities of Ephesus. The present town is called Selcuk. Ephesus III is the one associated with the Apostle Paul's ministry. It was built on the west and south of Mount Pion.

At that time it had a beautiful harbor—now all silted up —and was the chief commercial city of the east. It was the most populace and wealthy city in Asia Minor. Here was located one of the Seven Wonders of the Ancient World— the great temple of the goddess Artemis (Greek) or Diana (Roman). Her image was said to have fallen down from heaven and the temple was built where she fell. It was 377 feet long by 180 feet wide standing on an immense raised platform about 425 feet by 240 feet. It had over 100 columns 56 feet high and 6 feet in diameter. The temple was made of wood, marble and gold. Little or nothing remains of this great building at Ephesus today. Most of what was excavated is in the British Museum. Excavations of the Marble Street, with its many beautiful buildings as well as the great theatre, seating some 25,000 people, are most impressive after almost 20 centuries.

Paul came to Ephesus first on his second missionary journey (Acts 18:19-21). He stayed only a short time but returned for a period of two years on his third journey. At this time the Holy Spirit was poured out on believers in a special manner (Acts 19:1-7). Paul preached in the Jewish Synagogue, in the school of Tyrannus and also in private homes, and the Word of God spread throughout all the region (Acts 19:8-10; 20:20). It was in Ephesus the "special miracles" were wrought by the hands of Paul through "handkerchiefs or aprons" (Acts 19:11,12). God's power was mightily manifest in Ephesus (Acts 19:13-20) so that the worship of the great Diana suffered severely. The uproar instigated by the silversmiths, which overflowed the great theatre, testified to the influence of the Gospel in that city and area (Acts 19:23-41).

Paul's touching message to the Ephesian elders, who came to Miletus to meet him as he was on his way back to Jerusalem, is one of the apostle's three outstanding sermons which are recorded in the book of Acts (Acts 20:17-38). The Apostle John was one of the early leaders of the church at Ephesus. It is believed he brought Mary, the mother of Jesus, here (John 19:25-27). On Mount Selimisses, near Ephesus, one is shown a beautiful little chapel built on what some believe was the home where Mary spent her last days. It is called the Panaya Kapulu.

The Church at Ephesus was perhaps the most spiritual of the early Christian Churches. Certainly Paul's epistle to it contains some of the most exalted spiritual truth in the New Testament. Our Lord's commendation of this church, in His epistle, is indeed very gracious (Revelation 2:1-7).

Haran—In the northwestern part of Mesopotamia (Acts 7:2) is a prairie area called Padan-Aram (Genesis 28:5). In about its center, on the Balikh River a tributary of the Euphrates, is the city of Haran. In response to the call of God Abraham, with his father Terah, left Ur to go to Canaan, but they tarried at Haran, 600 miles north of Ur. Here he stayed until after the death of Terah (Genesis 11:31,32; 12:1-5; Acts 7:2-4). It was probably a flourishing city when Abraham was there.

In taking this long circuitous route to go to Canaan, Abraham was following the old caravan roads that led from Mesopotamia to Haran and thence southwest through Palmyra—Biblical Tadmor (II Chronicles 8:4)—a great

Fountain of Memnius on the Marble Street of Ephesus in Turkey.

A portion of the acropolis of ancient Pergamum, now called Bergama, in Turkey.

165

oasis. From there he would continue to Damascus and thence into Canaan where his first stop was Sichem or Shechem (Genesis 12:6). This ancient caravan route, which continues south to Egypt, has been called "The Fertile Crescent." Traders and armies have used it for thousands of years. Canaan thus has been a land bridge between Mesopotamia and Egypt.

Abraham sent his servant back to the area of Haran to find a bride for Isaac (Genesis 24:10). Later Jacob fled here and labored for 20 years (Genesis 28:10; 29:4). Here he married Leah, Rachel, Zilpah and Bilhah. All of his 12 sons were born here except Benjamin (Genesis 35:16-19).

Iconium—Konya—Eighty miles southeast of Pisidian Antioch, along the military road built by Augustus and called the Royal Road, lies the city of Iconium, now the modern city of Konya, in the center of the Antolian plateau—elevation 3,770 feet. The Royal Road extended on to Lystra. In apostolic days Iconium was one of the chief cities in the southern part of the Roman province of Galatia, which at that time included Phrygia.

When Paul and Barnabas were driven out of Pisidian Antioch, on their first missionary journey, they made their way to Iconium (Acts 13:51). Here they had great success preaching to both Jew and Gentile. They apparently stayed there for a "long time," but when the multitude of Jews and Gentiles sought to stone them they fled to Lystra, 18 miles south and west of Iconium (Acts 14:1-6; II Timothy 3:11). Jews from Iconium, as well as from Antioch, followed Paul and Barnabas and persuaded the people of Lystra to stone Paul (Acts 14:19).

Paul revisited Iconium as he returned to establish the churches and to appoint elders (Acts 14:21-23). He also probably visited the saints at Iconium on his second (Acts 15:36,41; 16:1,2) and third journeys (Acts 18:22).

Laodicea—Laodicea was the capital of Phrygia. It was located about 100 miles east of Ephesus, just a few miles northeast of the present good-sized town of Denizli. It was named in honor of Laodice, the wife of Antiochus II (B.C. 261-246) who rebuilt it on or near the site of a former city. It was destroyed by an earthquake in the first century and was rebuilt by Marcus Aurelius. There was a large colony of Jews here. It was the seat of a Christian Church (Colossians 2:1; 4:13,15,16). It was one of the seven churches of the Book of Revelation, and its letter is full of awesome warning (Revelation 3:14-22). It is now a heap of ruins called by the Turks Eski Hissar—"Old castle." Remains of the stadium, two theatres and some of the walls of old Laodicea can be seen.

Lystra—Lystra was a city in the province of Lycaonia (Acts 14:6) 18 miles south and a little west of Iconium on the Royal Road to Antioch in Pisidia. It was a Roman colony and at that time was part of the province of Galatia. It is on the high tableland north of the Taurus Mountains.

Paul and Barnabas came to Lystra after being threatened with stoning at Iconium. A man who had been a cripple from birth was marvelously healed through Paul's ministry here at Lystra. The people declared that the gods had "come down to us in the likeness of men." They called Barnabas Jupiter—supreme god of the Romans corresponding to the Greek's Zeus—and Paul was called Mercurias, "because he was the chief speaker." Mercury was a Roman god corresponding to Hermes of the Greeks, the son of Zeus. He was regarded as the god of oratory. Paul and Barnabas quickly corrected this attitude. When Jews from Antioch came to Lystra they persuaded the people against the apostles. Thus those who would have worshiped them now stoned Paul (Acts 14:8-19).

Later Paul was to return to this city (Acts 14:21). On his

third visit, during his second missionary journey, Timothy joined the evangelistic party (Acts 16:1-4). Paul referred to this young man as "my own son in the faith," and "my dearly beloved son" (I Timothy 1:2; II Timothy 1:2). The two Epistles to Timothy form an important part of the New Testament. Paul may have come through Lystra on his third journey (Acts 18:23).

No archaeological excavations have been made at the site of ancient Lystra. Only a few pillars are visible. The site is near the village of Hatunsaray.

Miletus—An ancient important seaport on the Aegean Sea about 36 miles south from Ephesus. It is now some distance from the coast, the harbor having become filled with silt. On his last journey to Jerusalem Paul stopped here and sent for the elders of the Ephesian church. When they were come he delivered the touching message recorded in Acts 20:17-38. He testified to these church leaders of his ministry among them, warned them of "grievous wolves" who would come among them "not sparing the flock," and told them that they would "see his face no more."

This is the third discourse of Paul which is reported by Luke in the book of Acts. The first was addressed to the **Jews** in the synagogue at Pisidian Antioch (Acts 13:16-41). The second was addressed to the **Gentiles** on Mars Hill in Athens (Acts 17:22-31). The third to the **Church** here at Miletus (Acts 20:18-35).

The village of Balat is now on the site of the old city.

Perga—Perga, modern Murtana, was the capital of the province of Pamphylia. It was a very important city in Roman times. Situated on the Kestros River, it was about 11 miles east of Attalia (Antalya). Its site lies a short distance north of the highway at the village of Aksu, 10 miles east of Antalya. Here may be seen extensive ruins including the theatre, stadium, baths, agora and basillica. It was the first city in Asia Minor to be visited by Paul and Barnabas during their first missionary journey (Acts 13:13). From here John Mark returned to Jerusalem, choosing not to accompany the two apostles any farther (Acts 13:13). After traveling as far east as Derbe, Paul and Barnabas retraced their steps and preached the Word of God in Perga (Acts 14:24, 25).

Pergamos—Pergamum—now called Bergama, is situated 68 miles north of Smyrna (Izmir) and 15 or 20 miles inland from the Aegean Sea. Its acropolis rises 1,100 feet high. At one time in its history, it was one of the most splendid cities in the Middle East, even rivaling Alexandria and Antioch. Under the Romans, Pergamum was proclaimed capital of the province of Asia. Revelation 2:12-17 records the letter written to the Christian church at Pergamos. Verse 13 of this passage speaks to "Satan's seat" being here. Pergamos was a center of idolatry. The great altar of Zeus on the acropolis has been suggested as fulfilling this name. It was 125 feet by 115 feet with 40-foot-high pillars and outstanding bas relief friezes. Extensive excavations have been carried on at Pergamum for many years by Germans from the Museum of Berlin. The altar of Zeus was found in an excellent condition and has been transported to Germany.

The excavations on the acropolis have uncovered vast remains of temples, palaces, libraries and the steepest theater in the ancient world seating 15,000. The outstanding library contained 200,000 volumes many of which were written on parchment, a new material invented here and called "pergamena." The library was removed by Mark Anthony and presented to Cleopatra. Nearby is an extensive temple of Aesculapius, the god of medicine. Antipas, called "my faithful martyr" (Revelation 2:13), was murdered in Pergamos. He was the first Christian put to death by the Roman State.

Philadelphia—The New Testament city of Philadelphia is now known as Alashehir. It is a picturesque town in a narrow valley about 26 miles southeast of Sardis. Philadelphia means "brotherly love." The city was built on a terrace some 650 feet above sea level. It was noted for its temples to several of the Roman emperors. It is said that Christianity was longer taking root here than in some other places. Many of its early Christians were martyred. The letter addressed to it, one of the seven churches in Asia Minor, is the only one containing no condemnation (Revelation 3:7-13). There is almost no evidence today of the city of John's time. No excavations have yet been made.

Sardis—About 58 miles east, and a little north, of Smyrna (Izmir) is the little village of Sart. Nearby are the ruins of ancient Sardis. It is about 36 miles south of Thyatira (Akhisar). Sardis was the capital of Croesus, king of Lydia, who was noted for his fabulous riches. It was he who minted the first coins in history. Christianity was brought to Sardis at an early period as it was one of the seven churches to which letters are addressed in the Book of Revelation (3:1-6). Excavations of the old city have been made by the University of Princeton. Outstanding of these is the temple of Artemis, measuring 300 by 148 feet.

Seleucia—Samandag—Seleucia Pierria, to distingish it from other cities named the same, was located about 5 miles from the mouth of the Orontes River. It served as the port of Antioch in Syria—16 miles up the river. It was one of the most important harbors of the Eastern Mediterranean during New Testament times. These cities are now in Turkey. Paul and Barnabas passed through Seleucia on their first missionary journey (Acts 13:4; 14:26). Probably also on the other journeys. It is now known as Samandag.

Smyrna—Smyrna, now the flourishing city of Izmir, is located 40 miles north of Ephesus on the Gulf of Izmir. It is the most important port of Asia Minor on the Aegean Sea. The city was recognized as one of the finest cities in Asia and was called, "the lovely—the crown of Ionia—the ornament of Asia." Here was located one of the seven churches to which the Risen Lord addressed epistles (Revelation 2:8-11). Polycarp, the noted bishop of the church of Smyrna, was martyred here about 169 A.D. The ruins of the Roman agora—the market place—take the visitor back to apostolic days. Of interest also is the citadel, known as the Kadifekale, built by Alexander the Great on Mount Pagos (elevation 525 feet), overlooking the city.

Tarsus—The city of Tarsus was the capital of the province of Cilicia in Southern Asia Minor—now a part of Turkey. It was built on both banks of the Cydnus River about 10 miles from the Mediterranean Sea and 30 miles south of the Taurus Mountains. It was noted in early days for its fine harbor, now silted up, which made it an important commercial center. It was also on the road connecting the Euphrates Valley to Asia Minor which passed through the Taurus Mountains by means of the famous "Cilician Gates"—a narrow pass between walls of rock—and one of the most important mountain passes in the ancient world. Tarsus was also famous for its university, being one of the three principal university cities of its day—along with Athens and Alexandria. It is said to have even surpassed these others in its intellectual eminence. It was at Tarsus that Anthony first met Cleopatra (38 B.C.).

Tarsus is the birthplace of the Apostle Paul (Acts 22:3). He speaks of himself as "a citizen of no mean city" (Acts 21:39). After his first visit to Jerusalem, following his conversion to Christ, he returned to Tarsus for several years (Acts 9:30). Barnabas went to get him to help in the rapidly growing church of Antioch in Syria (Acts 11:25). He no doubt visited the city on his second missionary journey (Acts 15:41) and possibly on his third (Acts 18:23).

Thyatira—Thyatira is on the road from Pergamos to Sardis about 44 miles southeast of Pergamos. It was particularly noted for its dyeing industry. At no place could scarlet cloth be so brilliantly or permanently dyed as here. Paul's first convert in Europe, Lydia, who accepted the Lord at Philippi, was a seller of purple from Thyatira (Acts 16:14). The Lord addressed one of the letters of Revelation to the church at this place (Revelation 2:18-29). The modern city of Akisar now occupies this site.

Troas—Eskistanbul—Troas is a seaport of Mysia in western Asia Minor. It is located 10 miles south of Homer's Troy, now known as Hissarlik. It was here that Paul, on his second missionary journey, and after being forbidden of the Holy Spirit to preach in Asia and Bithynia, saw the vision of the man of Macedonia inviting him to come and minister there. Sailing from Troas, Paul and his party, including Luke, stopped at the island of Samothrace in the Aegean Sea midway on their journey to Neapolis— modern Kavalla, which was the seaport of Philippi in Macedonia (Acts 16:8-12). This vision, and Paul's response, marked the beginning of his ministry in Europe. Thus the Gospel was taken to the West instead of the East. All subsequent history has been affected by this move.

Later, as he returned to Jerusalem on his third journey, Paul visited the church at Troas for one week. While he was preaching, a young man called Eutychus fell out of the window and died. Paul immediately embraced him and the Lord restored him to life (Acts 20:6-12). Note other references to Troas: II Corinthians 2:12,13; II Timothy 4:13.

The following information and suggestions are intended to be of help to those who are traveling abroad in Bible lands for the first time. Your travel agent or tour guide will help answer any further questions you may have.

LEGAL DOCUMENTS REQUIRED

It is necessary to have a valid United States passport This may be secured through the Passport Division of the Department of State. In order to apply for a passport you will need your birth certificate or other proof of your birth such as a baptismal certificate or expired passport. You should also secure two passport pictures—front view, 2½ by 2½ inches, on a white background. This passport will be valid for five years.

Visas for any country requiring them should be secured before leaving the United States. Your travel agent will advise and assist you in this.

For re-entry to the United States, and for entry to many foreign countries, you need a smallpox vaccination certificate. This should be obtained not less than eight days before leaving home, and it will be valid for three years. We suggest that you have your vaccination a month or six weeks before departure so that if you have any reaction you will have recovered in time to enjoy your trip.

U. S. CUSTOMS REGULATIONS

Residents of the United States are required to declare the full retail price of all articles purchased abroad. A customs declaration form will be given to you on your return flight. Fill it out in full.

If you are out of the country for at least 48 hours you

are allowed to import, duty-free, $100 worth of merchandise based on the retail price. Articles which are to be sent to you later must be included in your declaration.

In addition to this you may send home, duty-free, as many gift purchases as you desire providing the retail price of each does not exceed $10.00 and no more than one gift a day is sent to one address. These parcels must be marked "Gift," and cannot be sent to yourself. It is advisable to ask for a bill of sale with every purchase and to keep these to show to the customs agent if requested. Before leaving the United States, register all foreign-made items which you are taking with you, such as cameras, binoculars, tape recorders, etc. Otherwise you might be charged duty bringing them back into the country. Register these with the nearest U. S. Customs Office.

CURRENCY CONVERSION

Foreign currency is available at any bank and at foreign exchanges in the airports of each country.

It is recommended that you carry your money in low-value travelers checks—not larger than $10 or $20 amounts. Thus you will not be left with a large amount of local currency when you leave a country. You can convert it to U. S. funds, but a percentage charge will be made.

In addition to this, we suggest you take at least 25 one-dollar bills to use in the purchase of small items.

LUGGAGE

The airlines will carry free luggage weighing 66 pounds (30 kilograms) for First Class passengers, or 44 pounds (20 kilograms) for Economy Class passengers. Those traveling on tours should figure the latter amount. You may carry one large suitcase or two smaller ones. Small handbags, cameras and coats which are carried are not weighed.

You may check the weight of your luggage ahead of

time on your bathroom scale. An accurate way to do this is to weigh yourself first, then hold your baggage and note the weight. Subtract your weight from the whole. Remember to make allowance for gifts you may purchase abroad.

DRINKING WATER

The water in some foreign countries varies from that which you are used to drinking. You may be told that the water in a certain country, or a certain hotel, is safe to drink—i.e., that it is sanitary. However, some people contract diarrhea simply from the change of water. This also applies to ice cubes made from local water.

Consult your doctor as to what medicine you should take along. He may prescribe medication which will help prevent this familiar travel sickness. He will also suggest that which will cure it. Some travelers drink only bottled water. Excellent varieties are available in each country. It is also safe to drink the bottled carbonated beverages which are similar to those obtainable in the U. S.

ELECTRICAL APPLIANCES

Because of a wide variation in electrical voltages and outlets, appliances which are not adapted to both 110 and 220 volts will be of little or no use. They should be left at home. If you do have a razor or travel iron adapted to 220 volts, be sure to take a European plug adapter—round prongs. Most of the better hotels do provide an outlet for electric razors at 110 volts. However, this outlet should not be used for any other appliances.

THE METRIC SYSTEM

European and Asian countries use the metric system for indicating weights, distances and temperatures. Consider this when comparing with our measure system.

Temperature

Temperatures in Bible Lands are all reported in degrees Centigrade. On the Centigrade thermometer, freezing is 0 rather than 32 as on the Fahrenheit. 100 degrees Centigrade is boiling and corresponds to 212 degrees Fahrenheit. To convert from Centigrade to Fahrenheit, take 9/5 and add 32. For example: 30 degrees Centigrade divided by 5 equals 6, times 9 equals 54, plus 32 equals 86 degrees Fahrenheit.

Distances

The basic distance measure is the meter. One meter is equal to 3.281 feet. Highway distances are computed in kilometers rather than in miles. A kilometer is 1,000 meters or 3,280 feet. Thus it is ⅝ of a mile (5280 feet) or 0.6214 miles. Two simple methods of quickly converting kilometers to the approximate mileage are suggested: Take the number of kilometers and divide by 8 and multiply by 5. For instance: 80 kilometers divided by 8 equals 10. Multiplied by 5 it comes to an approximation of 50 miles.

Another suggested method is to multiply the number of kilometers by 6 and cross off one decimal. For example: 80 kilometers multiplied by 6 equals 480. Cross off the last decimal and you have 48 miles. The two systems result in slightly different results, but either gives a quick approximation.

Weights

Weights are computed by the kilogram or "kilo." One "kilo" is slightly more than two pounds.

Volume

Gasoline and milk are measured in liters. One liter is a little more than a quart.

CLIMATE

In planning his trip, the tourist asks "What weather conditions may be expected, and what clothes shall I take?" Much depends upon the time of year during which you will be traveling.

Generally speaking, the Middle Eastern countries, Cyprus, Israel, Lebanon, Syria, Jordan, Egypt and Turkey, have warm comfortable weather from April through November. Virtually no rain will be encountered between May and October. Weather conditions will be found to be very similar to that of Southern California. Men should bring a light sweater, and ladies should have a sweater and a lightweight top coat, inasmuch as the evenings are cool even though the days may be hot. From December to March, even though you will have many sunny days, cold and rainy weather may be encountered, and a warm coat and rain apparel should be provided. A light plastic raincoat is recommended even in the spring and fall for the occasional showers which may come.

Iran and Iraq can be very hot in summer and cold in winter. April to mid-June and mid-September to mid-November are recommended times to visit these countries.

Greece has a minimum of cold weather. In Athens the average winter temperature is around 52 degrees, and in the summer about 78 degrees. During July and August the thermometer may go up to 100 or more. However, a cool breeze usually springs up at night.

In Italy, temperatures are cooler in winter and not as warm in summer than those of Greece. In Rome, where warm weather begins in May and often lasts through October, the evenings are generally cool.

WHAT TO WEAR AND TAKE WITH YOU

Travel light. Do not burden yourself with hard-to-take-care-of clothes. Spare yourself the bother of carrying non-essentials. This means packing and unpacking will be much easier. Remember also that your luggage allowance is limited—44 pounds on tours.

Modern lightweight drip-dry clothes are ideal for traveling. They may be washed, hung and dried overnight. Several inflatable hangers are excellent for this purpose. A little travel clothesline is most handy. It can be strung up for drying clothes. Wash cloths are seldom provided in the hotels. Take one with you. Pre-moistened face cloths are refreshing during the day's sightseeing. Be sure to bring sturdy, comfortable flat walking shoes. You will be doing some climbing over uneven ground. Hats and gloves are unnecessary though a hat for protection against the sun is recommended for those whose skin is sensitive to the sun. Sun glasses should be taken. If you wear prescription glasses, be sure to take an extra pair if possible, and have your oculist write your prescription on your Health Certificate.

Ladies' Wardrobe

The following is a suggested list of clothing for your trip. If your trip is in the winter, the clothes suggested should be of a warmer quality. If in the spring or summer, everything should be of the lightweight variety.

Lightweight travel suit.

Lightweight water-repellent coat.

2 casual blouses.

1 cardigan-type sweater.

2 casual dresses.

1 informal dinner dress.

Several sets lingerie.

2 nighties.

2 lightweight skirts—full skirts will be much more comfortable.

6 pairs nylon hose

1 packable robe and slippers

1 or 2 scarves. These are necessary for entering churches or shrines.

1 bathing suit and cap if desired.

Your beauty kit should contain whatever you require of

cosmetics, toothpaste and toothbrush, hair-do gadgets, brush, comb and shower cap.

Men's Wardrobe

The following suggestions will help you plan your wardrobe. If your trip is during the winter months, warmer clothes should be taken and an overcoat should be added to the list. If you travel during spring or summer or in the early fall, the clothes should be lightweight. Dacron or similar wash and wear clothes are recommended.

1 lightweight raincoat.
1 business suit suitable for dinner wear.
1 sport jacket.
1 sweater.
2 pairs of slacks.
2 drip-dry dress shirts.
2 drip-dry sport shirts.
2 sets drip-dry undershirts and shorts.
2 pairs pajamas.
6 pairs hose.
1 bathing trunks.
Slippers.
Dress and walking shoes.
Several ties.
Handkerchiefs.
Dressing kit for toothbrush, toothpaste, brush, comb, etc.
Shaving kit. See notes under Electrical Appliances.

SIZE CHARTS

The following charts will assist those who wish to purchase wearing apparel in the countries visited. Please note that the size equivalents are approximate.

Blouses and Sweaters

American	34	36	38	40	42	44
English	36	38	40	42	44	46
Continental	42	44	46	48	50	52

Dresses and Coats (Misses')

American	10	12	14	16	18	20
English	32	33	35	36	38	39
Continental	38	40	42	44	46	48

Dresses and Coats (Children's and Junior Misses')

American	2	4	6	8	10	13	15
English	1	2	5	7	9	10	12
Continental	1	2	5	7	9	10	12

Men's Suits and Overcoats

American and English	36	38	40	42	44	46
Continental		46	48	50	52	54	56

Men's Shirts

American and English	14	14½	15	15½	15¾	16	16½	17
Continental	36	37	38	39	40	41	42	43

Men's Socks

American and English	9½	10	10½	11	11½
Continental	38-39	39-40	40-41	41-42	42-43

Men's Hats

American	6⅝	6¾	6⅞	7	7⅛	7¼	7⅜	7½	7⅝
English	6½	6⅝	6¾	6⅞	7	7⅛	7¼	7⅜	7½
French	3	3½	4	4½	5	5½	6	6½	7
Continental	53	54	55	56	57	58	59	60	61

Women's Shoes

American	4	5	6	7	8	9	10
English	2	3	4	5	6	7	8
French	36	37	38	39	40	41	42
Italian	32	34	36	38	40	42	44
Israeli	34½	35½	36½	37½	38½	40	41

Women's Stockings

American and English	8	8½	9	9½	10	10½
Continental	0	1	2	3	4	5

BIBLIOGRAPHY

Harriz, Michel. "A Story in Stone." Beirut: Harb Bijjani Press, 1963

Keyes, Nelson Beecher. "Story of the Bible World." New York: Hammond, 1959

Kopp, Clemens. "Holy Places of the Gospels." New York: Herder and Herder, 1963

Lapide, Pinchas E. "A Pilgrim's Guide to Israel." London: Harrap, 1966

Morton, V. "In the Steps of the Master." New York: Dodd-Meade, 1934

National Geographic Society. "Everyday Life in Bible Times." Washington, D.C., 1967

Olson, Arnold. "Inside Jerusalem." Glendale, California: Gospel Light Press, 1968

Patterson, Harriet Louise. "Around the Mediterranean with My Bible." Chicago: Judson Press, 1948

Peale, Norman Vincent. "Adventures in the Holy Land." Englewood Cliffs, New Jersey: Prentice-Hall, 1963

Pearlman, M. and Yannai, Y. "Historical Sites in Israel." Tel Aviv: Massadah-P.E.C. Press Ltd., 1965

Pfeiffer, Charles F. "Baker's Bible Atlas." Grand Rapids, Michigan: Baker Book House, 1961

Pfeiffer, Charles F. "Jerusalem Through the Ages." Grand Rapids. Michigan: Baker Book House, 1967

Pfeiffer, Charles and Vos, Howard F. "Wycliffe Historical Geography of Bible Lands." Chicago: Moody Press, 1967

Showker, Kay. "Travel Jordan, The Holy Land." Beirut: Librairie Du Liban

Smith, Wilbur M. "Israeli-Arab Conflict and the Bible." Glendale, California: Gospel Light Press, 1967

Thomson, W. M. "Land and the Book." London: Nelson, 1888

Unger, Merrill, F. "Archaeology of the New Testament." Grand Rapids, Michigan: Zondervan, 1962

Unger, Merrill F. "Archaeology of the Old Testament." Grand Rapids, Michigan: Zondervan, 1954

Unger, Merrill F. "Unger's Bible Dictionary." Chicago: Moody Press, 1957

Unger, Merrill F. "Unger's Bible Handbook." Chicago: Moody Press, 1966

Vilnay, Zev. "Israel Guide." Jerusalem: Sivan Press Ltd., 1967

Vilnay, Zev. "New Israel Atlas." Jerusalem: Israel University Press, 1968

Wolf, Betty Hartman. "Journey Through the Holy Land." Garden City, N. Y.: Doubleday, 1967

Yadin, Yigael. "Masada." London: Weidenfield and Nicolson, 1966

INDEX

184